A New
Economic View
of
AMERICAN
HISTORY

A New Economic View of AMERICAN HISTORY

SUSAN PREVIANT LEE

and

PETER PASSELL

W·W· NORTON & COMPANY

New York – London

For Louella Huebner Rich

Copyright © 1979 by Susan Lee and Peter Passell
Published simultaneously in Canada by George J. McLeod Limited,
Toronto. Printed in the United States of America.

All Rights Reserved

First Edition

Library of Congress Cataloging in Publication Data

Lee, Susan, 1943–
  A new economic view of American history.

  Includes bibliographical references and index.
  1. United States—Economic conditions.
I. Passell, Peter, joint author. II. Title.
HC103.L34 1979   330.9'73   79–15554
ISBN 0–393–95067–0

BOOK DESIGN & ILLUSTRATION: RFS Graphic Design, Inc.

1 2 3 4 5 6 7 8 9 0

Contents

80-02771

M

Acknowledgments

This book rests, in large part, on the ideas and work of economists and historians too countless to mention here. But we would like specially to thank two of them—Robert Fogel and Gavin Wright—whose careful reading and insightful criticisms have improved this work immeasurably.

Then, too, we would like to acknowledge those colleagues who have shaped our views on economic history and who have, in all meanings of the word, inspired our endeavor. Here we include William Alpert, Stuart Bruchey, Stephen DeCanio, Donald Dewey, Stanley Engerman, Woody Fleisig, Ron Findlay, Robert Gallman, Claudia Goldin, Kenneth Jackson, Hillel Jaffe, Merrill Jensen, Stanley Lebergott, Peter Lindert, Don McCloskey, Jacob Mincer, Richard B. Morris, Chris Norwood, William Parker, Jane Price, Joe Reid, Lloyd Reynolds, Hugh Rockoff, Maria Schmundt, Richard Sutch, Peter Temin, Jeffrey Williamson, and Kathryn Yatrakis.

We are grateful for the critical and editorial generosity of Edwin Barber and Donald Lamm of W. W. Norton, and for the forebearance of our agent, Don Cutler.

A debt is owed as well to Tony Cavin, Joan Plotkin, and Sandy Ratkowsky, who provided invaluable support in the mechanics of creation.

Finally, of course, we wish to thank our students, whose book this really is.

Introduction

It is customary to begin a book like this with the scholar's version of the pep rally. A couple of paragraphs on the importance of the field to the defense of civilization, a hand for the giants of the past who made it all possible, a suggestion that mastery of the subject will take a lot of work, but the rewards will be great.

It is equally customary for readers to skip these opening remarks, or, at best, take the opportunity to practice a previously mastered skill—the one they teach at Evelyn Woods'. We sympathize. Those in need of inspiration so close to game time generally learn from experience that book introductions are not the place to find it. The well-motivated, by contrast, resent the patronizing sentiment that usually wafts in with the lecture. At pep rallies, at least, the band plays "Hello Dolly" and the Coor's is chilled.

We think we have a better reason than custom or pedantry to pause a few pages before digging in. American Economic History is a subject in ferment, at once enjoying a glittering vogue and yet in danger of defining itself out of existence. Readers well-versed in political or social history are likely to be surprised—and perhaps offended—by the break with tradition embodied in much of the research called economic history these days. Economic history journals have been invaded and/or captured by aliens armed with productivity indices, simulation models, and consistent estimators, but decidedly lacking in readable prose styles or what is (admiringly) labeled common sense. And at the end of those articles, where any reasonable person would expect to find the conclusion, the authors instead call for a new round of cross-section data or suggest something about sensitivity analysis.

Even readers more at home with the jargon of modern economics may be in for a dose of culture shock. The approach will look familiar, the quick victories proclaimed over lightly armed historians gratifying.

But they will not be accustomed to dealing with the guerrilla counterattacks on cherished—and previously unquestioned—first principles: the virtue of very simple assumptions about the motives of consumers and producers, the practical value of step-by-step deductive reasoning, dependence on statistical hypothesis testing. For economists, history may appear to be an undisciplinable colony in which the natives are ungrateful, the terrain ideal for snipers and booby traps, the potential booty of victory unpromising. A brief introduction to where U.S. economic history has been and where the authors believe it is going may cushion the blow for the uninitiated student of both history and of economics.

A Short History of American Economic History

No unifying tradition or single school of thought dominates economic history in the United States. Before World War I few scholars were interested in the subject; fewer still would admit that a separate subject called economic history was worth studying. Some historians, clustered at Ivy League universities, wrote historical treatises on economics. A half dozen or so—Frank Taussig's *Tariff History of the United States,* Wesley Mitchell's *History of the Greenback,* David Dewey's *Financial History of the United States* among them—are remembered and read today. But only in the 1920's is it possible to find groups of American economic historians with similar interests or goals, and even here the identification of "schools" is a bit artificial.

At one end of the spectrum are economic historians who really were, at heart, political or social historians. They concentrated their attention on economic institutions because they believed that behind political and social movements lay economic causes. Charles Beard's *Economic Interpretation of the Constitution of the United States* exemplifies this approach. First published in 1913, Beard's book stunned contemporaries by arguing that the Constitution was framed for the purpose of protecting the interests of a moneyed elite, property owners financially threatened by government policies under the Articles of Confederation. In later works (some co-authored with Mary Beard) he also challenged conventional interpretations of the causes and impact of the Civil War, asserting that the War represented the final struggle between industrial capitalism and feudal plantation agriculture. The Beards' influence can be seen today in political historian Gabriel Kolko's interpretation of late 19th century government regulation as a device to protect big business and William A. Williams's work on the economic origins of American imperialism.

A related group of economic historians can be identified by their preoccupation with matching historical experience to predictable stages of economic development. Many "stage" theorists have been Marxists, organizing their investigation of political and social history to fit Marx's predicted historical evolution from feudal agriculture to industrial capitalism, thence to working class revolution. It is possible, of course, to believe in development stages without linking the stages to the struggle between social classes. Joseph Schumpeter suggested that socialism would follow capitalism as private enterprise lost its capacity to generate technological innovation. Walter Rostow directly challenged Marx with a stage theory of his own. Here the emphasis is on what triggers and sustains industrial growth, rather than on the identification of dominant social classes with types of economic systems. For Rostow, rapid expansion followed the emergence of a leading industry, like railroads or cotton textiles.

Very few economists today accept Rostow's notion that a single theory can explain the timing of development in many countries; the data collected on the growth process in the United States and Europe simply don't support it. However, the urge to explain great historical change by reference to discrete stages remains irresistible to many historians—Marxist and non-Marxist.

A larger group of economic historians have been less concerned with the broad sweep of history than with isolating the special features of the American experience. Unlike Beardian determinists and stage theorists like Rostow, they share the view that describing economic institutions—how banking systems are established, how industries are born and mature, and so on—is an end in itself. Many institutionalists focused on business and business leaders: Paul Gates on the Illinois Central Railroad, Thomas Cochran on the Pabst Brewery, Kenneth Porter on John Jacob Astor. Or they pieced together coherent descriptions of whole sectors of the economy. Though somewhat out of fashion, institutional economic history is alive and well and living in Cambridge, Massachusetts—much of the best work in the field is published in Harvard's *Business History Review*.

Yet another approach—the very opposite of the institutionalist stance—is to view history through statistics alone. Before the 1920's, quantitative information about the past was largely unavailable or organized so poorly that it provided limited insight. Few scholars had the interest, skills, or patience to make sense of the raw data accumulated by government agencies and private business. Thus historians knew there had been a bank panic in 1837 and a subsequent recession but had no fix on how this recession compared in severity to other business collapses; scholars were aware of farmers' discontent associated with falling prices in the late 19th century but couldn't measure the actual impact on total farm income.

The initial impetus to collect and organize the numbers was not curiosity about the past but the belief that historical data was necessary to solve pressing contemporary problems. Economists trying to understand the cause of business cycles—those maddeningly regular cycles of depression and boom in business activity—needed data on prices, output, employment and investment to test their theories. Hence the motive for organizing the National Bureau for Economic Research and later the International Committee on Price History, both sponsored by private foundations. Pioneers in the collection and analysis of the numbers include Wesley Mitchell, Arthur Cole, Thomas Berry, and Anne Bezanson. This early work made possible the kind of sophisticated national income accounting that we take for granted today. Though the nuts and bolts hard work of changing raw historical data into useful statistics carries with it little glamor, this critical task continues to occupy a dedicated minority. Numbered among their ranks, in fact, is the only economic historian to win a Nobel prize—Simon Kuznets.

As must be clear, these groups of economic historians—institutionalists, stage theorists, economic determinists, quantifiers—had diverse interests and approaches to the subject. Some would have denied that any other approach than their own was useful economic history; others would have denied that their own study of the past should be labeled economic history, as opposed to development economics or social history. Technical journals devoted to economic history were dominated by institutionalists; mainstream journals in economics and history in large part treated the subject like some tiresome great aunt— invited to attend family ceremonies, courteously remembered on her birthday, but otherwise ignored.

In the late 1950's, however, all that changed. Most observers mark the transition by a1958 article in the *Journal of Political Economy*. Two economists, Alfred Conrad and John Meyer, published estimates of the profitability of slavery on the eve of the Civil War.[1] Their conclusions— much will be said on this subject in later chapters—were less startling than the way they went about obtaining them. Instead of using traditional historians' methods—directly examining the motives or the perceptions of slave owners, reviewing the accounts of individual plantations, or assessing the record of individual slave owners in forcing work from unwilling conscripts—Conrad and Meyer approached the problem abstractly. If what one wishes to know is whether a typical investment in slaves paid off, then the issue of profitability turns on the same factors that determine the profitability of investments in, say, bulldozers, TV game show syndications, or jumbo jets. Slavery is profitable if the return on the cash outlay is at least as high as the yield on alternative investments. Economic theory supplies the concepts and the method for calcu-

[1] "The Economics of Slavery in the Antebellum South," *Journal of Political Economy* 66 (April 1958).

lating yields; historical data, filtered through a set of theoretical assumptions about agricultural production conditions, supplies the raw material. No messing with crumbling archives in dusty county courthouses, no fussing about what slaveholders *thought* they were doing. In short, Conrad and Meyer started a revolution in economic history by isolating the technical question within the slavery controversy and applying a strictly technical method to obtain a solution.

Whether the profession actually needed Conrad and Meyer to show it the way, or whether their approach to research in economic history was an idea whose time had come, is not clear. Nor, of course, is it very important. What is important is the response of the profession to the change. The years following produced a trickle, then a flood, of books and articles that adopted the Conrad and Meyer approach to economic history. At first these were written largely by economists who felt most at home with technical methods borrowed from economic theory and statistics. Today the mix of scholars is more balanced as growing numbers of economists and historians are learning the techniques of the other discipline.

Early practitioners were tabbed "Cliometricians"—Clio is the muse of history—though it was soon apparent that it was more than an interest in numbers and measurement that made them different from institutional historians. John Hughes coined the phrase "New Economic History," a label short on descriptive power but far more durable. Not all economic historians today identify themselves with this new wave. It is fair to say however that no one with the remotest interest in economic history can ignore the influence and accomplishments of New Economic History.

The New Economic History: What's It All About?

New Economic History has no exact definition. Unlike the U.S. Senate or the American Medical Association, there are no formal membership requirements and no official admissions committee to judge the virtues of applicants. Practitioners disagree among themselves about what makes the field special. Still, it's possible to isolate a few of the features that distinguish this approach from earlier work.

EXPLICIT USE OF ECONOMIC THEORY

Following the practice of the natural sciences, New Economic Historians test the consistency between facts that are known ("the data") and an explicit theory of how the system works that causes events to happen ("the model"). One researcher, for example, examined the hypothesis that the business boom and inflation of the 1830's was triggered by

Andrew Jackson's infamous bank veto, which terminated the Bank of the United States' power to limit private bank loans. Earlier generations of historians had casually inferred the bank veto-inflation relationship from the fact that the boom followed on the heels of the bank's neutering. But if this explanation were correct, economic theory suggests that private banks would have increased their ratio of loans-to-reserves.[2]

Another investigator wished to explain the time pattern of implementation of mechanical grain reapers on 19th-century farms. He hypothesized that the reaper would be adopted when the cost of mechanically harvesting an acre of wheat fell below the cost of harvesting by hand. Since harvesting costs were determined by wages, machinery prices, and farm size, it was possible to assemble the relevant data and then assess just how well his theory fit the facts.[3]

Explicit hypothesis testing is the centerpiece of the scientific method because it is such an efficient way of finding out how things work. With a clearly stated theory, it is possible to cut expensive and time-consuming data collection to the minimum needed to confirm or refute the hypothesis. Though in practice it is not, strictly speaking, possible to prove an hypothesis correct, explicit theory does allow the researcher to devise tests to rule out competing explanations. Thus economic theory allowed a direct comparison between the standard "Bank War" explanation of the 1830's boom, referred to above, with an explanation based on international financial events. And the new explanation of reaper diffusion based on relative costs could be matched against competing explanations—favorable conditions for mechanical harvesting in the West, changing attitudes toward technically advanced farm methods.[4]

Historians not at home with the methods of economists are often puzzled by this reliance placed on theory when scientific formality often appears to clutter arguments that can be stated in common sense terms. Turgid tracts revealing the obvious abound in social science; must economists pollute the prose of historians too?

Yet an examination of traditional historical writing reveals an equal reliance of theories; they are just kept under the carpet of historical assertion. Virtually any analytic historical statement—"Reduced railroad freight rates spurred the growth of western agriculture" or "New Deal fiscal policies shortened the Great Depression"—implies a theoretical framework. Sometimes the implicit theory is too obvious to bear much explanation; in truth, making explicit every premise behind an argument would be a waste of effort.

[2] See chapter 6 for the whole story.
[3] See chapter 7.
[4] As the bitter debate over the economics of slavery (discussed in chapters 8 and 9) illustrates, reliance on formal theories cannot transform economic history into an exact science. But we expect readers will see the clear advantages to explicit theorizing in context.

History "without theory," however, can mislead. Robert Fogel makes the case for explicit theory with an example from Eugene Genovese's essay on the effect of slavery on Southern economic growth.[5] Genovese argued that slavery retarded Southern industrial development by limiting the market for factory-produced goods. The small size of the market meant higher costs for southern firms and left them fatally exposed to competition from northern industry.

Genovese's argument is plausible. But, as Fogel points out, buried under such seemingly straightforward assertions are a myriad of theoretical assumptions, all of which must be correct for the case to stand. First, Genovese assumes that, without slavery, the demand for southern manufactured goods would have been higher; that assumption rests on a groundwork of subsidiary assumptions about what free workers, as opposed to slaves, would have consumed. Second, he assumes that southern industrial firms faced decreasing production costs and would have been able to reduce unit costs if the market were larger. Third, Genovese assumes that the northern competitive edge was so narrow in southern markets that it could have been overcome by southern firms operating in broader markets.

Genovese's package of assumptions, his model of how the southern market economy operated, may or may not be accurate. But as long as those assumptions remain implicit to his argument, the debate over its validity is likely to proceed in confusion, with little hope of resolution.

THE COUNTERFACTUAL HYPOTHESIS

Many scholars who are willing to make room for explicit theory in history resist opening the door to another innovation of NEH: the counterfactual hypothesis. Counterfactual hypothesizing is an attempt to measure the significance of what actually happened by pretending the event never occurred and asking how the world might have been different. Did the importation of slaves from Africa in the eighteenth century lead to the rise of cotton plantations in the early nineteenth century? A New Economic Historian might restate the question: If slaves had not been imported, yet other factors—the technology of cotton farming and textile production, restrictions on international trade, and so on—had remained the same, would cotton plantations have grown up in the South?

Perhaps the best-known example of counterfactual history is Robert Fogel's assessment of the contribution to income made by the national railroads.[6] Fogel measured the net value of rail services by estimating the

---

[5] "The Specification Problem in Economic History," *Journal of Economic History* 27 (Sept., 1967).
[6] See chapter 13.

extra cost of providing equivalent services by water and wagon transportation. Counterfactual experiments, however, can be found in dozens of other books and articles. For example, Claudia Golden measured the economic cost of the Civil War by estimating economic growth in the war's hypothetical absence.[7] Robert Thomas measured the costs and benefits of British colonial policies by estimating colonial income in the absence of imperial trade restrictions.[8] E. Cary Brown computed the impact of New Deal fiscal policies by comparing actual performance with a hypothetically drawn neutral fiscal policy.[9]

Opposition to counterfactual history is based on the idea that it is impossible to verify the effects of events that never took place. Traditional historian Fritz Redlich calls the results "quasi-history." Redlich writes that a "[counterfactual] model is never a piece of history because it is conjectural . . . a distortion of reality . . . If we were to accept it as history, the piece would be bad history . . ."[10]

In their own defense, New Economic Historians argue that virtually any attempt to analyze past events involves comparisons between what happened and a hypothetical alternative. Did Federal Reserve blunderings during 1929–31 cause unemployment to rise dramatically? The answer rests on what would have happened if the Fed had pursued wiser policies. Did Teddy Roosevelt's trust-busting policies slow the move toward industrial concentration? We can never know without examining what would have happened in the absence of these policies.

The virtue of explicit counterfactual history over implicit counterfactualizing is that it forces the analyst to make clear the hypothetical alternative. Explicit counterfactuals expose the exercise to criticism and possible improvement by laying bare any shaky assumptions or fallible deductions that lie beneath the surface. Thus Fogel could be criticized for his estimates of the cost of canal operations or the cost of storing inventories in the absence of railroads. Even more important, critics could question the value of such a sweeping counterfactual experiment, since the absence of the railroad would have affected the economy in so many unpredictable ways. These criticisms and serious questions quite possibly could have remained undefined, resting quietly under a carpet of observations that "proved" the railroads were the chief economic event in the late nineteenth century.

Whether Fogel's attempt stands up well or not, defenders of the method would claim credit for their approach. Counterfactual history, implicit and explicit, stands or falls on the reasonableness of the alterna-

---

[7] See chapter 11.
[8] See chapter 2.
[9] See chapter 16.
[10] "New and Traditional Approaches to Economic History and Their Interdependence," *Journal of Economic History* 25 (Dec., 1965).

tive. At the very least, explicit counterfactuals dramatically expose the weakness of an analysis where a more traditional weighing of the evidence based on the very same assumptions might slip by the reader.

SOPHISTICATED USE OF NUMBERS

Even a casual glance at the articles in the *Journal of Economic History* makes plain the dependence of NEH on statistics and mathematical methods for interpreting their meaning. Interest in the numbers is not entirely new to economic history; as we noted before, economists have been collecting historical data on the U.S. economy for several decades. What is new is the use of data within economic history for hypothesis testing as opposed to description, the sophistication of the data collection process, and the reliance on computer-assisted techniques for rigorous statistical inference.

NEH is avowedly analytical; it focuses on why events occurred rather than on description. Hence it is natural that practitioners would view data differently, shifting the emphasis from statistics that highlight chronologies to statistics that can help confirm or refute hypotheses.

An example might clarify the difference. A description of the rise of cotton textile manufacture in New England before the Civil War would surely require statistics on total production, perhaps broken down by region. However, if one wished to know why textile production settled in Massachusetts rather than in North Carolina, why American producers succumbed to British competition in one period but were able to hold their own in another, or whether large mills were more efficient than small mills, then data on production and costs for many individual mills would be needed. This follows from the way mathematical statistical techniques are used to confirm or refute hypotheses. The more data available, the less one need fear that random errors in numbers collection will influence the conclusion, and the greater the ability to distinguish between competing interpretations of the same historical event.

While the accuracy of statistics has always been important to historians who made use of them, the demands of hypothesis testing have forced researchers to be more ingenious in the search for good data and more critical of the quality of what they find. New economic historians, like other empirically oriented social scientists, bear special responsibility for the integrity of their facts since their methods put an extra barrier between the producer and consumer of research. The reader must trust the quality of the data that lies beneath the surface of statistical manipulations.

But unlike social scientists working on contemporary problems, economic historians rarely have much control over the data collection process. Department of Labor statisticians can (and do) fine-tune their monthly surveys on unemployment, adding or rewording questions, changing the sample of workers interviewed. Historians are trapped by past practices or, at best, limited by the availability of records in local historical societies and county courthouses.

Hence the premiums placed by good economic historians on (1) verifying the quality of their data and (2) finding alternatives to the use of poor (or nonexistent) data. Maintaining standards on the quality of data involves personal discipline as well as the application of scientific sampling methods. Alternatives to poor data often amount to an exercise in belt-tightening: economizing by substituting theory for fact where a few carefully chosen assumptions can fill in the gaps without destroying the value of the investigation; employing modern statistical methods that permit inferences from an absolute minimum of information.

The best numbers and most sophisticated techniques for wringing truth from them would often be useless without computers. Computers have changed the face of both the natural and social sciences over the past twenty years, allowing researchers to substitute the brute force of virtually instantaneous arithmetic manipulation for mind-numbing bouts with mechanical calculators. In many cases, problems that had no practical solution because they would have taken years now can be polished off in two or three minutes.

Specifically, computers permit economic historians to make complex inferences from masses of facts. For example, Gavin Wright was able to test the interrelations of more than a dozen variables that he believed influenced the price of cotton in the Old South.[11] The computer also allowed Wright to perform controlled experiments on his estimated cotton market model, mathematically simulating worlds that never existed to test the impact of government policies on economic development. DeCanio and Mokyr were able to select factors that determined nineteenth-century wage rates with the goal of isolating the effects of unexpected Civil War inflation of workers' standard of living.[12]

FOCUS ON NEW TOPICS

Most practitioners of the NEH would claim their differences with traditional economic history were based on method, rather than subject matter. New Economic Historians, by their own reckoning, have simply expanded the "tool kit," borrowing theory and econometrics from other specialties within economics; what they choose to analyze is merely a matter of personal interest.

Personal interests, however, can be shaped by training, and the skills of the New Economic Historians are better suited to study certain prob-

---

[11] "An Econometric Study of Cotton Production and Trade 1830–60," *Review of Economics and Statistics* 53 (May, 1971).
[12] See chapter 11.

lems than others. A case can be made that they have borrowed the special concerns as well as the methods of modern economics. Probably the most notable distinction is the shift away from institutions and toward the explanation of economic development. Economic development—the sources of growth—is a central concern of contemporary economics. New Economic Historians have extended that preoccupation to the past, concentrating on the period of greatest change, the nineteenth century.

Thus much of the NEH is about how growth happened. What factors increased labor productivity? How did economic sectionalism encourage or retard growth? What determined the pace of technical change? How did government activity influence output? Less in evidence is research about matters that can't easily be quantified—entrepreneurship, business and union power, relationships between politics and economics.

The New Economic History: What's in It for Historians?

Until very recently, a majority of historians would, no doubt, have answered: "very little." New Economic Historians were viewed as the enemy, con artists and opportunists attempting to do history without knowing any. Greek letters and regression equations look great on the printed page; who cares why Andrew Carnegie succeeded or why Populist reformers failed . . . ? Friction between economists and historians remains; some economists still tend to their computer programs mumbling "sour grapes" and some historians still claim superior access to Historical Truth via the route of liberal education. But for most, the divisions no longer look so important.

NEH is a complement to rather than a substitute for traditional institutionally oriented economic history. Andrew Carnegie's manipulations of capital markets, exploitation of immigrant labor, or success in subverting the political process is more interesting—not less—in the context of knowledge of the factors influencing productivity change in the steel industry. The political economy of the Populist movement becomes more important, given an understanding of the effects of falling prices on farmer-debtors.[13]

Similarly, NEH poses no genuine threat to political and social historians. Few historians today believe that political or social change can be studied in a vacuum, and recent work underscores that interdependence. New Economic Historians have challenged traditional interpretations in such diverse subjects as the effects of slavery on black culture, the economic roots of sectionalism, opportunities for social class mobil-

[13] See chapter 14.

ity, and the political motives behind New Deal Welfare programs. For all the ill-will generated by NEH, it seems clear already that the study of history has benefited. Historians, including those unconvinced by computer-brandishing invaders, are becoming better social scientists. Economists, in turn, are learning some history and even a little humility.

The New Economic History: What's in It for Economists?

This may seem a strange sort of question, since it is economists who led the attack on institutional economic history and are occasionally heard to proclaim imperial victory over the humanists. Yet a good number of economists disapprove of intellectual imperialism and prefer to see their colleagues at work at home, rather than out educating historians (or sociologists or political scientists). In spite of the renaissance in economic history, the general economics journals that make—or follow—professional tastes continue to ignore work in the field.

Donald McCloskey argues that history's foothold is so insecure because economists are hooked on the model of the natural sciences—physics, chemistry, biology. For decades economists have been working to shed their image as "soft" scientists by mathematizing every part of the profession and granting extraordinary prestige to the specialty least tainted by subjectivity—mathematical economic theory. History reminds economists of their origins in politics and philosophy, on the humanities side of the tracks. Visits to the old neighborhood can often be uncomfortable.

Such logic may explain the attitudes of economists, but it doesn't justify them. If the past is worth knowing about, history is important, and economic historians have much to contribute. However, even for economists who find nothing intrinsically interesting about the past, a good case can still be made for studying economic history. As Wesley Mitchell argued fifty years ago, understanding economic processes in the past makes it easier to analyze contemporary questions. The quantitative historians of the 1920's and 1930's who collected business cycle data were motivated by such practical considerations. A list of other subjects with contemporary relevance might include the determinants of technological change, the returns to public investment in education, the impact of government regulation on transportation, the role of international trade and finance on growth, the costs and benefits of liberal immigration policies, the effects of regional economic specialization, the impact of war on the national economy.

Economists, for all their desire to be objective scientists, are more or less prisoners of untested conventional views. Myths about the past become assumptions about the present. As a practical matter such conventions can't be avoided. But good history can give them a critical foundation.

Bibliography

*Ralph Andreano (ed.), *The New Economic History: Recent Papers on Methodology* (Wiley, 1970). A collection of essays from Explorations in Economic History. Good stuff, most notably from Lance Davis, Robert Basmann, and Alfred Conrad.

*Arthur Cole, "Economic History in the United States: Formative Years of the Discipline," *Journal of Economic History* 28 (Dec., 1968). Summary of traditional approaches, with a good bibliography.

*Albert Fishlow and Robert Fogel, "Quantitative Economic History: An Interim Evaluation," *Journal of Economic History* 31 (March, 1971). Sophisticated overview of the accomplishments of NEH, with suggestions of where the field ought to be heading.

*Robert Fogel, "The New Economic History: Its Findings and Methods," *Economic History Review* 19 (2d Series) (Dec., 1966). Summary (and defense) of the methods of NEH, with a now dated tabulation of NEH research.

*Robert Fogel, "The Specification Problem in Economic History," *Journal of Economic History* 27 (Sept., 1967). The first half of the article, written nontechnically, explains the virtues of explicit vs. implicit theorizing.

*John Hughes, "Fact and Theory in Economic History," *Explorations in Entrepreneurial History* 3 (2d Series) (Winter 1966). Readable essay by economist who wishes to make peace with traditional economic historians.

**Peter McClelland, *Causal Exploration and Model Building in History, Economics and the New Economic History* (Cornell University, 1975). A rigorous examination of the logical foundations of historical methods. Tough, but worth it.

**Donald McCloskey, "Does the Past Have Useful Economics?" *Journal of Economic Literature* 14 (June 1976). An economist's cogent defense of the relevance of NEH to contemporary economics.

**Donald McCloskey, "The Achievements of the Cliometric School," *Journal of Economic History* 38 (March, 1978). Up-to-date overview on the accomplishments of the New Economic History.

Notes: The references here are to historiography and methodology—how history has been done, and how it should be done. For references to specific issues discussed in this chapter, see the bibliography to the substantive chapters that follow.
Note: Here, and in the bibliographies to the following chapters, references are rated for the amount of knowledge the authors assume on the readers' part.

(*) = understanding of basic economic concepts, little formal knowledge.
(**) = solid understanding of introductory college economics; better yet, some intermediate-level economics training.
(***) = advanced undergraduate-level economics; better yet, some graduate-level economic theory.
(‡) = knowledge of, at minimum, the principles of econometrics.

**John Meyer and Alfred Conrad, "Economic Theory, Statistical Inference, and Economic History," *Journal of Economic History* (Dec., 1957). Why economic methodology should be applied to history, by two pioneer NEH'ers.

*Douglass North, "Economic History," in *International Encyclopedia of the Social Sciences* (Crowell, Collier and Macmillan, 1968). The basics, from the point of view of a New Economic Historian.

*William Parker, "From New to Old in Economic History," *Journal of Economic History* 31 (March, 1971). A witty defense of the importance of economic history by the self-styled "oldest new economic historian."

*Fritz Redlich, "New and Traditional Approaches to Economic History and Their Interdependence," *Journal of Economic History* 25 (Dec., 1965). The most thoughtful attack on counterfactuals in history, combined with a defense of the institutional approach.

*Fritz Redlich, "Potentialities and Pitfalls in Economic History," *Explorations in Entrepreneurial History* 5 (2d Series) (Fall, 1968). Here Redlich softens his views on the New Economic History.

*James Soltow, "American Institutional Studies: Present Knowledge and Past Trends," *Journal of Economic History* 31 (March, 1971). Survey of important institutional history studies.

*George Taylor and Lucius Ellsworth (eds.), *Approaches to Economic History* (University of Virginia, 1971). Brief, useful summary essays on traditional approaches. See particularly essays by Hugh Aitken, George Rogers Taylor, Robert Gallman and Lance Davis.

**Peter Temin, "General Equilibrium Models in Economic History," *Journal of Economic History* 31 (March, 1971). A practitioner's consideration of the use of complex models in historical research. Will mean more to advanced students.

‡**Gavin Wright, "Econometric Studies of History," in *Frontiers of Quantitative Economics,* ed. by Michael Intriligator (London: North Holland, 1971). An analysis of the quantitative studies in economic history, current to 1970. First-rate, but of limited usefulness since the survey is now dated.

The colonial economy

1

The first Europeans to settle in what is now the United States came to exploit the natural resources of the North American continent. During the last third of the 16th century, Spain, France, and England all fought over the right to colonize Florida. The prize, however, proved to be of little value to Spain, the winner. Florida had no mineral treasures comparable to those in Latin America or the Caribbean. And fierce resistance from the native Indians, combined with inhospitable soil and weather, made it impossible to generate an agricultural surplus that could be sold in Europe.

In the 1580's, adventurers with a mandate from Queen Elizabeth to establish an English presence in North America had an even more difficult time. Two outposts at the site of Roanoke, Virginia, were wiped out by the Indians. Settlers at Jamestown on the Chesapeake Bay had only marginally better luck—two-thirds of the members of the merchant-sponsored expedition died of famine and infection during the winter of 1608. But Jamestown did survive its terrible initial decade, and with the Maryland colony to the north, formed the nucleus of a successful economy based on the cultivation of tobacco.

Like Jamestown, the earliest New England colonies were also financed by English commercial interests with profits foremost in mind. Many of the actual settlers, however, were religious dissenters eager to put 3,000 miles of ocean between their homes and a capricious, intolerant government. Plymouth, the original Pilgrim settlement founded in 1610, suffered a casualty rate almost as high as Jamestown's. It was eventually absorbed by the larger, better-organized Massachusetts Bay Colony, which had been started a few years later by business-minded Puritans. Massachusetts prospered, anchoring its economy to subsistence

15

agriculture and port services for the growing American trade with Europe.

Virginia and Massachusetts were by far the most important mainland colonies in the mid-17th century; they were home to two out of three English-speaking Europeans in North America. Maine and New Hampshire were nothing more than conglomerations of small fishing villages of uncertain colonial ownership. In fact, Massachusetts managed to annex Maine in 1652 and did not relinquish control until the 1820's. New Hampshire, also coveted by expansionist Massachusetts, was luckier; it was granted independent status by the British government in 1680. Connecticut and Rhode Island were first settled in the 1630's—the former by Massachusetts farmers in search of land, the latter by religious dissenters driven from their Massachusetts homes by Puritan orthodoxy.

Of the mid-Atlantic colonies, only New York has any history to speak of before 1680. New Amsterdam—what is now the New York City area—was colonized by the Dutch in the 1620's with the goal of providing logistic support to Dutch commercial ventures in Latin America. Populated regions of the Hudson Valley and Long Island were loosely governed by the Dutch until England wrested control over the region in a series of wars ending in 1674. Thereafter the region grew quickly; fertile grain land and good water transportation along the river valleys attracted thousands of immigrants to New York, New Jersey, and Pennsylvania.

Development of the lower South also began during the last quarter of the 17th century. Virginia tobacco farmers, pressed by increased European demand and the depletion of suitable soils for growing the noxious weed, expanded into the northern coastal region of North Carolina. The development of South Carolina depended upon two specialized export crops. Inland swamp lands proved ideal for growing rice, while better-drained upland areas specialized in indigo, the plant used to make blue textile dyes. This latter crop, incidentally, could be raised profitably only when the overseas market was shielded from Latin American and Caribbean competition by means of trade restrictions or domestic production bounties. There will be more to say on this point in chapter 2. Georgia offered no equivalent commercial attraction during the 17th and early 18th centuries. In 1733, it was chartered as a colony to serve as a buffer against the Spanish presence in Florida and, secondarily, as a safe dumping ground for English paupers and petty criminals.

Maturation of the Colonial Economy

By the mid-18th century the colonial economy had matured along dimensions that are recognizable today. In reality, there was not one colo-

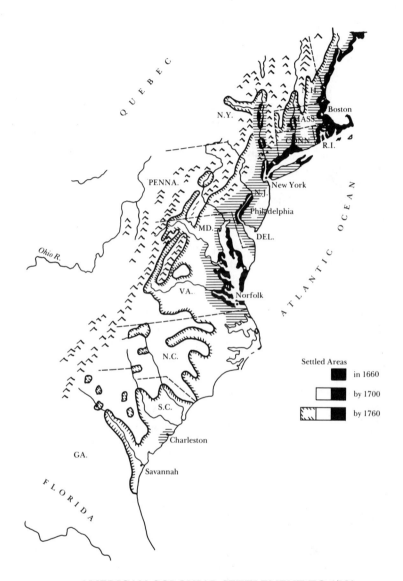

AMERICAN COLONIAL SETTLEMENT TO 1760

The coastal regions of the mid-Atlantic and New England, along with the nearby river valleys were settled first. Next came the less accessible hilly areas to the west. And, by the time of the Revolution, the Appalachian mountains were breached by farmers in search of land.

Source: Ross Robertson, *History of the American Economy* (Harcourt Brace Jovanovich, 1973), 52.

nial economy, but several, reflecting wide diversity in geography and weather.

Small port towns dotted the New England coast from Portsmouth, New Hampshire to Newport, Rhode Island. They supported a substantial fishing industry, as well as serving as regional marketplaces for food, timber, and manufactured goods. Boston, by far the largest New England city, was also the largest port for trade with the West Indies and Europe. The great majority of the population, however, worked as farmers on the coastal lowlands and interior river valleys of southern and central New England. As their numbers grew, they encroached on traditional Indian lands, finally leading to bloody confrontation. Several hundred colonial militia and several thousand Indians were killed during King Philip's War (1675–78).

In the long run, however, nature imposed greater constraints on New England agriculture than did the natives. Neither weather nor soil favored significant export crops; the farms of Massachusetts eventually could not compete with New York or Pennsylvania grain, surviving only by specializing in perishable meat, milk, and vegetables for sale in local markets. New England's potential for growth in an era dominated by agriculture was thus plainly limited. In 1720, approximately 171,000 people, 37 percent of the American colonists, lived in New England; sixty years later New England's population was substantially greater than that, but the relative attraction of other regions had reduced its percentage share to 25 percent.

No such constraints affected the middle colonies. Temperate weather and excellent river transportation favored the extension of wheat farming north along the Hudson Valley, west across the eastern tier of Pennsylvania, and south to the old tobacco regions of Maryland. The large surplus of grain and meat produced by the region was exported to Europe, as well as New England. This export trade stimulated the growth of two superb natural ports, Philadelphia and New York. By the 1760's, in fact, shipping, marketing, and processing of regional exports provided jobs for more people in each of those two cities than in Boston.

The upper South largely remained wedded to tobacco throughout the 18th century. Settlement progressed rapidly westward, as increased demand for the most important American export made cultivation profitable in ever more remote areas. By the time of the Revolution, tobacco was grown as far west as the hills of Virginia Piedmont, hundreds of miles from the Chesapeake. This movement, it should be noted, was not continuous; fluctuations in prices produced several boom and bust cycles in the local tobacco economy. Virginia was by far the largest colony and quite possibly the richest, supporting a wealthy plantation aristocracy as well as a large class of successful family farmers in the west.

In the lower South, South Carolina and Georgia thrived on trade in rice and indigo. During the late colonial period rice became the third largest export (following tobacco and flour), with total production increasing at least tenfold from 1715 to the Revolution. Indigo ranked fifth among exports, benefiting from exploding world demand for textiles and the cash bounty offered by Britain as an inducement to production.

North Carolina, by contrast, appears to have grown rapidly without equivalent dependence on foreign trade. James Shepard estimates that the colony's per capita exports—rice, indigo, turpentine, lumber—were one-fourth the level of Virginia's, just one-tenth the level of South Carolina's, in the late colonial period. These statistics may be distorted by the fact that North Carolina products shipped from Virginia ports were not counted in the totals. Nonetheless, it is striking that North Carolina managed to quadruple its population between 1740 and 1770 without emulating the economic structure of neighboring colonies.

Nearly two-thirds of all American exports originated in the South. One may note, however, that trade did not act as a catalyst for the growth of commercial service industries the way it did in the middle colonies and New England. In part this might be explained by the fact that tobacco, rice, and indigo required less processing for market than northern shipments of flour, fish, meat, and lumber. Such circumstances do not explain, though, why service industries like insurance and banking flourished in northern ports but not in southern ports. In the 18th century this regional distinction was not very important in terms of total value created or total employment—the entire colonial economy was overwhelmingly devoted to agriculture. But in later periods the failure of the South to develop commerce and industry parallel to agriculture had a profound effect on the destiny of the region.

Growth in the Colonial Economy

In 1640 the American colonies were a collection of farming villages barely self-sufficient in the essentials of life, and heavily dependent on Britain for protection against a hostile environment. One hundred and thirty years later these same colonies supported a population one-fifth that of England at roughly the same standard of living. The largest American city, Philadelphia, was only topped in size within the British Empire by London. Surpluses from American farms and plantations provided much of the world's tobacco and fed hundreds of thousands in the West Indies and Europe. When tested in the American Revolution, the colonial economy proved capable of both surviving without help from Britain and supporting a substantial armed force. It should thus come as no surprise that economic historians have spent much effort investigating the process of colonial economic growth.

What may be surprising, though, is how little is known about the rate of growth in the century and a half between initial settlement and independence. No statistics on output were systematically collected in the 17th or 18th century; we thus have no clear benchmarks by which to measure changes in the standard of living. Where numbers are not available, historians have been reduced to skilled guesswork based on qualitative accounts.

These accounts provide no reason to believe that per capita income increased significantly between the mid-17th century—when Massachusetts and Virginia had achieved a measure of economic stability—and the early 18th century. Total colonial income grew rapidly, but this growth was probably associated with an equivalent increase in total population.

What, then, do we know about income per capita in 1710? Working backward from fragmentary evidence about 18th-century growth, George Rogers Taylor estimated per capita income for the white population at about $28. More recently, Robert Gallman has argued that an income level this small would have been insufficient to sustain the modest but adequate life that we believe was enjoyed by a majority of free laborers. In terms of purchasing power, $28 would barely cover average expenditures for fuel and food at mid-19th-century levels. Since the colonists did not spend all their income on food and fuel, and since it is improbable that per capita expenditures rose markedly over the century, the $28 is surely too low. Gallman suggests that the actual level of income was probably somewhere between Taylor's estimate and English per capita income, known to have been about $45.

In contrast to the early colonial era, many historians believe that overall economic expansion in the last 65 years preceding the Revolution significantly raised living standards. By the mid-18th century, hundreds of plantation owners and merchants lived their lives in luxury. Equally important, thousands of family farmers and skilled artisans formed the nucleus of a substantial middle class.

A hard look at the numbers shows, however, that the growth of per capita income that made this transformation possible could not have been close to rates achieved after the mid-19th century. From 1839 to 1960, according to Raymond Goldsmith, average income in real terms increased at a 1.6 percent annual pace. Even if one makes the most favorable plausible assumptions—that income was very low in 1710 and very high in 1775—late colonial growth rates could not have exceeded one percent per year. If, more reasonably, one accepts Gallman's supposition of 1710 per capita income close to $45 and a 1775 per capita income at most one-third higher, the implied growth rate is about 0.4 percent. An explanation of why per capita growth rates were so modest by current standards awaits a closer look at the sources of 18th-century growth.

One misunderstanding related to the controversy over growth rates, however, is easy to untangle. Rapid extensive growth—which everyone acknowledges was taking place—need not have been associated with rapid improvement in living standards. Per capita income may have increased by only one-third between 1710 and 1775, but total output increased nearly tenfold. It is this extensive growth, driven largely by a population growth rate of over 3 percent per year, that allowed the colonies the luxury of buying an army capable of winning independence from Britain and the capacity to supply a hefty percentage of the world's trade in tobacco, rice, and indigo.

Those who consider the extraordinary dimensions of extensive growth in the colonial economy may be struck by the fact that the colonies were actually able to accommodate a 600-percent-plus population increase without a *decrease* in living standards. Today, economists believe that population growth in low-income countries seriously retards increases in per capita income. Since personal income is determined by labor productivity, more people virtually always means less output per person since the amount of land and capital per person correspondingly declines. For nations such as Bangladesh, Indonesia, and Haiti, unchecked population growth—at rates roughly equal to the American colonial rate—has made it all but impossible to raise living standards above a level considered inadequate in Europe 200 years ago.

One critical difference between Haiti in 1976 and colonial America in 1776 is the availability of land. When another Haitian enters the agricultural labor force, the amount of land per worker must fall, as must labor productivity. In the colonies, high-quality farmland was always available to accommodate a growing labor force. Labor productivity did not decline; the frontier was simply pushed westward. Nor did the market value of the product of the average worker fall. Elastic international demand for American products supported export prices as output expanded, while good water transportation made it possible to deliver goods to port at reasonable cost. It is even possible that extensive growth tended to increase average labor productivity by allowing colonists to take advantage of scale economies in transportation and distribution of goods. For example, ports at New York and Boston were probably able to store and dispense goods at lower cost per unit as the frequency of sailings to distant cities increased from a few each month to several each week.

As noted above, extensive growth dominated change in the colonial economy. It is still useful, though, to identify the sources of intensive growth, or changes in per capita income. An explanation of this change is interesting in its own right—by the standard of the preindustrialized world economy, a sustained growth rate of 0.4 percent is not inconsiderable. A fuller understanding of the process of American colonial growth, moreover, many provide some insight into the transition to more rapid modern growth. Herewith a primer on the sources of colonial per capita income growth.

TECHNICAL CHANGE

In the past century, growth has been identified with technical change. New techniques have permitted enormous increases in output from a given quantity of factor inputs. In fact, spectacular improvements—the introduction of steam power in water pumps, mechanization of cotton textile production—were taking place in Britain during the early 18th century. But such industrial changes had no direct effect on the American economy since colonial output was almost entirely agricultural.

Can any portion of colonial per capita income growth then be attributed to technical change? Some, surely, though far less than in later periods. Duane Ball and Gary Walton assembled extensive data on farm inputs and outputs for Chester County in the southeastern corner of Pennsylvania. They estimate that total factor productivity—a weighted index of the ratio of outputs to inputs—advanced at an average annual rate of just 0.2 percent from 1700 to the Revolution.[1]

Ball and Walton argue that data from this one county in Pennsylvania is representative of grain-and-livestock-producing areas of the middle colonies. Whether or not they are correct, it would certainly not be reasonable to generalize from this evidence about southern tobacco, rice, corn, hog, and indigo production. And for the South, unfortunately, these exists only qualitative evidence about agricultural technical change. Marc Egnal believes that tobacco technology remained stagnant, while productivity on rice plantations benefited somewhat from improved techniques of irrigation.

Apart from agriculture, shipping was the only section large enough for technical change to have had a significant impact on total income. As noted below, there was a considerable increase in productivity in ocean shipping, but Shepard and Walton find little evidence that this was due to changes in existing technology. What does seem apparent, though, is that the reduced danger of piracy in the 1750's permitted the use of lighter, more efficient ships lacking heavy armament. Such ships did not represent new technology—the Dutch first introduced these so-called fly-boats in 1595. The diffusion of "old" technology, however, may have resulted in considerable savings near the end of the colonial era.

[1] See the appendix to chapter 4 for an explanation of total factor productivity.

The indirect effect of technical change in Britain possibly had as great an impact on colonial income as the direct effect of technical change at home. Savings achieved in highly competitive British industries were passed on to customers, including American colonists. Egnal notes, for example, that a bushel of wheat worth 1.5 yards of wool cloth in 1740 could fetch 2.5 yards in 1760. Part of this improvement in what is called the "net barter terms of trade"—the ratio of export prices to import prices—resulted from reductions in distribution costs, discussed later in this chapter. But the long-term indirect effects that industrialization in Britain had on colonial income should not be entirely discounted.

INCREASED USE OF COMPLEMENTARY FACTORS

Output per capita can also be enhanced by increasing the quantity of land and/or capital available per worker. Reliable data simply aren't available to assess the impact of land and capital "deepening," but we have some indirect evidence. It is unlikely that land per worker increased during the 18th century. Quite the contrary: the average size of farms in the middle colonies and New England declined substantially over the century. Ball's evidence on Chester County shows the decline to be on the order of 75 percent. Average farm size is, of course, an extremely crude measure of available land per worker. It ignores changes in the number of workers per farm, in the percentage of total farm acreage prepared for crops, in the quality of acreage under cultivation. Still, one would be hard-pressed to defend the notion that land was the key to increased labor productivity.

How about capital? Relatively few opportunities existed in 18th-century America to change the mix of capital, land, and labor used in farming. Egnal does cite evidence of increased use of horsepower in New England and the middle colonies. But most of the physical capital in 18th century farms consisted of improvements to the land—fencing, drainage, removal of rocks and stumps. And here, there is no compelling reason to believe that farm practices changed much between 1700 and 1775.

If the ratio of capital to labor did increase, it was probably due to increased investment in livestock associated with a shift to grain feeding and to the increased use of "working" capital, those funds used to finance crops in production and inventories of crops between field and consumer. Working capital facilitated the growth of market-oriented agriculture; a farmer able to borrow money might profitably grow rice destined for Boston or Italy, instead of corn and hogs for the family dinner table. Quantitative evidence on the use of working capital is lacking, but contemporary accounts suggest that credit for export trade was easier to obtain in the middle of the century than at the beginning. Still, it is dangerous to make too much of this argument. Shepard and Walton's computations show that, on balance, the colonies borrowed little from Europe during the 18th century. Hence increases in working capital were limited by the savings rate of the colonists themselves.

SLAVERY

Slavery was of little importance to the colonies in the 17th century. The labor force consisted of free Europeans and a large class of white indentured servants. Indenturement—essentially a long-term labor contract between worker and boss—allowed impoverished English workers to trade several years of labor for ship passage to the colonies. The system also made it possible to rid England of "undesirables"—beggars, debtors, minor criminals—by transporting them to America at no expense to the Crown.

By the turn of the century, however, the economic return for the use of black slaves had increased. In part this may have been related to greater competition—and, thus, lower costs—in the business of importing slaves: The slave trade, formerly a monopoly of the English Royal African Company, was opened to all comers in 1698. In part the growth of slavery may also reflect the increasing cost of obtaining white contract labor, because wages in England were probably rising as a result of industrialization.

Undoubtedly the most important factor, however, was the expansion of tobacco and rice plantations in the South. In 1770 only a few percent of the work force in New England and the middle colonies consisted of slaves. By contrast, one-third of all workers in the upper South, and close to one-half in the lower South, were slaves.

From the point of view of colonial slave owners, slaves functioned like traditional forms of capital—machines, livestock—indirectly raising their income by complementing their input of managerial services, as well as providing the direct returns of asset ownership. The extent to which slavery is responsible for 18th-century gains in the per capita income of whites is not known. It is possible, however, that the impact of slavery was considerable. Not merely did the output produced by slaves (beyond that needed for their own subsistence) accrue to whites, but also slavery permitted the rapid expansion of the highest income sector of the economy, the sector devoted to the export trade—though, undoubtedly, some of the work done by slaves could and would have been done by additional white immigrants.

IMPROVEMENTS IN ECONOMIC ORGANIZATION

Shepard and Walton argue persuasively that an important source of improvement in colonial living standards was the reduction of marketing and distribution costs in overseas trade. Narrowing the gap between the price at which farmers sold their crops and the price consumers paid

made it profitable for regions—and individual farmers—to specialize in more productive activities. Hundreds of thousands of farmers, who would otherwise have grown food for themselves, instead produced grain, rice, tobacco, and indigo. These were ultimately exchanged for manufactured goods from Europe, rum, sugar, and molasses from the Caribbean, shipping, banking, and insurance services from colonial port cities. In the decade before the Revolution, exports and related services accounted for about one-sixth of colonial income.

The magnitude of productivity gains associated with improved distribution has been calculated by Shepard and Walton to be at least 0.8 percent per year over the century preceding the Revolution. Gains vary by commodity route, ranging from 0.6 percent on wine to 1 percent on bullion. Put another way, the real resources required to ship goods across the Atlantic were cut by more than half over the period. Since shipping and distribution expenses amounted to about half the total wholesale price of goods at their final destination, the impact of these gains on colonial income is quite significant.

Shepard and Walton's calculations are supported by the earlier work of Douglass North. North estimates average annual productivity increases in ocean shipping to have been 0.45 percent per year for the two centuries preceding independence. Since very little of the total change is believed to have taken place before 1675, North's figures confirm Shepard and Walton's.

Why did marketing and distribution costs fall so dramatically? The most important savings resulted from reduced risk in shipping, greater efficiency in distribution methods, and increased competitiveness in trade finance. Shipping risks were lower because fewer cargoes—and fewer crew members—were lost to pirates. This reduced risk was reflected in insurance premium reductions, estimated to average about 20 percent.

The sheer volume of trade allowed ships and ships' officers to specialize in specific cargoes and routes. Complex "triangular trade," mythologized in history textbooks (New England rum to Africa, African slaves to the Caribbean, Caribbean molasses to New England), was the exception rather than the rule in the late colonial period. By simply shuttling back and forth across the Atlantic or between northern ports and the Caribbean, shipowners cut waiting time in ports, hence reducing labor and overhead costs. A high volume of trade also reduced the unit cost of port services. More ship traffic meant cargoes spent fewer days in warehouses waiting for transport to the right place. Accumulated experience in trade—"learning by doing"—meant fewer mistakes in packaging, handling, and storage.

Shepard and Walton note, too, that interest rates on short-term financing of goods in transit were reduced during the period. The volume of trade partly explains this savings: Lenders found it easier to evaluate risks in well-developed trade and distribution channels. Expansion in the number of firms in commercial finance, moreover, is thought to have increased competition; Egnal points to the influx of Scots into the business of "factoring" Virginia and Maryland tobacco as the source of this competition.

Estimates of colonial growth, then, really amount to controlled conjectures based on fragmentary (and often nonquantitative) evidence. Our ignorance is not necessarily fated to last forever, however—data extracted from trade records and local legal records may yet yield a clearer picture of the way the colonial economy evolved. And as readers will discover in chapter 3, a better portrait of colonial economic change may pay dividends in the form of insights into the modern growth process.

Bibliography

**D. Ball and Gary Walton, "Agricultural Productivity Change in 18th Century Pennsylvania," *Journal of Economic History* 36 (March, 1976). Analysis supports view that colonial productivity change was very slow.

*P. Bidwell and J. Falconer, *History of Agriculture in the Northern United States 1620–1860* (Carnegie Institution, 1925). Classic reference work on pre-Civil War northern agriculture.

*Stuart Bruchey (ed.), *The Colonial Merchant* (Harcourt, Brace and World, 1966). Important resource material on colonial entrepreneurship.

*Marc Egnal, "The Economic Development of the Thirteen Colonies, 1720–1775," *William and Mary Quarterly* 32 (April 1975). Literate survey of basic material; comes to middle-ground conclusion on pace of development.

*Robert Gallman, "The Pace and Pattern of American Economic Growth," in Lance Davis, Richard Easterlin, William Parker (eds.), *American Economic Growth* (Harper and Row, 1972). First part of chapter cogently summarizes statistics on colonial growth.

*Lewis Gray, *History of Agriculture in the Southern United States* (Carnegie Institution, 1933). Remarkable companion volume to Bidwell and Falconer; still very useful.

*James Henretta, "Economic Development and Social Structure in Colonial Boston," *William and Mary Quarterly* 22 (Jan., 1965). Analysis of changes in the economic structure of Boston, as seen through the tax rolls.

*James Henretta, *The Evolution of American Society 1700–1815: An Interdisciplinary Analysis* (Lexington, 1973). Easy survey of colonial development.

*Alice Jones, "Wealth Estimates for the American Middle Colonies, 1774," *Economic Development and Cultural Change* 18 (July, 1970). Complements the New England estimate.

*Alice Jones, "Wealth Estimates for the New England Colonies about 1770," *Journal of Economic History* 32 (June, 1972). Useful in this context for estimating colonial income.

*David Klingaman, "The Significance of Grain in the Development of the Tobacco Colonies," *Journal of Economic History* 29 (March 1969). Argues that prosperity in the upper South in the late colonial period was due to diversification into grain farming.

*Aubrey Land, "The Tobacco Staple and the Planter's Problems: Technology, Labor, Crops," *Agricultural History* 43 (1969). Qualitative evidence on tobacco plantation productivity.

*John McCusker, "The Rum Trade and the Balance of Payments of the Thirteen Continental Colonies 1650–1775," *Journal of Economic History* 30 (March, 1970). Discounts the significance of rum in New England's trade, which was once thought as crucial to New England's prosperity.

**Douglass North, "Sources of Productivity Change to Ocean Shipping 1600–1850," *Journal of Political Economy* 76 (Sept./Oct., 1968). Analysis of the causes of falling shipping costs, using seminal methodology.

*J. Potter, "The Growth of Population in America 1700–1860" in D. Glass and D. Eversley (eds.), *Population in History* (Aldine, 1965). Excellent summary of colonial demography.

*Jacob Price, "The Economic Growth of the Chesapeake and the European Market 1697–1775," *Journal of Economic History* 24 (Dec., 1964). Descriptive material on economic conditions in the upper South.

**James Shepard and Gary Walton, *Shipping, Martime Trade and the Economic Development of Colonial North America* (Cambridge University, 1972). Contains research from their numerous journal articles; critically important overview of how colonial trade affected economic growth.

*J. Soltow, "Scottish Traders in Virginia 1750–1775," *Economic History Review* 12 (August, 1959). Explanation of why tobacco markets became more efficient.

*George Taylor, "American Economic Growth before 1840," *Journal of Economic History* 24 (Dec., 1964). Readable survey of colonial growth; less controversial regarding colonial development than postcolonial development.

Mercantilism and the american revolution

2

Colonial commerce was governed by a web of bounties, restrictions, and outright prohibitions intended to bind together the British Empire and reduce its economic dependence on other nations. The rationale for this system of laws and administrative directives is called mercantilism. Mercantilist policies dominated European economic philosophy for hundreds of years, beginning with the rise of strong central governments in the 15th century and ending only with the dramatic expansion of world trade in the 19th. It is interesting to American economic historians because of the role mercantilist policies played in the development of the colonies. Indeed, as this chapter will seek to elucidate, historians have spent much energy debating the proposition that mercantilist policies caused the American Revolution.

Whether mercantilism should get the blame—or credit—for precipitating revolt is almost impossible to decide. As the reader will discover, neither "new" nor "old" economic history really is up to the task of matching cause to this particular effect. What New Economic History can do, however, is provide a framework for measuring the impact of mercantilist policies on colonial income and fill in some of the numbers needed to measure that impact.

The Mercantilist System

The ultimate purpose of mercantilism—if in fact, it is reasonable to talk about the "purpose" of an economic system that evolved over centuries—was to use the economy to defend the power of the state. This meant shaping the economy so that it could provide maximum support in the event of war. Mercantilist legislation encouraged production of goods needed to make the country self-sufficient, to provide protection against foreign blackmail in an emergency. Subsidies were offered to industry, and tariff barriers or embargoes were imposed to protect these same industries from foreign competition. Protectionism had the secondary effect of reducing total imports, thus limiting the outward flow of gold and silver coins (specie) used to pay for imports.

Before the 19th century there was a practical purpose to such deliberate attempts to generate surpluses in the international balance of payments and thereby to accumulate specie. Precious metal was truly international money, vital for paying mercenaries, bribing neutral countries into alliance, and financing purchases of war goods from abroad. It would be giving too much credit to the mercantilists, however, to infer that their fetish with specie had a strictly rational basis. Mercantilists rather crudely connected gold with power. They almost mystically associated the rise of Spain in the 16th century with that country's discovery of gold in the New World. Before more relevant statistics like gross national product, per capita income, and growth rates were systematically collected, the abundance of specie served as a subjective bellweather of economic performance. Hence international payments deficits, which reduced the quantity of specie in circulation, were considered bad, while payments surpluses were considered good.

How do colonies suit the mercantilist scheme? In the 16th and 17th centuries, the prime lure of colonies was precious metals. The exploration of North America by the French, Dutch, and English was in large part motivated by hopes of matching Spain's good luck in Mexico and Peru. It was subsequently discovered that other natural resources could be as useful as bullion. Colonies could provide strategic military goods unavailable at home, like tall, straight tree trunks to make ships' masts. They might also provide materials in great demand—like sugar, and tobacco—that would otherwise be purchased from foreigners with the subsequent loss of specie.

A geographically scattered empire like England's or France's, moreover, stimulated the growth of an enormous merchant marine, which could serve as a training ground and source of peacetime employment for naval personnel needed in the event of war. Last and least important, colonies might be markets for home products shut out of foreign markets by other countries' competitive mercantilist policies.

British Mercantilism in Practice

Mercantilist regulation of British colonies dates from the 1620's, when steps were taken to prevent the importation into England of tobacco

from Dutch and Spanish colonies. A more complete system was instituted in the 1650's and 1660's, embodied in a set of laws called the Navigation Acts. These acts can be boiled down to four general categories.
First, to protect British shipping interests, vessels owned or built outside
the Empire were banned from the colonial trade and ships involved in
colonial trade were required to employ a crew consisting of no less than
three-fourths British subjects.

Second, a long, changing list of "enumerated" goods produced in
British colonies, including sugar, tobacco, indigo, furs, and naval stores
could only be shipped to Britain. This meant that even enumerated
goods bound for the continent had to be shipped initially to England
and then reshipped to their ultimate destination.

As part of a coherent mercantilist system, enumeration may or may
not have made sense. The obvious disadvantage was that the extra cost
of shipping through England made colonial exports less competitive in
world markets, and thereby reduced opportunities to earn foreign
exchange—that is, bullion—for Empire coffers. But the enumeration
requirement worked like a sales tax or export tariff, raising the price to
foreign buyers and lowering the revenues per unit to domestic sellers. If
continental European demand for colonial exports were inelastic, higher
consumer prices with the associated lower volume of sales would have
actually increased total Empire export revenues. Since the relevant demand elasticities are not known, it is not possible to calculate the net
impact of export enumeration on foreign exchange earnings. The contemporary mercantilist rationale for reexport requirements were not some
esoteric economist's argument, but the boost they provided to British
shipping, ship construction, and port facilities. Note, too, that enumeration generated healthy profits for English merchants in the business of
warehousing and transferring cargoes. Keeping these merchants happy
may not have been an objective of mercantilist doctrine, but it was good
politics.

Third, there were controls on imports that mirrored export enumeration. Enumerated imports were, by law, shuttled to England and
reloaded on British ships before they could be shipped to colonies.
Along with boosting British commerce, the requirement facilitated the
collection of stiff tariffs on imported goods that might have otherwise escaped detection.

And, finally, there was a set of direct controls and incentive payments to encourage imperial self-sufficiency. The grand design was
production specialization along rather sensible lines of "comparative advantage." England would produce manufactures, while the colonies
would produce raw materials. To that end, the colonies were forbidden
to export wool textiles and fur hats, even from one colony to another.
And, subsidies (bounties) for exports of indigo to England created an industry in South Carolina where none had previously existed.

Economic Impact on the American Colonies

Imperial regulation increased the income of some colonists, decreased that of others. On the benefit side, protection against non-British competition boosted the size of New England's ship building and shipping industries. Massachusetts shipyards, close to the forests of upper New England, had low costs compared to English shipyards. And once built, American colonial ships fared well in Empire competition, particularly between New England and the West Indies. As Shepard and Walton point out, colonial crews could be paid off and dismissed at home port; English ships were forced to bear the expense of frequently idle deckhands in those same ports.

A number of colonies benefited from the policy of subsidizing colonial production that complemented home manufacture. The six-pence-per-pound bounty on indigo paid after 1748 represented only a few percent of the wholesale price of the goods on the dock in Charleston, but many historians believe it had a critical impact on the growth of the industry. Bounties on other products—notably tar, pitch, turpentine, and lumber from North Carolina's forests—generated cash payments somewhat in excess of the indigo bounty. And finally, colonial exporters of unsubsidized goods benefited indirectly from mercantilist policies due to protection afforded them in the English domestic market. Colonial exports sold for a higher price in Britain because competing non-British products bore special, high tariffs.

Balanced against these benefits were the burdens of the Navigation Acts. First, the colonists had to pay higher prices for most goods imported from non-British sources, since a long list of these imports had to be routed through England. Enumerated non-British imports represented about 15 percent of colonial imports. Americans were also forced to pay premium prices for English manufactures protected by enumeration that might otherwise have been purchased from low-cost Continental sources.

Analogous to the import burden is the export burden generated by the Navigation Acts. Most of the tobacco and rice produced in the colonies was reexported from Britain, and a large portion of the reexport cost was borne by southern planters. Finally, colonial exporters paid higher prices for shipping services than they might otherwise, owing to the inability of foreign vessels to compete for the colonial trade. Part of the burden fell on foreign consumers forced to pay higher prices. But unless the supply of colonial exports and the demand for colonial imports were utterly unresponsive to price changes—an unlikely notion—colonists shared that burden. Note that this burden on export producers must be weighed against the benefits accruing to colonial shipowners if one is to compute the net impact on the colonial economy.

Historians have long debated the effect of the Navigation Acts on the colonies. Lawrence Harper changed the character of the debate, however, by offering actual estimates of some of the gross burdens and benefits in place of qualitative judgments about their importance.

Harper's analysis of the burden, shown in table 2.1, is limited to the direct costs of enumeration—the costs of rerouting exports and imports through England. The wide range of estimates for the year 1773 is derived from varying assumptions about the burden of enumeration per unit traded and the total volume of goods affected. Harper also computes one portion of the benefits of the Navigation Acts, the total subsidies paid on colonial exports of indigo, naval stores (tar, pitch, turpentine), and lumber.

Writing two decades later (1965), Robert Paul Thomas recomputed the impact of colonial regulation, working this time from an explicit counterfactual model of what economic life would have been like without the British presence. Thomas argued that it was unrealistic to speak of the burden of British Empire membership before 1763. Separation would only have led to domination by another power—France or Spain. After 1763, however, American independence was, at least in theory, practical. The French and Indian War resulted in the loss of Canada by France and Florida by Spain, spelling the end of significant continental influence over the lives of North American residents.

TABLE 2.1

**HARPER'S ESTIMATE OF BENEFITS AND BURDENS
OF NAVIGATION ACTS
(million $)**

	Low	Intermediate	High
Export Burden			
Tobacco	2.18	2.43	3.40
Rice	.19	.23	.52
Import Burden	.52	1.00	3.44
total*	2.88	3.66	7.36
Bounty Benefit			
Indigo	.12	.12	.12
Naval Stores	.18	.18	.18
Lumber	.03	.03	.03
total*	.32	.32	.32

*Columns do not sum due to rounding errors in the individual entries.

Source: Lawrence Harper, "The Effect of the Navigation Acts on the Thirteen Colonies" in Harry Scheiber (ed.), *United States Economic History* (Knopf, 1964), p. 37.

Thomas then calculated the impact of trade regulation in one year, 1770, and alternatively for an average year over the 1763–72 period.

THE REEXPORT BURDEN

Colonists were paid lower prices ("the direct burden") and were able to sell less ("the indirect burden") due to reexport requirements of the Navigation Acts. To calculate a hypothetical free market price for exports, Thomas assumes that, in the absence of regulation, the ratio of American to Continental prices for each export prior to the Revolution would have been the same as the ratio that actually prevailed after the Revolution. He then multiplies his hypothetical, unregulated price by the actual volume of pre-Revolution exports to obtain the direct burden.

The size of the indirect burden depends critically upon how responsive American export suppliers would have been to the higher prices prevailing in a hypothetically unregulated market. Thomas assumes separate supply elasticities for tobacco, rice, and a category called "other exports" to generate hypothetical increases in total export revenues. He then subtracts half that amount to net out the added cost of diverting additional labor and land resources into hypothetical export production.

THE IMPORT BURDEN

Americans paid more and bought less due to Empire restrictions on imports. Thomas computes these direct and indirect import burdens analogously to the export burdens, again using actual post-Revolutionary import prices as a hypothetical benchmark. The burden does not end here, however. Americans also paid more for English goods that were protected against Continental competition by tariffs, and Thomas makes an effort to estimate this loss as well.

EXPORT PREFERENCES

Just as English exports to colonial markets were protected against continental competition, American exports to Britain were protected against competition from non-Empire sources. Thomas calculates the positive price impact on colonial exports by creating an index of the average value of such tariff preferences. By assuming an average supply elasticity for the goods subject to this preference, he is able to estimate both the direct benefit of higher prices and the indirect benefit of an increased volume of exports.

EXPORT BOUNTIES

Bounties raised colonial income, but by less than the total cash payment to producers. This follows from the fact that bounties stimulated the production of certain goods—indigo, naval stores, and lumber—and thereby reduced the amount of land and labor available to produce other goods. To adjust for this resource reallocation, Thomas assumed that (1) the supply elasticity for lumber and naval stores was equal to one, and (2) without bounties, no indigo at all would have been exported.

SHIPPING BENEFITS AND BURDENS

The Navigation Acts tended to increase the earnings of colonial shipowners by blocking direct competition from non-Empire vessels. They tended to decrease ship earnings, however, by reducing the total volume of foreign commerce. In the absence of data needed to quantify these effects, Thomas ignores them. This is equivalent to assuming that the benefits equaled the burdens.

Table 2.2 summarizes Thomas's results.

Although calculated quite differently, the magnitude of Thomas's estimate of the gross burden of the Navigation Acts isn't very different from Harper's "intermediate" estimate. What makes Thomas's net burden so much smaller is, of course, the offsetting military defense benefit, included to provide a more realistic measure of the overall impact of mercantilism.

TABLE 2.2

**ANNUAL NET BURDEN ON
COLONIAL FOREIGN COMMERCE
(million $)**

	1770	1763–1772
Burden		
Exports		
tobacco	1.63	1.04
rice	.60	.70
other	.27	.18
Imports	.61	.72
total*	3.10	2.63
Benefit		
Tariff Preference	.28	.20
Bounties	.17	.18
total*	.44	.37
Net Burden	2.66	2.26

*Columns do not add up due to rounding errors in the individual entries.

Source: Robert Thomas, "A Quantitative Approach to the Study of the Effects of British Imperial Policy on Colonial Welfare," *Journal of Economic History* 25 (Dec., 1965), p. 626.

Thomas's interpretation of the impact also differs from Harper's. Harper argued that a $3 million burden was, in some important sense, large—larger, in fact, than the entire budget of the United States' national government in the 1790's. Just why this comparison is relevant, however, is not clear. The best explanation is that Harper had no alternative standard by which to compare the estimated burden.

Thomas, by contrast, does; he uses per capita income as a reasonable basis for comparison. If, as Thomas assumes, income was about $100,[1] the net burden would be far less than one percent. From such an estimate it would be difficult, Thomas concludes, to infer that the British presence was a serious hardship for the colonists.

Far from settling the matter, Thomas's estimate of the impact of British imperial policy has called forth from the economic history profession a series of rebuttals, corrections, and reformulations. Among the most significant points made by Thomas's critics and critics of Thomas's critics include the following:

(1) *Choice of the Appropriate Counterfactual Hypothesis.* Roger Ransom challenges the analytic value of Thomas's *net* burden computation on the grounds that the benefits of military protection were politically separable from the cost of the Navigation Acts. What Ransom is really challenging is the basis of Thomas's counterfactual hypothesis. The choice facing the British Empire need not have been simply "business as usual" or total independence for the colonies. It would have been possible, Ransom argues, for Britain to do away with the Navigation Acts without eliminating military protection for the colonies. By the same logic, there is no reason to believe that the Navigation Acts could not have been selectively dismantled, retaining the portions that were viewed as mutually beneficial to England and the colonies—bounties and, perhaps, tariff preferences—while abandoning reexport and reimport provisions. From this perspective, the relevant burden is the gross burden of import and export losses totaling $3.1 million.

(2) *Interpretation of the Magnitude of the Burden.* Even if one accepts $3.1 million as the most appropriate measure of the burden, it doesn't seem like much compared to total national income. As Ransom points out, however, the burden was not shared equally by regions in proportion to regional income. The South bore most of the impact, suffering losses on tobacco and rice exports. The burden is even more concentrated because not all individuals had equal stakes in foreign trade. If, in fact, just a few percent of the population—plantation owners—bore the lion's share of the burden, the political impact of the Navigation Acts might have been significant indeed.

---

[1] Gallman suggests that it was somewhat less.

One should not make too much of this specific argument however—agitation against mercantile restrictions was actually stronger in New England than in the South. On the other hand, it is simplistic to argue that a small per capita burden meant that the Navigation Acts were unimportant.

In addressing the impact issue, Thomas and Harper both compute one year's burden. This convention, on first glance, seems reasonable; the year eliminates seasonal fluctuations while presenting a picture of the flow of economic losses associated with the Navigation Acts. On reflection, though, this choice seems arbitrary since the colonists were not asking for a year's suspension of the Acts, but—one must assume—their permanent abolition.

A more logical approach, then, would be to calculate the "present value"[2] of the future burden extended indefinitely. This approach would, of course, increase the estimated burden many times over. At a ten percent discount rate—conservatively high for the period—a projected $3.1 million annual burden has a "present value" of $31 million. Still, if the object of the exercise is to measure the economic stake of the colonists in obtaining reform of the Navigation Acts or in achieving independence, this present value calculation is most relevant. A war of independence that involved a once-and-for-all-investment of less than the present value burden could be rationalized in purely economic terms.

(3) *Statistical and Conceptual Errors in Measurement.* As we've seen, measurement of the direct cost of reexport and reimport regulations depends upon assumptions about the price of goods in the absence of trade restrictions. Thomas assumed that the cost markup of exporting goods to Europe in percentage terms would have fallen to post-Revolution levels. Joe Reid, however, has demonstrated that this technique would not yield an analytically acceptable estimate of hypothetical pre-Revolution prices unless a variety of assumptions about market conditions were correct. Both Gary Walton and Peter McClelland have inconclusively examined these assumptions to assess the quantitative importance of Thomas's failure to match assumption to reality.

Other economists question a yet more fundamental aspect of Thomas's computation. Thomas uses Philadelphia and Amsterdam data to measure American-European price differences. Unfortunately, it is doubtful that the sample of prices from these individual cities is representative of import/export prices generally. The issue is not a trivial one; McClelland notes that, while Philadelphia rice prices rose 28 percent between 1760 and 1789, Charleston prices *fell* by 72 percent.

(4) *Estimation of an Upper Bound.* Computation of the Navigation Acts burden can produce only rough estimates of the actual burden since the data are untrustworthy. This sort of problem is not unusual in the social

---

[2] See this chapter's appendix for an explanation of the term and how it is calculated.

sciences, and the standard method for dealing with it is to stack the case against the hypothesis one is trying to prove. If the evidence then supports the hypothesis, one may then be confident that it is correct.

Hence, since Thomas believed that the burden was, in some useful sense, small, he made an effort to identify an "upper bound" of all reasonable estimates. Since the upper bound of the burden that he then measured was small, Thomas felt justified in drawing strong conclusions from weak evidence.

McClelland however challenged the assertion that Thomas had properly stacked the deck against his own case. Thomas's estimates may or may not be correct, but there is no reason, in fact, to believe that he systematically biased the computation against the hypothesis that the burden was small. Hence, McClelland re-estimates the data, arriving at an alternative upper bound estimate of 3 percent of national income—much more than Thomas's estimate, but in the context of the debate, still relatively small.

What can one conclude from this debate? Herman Krooss summarized the view of many in his remark that "the cost of the Navigation Acts has become a great bore."

It is surely true that economic historians have spent a disproportionate amount of energy on the narrow issue of the financial burden of colonial import and export regulations. Much of the literature interpreting Thomas's technique can best be defended as intellectual games economists enjoy playing for their own sake. McClelland's simply derived upper bound is probably the last word on the technical issue of measuring the Navigation Acts burden that will be of interest to historians.

From the viewpoint of history, estimation of the Navigation Acts burden is a starting point, not an end in itself. What really concerns historians is measuring the importance of mercantile restrictions as a cause of the American Revolution. There is no definitive analysis of that issue, nor is it reasonable to expect historians ever to generate one. The American Revolution, like most wars in history, was in large part a product of misperceptions and unilateral decisions. Superimposing a rational framework on the conflict then, simply because rational behavior is easier to explain than irrational behavior, begs the issue. It is possible, however, to draw a plausible, if unprovable, scenario of the origins of the war and the role played by mercantile restrictions.

For the first half of the 18th century Britain and the American colonies coexisted on satisfactory, if somewhat uneasy, terms. Trade restraints imposed by the Empire, as we have seen, probably had only modest impact on colonial incomes, and most of the burden was born by tobacco and rice planters. The burden would have been greater and rested more heavily on middle and northern colonists if trade laws had been uniformly enforced. In fact, England did not have the will to intervene in illegal, though flourishing, trade between New England and the non-British West Indian sugar islands. High tariffs, embodied in the Molasses Act of 1733, were never paid on the bulk of imported sugar because it suited the Crown to avoid political friction with the colonies. The obvious benefits to the colonies of Empire membership—bounties, tariff preferences, naval protection—also helped to smooth over inherent conflicts.

The year 1763 marked a turning point in the relationship. Before that year the perceived benefits of Empire membership dominated perceived costs. After 1763 colonial arrangements became increasingly unsatisfactory for both sides. England had just emerged victorious in a long war with France. But the war left Britain with a huge public debt and a growing conviction that the colonies must bear a greater share of the cost of maintaining the Empire. Effective rates of taxation in England were many times higher than tax rates in the colonies. Thus, to raise revenues, the Crown imposed a series of new taxes on the colonies and reformed colonial administrative practices to better enforce new and existing taxes.

For their part, the colonists saw the destruction of French power in North America as one less reason for suffering the restrictions of membership in the Empire. With the French gone from Quebec and the Great Lakes region, the colonists had much less to fear from external military power. The British victory actually created a new source of conflict: Americans wanted access to Indian lands formerly protected by the French, while the British wanted only peace with the natives and smaller military expenditures. English efforts to prevent colonial encroachment on Indian territory never amounted to much, but division over land policy hardly strengthened the bond between England and America.

British attempts to raise revenues both broadened the economic base of hostility to the home country and provided valuable lessons to the colonists in the art of collective resistance. A succession of revenue-related measures—the Sugar Act of 1764, the Stamp and Quartering Acts of 1765, and Townshend Acts of 1767, the Tea Act of 1773—were passed by Parliament. And colonial administrators were given increased power and personal financial incentives to enforce the revenue laws. Before 1763 only southerners had much reason to chafe under Empire regulations. But enforcement of Sugar Act restrictions on trade with the West Indies alienated articulate northern merchants, as well, while the highly visible Stamp Act tax on documents irritated just about everyone in business.

Colonial response to Parliament's revenue initiatives was active resistance. The Sugar Act sparked a boycott on imports from Britain. It succeeded in part because "patriotic" gangs called the Sons of Liberty were able to coerce unsympathetic local merchants. Parliament bowed to colonial sentiment, but tried again in 1767 by passing a flock of revenue measures known as the Townshend Acts. And as might be expected, the colonists responded with another nonimportation agreement, one that this time round received the official backing of the increasingly radicalized colonial legislatures. Imports were cut by one-third in 1768, and once again Parliament's will faltered; the Townshend Acts were repealed in 1770.

The net impact of these skirmishes was to polarize opinion over the right of England to govern the colonies. The colonists learned that resistance worked, and they gradually developed a popular philosophical rationale for that resistance. The British learned that decentralized rule would no longer work. They responded by increasing the legal authority of colonial administrators and by sending troops to back that authority.

By 1773 the psychology of conflict had escalated to the point that both sides were just as willing to do battle over the symbols of British authority as they had been earlier to contest actual attempts to raise revenue. Thus in response to a comparatively innocuous attempt by Parliament to grant a monopoly on the colonial tea trade to the East India Company, merchants organized the Boston Tea Party. Parliament then closed Boston harbor. A renewed British attempt to block settlement of Indian lands evoked a third import boycott from the First Continental Congress and a virtual declaration of economic autonomy. Last-minute attempts by Lord North in March, 1775, to compromise on basic issues crumbled under the weight of revolutionary rhetoric and mutual preparations for war.

What part, then, did mercantile restrictions play on the road to rebellion? As noted before, they had only modest direct effect on the lives of most colonists. A mercantilist concept—the notion that the basic purpose of colonies was to enhance the well-being of the home country— did, however, lead England into conflict with its colonies after 1763. Moreover, the generally benevolent impact of the mercantile system on colonial income need not mean that it would have remained benevolent. The colonists quite correctly perceived that the Navigation Acts were a potential vehicle for economic exploitation, and probably also perceived that Parliament would not pass by that opportunity for exploitation indefinitely. Hence, although the Navigation Acts did not precipitate the Revolution, they were a potent symbol of the economic differences that underlay the conflict.

The Economic Impact of the Revolution

From the perspective of the 20th century, in which war is associated with great economic upheaval, the American Revolution looks peculiar indeed. Though the Revolution did disrupt the lives of many and de-

stroyed a great deal of property, it never placed huge demands on economic resources the way the American Civil War or World War II did.
The colonial population numbered about 2.5 million in 1775; perhaps
one-third of that number were men of fighting age. Thus, in theory, the
colonial military could have drawn volunteers from a pool of about
800,000. In fact, the Continental army never exceeded 20,000. Another
10,000 may have served at any one time in the small American navy or
the much larger fleet of quasi-military privateers. But the vast majority
of colonial males either performed temporary services or were never involved at all in the patriot cause.

The explanation for this restraint is that the war effort had comparatively few ideologically committed supporters. On one side were the Pa-
triots, an articulate middle class of lawyers, merchants, and planters
leading an under-class of farmers and urbanites enticed by radical ideas
regarding the evils of aristocratic privilege. On the other were the Loyalists—civil servants of the Crown, northern landed wealth, Anglican
clergy—who strongly opposed the break with England. In between was
the majority, with no preferences based on perceived economic interest
or political theory. This group could not be called on to make great sacrifices. They acted as a buffer during the war, maintaining production out
of purely private economic interest and preventing the institution of
"total" war.

The war on the land spanned seven years, from Lexington to the last
skirmish at Combahee, South Carolina in August, 1782. But little of that
time was spent fighting. The British were mostly content to control a few
major ports. And General Washington was usually too busy keeping
together his ill-fed, poorly paid army to be able to threaten the passive
Redcoats.

By contrast, the war at sea was pursued aggressively and successfully
by colonial privateers, who got to keep what they captured. The Royal
Navy was spread too thin and operated too far from home port to offer
much protection to its merchant fleet. One estimate marks the war loss in
British ships and cargo at $80 million. This figure is probably much too
high; Richard B. Morris puts the total at a more realistic $18 million. In
either case, though, the redistribution of wealth from British to American pockets was considerable.

What happened to the colonial economy in the meantime? Predictably, small farmers living out of the range of battle and producing only
food for local markets, were virtually unaffected by the conflict. More
surprisingly perhaps, farms in contested regions or in British-occupied
territories often prospered, selling their crops to the highest bidder. Attempts by the British to interdict exports of tobacco and rice disrupted
the plantation economy of the South, as did seizure of some 25,000
slaves. But total exports of major crops remained substantial. Ships bear-

ing tens of millions of pounds of tobacco ran the British blockade and sold their cargoes in Europe. Since British merchants were more interested in getting by than winning the war, much of this tobacco actually ended up in England.

Comprehensive trade statistics are not available for the war period, though it is generally believed that exports were reduced more than imports. The increased trade deficit was at least partially balanced by what economists call "invisible earnings"—the income of privateers, expenditures by French and British troops on American soil who paid their bills in specie. Late in the war, the Continental Congress was also able to obtain credit from the French government and private Dutch banks that offset the negative impact of the blockade on export earnings.

Not everyone profited from the conflict, of course. Armies, even small armies like Washington's, cost a great deal to keep armed, clothed, fed, housed, and transported. Individual colonies were loath to pay their share of the army's bills through taxation, and the Continental Congress had no power to force them to see their duty. Instead, the government resorted to two ancient, if not honorable, methods of war finance: inflation and confiscation.

Congress printed paper money which, at least at first, they intended to redeem for specie at a later date. People who sold goods for government paper—in lieu of coins—were badly burned; by 1781 the Continental currency was worth less than one percent of its issue value. The alternative to peddling bad debts to unwary merchants was to confiscate goods from the well-informed. Loyalists, the first victims, had their lands seized by the state and resold as a source of revenue. After 1781, the army mostly fended for itself, scavenging food and work animals from unlucky farmers in its path.

The Transition to Independence

Not long ago, most American historians believed that the period between the Revolutionary War and the adoption of the Constitution in 1789 was one of serious economic decline.[3] England, after all, shut its markets to American exporters and abandoned American shipping to southern Europe to the mercies of Mediterranean pirates. Spanish mercantilist regulations made it difficult to make up lost trade elsewhere in Europe. Hence, with imports exceeding exports, specie drained from the country; shortages of money spread the depression beyond export industries into local market economies.

---

[3] A view disputed—to their great credit—by a few historians. See works by Jensen, Main, and Ferguson listed in the bibliography.

Problems beyond the control of a small country, according to the conventional view, were exacerbated by the weak decentralized government embodied in the Articles of Confederation. States retained the power to print money, issue debt, and restrict the flow of interstate commerce, all of which they did with little regard for the greater interests of the nation. Former colonies openly squabbled with each other over land claims west of the Appalachian mountains. In Massachusetts, mobs of poor farmers protesting high taxes and a lack of credit attacked state militia. National representatives were unable to negotiate trade treaties with Spain and England because the states could not agree on necessary concessions.

Enter the Constitution. The new federal system centralized authority to print money and regulate internal and external trade. In effect, the Constitution prepared the way for America to create a mercantile system of its own and thus compete more successfully with European systems organized along similar lines. Given effective power to make foreign policy, President Washington was able to remain free of entanglement in the Napoleonic Wars and thereby was able to establish lucrative European markets for U.S. shipping. At home, the Constitution enabled Treasury Secretary Alexander Hamilton to set public finance on a firm footing, with the federal government accepting responsibility for debts of the states and creating confidence in the national fiscal system.

The above interpretation of the Confederation period endured for two reasons. First, it *seems* to fit the economic facts. Trade did appear to decline in the post-Revolution years and shipping interests did indeed complain bitterly of their plight. Second, it justifies the shift to strong centralized government under the Constitution. The Constitution is a symbol of unity and national success; historians have therefore generally been eager to interpret the motives of its creators and the record of government after its adoption in the best possible light.

A close look at the evidence suggests, however, that postwar economic dislocation was minor, or at least less serious than once believed. Gordon Bjork's reconstruction of trade statistics for the Confederation period argues that export revenues quickly regained prewar levels and that the terms of trade swung in favor of the Americans. The United States did lose its special status within the British Empire and was excluded from legal trade with the British West Indies but continued a strong export trade with England itself. The real value of U.S. exports to England from 1784 to 1789, by Bjork's reckoning, was equal to 94 percent of the real value of colonial exports from 1770 to 1775.

Trade with the French West Indies, moreover, increased substantially, and illegal trade with British islands in the Caribbean is also thought to have flourished. It is probable that between them, they did not account for as much revenue as legal trade with the West Indies before the war. But in combination with increased commerce with southern Europe, the total value of U.S. exports was roughly the same magnitude as before the war. Shepard and Walton estimate that average annual colonial exports between 1768 and 1772 equaled $15.3 million. Bjork's reconstruction of average annual exports from 1784 to 1790, the Confederation period, equals $15.8 million.

Moreover, the relative movement of import and export prices suggests that, by comparison with the last six years of colonial rule, the Confederation paid less to buy more. According to Bjork's estimates, the average price of imports fell slightly, while the price of U.S. exports, led by tobacco, were sharply higher. In part, this change in the terms of trade reflects the benefits of being able to buy and sell abroad without the need to divert trade through England. In part it may also reflect a slow upward shift in the supply function for tobacco, as soil exhaustion in eastern Maryland and Virginia pushed tobacco cultivation onto the Piedmont.

One should not infer from Bjork's findings, however, that the Confederation period consisted solely of days of wine and roses. First, there is risk in accepting Bjork's trade statistics without qualification. Albert Fishlow and Shepherd and Walton argue that there is considerable room for error in his estimation procedure. Colonial export figures are based on extrapolations from just a few states, which may or may not be representative. Also, it must be remembered that recovery in the total value of trade was not matched by recovery in per capita terms. The explosive population growth characteristic of the late colonial period continued unabated in the two decades from 1770 to 1790. An average annual population growth rate slightly above 3 percent meant that 83 percent more people lived in the thirteen states in 1790 than 20 years earlier. Hence the export recovery in gross terms estimated by Bjork still implies a reduction of exports per capita of 59 percent and some parallel decline in living standards.

Exporters, moreover, did not all benefit equally from the post-war recovery. Trade patterns of the lower South and New England were clearly disrupted by the break with England. New England's fishing industry recovered slowly; South Carolina's indigo industry not at all. And neither region was in a position to take advantage of high postwar prices for tobacco and grains. The middle states, which did benefit from the grain boom, still suffered from the uncertainty of rapidly fluctuating foreign grain demand. Pennsylvania exports fell 45 percent from 1784 to 1786, then rose 71 percent from 1786 to 1790. Uncertainty is a cost, as every farmer with a mortgage understands well.

How, then, might one generalize about the health of the Confederation economy? Adjustment to independence benefited some and hurt others; losses surely outnumbered gains, but it is hard to go much beyond that qualitative statement. Reduction in trade per capita, noted previously, does not necessarily imply a comparable reduction in output per capita; the export sector, after all, never accounted for more than 10 percent of national income. And capital and land diverted from the export sector might have been almost as valuable creating goods for domestic consumption.

Another much discussed trend, the reduction in the quantity of specie in circulation, also has an ambiguous meaning for the economic well-being of the Confederation. The loss of coins was a result of an excess of payments for imports over revenues from exports—in other words, a balance of payments deficit. This loss does not necessarily imply a loss of total wealth to the economy: The money was exchanged for goods of equal value which were either consumed or invested. Nor can we be sure that the specie reduction affected total output, or impeded the efficiency of markets for goods or factors of production. Prices probably fell in terms of specie, thus probably restoring the total purchasing power of the remaining coins. And other forms of money and what economists call "near money"—paper notes issued by the states, private warehouse receipts on crops ready for sale, personal IOU's—served then (as they do today) as substitutes for species. Price level changes undoubtedly shuffled the ownership of wealth. A mortgage payable in specie, for example, became more valuable while farms encumbered by such mortgages became less valuable.

The number of people whose lives were altered by independence—for better or worse—does however provide a clue to why historians looking for signs of serious economic discontent had no trouble finding them. Those who benefit from political and economic events have no particular motive to alert the world to their good fortune. But those who lose are apt to complain, particularly if their expectations were quite different. Boston merchants did not believe that the fruits of successful revolution should end up in the hands of Philadelphia and New York merchants. Small farmers, once encouraged to identify their troubles with arbitrary rule from England, did not understand why their debts should become more burdensome after independence had been won.

Does this revisionist view of the Confederation justify skepticism about the economic impact of the Constitution? It is very clear that the revival of foreign trade after 1790 was more a result of European wars than the new Constitution. By virtue of American neutrality during the European wars, American ships could trade with both sides. The demand for American products increased substantially, and the demand for American shipping services increased yet more dramatically. A special feature of U.S. trade was the booming new business in reexports. In an ironic reversal of pre-Revolution mercantile roles, British West Indian products were shipped to the United States, relabeled as American, and then shipped to Britain without much risk of confiscation by the French Navy. U.S. reexport trade grew from nothing in 1790 to over $45 million in 1800, while ordinary exports increased from $19 million to over $40 million.

With respect to the economic advantages of the Constitution, then, the burden of proof properly rests on those who see in the document special incentives to growth. In the 20th century, we have become quite dependent on government institutions to regulate the economy. One should not infer from this modern experience, however, that government had an equivalent role to play early in the 19th century.

A clear advantage to the new system was that it gave the federal government the right to tax. The Confederation government, dependent on voluntary contributions from the states, was unable to raise revenue for public goods like national defense. It was, after all, in the interest of individual states to resist contributions since they would receive benefits from total national expenditure whether they contributed or not. The quantitative importance of this reform is not certain, though. Revenue requirements of the central government were quite small by modern standards; discretionary power to tax, short of the blanket authority granted by the Constitution, could have served as well.

The constitution removed power from the states to tax imports, granting this right only to the federal government. In practice, states within the Confederation couldn't very easily impede imports through tariffs, because foreigners could easily transfer their business to competing ports in other states. Under the Constitution, the federal government could restrict imports. Hence the benefit, if any, of this constitutional provision depends upon the debatable returns to protective tariffs and other trade restrictions (see chapter 5).

The other important economic provision of the Constitution was the elimination of state authority to print currency. Centralization of the power to create money is extremely valuable if the government wishes to control the quantity of money in circulation. But the government had no such wish; the very concept of central banking as an instrument of "monetary policy" had no meaning in the early years of the Republic.

In the absence of central banking, the major effect of eliminating state-printed money was to bind the state economies together through a common legal medium of exchange. This sounds more important than it really was. On the plus side, adoption of common currency reduced one cost of doing business in the same way it would be more convenient today to buy and sell goods abroad if foreigners used dollars as money. The common currency meant that businesses did not have to keep track of exchange rates between state currencies, or keep special forms of money on hand to buy or sell in other states. On the minus side, however, the common currency probably meant that economic shocks—a fall in the price of tobacco, for example—were transmitted through the national economy more rapidly. The benefits of economic centralization may thus have been outweighed by the costs.

For the moment, then, history allows no easy generalizations about the economics of government under the Constitution. The triumphs— or failings—of the founding fathers can be scrutinized only through a glass darkly.

Appendix A: Measurement of the Navigation Acts Burden

Thomas measured the burden of the Navigation Acts by analyzing their effect on what economists call "producer's surplus" and "consumer's surplus". The impact of reexport requirements, reimport requirements, and bounties can all be illustrated using figure 2.1.

First, the case of exports. S_{FOB} is the supply function for colonial exports on the dock in America; D_{CIF} is the demand function for colonial goods landed in Continental Europe. The unit cost (T) of transporting the goods from the colonies to Europe, via England, lowers the effective European demand curve facing the colonists to D_{FOB}. In market equilibrium, then, the colonists sell Q units at price P_C. Europeans pay P_E, the difference $(P_E - P_C)$ going to pay for transportation.

How much better off would colonial exporters be in the absence of the reexport requirement? Suppose direct trade would reduce the cost of transport by ΔT. This would raise the effective demand for colonial exports to D'_{FOB}. In the new equilibrium, the colonists would sell Q' units and receive P'_C per unit. Colonial income increases by the addition to revenues in excess of the "opportunity cost" of the additional resources used in producing $(Q - Q')$ extra exports. The addition to total revenues equals the difference between the rectangle $(P'_C WQ'O)$ and the rectangle $(P_C SQO)$. The opportunity cost of the added resources equals the area under the supply curve $(QSWQ')$. Hence the addition to producers surplus equals the shaded trapezoid $(P_C SWP'_C)$. Note that the change in selling price $(P'_C - P_C)$ is less than ΔT because a portion of the savings on transportation accrues to the buyer.

In measuring the trapezoid, Thomas needed to know, P_C, and P'_C, as well as the elasticity of supply to derive $(Q'-Q)$. P_C and Q are derived from trade data. P'_C is a hypothetical price that Thomas estimates from post-Revolution evidence. Thomas makes separate assumptions about the supply elasticity for each major export category.

To analyze the benefit of bounties, one need only think of ΔT as a unit subsidy that exporters can use to offset unit transportation costs. The subsidy raises effective demand from D_{FOB} to D'_{FOB}, and thus

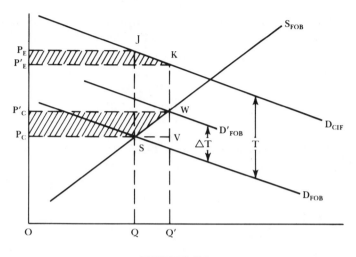

FIGURE 2.1

BURDENS AND BENEFITS OF EMPIRE MEMBERSHIP

Source: Peter McClelland, "The Cost to America of British Imperial Policy." *AER* (May 1969).

changes price and output in America from $P_C Q$ to $P'_C Q'$. The shaded trapezoid now becomes a measure of the benefits of Empire membership; measurement problems are equivalent to those in estimating the cost of reexport requirements.

Thomas assumed that foreign demand for bountied goods was perfectly elastic since England continued to import all bountied goods from non-American sources. It then follows that $(P'_C - P_C) = \Delta T$; the entire bounty ends up in the pockets of suppliers. ΔT is known; Q' comes from trade statistics. The resulting increase in output, $(Q' - Q)$ depends upon the supply elasticity. Thomas assumed that the supply elasticity equaled one for naval stores. He also assumed that, in the absence of bounties, indigo and lumber would not have been exported $(Q = O)$.

An analogous procedure is used to estimate the direct loss in real income associated with paying extra for non-Empire origin imports routed through England. Let S_{FOB} now be the supply of imports on the dock in Europe, and D_{CIF} the colonial demand for imports in America. If transporting goods to America via England cost T per unit, equilibrium is achieved with Q units at price P_E. If transport costs are reduced by ΔT by direct routing of imports, the colonists buy more (Q') and pay less (P'_E). Then real colonial income is increased by the shaded trapezoid $(P_E J K P'_E)$, the change in consumer surplus associated with lower import prices. Measurement of the trapezoid requires knowledge of actual prices (P) and quantities (Q), hypothetical prices (P'_E), and the elasticity of demand.

McClelland's approach, estimating an upper bound on the impact of reimport and reexport requirements, is designed to minimize the need for data. By definition, the fraction of national income lost due to trade route requirements equals

$$Z = \frac{(x-j)\ sE + ytM}{GNP}$$

where

> Z = the burden as a fraction of GNP
> x = fraction of colonial exports sent to Britain
> j = fraction of exports to Britain reexported to third countries
> s = fractional increase in average shipping costs for rerouted exports
> E = total value of colonial exports
> y = fraction of colonial imports from foreign countries routed through Britain
> t = fractional increase in average shipping costs for rerouted imports
> M = total value of colonial imports
> GNP = gross national product of the thirteen colonies

Since it is known that the fraction of reexports $(x-j)$ was greater than the percentage of reimports (y), and the rerouting markup on exports (s) is greater than the rerouting markup on imports (t):

$$(x-j)(s)\ [(E+M)/GNP] > Z$$

McClelland then makes upper-bound estimates for each of the components of the upper bound of Z:

$$0.5 > (x-j)$$
$$0.4 > (s)$$
$$.15 > (E+M)/GNP$$

Substituting in the formula:

$$.03 > Z$$

In other words, the upper bound of the burden is 3 percent of GNP.

One might criticize this procedure from two perspectives. By simplifying the computation McClelland may have discovered an upper bound that is unnecessarily high. In the jargon of econometrics, the procedure may be "inefficient." For McClelland's purposes, however, this is irrelevant. If 3 percent is "small" in the context of his argument, it is not necessary to use a more efficient procedure.

A more serious objection is raised by Walton, who argues that $(.15)$ is not a reasonable upper bound for $(E+M)/GNP$; it might be substantially higher. McClelland bases his upper-bound estimate on data for the 1830s. Walton asserts, however, that if per capita GNP were as small as

$55 at the time of the Revolution, (E + M)/GNP might have been as high as (.06), or 6 percent of GNP.

Just how damaging one finds this point depends upon how significant one believes a 6 percent burden would have been.

Appendix B: Calculating Present Values

When General Motors considers building a new assembly line, it must compare the cost to the expected revenues the plant will produce. It would not make sense, however, simply to add up the costs and add up the expected revenues to see which is larger. For, as will become clear, the timing of the revenues (and the costs) may be critical to the profitability of the investment.

Suppose the plant costs $100 million to build, and is expected to produce $11 million a year in profits each year for 10 years, whence it will become obsolete and worthless. The total revenues would exceed the construction cost—at the end of the ten years, GM would have $110 million ($11 million × 10) in the bank. But note that the company could do better financially simply by putting the $100 million in a savings account. At 5 percent interest, compounded annually, GM could turn its initial $100 million into $163 million without lifting a finger.

How, then, might General Motors decide whether a projected income stream is sufficient to merit an investment? It must adjust (discount) future income to account for alternative uses of the investment principle. If money invested now could earn 10 percent a year elsewhere, the "present value" of a dollar earned a year from now equals just about 91¢ ($1.00/1.10). Similarly, the present value of a dollar received two years from now equals just 83¢ [($1.00/(1.10)^2] because 83¢ earning a 10 percent return for two years would equal $1.

Now go back to the first example. What is the present value of $11 million a year received for ten years, if the return to alternative investments is 5 percent?

$$P.V. = \frac{\$11 \text{ million}}{(1.05)} + \frac{\$11 \text{ million}}{(1.05)^2} + \ldots \frac{\$11 \text{ million}}{(1.05)^{10}} = \$84.95 \text{ million}$$

It would thus not pay GM to build the plant because $100 million in the bank today is greater than $84.95 million, the present value of the expected income stream.

As one can see from this computation, the arithmetic of finding a present value, given the income stream and the interest rate, can become quite involved. One shortcut, however, can help: the present value of a constant revenue stream expected to last indefinitely equals the annual revenue divided by the interest (or "discount") rate. For example, $11 million a year forever, discounted at 5 percent, is equal to a present value of $220 million (11/.05).

Present value computations can be used to evaluate any problem in which one must compare costs or revenues received over time. In this chapter, for example, we argued that a projected $3.1 million annual economic burden arising from the Navigation Acts had a present value of $31 million when discounted at 10 percent. In other chapters we use the concept, among other ways, to measure the value of returns to rail construction.

Bibliography

MERCANTILISM AND THE BURDEN OF
THE NAVIGATION ACTS

*Frank Broeze, "The New Economic History, the Navigation Acts, and the Continental Tobacco Market, 1770–1790," *Economic History Review* 26 (Nov. 1973). Questions the use of tobacco prices by Thomas and others in computing the Navigation Act burden.

*Oliver Dickerson, *The Navigation Acts and the American Revolution* (Barnes, 1963). Standard defense of the Navigation Acts, as they affected the colonies.

*Stanley Finkelstein, "The Currency Act of 1764: A Quantitative Appriasal," *American Economist* (Fall, 1968). Suggests that the actual burden of the Currency Act was modest.

*Lawrence Harper, "Mercantilism and the American Revolution," *Canadian Historical Review* 3 (March, 1943). Interprets the burden as it might have influenced the Revolution.

*Lawrence Harper, "The Effect of the Navigation Acts on the Thirteen Colonies," in Harry Scheiber (ed.), *United States Economic History* (Knopf, 1964). Reprint of the original article computing the burden of the Navigation Acts.

*David Loschky, "Studies of the Navigation Acts: New Economic Non-History," *Economic History Review* 26 (Nov. 1973). Vigorous attack on the "numbers game" associated with the Navigation Acts issue.

**Peter McClelland, "The Cost to America of British Imperial Policy," *American Economic Review* 59 (May, 1969) and comments by Hughes and Kroos. The reconstituted, rigorous version of Thomas.

**Peter McClelland, "The New Economic History and the Burdens of the Navigation Acts: A Comment," *Economic History Review* 26 (Nov. 1973). Reply to Walton's defense of the original Harper estimates.

*Curtis Nettels, "British Mercantilism and the Economic Development of the Colonies," *Journal of Economic History* 7 (Spring, 1952). The classic non-quantitative article linking mercantilism to colonial hardship.

**Roger Ransom, "British Policy and Colonial Growth: Some Implications of the Burden from the Navigation Acts," *Journal of Economic History* 28 (Sept., 1968). Points out the inherent weaknesses of Thomas's aggregate approach to measuring the burden.

**Joseph Reid, "Economic Burden: Spark to the Revolution?" and "Comment" by Stephen DeCanio, *Journal of Economic History* 38 (March, 1978). Defends the importance of economic factors; largely based on an analysis of political events post 1763.

**Joseph Reid, "On Navigating the Navigation Acts with Peter McClelland," *American Economic Review* 60 (Dec., 1970) and reply by McClelland. Corrects an analytical oversight by McClelland and Thomas.

**Robert Thomas, "A Quantitative Approach to the Study of the Effects of British Imperial Policy on Colonial Welfare," *Journal of Economic History* 25 (Dec., 1965) and discussion by Jacob Price. The first New Economic Historian's attack on Harper.

**Gary Walton, "The New Economic History and the Burdens of the Navigation Acts," *Economic History Review* (Dec., 1971). An economist defends Harper.

THE CAUSE AND IMPACT OF THE REVOLUTION

*Charles Beard, *An Economic Interpretation of the Constitution* (Macmillan, 1913). The famous attack on the class motives of the framers of the Constitution.

*Gordon Bjork,, "The Weaning of the American Economy: Independence, Market Changes, and Economic Development," *Journal of Economic History* 24 (Dec., 1964) and discussion by Fishlow. Pathbreaking critique of the conventional wisdom regarding the economic problems of the Confederation.

*Marc Egnal and Joseph Ernst, "An Economic Interpretation of the American Revolution" *William and Mary Quarterly* 29 (1972). Careful analysis of what can be surmised about the impact of economics on the Revolution.

*James Ferguson, "The Nationalists of 1781–83 and the Economic Interpretation of the Constitution," *Journal of American History* 56 (1969). Historian attacks the conventional interpretation of the Confederation period.

*Merrill Jensen, *The New Nation* (Knopf, 1958). Early skepticism about the Confederation-Constitution interpretation by a famous historian.

*Jackson Main, *The Anti-Federalists: Critics of the Constitution* (University of North Carolina, 1961). Influential revisionist history questioning the standard interpretation of the need for the Constitution.

*Forest McDonald, *We the People: The Economic Origins of the Constitution* (University of Chicago, 1958). Attack on Beard's interpretation of the Constitution.

*Curtis Nettels, *The Emergence of A National Economy* (Holt, Rinehart, and Winston, 1962). Readable institutional history of the early national economy.

*James Shepard and Gary Walton "Economic Change After the American Revolution: Pre and Post War Comparisons of Maritime Shipping and Trade," *Explorations in Economic History* 13 (Oct., 1976). Examination of changes in trade patterns; new evidence of severe trade disruption in post-Revolution period, tending to support conventional view about the Confederation.

Economic growth before 1860

3

In 1790 the United States was a relatively prosperous, but fundamentally underdeveloped, economy supporting a population of four million in a few hundred-mile-wide band of farmland from southern Maine to Georgia. Almost everyone earned a livelihood working the land or providing processing and commercial services to those who did. Seventy years later, over 31 million resided in the United States at a far higher standard of living. Agriculture still dominated economic activity. Much of the arable land within a thousand miles of the Atlantic was in cultivation; farming had long since spilled over the Mississippi River into Texas, Arkansas, and the Great Plains. But by 1860, commercial agriculture was complemented by a booming manufacturing sector in the Northeast and was tied to major markets by an extensive system of canals and rail lines.

Explaining the pace and pattern of this early growth is a major preoccupation of economic historians. This preoccupation does not really need special justification: Growth is the essence of modern economic history. The political and social fate of nations in the last three hundred years has turned on their success or failure to grow. But early U.S. growth has attracted the attention of economists in the last few years for other reasons. Until very recently, theories of economic growth—explanations of the timing and determinants of growth not specific to one country or one epoch—were much in vogue. Development economists hoped to discover the general preconditions of growth, so that poor countries today might imitate the success of the rich. The United States' experience seemed both a good source of ideas—a springboard for theories—and a source of information to test the consistency of those theories. So too, in the era of the Cold War when such things seemed to matter more, U.S. development was studied as a model which proved that centralized economic control was not the only road to material success.

Early Growth: When and How Much

Economic historians searching for evidence on growth rates before 1840 are forced to play archeologist. After that date, reliable estimates of national and regional output can be assembled, albeit painfully, from a substantial base of data. But evidence from earlier years is so scanty that historians must speculate about what the dinosaur ate for breakfast from the size of his jawbone. This produced a certain diffidence on the part of researchers when asked for hard numbers—GNP, output per capita, rates of growth, and so on. Estimates were (and are) tentative. And not surprisingly, they vary almost as much as do descriptions of the dinosaur's lifestyle.

Curiously enough, though, this lack of specifics did not yield an equal measure of diffidence about the qualitative pattern of the growth process. The conventional wisdom, pre-1967, went something like this: After 1790, the American economy prospered mightily as a result of the trade boom of the Napoleonic war era. Then the withdrawal of the United States from world trade, due to President Jefferson's decision to suspend commerce with the warring parties, produced a sharp drop in per capita income after 1807.

Thereafter the stories diverge a bit, but plot lines remain similar. An early study by Robert Martin suggested that per capita income continued to decline for almost three decades, bottoming out in the 1830's, and then commencing a period of sustained rapid growth. No one accepted Martin's work without reservations after his methods were challenged by Simon Kuznets, William Parker, and Frank Whartenby. But, then, no one totally bought Kuznets's radical speculation that per capita income might actually have risen during the period. Marvin Towne and Wayne Rasmussen plausibly argued that rapid agricultural expansion represented a serious drag on labor productivity in what was clearly the dominant sector of the economy. The economy, of course, grew extensively under pressure from a rapidly growing population. But the United States had to run hard just to stay in place, as farmers were increasingly burdened by soils depleted through cultivation of tobacco and later cotton. Cost increases in hauling crops to ever more distant markets were barely offset by improving water transportation.

Reaching a similar conclusion, Douglass North emphasized another aspect of the decline precipitated by the trade embargo. The collapse of trade was so fundamental, according to North, that significant growth only recommenced in the 1830's. Per capita income was thus less in 1835 than it had been in 1800. George Rogers Taylor, seeking middle ground between North and Towne and Rasmussen, sees the whole 1775–1840 period as one of no overall progress; the productivity gains of the late colonial period barely held against the depressing forces of geography and population expansion.

Each of these necessarily impressionistic scenarios leads to the same conclusion. Sometime in the 1830's or 1840's there was a sharp discontinuity in the growth process. A long period of ups and downs without clear progress gave way to another development stage: sustained growth that more than doubled real per capita income in the sixty years and increased it sixfold in 120 years. A great puzzle for a generation of development economists thus becomes evident: What happened in the 1830's or 1840's that precipitated this leap to modern growth?

Walter Rostow, writing in the late 1950's, believed he had divined the answer. In the early 1840's, it seems, the United States met the preconditions for "takeoff." These included a high rate of national savings and the emergence of a leading productive sector—the railroads, in this case—that both increased output directly and stimulated expansion in other productive industries. The "takeoff" thesis is particularly enticing because it seems to explain growth spurts in many countries. The Industrial Revolution in England, for example, appears to have been led by the cotton textile industry. Note that U.S. per capita income grew about 1.5 percent annually after 1840. England grew at an annual rate of 1.3 percent from 1780 to 1880, while Japan managed 2.4 percent (1880–1960) and Sweden 2.5 percent (1863–1961). In each case, Rostow suggested, rapid, sustained growth followed a long dormant period.

Rostow's takeoff, and a handful of other development theories that start from the premise of discontinuity in growth, fit nicely into a commonsense description of the pre-Civil War period. On close inspection, however, American history fails to cooperate with the development theorists. Paul David's indirect analysis of changes in per capita output, which combines the use of "hard" data with carefully constructed assumptions, suggests a very different picture. Although per capita income before 1840 fluctuated widely, after 1840, the underlying trend was growth at about the same rate.

Perhaps the most startling aspect of David's analysis is how his simple approach could produce such a radically different result from the convention. Rather than attempt to measure per capita output directly from inadequate data, David makes use of simple arithmetic identities as a framework for careful conjectures. Output per worker for the economy as a whole must, by definition, equal the average of output per worker in each sector, weighted by the proportion of workers in each sector. Similarly, output per capita must equal average output per worker times the fraction of the population working.

David was able to obtain good estimates of the proportion of workers in the agricultural sector for every tenth year between 1800 and 1860 by revising figures originally prepared by Stanley Lebergott; the remaining fraction of the workforce was assigned to a catchall "non-agricultural" sector. The proportion of the population in the work-force—what economists call the labor force participation rate—was also derived from Lebergott's estimates.

Robert Gallman's research allowed David to compute output per worker in each of the two sectors for 1840. For earlier dates, output per worker for one sector, agriculture, can be derived from estimates of total farm output made by Towne and Rasmussen. But no equivalent data are available for output per worker in non-agricultural pursuits. In lieu of facts, David assumes that a rate of change of labor productivity was the same in farm and non-farm sectors. In other words, the relative productivity of labor remained constant as productivity improved overall.

What do the computations reveal? Table 3.1 shows an index of David's best per capita income estimates (1840 = 100), and the average annual rates of growth they imply. For purposes of comparison with the later period, an index of Gallman's direct estimates of output per capita are shown for 1840–60.

The decade averages show no particular break in the 1830's or 1840's. Progress is far from uniform—per capita output declined from 1800 to 1810—but the first forty years of the century, taken as a whole, are clearly years of substantial growth.

Using additional reference points, David distinguished three sepa-

TABLE 3.1

INDICES OF ECONOMIC GROWTH
1800–1860

	Per Capita Output Index	Annual Per Capita Growth (%)
1800	64.4	—
1810	61.9	−0.4
1820	67.6	0.9
1830	84.0	2.2
1840	100	1.8
1850	110.4	1.0
1860	137.0	2.2

Source: Paul David, "The Growth of Real Product in the United States Before 1840: New Evidence, Controlled Conjectures," *Journal of Economic History* 27 (June, 1967).

rate episodes of growth between 1790 and 1860. The first extends from 1790 into the opening few years of the 19th century. Per capita income grew, David speculates, at about 1.6 percent a year until the expansion was interrupted by the trade embargo and the War of 1812. The second burst of growth started in the 1820's and lasted until the mid-1830's; per capita growth from 1820–35 averaged 2.5 percent. The growth rate then slowed to 0.6 percent annually (but remained positive) for the next decade. The third and last pre-Civial War boom, starting roughly in 1845, produced an annual growth rate of 2.1 percent. David believes that, in the last few years before the Civil War, the economy continued to expand in per capita terms, though at a relatively slow pace.[1]

This leaves Rostow and Company without much to support their theories. The first few decades of the century mark no pause before the great expansion, the last few before the Civil War no "takeoff" into sustained development. Scholars partial to stage theories may be tempted to look for a discontinuity at some other convenient spot—notably the Civil War. This fits well into Marxist development theories, but as we shall see in a later chapter, the evidence is not very convincing. American growth is apparently too complicated a process to be so simply reduced.

Sources of Productivity Growth

The bare outline of David's analysis raises more questions than it answers. Earlier "guesstimates" about per capita growth rates were heavily influenced by conjectures about the difficulty of raising living standards in the face of rapid population growth and the geographic extension of agriculture. But David's work suggests that per capita income increased by about 55 percent from 1800 to 1840. How did they manage it?

When David's analytic framework is used, the growth can be easily broken down into its component parts:

INCREASED LABOR FORCE PARTICIPATION
One way to get more output per person is to put a higher percentage of people to work. Kuznets, one of the few "pre-David" optimists about early U.S. growth, based much of his optimism on an estimated 10 percent increase in labor force participation from 1800 to 1840.

---

[1] It should be noted that David's ingenious interpolations have recently been challenged by the principle source of his data—Robert Gallman. Gallman's revised data on the growth of the agricultural labor force—and subsequent necessary revisions in the estimate of the rate of change of agricultural labor productivity—suggest somewhat slower economic growth before 1850 and somewhat faster thereafter. This is not, however, an invitation to mark 1850 as a turning point. Gallman believes that the growth rate had been accelerating since 1800, leading to substantially faster growth near the end of the century than near the beginning, but no defined discontinuity in between.

Lebergott's more comprehensive work on the subject shows that Kuznets was wrong on this count, however. Labor force participation did increase before the Civil War by the full 10 percent, but two-thirds of the increase was concentrated in the last two decades. The major sources of fluctuation in the fraction of people at work were (1) the percentage of slaves in the population, (2) the rate of immigration, and (3) the birth rate among white Americans.

Slave population growth did not keep pace with total population growth—the proportion of slaves in the population fell slightly from 16.9 percent in 1800 to 14.5 percent in 1840. This reduction tended to *lower* labor force participation, since all slaves, male and female, were put to work as early as possible. By contrast, a gradual shift in the source of white population growth—from natural increases to immigration of working-age adults—tended to raise labor force participation. On balance, these forces raised participation—and per capita output—by just 3.5 percent before 1840, another 6.5 percent between 1840 and 1860.

SHIFT TO NON-AGRICULTURAL JOBS

The period 1800 to 1840 marked a dramatic shift in the percentage of the population employed outside agriculture. According to David, that percentage rose from 17 percent to 37 percent. David believes that the shift raised per capita output because workers in agriculture produced only about half as much—more precisely, between .399 and .551 as much—as non-agricultural workers. By this reckoning, the transition from virtually total dependence on farming to modest diversification accounted for an increase in output per capita of at least 16 percent.

It is easy to mistake David's manipulation of data and accounting identities for an analysis of the underlying cause of increasing labor productivity. David, however, did not ask *why* output per worker was much higher outside agriculture. He only demonstrated that, if relative labor productivity in the two sectors remained constant over the forty years, the observed shift of a substantial fraction of the work force to the more productive sector would raise overall average output by 19 to 27 percent.

But why was non-agricultural labor productivity so much higher during this period? The obvious answer is that, outside agriculture, laborers produced more because they had more capital—machines, buildings, and so on—to help do their work. The obvious answer, alas, is wrong. In that pre-modern age of technology, the average non-agricultural worker had little physical capital at his/her disposal.

Gallman suggests two other factors that may explain the gap in average productivity. First, average skill levels—human capital—were probably much lower in agriculture than in manufacturing or service jobs. Farming required little training, while many specialized non-farm jobs—blacksmithing, clothing manufacture, shoemaking—demanded considerable skill. Note one implication of this argument: The shift away from agriculture was not in itself the cause of increased productivity. Investments in training and capital were also needed if the shift was to raise overall output per worker. Second, the gap probably reflects a failure of markets to allocate labor to its highest value use. This should not really be surprising. Markets take time to adjust to changing conditions. And where change is rapid, it is almost inevitable that the market will always be in the process of catching up to current conditions.

INCREASED AGRICULTURAL PRODUCTIVITY

Four-fifths of all jobs in 1800 were in agriculture. Four decades later, despite the big shift toward manufacturing, that figure was still as high as two-thirds. Hence it should come as no shock that the arithmetic key to per capita income changes lay in the trend of farm labor productivity. Towne and Rasmussen simply assumed that average agricultural productivity must have remained constant, basing their assumption on the notion that falling transport costs, more efficient markets, and minor improvements in farming technique would roughly cancel out the adverse impact of increasing the distance between farm and consumer.

On reflection, however, this was a highly dubious assumption which clashes with other commonly held views. As noted previously, productivity increases caused by the structural shift toward manufacturing, plus the modest change in labor force participation, raised per capita output by at least 19 percent. Higher per capita income, under ordinary circumstances, should lead to higher average consumption of farm products. But with a smaller percentage of the labor force in agriculture, Towne and Rasmussen's assumption would imply a *decline* in per capita farm product consumption. David's revised productivity estimate based on Towne and Rasmussen's estimate of total farm output, suggests an increase in average farm labor productivity of 31 percent.[2]

What explains this productivity increase? Clearly, westward expansion did not have a significant depressing effect of farm productivity. Richard Easterlin's estimate of output per worker in 1840, broken down geographically, shows that the newer farming regions west of the Appalachian mountains were much more productive than areas close to the Atlantic coast. The very richest farming area in the nation was the cotton and sugar growing region of Mississippi and Louisiana. Transportation was apparently adequate to permit the development of successful specialized commercial farming at great distance from the East. This regional shift alone accounts for an 8 percent increase in average farm

[2] Note that the Gallman revisions of the David-Lebergott labor force estimates suggest that the agricultural labor force was actually 12 percent larger than previously believed; subsequently, agricultural productivity growth was somewhat less than David originally computed.

productivity, nationwide. The rest of the productivity change thus must be attributed to (1) reduced transport and marketing costs, which allowed specialization, and (2) hitherto underrated improvements in agricultural technology.

Each component of change in table 3.2 is estimated by holding other components constant. Thus, if the percentage of labor in agriculture and average agricultural labor productivity had remained unchanged between 1800 and 1810, increased labor force participation would have raised per capita output by 0.3 percent. If, between 1830 and 1840, labor force participation and agricultural productivity had remained unchanged, the shift of labor out of agriculture would have raised per capita output by 5.5 percent. Note that by this intuitive method of apportioning change to contributing factors, the sum of the sources of change for any given decade do not exactly equal the total change shown in the last column.

The debate over the rate and sources of early 19th-century growth is probably not over. For the moment, data limitations force the sort of controlled conjectures—that is, educated guesses—that beg for rebuttal. But economic historians are not likely again to be seduced by facile (though attractive) explanations of American development.

TABLE 3.2

SOURCES OF CHANGE IN PER CAPITA OUTPUT 1800–1860

	Percentage Change Attributed to:			
Decade	(a) Labor Force Participation	(b) Shift Out of Agriculture	(c) Increased Agricultural Productivity	Total
1800/10	0.3	−1.0	−3.3	−3.9
1810/20	1.9	3.9	3.7	9.2
1820/30	−1.2	6.6	17.5	24.3
1830/40	2.5	5.5	11.1	19.0
1840/50	6.5	6.1	0	13.0(10.4)
1850/60	0	1.1	21.5	22.1(24.5)
1800/40	3.5	15.8	32.2	55.3
1840/60	6.5	7.2	21.5	38.0(37.0)

Source: Paul David, "The Growth of Real Product in the United States Before 1840: New Evidence, Controlled Conjectures," *Journal of Economic History* 27 (June, 1967). Based on "Variant II" in 1840 prices. Figures in parentheses are directly estimated changes in per capita output, reproduced here for purposes of comparison. Other figures are David's conjectural estimates, based on the assumptions of constant relative productivity between agricultural and non-agricultural sectors.

Appendix: David's Method of Computing Output per Capita 1800/40

David makes use of the simple accounting identity

$$V = r[S_a P_a + (1 - S_a)P_n]$$

where V = output per capita

    r = fraction of the population in the labor force
    S_a = fraction of the labor force in agriculture
    P_a = output per worker in agriculture
    P_n = output per worker in non-agricultural production

If the value of each parameter (r, S_a, P_a, P_n) were known for each date, it would be easy to calculate output per capita (V), or an index of per capita output (V_t/V_o) for each date (t).

P_n is not known, however, for dates before 1840. Hence David assumes that the ratio of output per capita in the two sectors (Z) remained constant during the entire 1800/40 period:

$$Z = [P_n/P_a]_{1840}$$

Note that if Z is constant for all periods, the index of output per worker in each of the two sectors must be equal:

$$\frac{(P_a)_t}{(P_a)_o} = \frac{(P_n)_t}{(P_n)_o}$$

substituting:

$$\frac{V_t}{V_o} = \frac{r_t}{r_o} \frac{(P_a)_t}{(P_a)_o} \frac{Z - S_a(Z-1)_t}{Z - S_a(Z-1)_o}$$

TABLE 3.3

VALUES OF COMPONENT INDICES

Year	Z	S_a	$(P_a)_t/(P_a)_o$	r_t/r_{1840}	V_t/V_{1840}
1800	1.957	.826	.764	.966	.644
1810	"	.837	.739	.970	.619
1820	"	.790	.766	.987	.676
1830	"	.707	.900	.976	.840
1840	"	.634	1.00	1.00	1.00
1850	"	.548	1.00	1.065	1.130
1860	"	.532	1.215	1.065	1.380

Source: Paul David, "The Growth of Real Product in the United States Before 1840: New Evidence, Controlled Conjectures," *Journal of Economic History* 27 (June, 1967).

The productivity index thus depends only on the values of the index of labor force participation (r_t/r_0), the agricultural productivity index $(P_a)_t/(P_a)_0$, the value in each period of S_a (the fraction of the labor force in agriculture), and the parameter of relative labor productivity (Z). Table 3.3, derived by David from the work of Lebergott, Gallman, and Towne and Rasmussen, shows the values of the component indices.

Bibliography

*Clarence Danhof, "Comment on Towne and Rasmussen" in National Bureau of Economic Research (NBER), *Trends in the American Economy in the 19th Century*, Studies in Income and Wealth Series vol. 24 (Princeton, 1960). Evidence on technical progress in early 19th-century agriculture.

**Paul David, "The Growth of Real Product in the United States Before 1840: New Evidence, Controlled Conjectures," *Journal of Economic History* 27 (June, 1967). The basic source for the revisionist view of pre-1840 growth.

**Richard Easterlin, "Regional Income Trends 1840–1950" in Robert Fogel and Stanley Engerman (eds.), *The Reinterpretation of American Economic History* (Harper and Row, 1971). Regional income breakdown shows the positive impact of southwestern expansion on national income.

**Albert Fishlow, *American Railroads and the Transformation of the Ante-Bellum Economy* (Harvard, 1965). Critique of Rostow; see chapters iii and iv.

**Robert Fogel, *Railroads and American Economic Growth: Essays in Econometric History* (Johns Hopkins, 1964). See pp. 111–29 for critique of Rostow.

**Robert Gallman, "Gross National Product in the United States, 1834–1909" in NBER, *Output, Employment and Productivity in the United States after 1800*, Studies in Income and Wealth Series vol. 30 (Columbia University, 1966). Much-used estimates of 19th-century GNP.

**Robert Gallman, "The Agricultural Sector and the Pace of Economic Growth: U.S. Experience in the 19th Century" in David Klingaman and Richard Vedder (eds.), *Essays in 19th Century History* (Ohio University, 1975). Revisions of David's interpolations, based on new labor force data.

*Robert Gallman, "The Pace and Pattern of American Economic Growth" in Lance Davis, Richard Easterlin, William Parker (eds.), *American Economic Growth* (Harper and Row, 1972). Superb summary of the statistical evidence.

**Simon Kuznets (ed.), *Income and Wealth of the United States, Trends and Structures* (Bowes and Bowes, 1952). See appendix on pre-1870 trends for speculation on changes in per capita income prior to 1840.

**Stanley Lebergott, "Labor Force and Employment 1800–1960" in NBER, vol. 30. The basic source of early labor force data.

*Robert F. Martin, *National Income in the United States 1799–1938*, National Industrial Conference Board Study #241 (NICB, 1939). The "original" estimate; suggests that per capita income stagnated in the early 19th century.

** Douglass North, *Economic Growth of the United States, 1790–1860* (Prentice-Hall, 1961). North's reinterpretation of the early growth process. One of the first New Economic Histories.

* Douglass North, *Growth and Welfare in the American Past: A New Economic History*
**   (Prentice-Hall, 1974). A short, easy textbook incorporating then recent findings. Chapters 5 and 6 summarize North's views on early growth.

** William Parker and Judith Klein, "Productivity Growth in Grain Production in the United States, 1840–60 and 1900–10" in NBER vol. 30. Evidence that labor productivity was high in western areas.

** William Parker and Frank Whartenby, "The Growth of Output Before 1840" in NBER vol. 24. Importance of agricultural sector in the determination of pre-1840 per capita output.

* Walter Rostow, *The Stage of Economic Growth* (Cambridge University, 1960). The "takeoff" thesis exposited.

* George Taylor, "American Economic Growth before 1840: An Exploratory Essay," *Journal of Economic History* 24 (Dec., 1964). Highly readable essay summarizing the pessimistic evidence about pre-1840 growth.

** Marvin Towne and Wayne Rasmussen, "Farm Gross Product and Gross Investment in the 19th Century" in NBER vol. 24. Nuts-and-bolts overview of the farm sector; origin of pessimistic views on farm productivity early in the century.

Westward expansion
and the
transportation
revolution

4

The Economics of Expansion

The peace treaty signed by Britain in 1783 ceded to the United States all of the territory south of Canada, east of the Mississippi River, and north of Florida. At the time of the treaty, just one-third of this land was settled by Europeans and their descendants. Barely forty years later, however, farmers in search of land were spilling over the borders of that original United States into the West. From then on, luck and the realities of geopolitics allowed the nation to expand its borders as rapidly as it wished. But the legal right to settlement alone did not make settlement economically desirable or even feasible; improvements in transportation were also needed.

Before 1830, water transportation (or lack thereof) determined the path of settlement. Water transport was relatively cheap, even when great distances were involved. No matter how productive the land, however, farmers could not usually produce crops for regional or national markets at a profit if they worked more than forty or fifty miles from a navigable river or lake. At greater distances the high cost of hauling goods overland by wagon usually swallowed the surplus a farmer might otherwise earn above the variable costs—labor, animals, seed, tools—of growing the crop.

East of the Appalachian mountains, this was not a serious constraint on land development; most fertile areas of the eastern seaboard lie within reach of a navigable river. Much the same conditions prevailed on the other side of the Appalachians. But on the western side of the mountains there was one big difference: Virtually all the important waterways flowed into the Mississippi. Hence cargo for the East and Europe had to follow the river system to New Orleans. As long as the seaport was controlled by foreigners—Spain, then France after 1800—the development of the western half of the original United States depended upon foreign good will.

Not wishing to trust the economic viability of the West to continuing diplomatic negotiation, President Jefferson attempted in 1803 to settle the matter by purchasing permanent transit rights along the river and through the port of New Orleans. He ended up instead with the entire Louisiana territory, a land mass of 828,000 square miles, roughly the size of the rest of the country. From the point of view of the French, the deal was sensible. It would not have been possible to defend the territory against British naval power without a considerable military investment, which Napoleon was unprepared to make. Far better to sell it to the neutral Americans for cash than to have it wrested away by France's perennial enemy. Moreover, as both the French and the Americans well understood, the territory itself was valueless without guaranteed access to New Orleans. Control of the Mississippi seaport and the middle third of the American continent where thus inextricably linked.

Jefferson's decision to buy Louisiana made a lot of Americans unhappy in 1803. And today there is a tendency to patronize opponents of the purchase, as if Jefferson's detractors were primarily angry because he paid too much. What was really on their minds was politics: Federalists from the Northeast were afraid the new territory would eventually guarantee political hegemony for the Antifederalist, agrarian west. Some Federalists might have been displeased by the Louisiana purchase if it had cost $15 instead of $15 million.

The purchase of Louisiana did not secure the entire southern flank of the United States. Spain continued to control what is now the state of Florida, plus the coasts of what are now the states of Alabama and Mississippi. Florida itself was of no great economic consequence at the time, but the western extension of Spain's territory along the Gulf of Mexico blocked river access to the sea for much of Alabama.

The value of this western extension of Florida became clear once settlement began west of the Appalachians and American acquisition became irresistible. In 1810, a revolt by local settlers gave President Madison the pretext to occupy the coastal region of Louisiana and Mississippi; two years later the U.S. Army seized the rest of West Florida. Spain, no longer a power capable of defending an overseas empire against determined opposition, reluctantly ceded the last remaining chunk of Florida in 1819. As a face-saving gesture, the United States as-

WESTWARD EXPANSION OF THE FRONTIER, 1800–1860

Population pressure, improved transportation, and increasing national market orientation pushed the frontier into the Great Plains by the Civil War.

Adopted from Ross Robertson, *History of the American Economy* (Harcourt Brace Jovanovich, 1973), p. 114.

sumed responsibility for local residents' financial claims against the Spanish government.

Acquisition of the western third of the continent was not quite as easy. As part of the agreement over Florida, the United States recognized Spain's ownership of Texas. This, however, did not stop thousands of Americans from settling in East Texas in the 1820's; nor did it prevent those settlers from securing their independence from Mexico in 1836 after local authorities attempted to block further American cultural and economic intrusion. Texas remained a sovereign nation for nine years, owing to northern opposition to its annexation, which would add another slave state to the union.

This opposition was finally overcome in a great wave of chauvinist

1789–1860

OREGON
COUNTRY
1846

LOUISIANA
PURCHASE
1803

AREA OF THE
ORIGINAL
UNITED STATES
1783

MEXICAN
ACQUISITION
1848

GADSDEN PURCHASE
1853

TEXAS
ANNEXATION
1845

ALASKA
PURCHASE
1867

FLORIDA
ACQUISITION
1819

HAWAII
ANNEXED
1898

TERRITORIAL ACQUISITION OF THE UNITED STATES

The Louisiana Purchase alone nearly doubled the area of the country. A land
mass virtually the equal of Louisiana was added in short order during the
1840's—courtesy of Mexico and Great Britain.

Adapted from Ross Robertson, *History of the American Economy* (Harcourt Brace Jovanovich,
1973), p. 106.

sentiment created in part by a dispute with England over title to the Pacific Northwest. Fearing English encroachment on America's divine
right to rule the continent, Congress annexed Texas in 1845. Mexico
naturally took offense: It preferred dealing with the Texas republic than
the imperial-minded United States. Relations deteriorated rapidly when
Mexico refused to yield to U.S. demands for the quick sale of California
and New Mexico, or to recognize U.S. claims to a disputed chunk of
Southern Texas.

Mexico's unwillingness to sacrifice territory without a fight can probably be explained by its miscalculation of Britain's stomach for conflict with the United States. Mexico believed that the United States would
ultimately be forced to go to war with Britain over Oregon, and thus
based its dealing with the Americans on the premise of countervailing
British power. However, when President Polk accepted a compromise
over Oregon, Mexico lost its only significant ally. It did not adjust quickly

to this reality, preferring war with a vastly more powerful country to diplomatic concessions.

Both countries paid dearly for this miscalculation. About 13,000 Americans and a far larger number of Mexicans died in the war—mostly from disease. Direct U.S. military expenditures for the two-year adventure totaled $97 million. As part of the peace settlement, Mexico sold California, Nevada, Utah, and the northern tier of Arizona and New Mexico for $18 million. Five years later, Mexico ceded the rest of Arizona and New Mexico for another $10 million. The territory comprising the first 48 states was now complete.

Private Settlement of the Public Domain

National acquisition of territory is only one step in the process of economic expansion. In a society committed to individual ownership of land—feudal and communal landholding had been attempted and discarded during the early colonial period—it was necessary to devise a system for transferring land from public to private hands. The creation of a mechanism for land distribution was simple; deciding who should get how much land (and when) was not.

After the Constitution was adopted, the states agreed to cede their much-disputed claims to some 283 million acres west of the Appalachians to the federal government. The Louisiana Purchase added 433 million acres to the public domain in 1803, while purchases and annexation of the rest of what would become the 48 states accounted for another 700 million acres.

Land is wealth, and the most obvious issue facing Congress was who should receive it. One option was to sell the land at full value, thereby retaining the wealth for the nation. Another option was to give the land away, thereby distributing the wealth to those deemed worthy. Before the Civil War, Congress nominally chose the first option but failed to provide an adequate mechanism for implementing it. As a result, the federal government received a portion of the value, while the rest went to purchasers.

Parcels of land were surveyed and then put up for auction. If no one bid on the land at the initial auction, it remained on sale at a legal minimum price. By auctioning land to the highest bidder, the government could, in theory, have captured the full market value of the land it sold. The system didn't work very efficiently, though, for a variety of reasons. Foremost was corruption: Land office officials could be bribed to bypass the auction or misrepresent the land's value; the parcels in question would then pass into private hands at the legal minimum price. Bidders could also conspire among themselves to withhold competitive bids, or

THE CHANGING PUBLIC LAND LAWS 1785–1916

A variety of motives were at work in the evolution of a national land policy. But the trend is very clear: easier and easier access. The price and purchase conditions imposed on public land settlers gradually became a minor barrier to land acquisition.

Year	Price (per acre)	Size (acres)	Conditions
1785	$1 minimum	640 or more	Cash sale; amended in 1787 to provide for payment of one third in cash, the remainder in three months
1796	$2 minimum	640 or more	One half of purchase price paid within 30 days, the remainder within one year
1800	$2 minimum	320 or more	One fourth of purchase price paid within 30 days, then annual installments of one fourth for three years, at 6 percent interest
1804	$2 minimum ($1.64 for cash)	160 or more	Credit as in act of 1800; discount to $1.64 per acre for cash payment
1820	$1.25 minimum	80 or more	End of credit system; cash payment only
1830	$1.25 minimum	160 maximum	Squatters on public domain land allowed to purchase their tracts at the minimum price (preemption); temporary act, had to be renewed biennially
1832	$1.25 minimum	40 or more; 160 limit on preemption	Cash purchase only; right of preemption reaffirmed
1841	$1.25 minimum	40 or more; 160 limit on preemption	Cash purchase only; established right of preemption, doing away with necessity of renewing legislation
1854 (Graduation Act)	12.5 cents minimum	40 or more	Reduction of the sale price of land in proportion to the length of time it had been on the market; price ranged from $1 for land unsold for ten years to 12.5 cents for land unsold for thirty years

Source: Lance Davis, Richard Easterlin, William Parker (eds.), *American Economic Growth* (Harper & Row, 1972), pp. 104–5.

Year	Price (per acre)	Size (acres)	Conditions
1862 (Homestead Act)	Free	160 or less	Payment of an entry fee and five years continuous residence; land could be preempted after six months' residence for $1.25 per acre cash
1873 (Timber Culture Act)	Free	160	Cultivation of trees on one quarter of a 160-acre plot gave the settler title to the whole 160 acres; amended in 1878 to require the cultivation of trees on only one sixteenth of the plot
1878 (Timber and Stone Act)	$2.50	160 or less	Sale of lands chiefly valuable for timber or stone resources to bona fide settlers and mining interests
1877 (Desert Land Act)	$1.25	640; reduced to 320 maximum in 1890	Sale of a section of land to a settler on condition that it be irrigated within three years; amended in 1891 to increase the amount of improvements required, with one eighth of the land to be under cultivation; payment to be 25 cents at time of entry, $1 at the time of making proof of compliance with the law
1909 (Enlarged Homestead Act)	Free	320 acres	Five years' residence with continuous cultivation; designed for semiarid lands that were nonirrigable and had no minerals or merchantable timber
1916 (Stock-Raising Homestead Act)	Free	640 acres	Designed for land useful only for grazing; conditions similar to previous Homestead laws

Sources: Benjamin H. Hibbard, *A History of the Public Land Policies* (University of Wisconsin, 1965), *passim;* and Roy M. Robbins, *Our Landed Heritage: The Public Domain, 1776–1936* (University of Nebraska, 1962), *passim.*

they could coerce or bribe potential competitors to refrain from offering higher bids.

Equally important, the auction system often failed to match land to the potential buyers who valued it most highly. This should not be surprising: Very few markets operated efficiently in the early nineteenth century, least of all for commodities as diverse and complex as land. It takes a great deal of information to match specific properties with specific buyers, and such information was typically too expensive to obtain in an age before telephones and rapid mail service. As a result, rapid land distribution necessarily led to a loss in potential federal revenue.

Government policies, moreover, compounded the problem. After 1820 all land sales were made for cash only, preventing the vast majority from bidding, even when they knew what they wanted. The auctions were thus left to those who had money, or access to private credit. With relatively few people in the market for land, speculators were sometimes able to buy large parcels cheaply and then resell the property for much more by accepting mortgages from farmers. This need not have meant that speculators became rich at "public expense". They performed a service that the government chose not to perform, providing credit where it was needed. But the evidence tentatively suggests that the lack of competition among speculators allowed them returns in excess of the competitively determined value of their services.

Land issues based on the distribution of wealth very early on became tangled with other ideological issues. The Federalists, influenced by Alexander Hamilton, viewed the public lands primarily as a source of revenue for the central government. Such revenues would permit the expansion of the role of the federal government, quite possibly at the expense of state power. The Antifederalists, led by Thomas Jefferson, saw in the public lands the opportunity to create a nation of small landed farmers. Jefferson believed that these sturdy settlers would be the bulwark of democracy, protection against arbitrary government power.

The Antifederalists thus believed in rapid land distribution at the lowest possible cost to settlers. The interests of the Federalists were less clear. Rapid settlement, other factors equal, meant a smaller population for the east coast and less influence for the Federalist Party. Revenue considerations turned on implicit assumptions about the elasticity of demand for land. If land prices and minimum parcel sizes were set very high, little revenue could be collected. If, by contrast, terms were liberal, a high volume of sales would be offset by low prices. Revenues would be maximized at the point where the volume gain from an additional small reduction in price just equaled the resulting loss in revenue per acre—in economics jargon, where the elasticity of demand equaled one.

No one, of course, knew what the demand curve for land looked like, or really understood the problem in these terms. Conceptually, the issue is clouded by the fact that land is not a uniform factor; characteristics such as soil type, climate, and location make every parcel unique. Hence it would have been difficult to talk about the elasticity of demand for land, even if the problem had been understood in these terms. At first, under Federalist pressure, prices were set very high ($2 per acre) and the minimum purchase was 640 acres. Very little land was sold at this price, so the acreage requirement was halved in 1800, and halved again in 1804. The minimum price was ultimately slashed to $1.25 in 1820. Land sales were still quite modest until the 1830's but then exploded under the influence of high crop prices in the 1830's. They constituted a major source of revenue for the federal government in those years and, incidentally, a source of embarrassment to those whose politics called for liberal land distribution but distrusted the impact of land revenues on federal power.

Public land issues were often the cutting edge of political conflict in the 70 years before the Civil War, with ideology and sectional politics becoming increasingly confused. From the perspective of a century, however, one can quite easily generalize about the trends in policy and their impact. Liberalization of the terms of land sales was virtually continuous, and revenue considerations of decreasing importance as time passed. After the 1820's the price of land was probably a minor barrier to westward expansion. At $1.25 per acre, other costs of setting up a farm—clearing land, maintaining a family until the first crop—dominated. Hence other factors, those determining the profitability of farming and the availability of farm labor determined the pace of expansion.

The Transportation Revolution

At the beginning of the 19th century the only cheap dependable transportation in the United States was by river or ocean. As noted previously, this effectively limited production of all but a few valuable goods (like furs and naval stores) to coastal areas and land within a short distance of navigable rivers. This proved little handicap in the South, where fertile land was well served by natural waterways. It was a major obstacle, however, to the development of the interior of Ohio and the upper Midwest.

Change in transportation came in several forms. The first and probably least important innovation was the turnpike. Like common roads, turnpikes in this era were generally poorly surfaced. But unlike common roads, tolls provided funds for more ambitious grading and for frequent maintenance. A good estimate is that they cut the resource cost—labor and capital input—of moving heavy freight by half.

Virtually all turnpikes were built in New England and the middle

Atlantic states. A few made money for their sponsors—usually private corporations—but most probably did not. George Rogers Taylor found evidence that as few as 5 of New England's 230 turnpikes clearly operated in the black. Profitability is an inaccurate measure of the net benefits to society provided by improved roads, however. For much of the benefits were captured by users in the form of reduced transport costs, rather than by the owners of the turnpike. Evidence on just how substantial the total benefits to society might have been is lacking, however, since records of construction costs and freight hauled exists only for a few road segments.

Albert Fishlow suggests that the long haul turnpike connecting the East with Ohio and western New York probably yielded a high rate of return on investment, when both the benefits to the canal users and the canal owners are included. Although construction was extremely expensive, these turnpikes had little competition in their first years of existence and were thus heavily traveled. Based on reports that the Pennsylvania and National turnpikes hauled 40,000 tons of freight per year and cut freight costs in half, Fishlow figures they generated a social return on capital of about 15 percent. This compares favorably with virtually any contemporary private investment return. By contrast, the turnpikes in the East were probably overbuilt and suffered from competition by water almost immediately.

The construction of canals in the United States was seriously contemplated in the 1790's, but it was only in 1825 that the first major route—the Erie Canal—was completed. The lag was probably not due to a lack of technical knowledge; canals were in widespread use in England by the late 18th century. More likely, it was a reasonable response to economic conditions. Canals cut the variable costs of heavy freight transport; one work animal could haul as much tonnage by water as fifty animals hauled by turnpike. There was, however, no practical way to build a canal with a small capacity. Long canals were massive undertakings, the largest capital projects of their time. Hence they were only economically justifiable on routes where the burden of huge fixed construction costs could be spread over a great deal of freight traffic.

By the time it was built, the Erie Canal linking the Hudson River to Lake Erie, certainly qualified. The canal was an immediate success, opening up a vast interregional trade between the port of New York City and the upper Midwest. Its sponsor, the State of New York, was able to recoup the original $9 million investment quite quickly—Fishlow reports that the net return over the Canal's first ten years of operation was about 8 percent. The social rate of return—including both the internal financial return to the backers and the advantage to shippers—was many times greater.

The achievement of the Erie brought forth a wave of imitators.

Other states saw the success of the Erie and overcame previous reluctance to put their own residents in debt. In part their motives were based on underlying competition among eastern cities for western trade. Philadelphia, eager to sustain its position as the premier East Coast port, pushed construction of a canal across the Appalachians to Pittsburgh. This would have allowed midwestern farmers to send their goods east via the Ohio River, rather than via Lake Erie. Maryland entrepreneurs, equally eager to make the Potomac River an outlet for midwestern freight traffic, received federal and state support for a canal link through Cumberland, Maryland to the Ohio Valley.

Neither the Pennsylvania nor the Chesapeake and Ohio Canals lived up to the expectations of their promoters. The Pennsylvania Canal, perhaps the most daring engineering design of the early 19th century, was very expensive to build. And because its middle link over the Appalachians was actually by cog railroad, shippers were forced to pay the added cost of unloading and reloading their barges in the eastern and western mountain foothills. The C and O Canal, long delayed by construction problems and cost overruns, never made it to the Ohio River system. It finally was completed as far west as Cumberland in 1850. But by that time, the railroad was a serious competitor, luring traffic away from the canal.

The narrow private and broader social fortunes of other canals present a mixed picture. Less ambitious intraregional canals built very early (in the 1820's) to haul coal from the mines of eastern Pennsylvania were generally very successful. A second wave of intraregional canal construction, late in the 1830's, connected the Ohio River to Lake Erie and extended the New York and Pennsylvania systems. These intraregional efforts were generally financial failures; their social rate of return, including the benefits to shippers, may have exceeded the cost of capital, however; we don't really know enough today to say for certain. Yet a third wave of construction, begun after the economic downturn of the early 1840's, was very obviously a financial disaster for their governments and private backers. Most of this late investment was made to complete major projects like the C and O, which had been planned long before the recession. Many of these later projects operated for a few decades after their completion in competition with the railroads. Once the canals were built, after all, variable operating costs were quite low. But in general these later, shorter canals were of little economic importance.

It is clear that late canal construction was a mistake. These failures tend to be given too much weight, however, in historical analyses of the canal era. The economic achievements of the canals considered as a group, were considerable. They drove down the cost of shipping from about 20¢ per ton/mile to 2–3¢ per ton/mile in the 1830's, and later on to as little as a penny. Fishlow's estimate of the social (shipper, consumer,

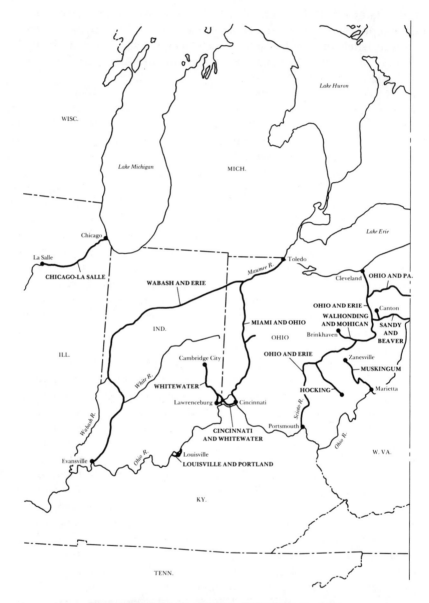

THE PRINCIPAL CANAL SYSTEMS IN 1860

Major canals connected the major farming regions of the North with the Great Lakes and the important navigable waterways. By the eve of the Civil War, however, many were losing their share of the market to the railroad.

Source: Adapted by Ross Robertson, *History of the American Economy* (Harcourt Brace Jovanovich, 1973), p. 150; from Carter Goodrich, *Canals and American Economic Development* (Columbia University, 1971), p. 184.

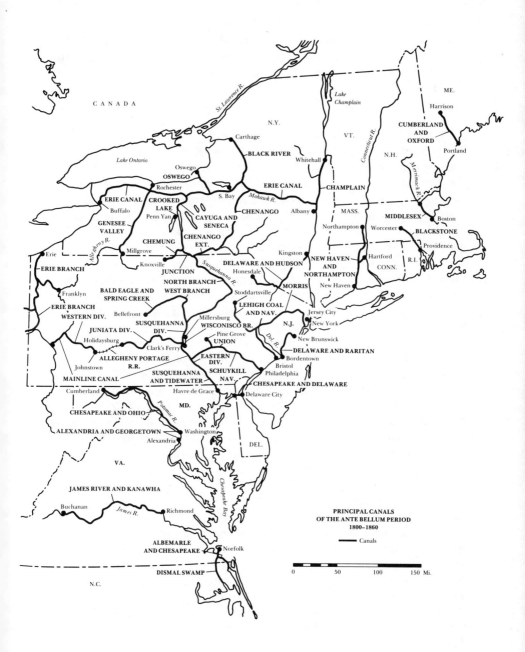

**PRINCIPAL CANALS
OF THE ANTE BELLUM PERIOD
1800–1860**

━━━ Canals

0   50   100   150 Mi.

owner) rate of return on all canal construction, based on the conservative assumption that canals cut freight rates from an average 17¢ before
1846 to 2¢ thereafter, exceeds 50 percent. Much of their collective success was of course due to the spectacular fortunes of the Erie. But, according to Roger Ransom, even a noted financial failure like the Ohio
Canal yielded a respectable social rate of return on the order of 10 percent.

Canals were not the only advance in water transportation during the
antebellum era. Even after the completion of the major inter- and intraregional canals, most cargo was still dependent on transport by river,
lake, or sheltered coastal waters. At the beginning of the 19th century,
western river vessels consisted of keelboats—substantial craft steered by
rudders—or cruder, raft-like flatboats. They served well enough taking
freight downstream, but were a wildly inefficient means of hauling
goods back upstream. Mississippi flatboats were actually constructed for
a single downstream voyage, then broken up for lumber in New Orleans. Keelboats were literally hauled upstream by human muscle power.
The amount of trade sustained this way was naturally quite limited.

Steam power made an enormous difference. First demonstrated by
Robert Fulton in 1807, the steamboat proved its feasibility carrying
cargo upstream on the Mississippi in 1815. Early designs were relatively
primitive and, in terms of freight-hauling capacity, were quite inefficient. However, advances in steam technology soon thereafter allowed
for the use of small, light, high-pressure steam engines that permitted
more space for freight and much faster upstream speeds. Complementing major increases in payload and speed were improvements in engine
safety that cut insurance costs and reduced maintenance time. Increased
navigation experience by river pilots, plus a considerable investment in
the elimination of navigation hazards also made it possible for steamboats to operate at night.

Mak and Walton estimate that from 1817 to 1848 total factor productivity for western river steamboats—the ratio of the value of transport services to a weighted average of factor inputs—increased at an
average annual rate between 6 and 7 percent. This sustained rate of productivity improvement is almost unprecedented in the history of technology. By comparison, ocean shipping productivity increased by just
3.5 percent annually (1815–60), canal and turnpike transport hardly at
all. Competition among steamboat operators meant that productivity
gains would be translated into declining rates; freight that cost more
than 4 cents per pound delivered upstream from New Orleans to Louis-
ville in 1816 cost only ⅝ of a cent per pound in the 1830's.

Steamboats naturally drove keelboats off the waterways that were
deep enough to support steam-powered craft. Curiously, though, steamboats had no adverse impact on flatboat commerce. More than twice as

many "flatboats"—really just wooden rafts—reach[
1846 than in 1816. The explanation for this persi:
obsolete technology is simple. Flatboats were able
steamboats downstream—they were slow, but rec
vestment and utilized cheap, abundant off-seasc
build and operate. And once downstream, flatboats wei
leaving the return of the crew upstream as the remaining expense. But
this critical bottleneck in flatboat operation was actually solved by the
rival steamboat technology. A trip for the flatboat crew from New Orleans to Ohio that had taken several months in 1815, took just 10 days by
steamboat in 1840. In fact, Mak and Walton estimate that, due in large
part to this technical complementarity with steamboats, total factor productivity for flatboats rose at an average annual rate of about 2 percent
from 1815 to 1850.

Steam engine technology gave the steamboat a huge advantage over
traditional keelboats in river transportation as early as 1820. Sailing
ships on the Great Lakes and on ocean routes, however, proved more
difficult to displace. As late as 1850, steamboats represented just one-
third the tonnage working the Great Lakes, one-tenth the tonnage on
coastal routes, and barely 4 percent on international routes. Fishlow
suggests that sail power held its own against steam in these areas for a
number of reasons. The construction costs of sailing ships were much
lower than steamships, and the ratio of cargo space to total ship tonnage
was much higher. River steamboats could—and did—stop for fuel
frequently; by contrast, space set aside for fuel on lake and oceangoing
steamships necessarily depressed productivity. Steamboats were faster
than sailing vessels, but the difference was not nearly as great on open
water as it was fighting the current of a river. For that matter, specially
designed sailing ships—the famous clipper ships—could beat steam-
powered boats and still match their cargo-carrying capacity. Steam-
powered ships would gradually narrow these productivity differences
after the Civil War as steam engines became yet lighter, cheaper, more
dependable and fuel efficient. But is would take the rest of the 19th century to make ocean-going sailing ships obsolete.

The last and most celebrated change in antebellum transportation
was the railroad. Railroads had enormous technical advantages over
water transport alternatives. They were faster, more flexible and could
deliver cargo from the point of production to market without multiple
loading and unloading. They could be built through rugged terrain at a
minute fraction of the cost of canals and could deliver cargo year round,
even in cold climates. In retrospect, then, it might seem surprising that it
took at least a quarter of a century from the initial rail construction for
railroads to dominate water in interregional transportation. Half the
grain reaching New York in 1870, for example, still arrived by water.

The first major railroads were actually planned as defensive measures against water competition. Construction of the C and O Canal meant the displacement of port traffic from Baltimore to Washington, while the Erie Canal diverted freight to New York City that might otherwise have gone through Boston. It is no surprise, then, that Baltimore and Boston pioneered interregional rail links as means of recapturing lost business. The Baltimore and Ohio Railroad, started in 1828, was intended to connect Baltimore with the Ohio River at Wheeling, West Virginia, about 250 miles away. The Boston and Worcester line was seen as a strategic link in providing cheap transport between Boston and Albany, the eastern terminus of the Erie Canal. A third early rail line from Charleston, South Carolina to the interior was intended to draw cotton traffic away from Savannah, Georgia.

By 1839, when rail construction was halted virtually everywhere due to a national business recession, some 3,000 miles of track were in service; yet major interregional water transport was not threatened by rail because much of the track lay between east coast cities, thus carrying passengers rather than freight. The other component of intraregional track consisted of short feeder lines serving dense industrial regions around Boston, Philadelphia, and Baltimore. These lines required relatively modest financial backing and paid for themselves quickly.

The ambitious east-west lines, by contrast, were extremely vulnerable to financial upheaval. They were not pay-as-you-go projects; profitable traffic depended upon completion of the original interregional design. Hence, after the economic upturn in the 1840's construction was not immediately completed; only in 1849 did freight revenues exceed passenger revenues. The East Coast-Great Lakes connection was finished in 1850. Direct rail service to the midwest waited for the completion of the New York Central to Chicago in 1853, the Baltimore and Ohio to St. Louis and the Central Virginia to Memphis in 1858.

Once completed, the interregional railroads did make money. But there is reasonable doubt whether this would have been possible if the railroads had somehow been constructed in the 1830's. According to Fishlow, the railroads were twice as productive in terms of service provided per weighted average of factor inputs in 1859 than they had been in 1839. About half of this jump in productivity was simply the result of the growth in the use of an underutilized system of tracks. But the other half can be attributed to technical improvements in the construction and use of rails, locomotives, rolling stock, and terminal facilities. Thus, while the delays in the expansion of the rail system into the west were largely unplanned, they may have been fortuitous.

There is another reason, apart from delays in completing the east-west links, that allowed canals to operate long after they represented obsolete technology. Canals required enormous initial fixed investments to construct but functioned with low variable operating costs. It thus paid to keep a canal operating as long as it could recover a small fraction of the average cost of moving freight. In the late 1850's no one with any sense would have invested in a new canal rather than a new railroad. By virtue of already being there, however, canals were able to match the tariffs charged by railroads and still cover operating costs. Second, for high-bulk commodities moving long distances—coal and iron ore, for example—the actual resource cost involved in water transport remained lower than rail costs into the twentieth century. Thus it should not be surprising that while canals continuously lost ground to railroads, they shared in the absolute growth of interregional traffic until the 1880's.

Appendix: The Computations of Total Factor Productivity

Economic historians frequently wish to measure differences in output that cannot be explained by differences in the quantity of productive inputs employed. If only one factor of production is used, the notion of a factor productivity index is conceptually (and computationally) simple. Thus if an output of weeds (W) are grown only with the use of land (R), an index of land productivity can be constructed merely by comparing the weed-to-land ratio (W/R) at any time (t) with a "benchmark" period (o).

$$F = \frac{(W/R)_t}{(W/R)_o}$$

Land that grows twice as many weeds per acre is twice as productive, and so forth.

Suppose, however, both land (R) and labor (L) are used to cultivate carrots (C). Intuitively, one wishes to measure factor productivity by comparing carrot output with some combined measure, or index, of the two factor inputs (I)

$$F = \frac{(C/I)_t}{(C/I)_o}$$

This still leaves, however, the problem of choosing a way to combine the two factors into the index of factors. By definition, the index must make it possible to compare disproportionate bundles of factors—say 7 units of land and 3 units of labor with 6 units of land and 4 units of labor. The choice of a mathematical formula for making the comparison comes from the underlying economic problem—measurement of output changes not entirely attributable to input changes—that prompted the total factor productivity index in the first place. If, for example, under identical conditions, 7 units of land plus 3 units of labor produce 25 percent more carrots than 6 units of land and 4 units of labor, the index value (I) of 7 land + 3 labor should be 25 percent greater than the index value of 6 land plus 4 labor.

Hence I is constructed from reasonable assumptions about the way factor inputs combine under standard production conditions to make output

$$I = R^a L^b$$

where a and b are "geometric" weights. This gives us a mathematical structure for the index, but it doesn't provide much help about how to choose the specific numerical values for the weights, a and b. It takes more reasonable assumptions this time about the way in which owners of factor inputs are rewarded for the use of their services. It turns out that factor shares in total output serve as proxies for a and b. If, for example, laborers receive 70 percent of the carrots as their wages and landowners receive the other 30 percent as rent, a = .3 and b = .7

An index based on geometric weights is particularly convenient to manipulate mathematically. Since

$$F = \frac{C}{R^a L^b}$$

it follows that

$$F^* = C^* - aR^* - bL^*$$

where (*) indicates percentage changes.

Thus the percentage change in total factor productivitiy simply equals the observed percentage change in output, less the percentage changes in the quantities of factors used multiplied by their respective weights. Suppose carrot output rises 80 percent, the amount of land in production declines by 10 percent, and the amount of labor increases by 70 percent:

$$F^* = 80\% - (.3)(-10\%) - (.7)(70\%)$$
$$F^* = 80\% + 3\% - 49\% = 34\%$$

Total factor productivity has risen 34 percent.

Total factor productivity indices are a powerful, intuitively meaningful tool for measuring productivity change. One should remember, however, that a total factor productivity index is no better than the data and the assumptions that go into its construction. They are probably most valuable in the sorts of computations made by Mak and Walton that are cited in this chapter, computations showing productivity trends in a single well-defined industry. Total factor productivity is also used commonly to measure differences in productivity over time for an entire economy, or to compare productivity in two different economies at the same time. And here, as we shall see in other chapters, the economic meaning of the indices are less clear.

Bibliography

** Albert Fishlow, "Internal Transportation" in Lance Davis, Richard Easterlin, et al., *American Economic Growth: An Economist's History of the United States* (Harper and Row, 1972). Indispensable summary of the economics of pre-Civil War transportation.

** Albert Fishlow, "Productivity and Technical Change in the Railroad Sector 1840–1910" in National Bureau of Economic Research, *Output Employment and Productivity Change after 1800,* Studies in Income and Wealth, vol. 30 (Princeton, 1966). Measurement of total factor productivity change in pre-Civil War era.

** Albert Fishlow, *Railroads and the Transformation of the Ante-Bellum Economy* (Harvard, 1965). Pathbreaking work, analyzing the direct and indirect effects of the railroad on national income.

** Erik Haites and James Mak, "Ohio and Mississippi River Transportation 1810–1860," *Exploration in Economic History* 8 (Winter, 1970). Shows evolution from keelboats to flatboats to steamboats.

** Erik Haites and James Mak, "The Decline of Steamboating in Antebellum Waters," *Explorations in Economic History* (Fall, 1973). Analysis of competition between steamboats and rail transport.

** Eric Haites, James Mak, and Gary Walton, *Western River Transportation: The Era of Early Internal Development 1810–1860* (Johns Hopkins, 1975). Industry study, incorporating much of the material in their journal articles.

* Benjamin Hibbard, *History of Public Land Policies* (University of Wisconsin, 1965). Standard reference source on federal land policy.

* Louis Hunter, *Steamboats on the Western River* (Harvard, 1949). Basic descriptive material on the evolution of steamboat transport.

** James Mak and Gary Walton, "Steamboats and the Great Productivity Surge in River Transportation," *Journal of Economic History* 32 (Sept., 1972). Estimate of the rate and causes of productivity change in inland steamboats.

** James Mak and Gary Walton, "The Persistence of Old Technologies: The Case of Flatboats," *Journal of Economic History* 33 (June, 1973). Why flatboats were able to survive the introduction of steamboats.

** Albert Neimi, "A Further Look at Interregional Canals and Economic Specialization 1820–1840," *Explorations in Economic History* 7 (Summer, 1970). Rebuttal to the regional specialization argument offered by Ransom.

** Douglas North, "Sources of Productivity Change in Ocean Shipping, 1600–1850," *Journal of Political Economy* 76 (Sept./Oct., 1968). Pioneering application of total factor productivity analysis to transportation efficiency.

** Peter Passell, *Essays in the Economics of 19th Century American Land Policy* (Arno, 1975). First essay analyzes the market for public lands in the South 1820–60.

** Roger Ransom, "Interregional Canals and Economic Specialization in the Antebellum United States," *Explorations in Economic History* 5 (Fall, 1967).
Argument that canals were largely responsible for regional economic specialization.

** Roger Ransom, "Interregional Canals and Economic Specialization in the Antebellum United States," in D. Klingaman and R. Vedder (eds.), *Essays in
19th Century Economic History: The Old Northwest* (Ohio University, 1975).

** Roger Ransom, "Social Returns from Public Transport Investment: A Case
Study of the Ohio Canal," *Journal of Political Economy* 78 (Sept./Oct., 1970).
Measurement of the economic rent accruing the users of the Ohio Canal.

* Roy Robbins, *Our Landed Heritage* (Princeton University, 1942). Useful descriptive material on the institutional evolution of land policy.

* Malcolm Rohrbough, *The Land Office Business* (Oxford University, 1968). Details of how the land office functioned, with evidence of corruption.

* Harry Scheiber, *The Ohio Canal Era* (Ohio University, 1969). Intensive analysis
of the impact of one major canal system.

* Harry Scheiber, "The Ohio-Mississippi Flatboat Trade: Some Recon-
siderations," in David Ellis (ed.), *The Frontier in American Development* (Cornell University, 1970). Why flatboats benefited from steamboat development.

* Harvey Segal, "Canals and Economic Development" in Carter Goodrich (ed.),
Canals and American Economic Development (Columbia University, 1961).
Initial presentation of the argument that the social rate of return on
canals was very high.

* Harvey Segal, "Cycles of Canal Construction" in the Carter Goodrich (ed.)
Canals and American Economic Development (Columbia University, 1961).
Data on waves of canal construction.

* George Taylor, *The Transportation Revolution 1815–1860* (Holt Rinehart,
1962). Still the standard reference work on pre-Civil War transportation.

* Mary Young, *Redskins, Redshirts and Rufflenecks* (University of Oklahoma,
1961). Account of land policy during Jackson's administration.

Industrial change
before the civil war

5

National income was twelve times greater in 1860 than it had been in 1800. Much of this growth was extensive, reflecting vast increases in the size of the labor force and the expansion of agriculture as far west as the great plains. It was nourished by dramatic improvements in transportation, the fertility of western farmland, an almost insatiable foreign demand for America's export crops, and—not least—the availability of slave labor to do the backbreaking work on southern plantations.

But growth was intensive as well as extensive, reflecting increased productivity. Much of the increase in productivity is associated with the rise of mechanized manufacturing, a trend loosely referred to as "industrialization". It is difficult to dissect the process of industrialization scientifically. "Industry" really comprises many separate industries, each having its own beginning, its own development. It is possible, though, to describe some of the historical landmarks in the rise of American manufacturing, and, then, using recent research of economic historians, to look closely at change in a few key sectors.

The Growth of Manufacturing

In the earliest years of independence, manufacturing hardly counted. What few manufactures were produced—there are no accurate records—took shape for the most part in small workshops and private homes. The high cost of transportation in this pre-canal, pre-steamboat era usually limited the market for manufactures to local areas. The technology of manufacturing—sources of power, tools—had been roughly the same for a century.

Some Americans were aware, however, of the major technical innovations that were revolutionizing textile manufacture in Britain. And experimental factories, using new British cotton textile machinery, are known to have been set up as early as 1787. The factory system in America is typically dated, though, from the construction of a commercially viable cotton mill by Samuel Slater and Moses Brown at Pawtucket, Rhode Island in 1790. Slater was among the first of many English technicians who learned their trades in British mills and emigrated to countries where their skills were most valued.

Why did the first commercially successful factories in America make cotton cloth? For several reasons. First, a potent new technology that could increase tenfold the amount of cotton thread a worker could spin in a day was just begging to be borrowed. To be sure, English law prohibited the export of spinning machinery, but the law could not prevent Slater and his colleagues from exporting their skill in building the machines. Cloth was expensive relative to its weight and bulk, so transportation costs were not a critical barrier to centralized production. And, unlike many goods, the price elasticity of demand[1] for cotton cloth was substantial. New techniques that lowered manufacturing costs tapped into a huge market capable of supporting large-scale textile production.

Slater's mill employed water frames, a mechanical, water-driven device for spinning many threads at once. The new spinning techniques, substituting capital for labor, were so clearly cheaper that the mills soon spread to dozens of New England towns with adequate water power. Spinning mills, moreover, received a welcome boost of protection from foreign competition during their critical shakedown period. From 1807—the beginning of President Jefferson's embargo against trade—to 1815 and the resolution of the War of 1812, imports virtually vanished.

Spinning, of course, was only the first stage in cloth manufacture; the second, more complex step consisted of weaving the thread or yarn into fabric. For a short period in England after the introduction of new spinning technology, weaving stood as a bottleneck in textile production. With the textile industry dependent on skilled hand weavers to make cloth, the weavers were able—through high wages—to reap a portion of the cost savings associated with mechanized spinning, and thereby, also, to provide the means of their own undoing. Mechanized weaving was well within the technical capabilities of contemporary engineers, and the windfall gains reaped by hand weavers presumably increased the incentives to develop this nascent weaving technology. Before long, the power loom had replaced hand-driven models, and the skills of the hand weavers were rendered obsolete.

---

[1] The responsiveness of demand to changes in price—formally the percentage change in the quantity demanded divided by the percentage change in price, as one moves along the demand curve.

In the United States, the adoption of power looms came rapidly after the end of wartime import protection. Hence in America, too, the timing of the diffusion of new technology appears to have been no accident. According to Temin, cost-cutting power looms were probably needed by textile manufacturers merely to survive the onslaught of cheap British cloth that arrived with the peace treaty in 1815.

Francis Lowell's Boston Manufacturing Company in Waltham, Massachusetts was one of of the first to use the power looms. Lowell's factory is better remembered, however, for organizational rather than technical innovation. His Waltham mill, huge by contemporary standards, was built in 1814 at a cost of $300,000. It integrated spinning and weaving in one plant, a system that allowed for considerable economies in the use of labor. New questions of inventory handling and distribution were answered with a degree of skill previously unknown in American enterprise. Lowell, moreover, solved the problem of finding dependable, inexpensive labor both strong enough to operate the machinery and willing to spend endless days in the factory. His firm recruited young single women—the surplus labor of New England farms—who were willing and able to work long hours while living chastely in special dormitories near the plant. After a few years they could return home with tidy dowries.

Cotton textiles were the most spectacular example of the growth of manufacturing prior to the Civil War. Cotton cloth output grew at an average annual rate of 15.4 percent from 1815 to 1833 and a still respectable rate of 5.1 percent from 1834 to 1860. The industry employed 115,000 on the eve of the Civil War, producing about 7 percent of manufacturing income and over 2 percent of total commodity production in what had become a very large economy.

Cotton, however, was not the only industry to grow in this period. Wool textiles benefited from some of the same technical and organizational improvements that generated explosive growth in cotton. The application of water power and mechanical devices transformed wool cloth manufacture into a factory industry. Wool steadily lost ground to cotton, however, for two reasons. First, the technical problems involved in reducing production costs were inherently harder to solve; applications of new technology came early, but animal fibers proved more difficult to handle with machines, and thus mechanization advanced more slowly. Second, the potential market for wool was more limited; the financial incentives for mechanization were less apparent because sales were less responsive to price reductions. Wool remained more expensive to manufacture and wool clothing harder to clean; it could not hope to compete directly with cotton in the great market for cheap, lightweight clothing.

Other pre–Civil War industries reflect the diversity of experience in this age of mechanization. "Low-technology" labor-intensive methods dominated in the production of shoes and clothing, industries where mechanization was difficult and consumers were biased in favor of goods made to order. The flour industry, by contrast, used machinery extensively in high-volume mills as early as 1810. Thanks to mechanization, the value of output per worker in flour milling was four times as high as in shoe production in 1860 and nearly three times as high as in cotton textiles![2]

If the preceding explanations of technical change in various industries seem a bit ad hoc, it's because they are. It is easy enough to recognize the great economic forces shaping the manufacturing sector—labor-saving innovation as a response to a scarcity of cheap labor; borrowed technology adopted when it could save money; improved transportation that allowed the construction of large factories hundreds of miles from raw materials and equally far from consumers. But, as one can see from the following sections, it takes a much harder look at industrial development to analyze the quantitative importance of these factors.

Productivity Change in Cotton Textile Production

Technical change in cotton textiles is a symbol of the critical role technology can play in growth. Innovations in textile production, embodied in new machinery and new factories, changed the landscape of England in the late 18th century and performed similar miracles in New England in the early 19th. Note, however, that the great technological benchmarks of the American textile industry—Slater's mechanized spinning mill, mechanized weaving, the big integrated factory at Waltham—all came in the first quarter of the 19th century, yet cloth output continued to grow at a dramatic pace after 1825. This had led some historians to assume that technology, after the initial surge, must have taken a back seat to other productivity-increasing factors.

Casual historical associations between discrete technical improvements—or lack thereof—and the rate of productivity change are easy enough to understand. We generally think of new technology as being embodied in new machines: On day number one, the weaver sweats over a hand loom to produce a few yards of cloth. On day two, the wily engineer arrives and hooks up a new loom to a water wheel. Now the same

---

[2] The success of "low-technology," labor-intensive manufacturing as well as capital-intensive manufacturing suggests that much more was at work in the rise of New England industry than technical change or water power availability for mills. Alexander Field argues that New England labor costs may have fallen, as east-west transport improvements destroyed the viability of infertile eastern agricultural lands without simultaneously providing an outlet for redundant agricultural workers.

weaver (or perhaps even a less skilled worker) can produce three or four or ten times as much cloth in an afternoon.

Sometimes that does happen—and, indisputably, it did happen to the textile industry before 1825. But it isn't the only technological road to higher productivity. In 1966, Lance Davis and Louis Stettler examined the records of early New England cotton textile mills in detail and discovered that technical progress apparently continued long after the shiny new machines were in place. They attributed this continuing growth in productivity to improvements in manufacturing technique gained through experience—a process known to economists as "learning-by-doing." It then fell to Paul David to measure the importance of Davis and Stettler's learning-by-doing hypothesis.

Drawing upon earlier unpublished work by Robert Zevin and the data amassed by Davis and Stettler, David econometrically estimated the sources of growth in average labor productivity (output per worker-hour). His results are shown in table 5.1. Note that in the earlier period, labor productivity was increasing at a rate of 6.67 percent per year. Much of this increase, David estimates, took place because each worker

TABLE 5.1

SOURCES OF LABOR PRODUCTIVITY GROWTH IN COTTON TEXTILES

| | 1833–39 | | 1855–59 | |
	Average Ann. Growth (%)	Portion of Total Productivity Increase (%)	Average Ann. Growth (%)	Portion of Total Productivity Increase (%)
Increased Capital per Unit of Labor	0.74	11	0.43	13
Increased Raw Material per Unit of Labor	3.33	50	1.60	50
Improvements in Labor Force Quality	0.33	5	0.33	10
Improvements in Machinery Technology from External Sources	0.25	4	0.30	9
Learning-by-Doing	2.02	30	0.54	17
Total	6.67	100	3.20	100

Source: Paul David, "Learning by Doing and Tariff Protection: A Reconsideration of the Case of the Antebellum United States Cotton Textile Industry" in *Technical Choice, Innovation and Economic Growth* (Cambridge University Press, 1975), p. 162.

tended more machines and processed more raw cotton per hour. Changing factor proportions within existing technical knowhow thus raised labor productivity by a total of $3.33\% + .74\% = 4.07\%$. Such a result is not surprising. In periods of rapid growth, the diffusion of state-of-the-art technology to old facilities can account for great productivity increases.

What is surprising, though, is the rate of technical progress—the difference between the 6.67 percent overall productivity gain and the 4.07 percent attributable to increases in raw cotton and machinery per worker. That net 2.60 percent average annual gain is equal to (or better than) the productivity gains achieved by modern industry since World War II and hardly conforms to the portrait of a technically stagnant industry. More striking still, is the way technology improved. Of the 2.60 percent, David attributes only 0.58 percent to improvements in labor force quality and in textile machinery.[3] The rest (2.02 percent) came from "learning-by-doing"—subtle improvements in organization and efficiency achieved through accumulated experience in operating textile mills. The overall rate of productivity increase (3.20 percent) is much lower in the 1855–59 period, as is the proportion of productivity gain attributable to learning-by-doing. This latter finding can be attributed to the fact that by the 1850's textile output was expanding at a much slower rate, so one would expect the learning process, based on accumulated experience in production, to have slowed, too.

Is there a moral to David's econometric tale? On first glance, it appears to offer weight to the view that protective tariffs played an important role in early 19th-century American economic growth. The debate over the virtues and vices of tariffs is an old one. Ever since the great English economist David Ricardo wrote more than a century ago on the value of importing grain rather than growing it at home, Anglo-American economists have seen free international trade as a way of improving the lot of all parties concerned. Trade, unfettered by tariffs and quotas, allows each country to specialize in what each does best, and then export the surplus at advantageous terms.

But, as modern economists point out, the gains from trade can be outweighed by the losses. A young, potentially efficient industry may need time to adjust to foreign competition. If in the first stages of development it is allowed no breathing space, the "infant" industry may be stillborn. As a result, the economy will go on importing goods that could be produced more cheaply at home.

Applied to the American cotton textile industry of the 1820's and 1830's, the argument has some appeal. With protection from competi-

---

[3] Pamela Nickless has pointed out that David's labor force quality adjustments, solely based on changing ratios of male and female workers, are probably inaccurate. This does not change the thrust of David's argument, however.

tion, manufacturers had a chance to "learn" to produce efficiently. Once trained, mechanics and managers could (and did) leave their employers and start new factories, taking with them the accumulated experience of the old factories. If these "infant" factories hadn't been protected after 1820, the American industry would have grown less rapidly (or not at all), and the experience gained by individual producers would have been lost to the economy as a whole.

Early protection of textiles probably was, on balance, a net plus to the American economy. David's evidence of rapid learning-by-doing suggests that the gains in the form of lower-cost cloth in the future outweighed the immediate loss coming in the form of higher cloth prices in the 1820's. Similar gains in efficiency, at lower cost to consumers/taxpayers, could have been achieved by selective government subsidies of a small number of innovative firms. Excluding this option, however, cotton textile tariffs may well have been better than no tariff. But, as David points out, the efficiency rationale for protection declined as the American industry matured, and learning-by-doing added only marginally to productivity. Thus, it is hard to make the case for continuing tariffs in the 1840's or 1850's—a period, incidentally, in which the tariff loomed ever larger as a political issue dividing sections of the economy. Indeed, the tariff returns to haunt in the chapter on the origins of the Civil War.

The Growth of Cotton Textile Output

Since the huge increases in cotton textile production came at the same time that the factory system was sharply reducing the cost of making cloth, it is reasonable to assume that the cost reductions were the cause of the increased sales. The inference is simple: In a competitive marketplace, lowered costs are passed on to consumers in the form of lowered prices. If the quantity of cotton cloth demanded was sensitive (that is, elastic) to price, technical improvements would yield the observed increase in output. The cotton cloth market could thus look like figure 5.1, output increasing from A to B as supply shifted outward on an elastic demand curve. By the logic of figure 5.1, productivity change assumes an enormous independent role in economic development: The cut in production costs, associated with new technology and capital investment, alone propels the growth of the largest industry in the young industrial sector. To put it another way, if productivity changes hadn't lowered textile prices, output would not have increased and the industry would have languished.

This "supply-driven" explanation of cotton textile growth is not, however, the only explanation consistent with falling prices and rising output. Theoretically, textile expansion could be driven by demand

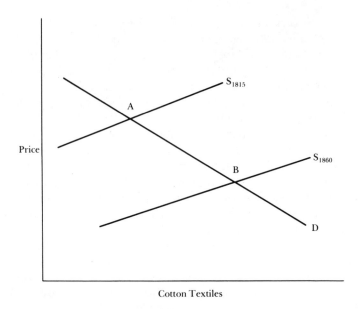

Price

Cotton Textiles

FIGURE 5.1

Supply-Driven Growth: Technical improvements shift down the supply curve
for cloth, lowering price and raising output from A to B.

alone, as depicted in figure 5.2. That, however, would only be possible if
the supply curve for textiles was sloped downward—a highly implausible
condition. But the facts do not rule out a scenario somewhere in between
the all-supply and all-demand explanation; changes in both supply and
demand could have contributed to the industry's expansion. Figure 5.3
shows what we mean.

How much of a role did demand changes play in the industry's early
growth? Robert Zevin, utilizing the limited available data, fits together
the pieces of the puzzle to arrive at a most likely explanation. Zevin lists
factors that might tend to increase the demand for American cloth at a
given price:

(1) *Import Substitution*. Tariffs certainly reduced the competitive position of British producers in the American market in the 1820's, effectively shifting outward the demand for American-made goods.[4] Zevin
argues, however, that the tariff affected only timing of the shift in demand; with or without a tariff, American producers would have eventu-

[4] It is easy to misinterpret this argument. Zevin is implicitly comparing the 1820's with a
counterfactual world in which there is no tariff at all. In fact, the 1820's tariff constituted a
more moderate trade restriction policy than the wartime import embargo that preceded it.

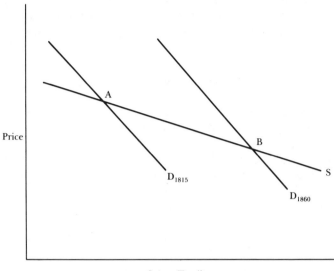

FIGURE 5.2

Demand-Driven Growth: An outward shift in demand alone (due to income growth, reduced distribution costs, population growth) increases output from A to B.

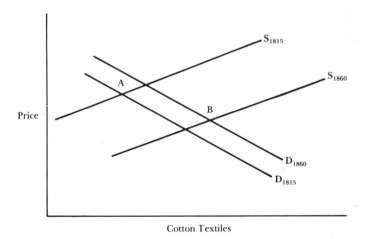

FIGURE 5.3

The Most Plausible Scenario: Both supply and demand shift to increase output and lower the textile price.

ally captured the same share of the total market. Hence the long-run contribution of the tariff to demand growth was nil. (Note, of course, that this does not rule out the possibility that the tariff shifted the *supply* function through the infant industry effects discussed in the previous section.)

(2) *Shifts in the Size and Distribution of the Population.* The more people, other factors held constant, the more demand for cotton clothing. Since the population grew at about 3 percent a year over the 1815–40 period, this factor alone should have shifted demand outward at a 3 percent rate. Actually, the impact of population was probably much greater. Population growth was proportionately greater in urban areas and in the West, where people were less likely to have access to home spinning and weaving tools for making their own cloth. Zevin thus suggests that demographic factors accounted for substantially more than 3 percent output growth.

(3) *Income Growth.* Rich people buy more clothing (and more of practically everything else) than do poor people. Therefore one component of growth in demand is the growth of per capita income. Using Robert Martin's research—now believed to be unduly pessimistic for this early period (see chapter 3)—Zevin computes an average annual per capita income growth rate of one percent. Assuming that people spent a constant proportion of additions to income on clothing (that is, had an income elasticity equal to one) Zevin figures this factor accounted for a one percent average annual outward shift in demand.

(4) *Transport Improvements.* By cutting the difference between what manufacturers received at the factory gate in Massachusetts and what farmers in Michigan or Illinois ended up paying, falling transport costs effectively shifted outward the demand for textiles. Through a series of educated guesses about how much transport costs went down due to the introduction of the steamboat and completion of the Erie Canal, and how consumers responded to lower delivered prices, Zevin assigns an average annual demand growth rate to this factor of one percent a year for 1815–24. After 1823, Zevin argues, improvements had little effect on the average costs of getting textiles to consumers, and thus had little impact on demand.

Taken together, Zevin's various influences on demand account for a 9 to 10 percent average annual demand shift from 1815–24, and 7 to 8 percent from 1825–33. Since total cotton cloth sales increased by a 15.4 percent average rate over the entire period, it appears that demand changes alone accounted for more than half the expansion of the industry. From 1834–60, Zevin argues, western and urban areas grew at a far slower pace, and increasingly affluent Americans spent a smaller fraction of their income gains on inexpensive cotton clothing. As a result, demand shifted out at just 3 to 4 percent a year. But the rate of expansion in the maturing cotton cloth industry declined yet more, to an annual pace of 5.1 percent. Hence demand explains an ever higher proportion of output growth in this period.

Assuming Zevin is even close to the ballpark, his work puts a very different cast on the "supply driven" explanation of early industrial growth. Even if the price of cotton cloth had not fallen by three-fourths in the 1815–60 period, the industry would have expanded enormously in response to national economic growth. (Actually, lumping together of various supply factors masks an additional revelation. The establishment of high-technology integrated mills from 1815–33 explains most of the fall in cotton textile prices, but not all. About one-sixth of the cost savings was due to a sharp decline in raw cotton prices.)

Thus by itself, the technological revolution in textile manufactures was responsible for about one-third of the 15 percent annual growth in output in the early years. One should take care in generalizing from this startlingly small number to discount the importance of technical change in early growth, however. Zevin's research may not be the last word on this subject. And besides, cotton textiles is just one industry among many. But surely Zevin's work damages the conventional wisdom that technical change was the single important factor setting the stage for economic development.

The Growth of the Iron Industry

Iron is as intimately connected to 19th-century industrial development as Big Macs are to McDonald's. The shift from labor-intensive manual production was based on iron machinery. Steam engines made from iron powered the water pumps that revolutionized coal mining and the steamboats that opened western rivers. Iron pipe allowed the construction of durable water and sewage systems for urban areas; iron rails made the railroad a practical means of transport.

But iron output did not grow anywhere near as rapidly as cotton textiles—an average of just 6 percent annually in the three decades before the Civil War. Nor did the American iron industry adopt state-of-the-art British production techniques with the aggressiveness of the cotton textile industry. The probable explanation for this less-than-spectacular performance, Peter Temin suggests, lies in the peculiarities of iron technology, rather than in esoteric analysis of entrepreneurship or market conditions.

To make iron products, one must first make pig iron. Iron ore, a combination of iron, oxygen, and impurities, is transformed into the element iron by heating it in a blast furnace in contact with a carbon fuel.

The carbon draws off the oxygen, leaving behind a mixture of iron, carbon, and impurities called pig iron. Molten pig can be cast in various shapes—if the impurities it contains are the right kind in the right proportion. But to make rolled or hammered shapes which can resist shock without cracking, the carbon introduced when the pig iron was created has to be removed, leaving so-called wrought iron.

For centuries, pig iron was made with charcoal as the iron ore oxygen reduction agent in small blast furnaces, and then transformed into wrought iron by removing the carbon on local forges. In 18th-century England there were substantial advances, though, in iron technology directed toward paring the amount of fuel and labor per ton of finished product. Coke, a refined version of coal, was substituted for charcoal, permitting the use of larger furnaces. And new techniques for removing carbon from pig iron, called "puddling," greatly reduced the labor requirement for making wrought iron. Puddling was quickly adopted in the United States, but coke technology did not catch hold until after the Civil War. The pig iron industry in antebellum America mostly stuck by the old charcoal-fired furnace.

This American failure to adopt new iron technology—in contrast with the rapid transfer of textile technology—has inspired historians to speculation. The most common explanation, that wood to make charcoal was plentiful in America and scarce in England, sounds plausible, but probably isn't correct. Most of the cost of making charcoal was the cost of labor needed to cut down trees and haul the wood to the charcoal kiln, not the wood itself. There is little evidence, moreover, that American labor was cheaper than English labor; the correct explanation is subtler.

British iron makers used coke that was processed from local coal mines. All coal is not alike, however. The kind needed to make coke—bituminous coal—was only found in the United States west of the Appalachians, and the bituminous deposits then known to exist contained too much sulphur impurities to yield high-grade pig iron. So Americans continued to use charcoal exclusively until means were discovered in the 1840's for utilizing the anthracite coal deposits of Eastern Pennsylvania in pig iron production.

Even after 1840, it is not clear that the growth of anthracite pig iron at the expense of charcoal pig iron could be attributed to technologically based cost savings. Robert Fogel and Stanley Engerman have econometrically estimated supply and demand curves for pig iron between 1842 and 1858. They calculate that the rapidly changing composition of demand for iron favored the anthracite form. Better suited for heavy construction, anthracite iron benefited from strong investment-related demand. This demand grew at an average annual rate of 5.5 percent, while the demand for charcoal iron actually slipped. To put it another way, without the observed expansion of demand, anthracite iron production would have been only half as large by the end of the period.

Emphasis on technical change in explaining the growth (or rather, the lack of growth) of the pig iron industry has generated other issues, too. The tariff on pig iron was lowered in 1846, and as a consequence, competition from imports increased. Domestic production of anthracite iron continued to grow rapidly, but production of charcoal iron fell. Historians, influenced by the ideology of free trade, directly connect the decline of charcoal iron to competition from coke-based pig iron—the new modern technology driving out the old. But, Fogel and Engerman argue, the truth is more elusive. Foreign competition surely hurt charcoal iron, but even if high tariff barriers had been maintained, they estimate that slackening demand would have cut into sales. All American producers would have been helped by higher tariffs. However the biggest beneficiaries would have been anthracite ironmakers, whose product was closer in composition and use to imported coke iron.

The Diffusion of the Steam Engine

American textile manufacturers adopted mechanized spinning and weaving as rapidly as they could be put to use. By contrast, American pig iron producers bypassed English coking technology for many decades—not because they were trapped by traditional production methods, but because the right kind of coke wasn't available in the East. Another major technological innovation that would eventually revolutionize 19th- century manufacturing—the steam engine—also had a mixed reception. In certain industries and certain regions, steam dominated the alternative power source, water, which had made possible much of early 19th-century mechanization. Yet in others, steam engine technology was virtually ignored. Peter Temin's work on the "diffusion" of the steam engine provides a convincing explanation.

Steam power was used in Britain in the 18th century largely to operate water pumps in deep mines prone to flooding. The early steam engines were extremely inefficient, requiring huge amounts of heat to achieve a given amount of physical work. Their application to machinery was thus extremely limited; Britain's first textile mills, like America's, were powered by waterfalls on local streams and rivers. Two important technical advances around the turn of the century, however, opened the way to the age of steam. The English mechanic-engineer James Watt was able to improve the basic design of the older Newcomen steam engine sufficiently to allow broad industrial applications. And, less well remembered but probably just as important, the first high-pressure steam engines using radically different technology were introduced.

High-pressure engines opened the possibility of enormous efficiency improvements, raising the ratio of work produced to fuel burned. Equally significant, the engines themselves were smaller and lighter for a given horsepower capacity, and were thus well-suited as power plants for boats and trains. During the first four decades of the 19th century, low and high pressure steam engines continued to be built, neither proving sufficiently superior in operation to dominate the other. British manufacturers preferred the low-pressure engine which was safer and perhaps more reliable. American producers frequently opted for high-pressure designs that required more technically sophisticated manufacturing; 95 percent of the 1,200 stationary steam engines in the United States in 1838 were of the high-pressure variety.

As noted before, though, steam technology was not uniformly welcomed. This fact Temin attributes to varying cost considerations in different industries and regions. First, water power could only be used where there was a stream to dam. In dry or flat land the real choice was thus between no power and steam power, rather than between water power and steam. Where water power was feasible, however, steam still might be cheaper; each power source had advantages and disadvantages.

The use of water power meant a large initial investment in building a dam and putting a waterwheel in place. But once built, power was almost "free." Steam, on the other hand, required a relatively small initial outlay, but fuel consumption meant continuing expense. Even within regions with plenty of fast-moving streams, water power sites were limited. Hence raw materials for processing in water-powered mills might need to be hauled dozens of miles from the nearest convenient water transport, and finished products would have to return the same way. Steam power gave the mill owner the freedom to locate near low-cost transportation. But transportation bills might be large nonetheless, since fuel would have to be brought to the factory to feed the engines.

Temin's research suggests that early 19th-century manufacturers understood these considerations very well. And, in a satisfyingly high proportion of cases acted in the way economists would predict, choosing the cheapest power source to suit specific needs. Textiles dominated manufacturing in New England. Water and steam power were sufficiently close in cost (about $50 per horsepower per year) that the choice of power turned on mill location, rather than vice-versa. The cotton mills around Lowell, Massachusetts, took advantage of the exceedingly good water sites and accepted the fairly moderate costs of transporting raw cotton to the factories. Along the Atlantic coast, however, mills were driven by steam and fed by coal hauled at relatively low cost from Pennsylvania.

Two industries outside New England—sugar refineries and saw mills—were major users of steam power, and for good reason. The perishability of raw sugar cane required that refineries be located near the cane fields of southern Louisiana, a region lacking adequate water power sites. Saw mills were somewhat less limited in choice of location. They did have to be placed on rivers downstream from a source of timber. Presumably, though, entrepreneurs could choose river sites near waterfalls. Temin argues that high interest rates in the West, where many mills operated, raised the cost of capital-intensive water power above that of steam. This explains, at least in part, why the lumber industry used more steampower than any other in the 1840's.

The iron industry represents an interesting hybrid in which changing manufacturing technology in the 1840's, rather than the economics of engines, led to a shift from water to steam. Before the 1840's, blast furnaces were generally located on streams in heavily wooded areas. Water was needed for cooling, and wood for making charcoal; water power would often be the bonus for picking a site largely for other reasons. After the 1840's, however, pig iron made with mineral fuel (anthracite, occasionally low sulphur bituminous coal) began to overtake charcoal iron, and new furnaces were located near coal fields. The availability of suitable water power—never an overriding economic priority in the iron industry—became even less important, and water power gradually gave way to steam.

Labor Scarcity and the Choice of Technology

England at mid-19th century was the greatest industrial economy in the world, a fact which pleased the English rather immodestly. Hence it was both surprising and profoundly disturbing for the self-satisfied Victorians to discover that, in certain industries, American technology was apparently more modern than British technology. An American display at the Crystal Palace exhibition in 1851 demonstrated what came to be known as the "American System"—the technique of interchangeable parts in firearm construciton. Production based on interchangeable parts, unheard of in England at the time, was in fact fairly widespread in light manufactures in the United States. By mid-century, manufacturing using interchangeable parts had spread beyond firearms to dominate fabrication of important consumer goods such as clocks and hardware.

The use of interchangeable parts was not the only benchmark of advanced American technique. Americans took an early lead in what is now called the machine tool industry—the production of machines for manufacturing. This specialization of function, in which separate businesses made tools for other industries, allowed for enormous economies in the creation of new technology. Mechanics who worked on design problems in one industry—say handguns—would find broad applications of their engineering solutions in other industries. And, as Nathan Rosenberg has pointed out, machinery producers were in an ideal position to provide expertise to emerging industries. The first locomotive manufacturers, for example, cut their technological teeth on textile machinery production.

Early 19th-century American manufactures were also notably advanced in the use of assembly lines. Using the first conveyer belts, Oliver Evans's turn-of-the-century mill processed grain into flour in one continuous chain. Slaughterhouses in Cincinnati employed an assembly line strategy in dismembering hogs as they moved from station to station by overhead rail. This permitted specialization of labor and saved human effort in hauling the carcasses.

English experts, commissioned to investigate the rather rude American challenge to British technological leadership, explained the American advances in terms familiar to 20th-century economists: Differences in technology, they believed, were based on differences in the cost of labor. With abundant land available for farming to anyone who could afford the initial investment in clearing and planting, American industry had to pay high wages to keep workers. High wages induced manufacturers to use the most capital-intensive, labor-saving techniques available. Two modern economists, Erwin Rothbarth and H. J. Habakkuk, have expanded this argument, attributing American technology to the scarcity of labor.

As inherently appealing as this explanation is, the truth may not be so simple. The abundance of land in the United States surely raised the productivity of labor above what it would otherwise have been, thereby requiring the payment of high wages in competitive labor markets. But farming was not conducted wholly without capital, and therefore, land abundance would also tend to raise the return on capital. America was thus both "labor scarce" and "capital scarce"; the observed use of large amounts of machinery in some industries cannot so casually be explained as a natural business response to labor scarcity.

Peter Temin resurrected the debate over labor scarcity in 1966 with his own explanation, which turned Habakkuk upside down. He suggested that the capital intensity of American industry was an illusion, leaving nothing real to explain. American machines were flimsier and had a shorter life than British machines, and thus represented less capital, not more, than British machines. The high wages paid to labor may not have been so high after all, but only a statistical error derived from equating money wages with real wages; adjusted for purchasing power, the American wages may not have gone as far.[5]

[5] The following discussion is not really fair to Temin. He argues—convincingly, in a 1971 article reviewing the debate—that his objective was to outline the problems inherent in Habbakuk, rather than to defend the hypothesis that American industry was actually relatively labor-intensive. It serves the purpose of clear exposition, though, to use the argument as a straw man. Consider the device as a fiction with socially redeeming significance.

Temin might be right. But, as the appendix shows, the economic model underlying his analysis of Habakkuk is flawed. An equally plausible explanation of what the British saw in America can be attributed to Nathan Rosenberg. The British visitors were struck by the number of guns each worker at the Springfield Arsenal could assemble in a day. With the elimination of the "fitting" process—the individual tailoring of metal and wood parts for each musket—assembly time was reduced from a few hours to a few minutes.

Can we then say that American gun manufacture was more labor-saving than British manufacture? Yes and no. There is no question that interchangeable parts cut the amount of labor needed to make—or repair—the standardized weapon. But the British product was not only made differently, it was different. British guns were thought of as fine instruments, handcrafted to the specifications of each buyer. Unless owners were willing to accept a musket exactly like their neighbors', the American System was not practical.

Hence it is possible that differing tastes explain different manufacturing techniques in some of the industries that so upset the English. In the United States, guns were primarily made for citizen-soldiers and frontierspeople—the emphasis was on plain and cheap. In 1851 much of the British demand was for higher-quality weapons that required labor-intensive processes, no matter where they were made.

An alternative (but not uncomplementary) "supply-side" explanation can be attributed to C. K. Harley. Harley suggests that the relative abundance of skilled labor explains Britain's failure to mechanize. If skilled labor is a good substitute for machinery in production, cheap skilled labor may have made it unprofitable to adopt capital-intensive methods. In America, by contrast, the relative scarcity of skilled workers may have required the adoption of machines that could be operated by the relatively abundant unskilled workers. Either way—the demand approach, or Harley's skilled labor supply approach—we are freed from the constraints imposed by the Habbakuk-Temin dilemma.

Appendix: Factor Scarcity and Technical Change

The labor scarcity explanation of differences in technology between Britain and the United States is buried under a mountain of ambiguous language and unstated assumptions. A particularly important ambiguity is what is meant by "differences" in technology. Two interpretations are possible.

We might mean different techniques chosen from a common pool of knowledge about production processes, from the same production function. Or we might mean different techniques associated with different

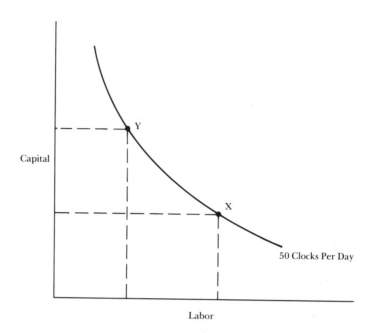

FIGURE 5.4

The relative cheapness of labor leads French manufacturers to use a lot of labor and little capital (choice X). German manufacturers with access to the same production technology choose Y because labor is relatively expensive in Germany.

production functions. An illustration should help to make the distribution. Suppose French and German clockmakers each have the same information about how to make clocks. When they build clock factories they confront the same set of choices about how to combine labor and capital to create the finished product. Assuming that the sole objective of all clockmakers is to minimize production costs, different choices of technique will be based entirely on differences in the cost of production factors.

In figure 5.4 the French manufacturer chooses combination X from the technology menu (economists call it an isoquant). The factory employs a lot of labor and a little capital to make 50 clocks a day because labor is relatively cheap, compared to capital. The German manufacturer, by contrast, chooses combination Y—a lot of machines and a little labor—because the going wage rate is relatively high (compared to the cost of capital). Both factories make 50 clocks a day and have access to the same production technology. But, to minimize production costs, each chooses a different manufacturing approach.

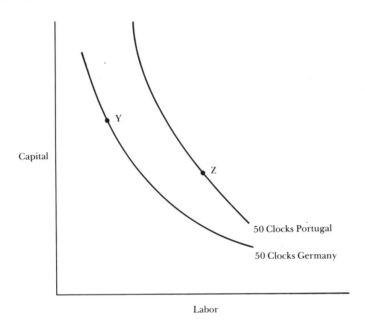

FIGURE 5.5

Portuguese manufacturers do not have the latest information on capital-intensive technology that is available to the Germans. Thus, even though labor is expensive in Portugal, technology forces them to use labor-intensive methods
(choice Z).

Consider now a third clock factory, in Portugal. The relative costs of
labor and capital, let us assume, are identical to Germany's. But the Por-
tugese do not have access to the latest information on clockmaking.
Their clock factory's production alternatives, shown in figure 5.5 are virtually limited to labor-intensive methods. Thus, even if labor is expensive, as in Germany, they use a labor-intensive process, represented by Z
to make 50 clocks a week.

Different factor costs (as in figure 5.4) or different production functions (as in figure 5.5) can explain different choices of technology.
Which figure could apply to Britain and America in 1850? Both are consistent with the known facts, but a figure 5.5 world would surprise most
economic historians. In order for different production functions to
persist for any length of time, something must prevent the flow of information between the two countries. And it is difficult to believe that British manufacturers were not capable of borrowing labor-saving techniques that reduced costs.

Perhaps the best—though not the only—case to be made for the existence of different production functions turns on the rapidly changing

nature of technology in both countries. Suppose American manufacturers searched more aggressively than their British counterparts for new techniques (that is, superior production functions) that would reduce the amount of labor needed. These techniques would eventually make their way east across the Atlantic. But since the process of invention and adoption of new technology was continuous, at any one moment the British would be behind the Americans. There is certainly plenty of casual evidence that American innovations were labor-saving in nature—one need look only as far as the firearms, grain-milling, and hog-processing industries previously discussed. Paul Uselding and Bruce Juba have attempted to measure this presumed bias toward labor-saving technology, with mixed econometric results. For the moment, we are left to speculation and intuition.

Another confusion in the "labor-scarcity" controversy is based on what evidence is really needed to pin down the explanation of differing technology. Temin argued that the availability of land for agriculture in the United States could not explain the use of labor-saving technology. The amount of capital used per unit of labor, Temin asserted, would be solely a function of the interest rate. Interest rates, however, were higher in the United States in the 1850's—not lower—leaving Temin with little choice but to deny the fact that American industry was more capital-intensive.

Temin's case rests on a set of assumptions about underlying production relationships in the manufacturing and agricultural sectors of the American economy. These allow him to derive a simple mathematical relationship between the return to capital (the interest rate), the return to labor (wages), and the capital-labor ratio chosen by a cost-minimizing business. The relationship, called the factor-price frontier, is shown graphically below as figure 5.6

Each point on the frontier represents a wage rate, an interest rate, and a capital-labor ratio. So long as Britain and the United States are operating on the same produciton function, both countries will have the same factor-price frontier. Thus, if interest rates are higher in the United States, wages and the capital-labor ratio must be lower.

The trouble with Temin's analysis is that it is no better than the assumptions needed to insure identical British and American factor-price frontiers. Yet, as Robert Fogel has pointed out, these assumptions are highly suspect. The most obvious questionable assumption is the identity of the American and British production functions. If American producers have access to superior knowledge, the factor-price frontiers might look like figure 5.7. By dint of superior technology, the United States could have higher wages *and* higher interest rates—and still have a higher capital-labor ratio.

Less obvious, but probably more damning, Temin's analysis depends

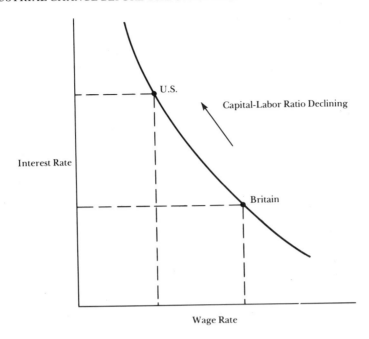

FIGURE 5.6

For two countries with access to the same technological information, the competitive return to capital (interest rate) and the return to labor (wage rate) are determined by the ratio of capital to labor. Thus both countries operate on the same "factor-price" frontier. Where they operate is determined by the amount of labor and capital available.

upon the absence of land (or agricultural output) from the manufacturing process. We know, in fact, that manufacturers used "land" in the form of abundant lumber and minerals in a number of industries. Cheap agricultural commodities—grain, raw cotton, sugar—moreover, were inputs in major manufacturing industries. If raw materials and agricultural products cost less in the United States than in Britain, wages and interest could look like figure 5.7, even if identical technology was employed in each country.

Finally, Fogel notes, Temin has subtly distorted his argument by labeling the horizontal axis of his factor-price frontier as "wages". It really should be labeled as the return to labor, denominated in terms of manufactured goods. If workers consumed mostly agricultural goods, rather than manufactures, very different conclusions are possible. Suppose Britain and the U.S. have identical factor-price frontiers, as in figure 5.6. Relatively high American interest rates will lead to a relatively low return to labor in terms of manufactured goods. But, since food was

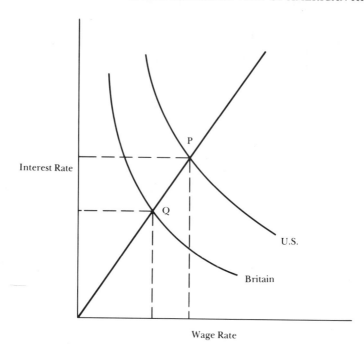

Interest Rate

Wage Rate

FIGURE 5.7

The United States, operating at point P, and Britain, operating at point Q, use the same ratio of capital to labor in manufacturing processes. But note that the United States is able to pay higher interest rates and higher wages than the British. See the text for reasons why the factor-price frontiers for the two countries may have diverged in the manner illustrated.

relatively cheap in America, the "lower" wage would buy more of what workers wanted to consume. In other words, higher observed interest rates in America would be consistent with higher *real* wages. Moreover, if we denominate interest payments in terms of how much of the agricultural goods they can buy, "higher" interest rates are paradoxically also consistent with more capital-intensive produciton processes.

Where does this leave the debate? In need of more detailed empirical information about production processes and returns to capital and labor. Only with this information would it really be possible to explain the reasons—if any—that Americans used more capital-intensive manufacturing processes than the British.

Bibliography

**Edward Ames and Nathan Rosenberg, "The Enfield Arsenal in Theory and History," *Economic Journal* 78 (Dec., 1968). Seminal history leading to more complex analysis of the "labor scarcity" hypothesis.

***D. L. Brito and Jeffrey Williamson, "Skilled Labor and 19th Century Anglo-American Managerial Behavior," *Explorations in Economic History* 10 (Spring, 1973). Yet another approach to explaining the labor-scarcity paradox—this one anchored on differing costs for capital goods.

*Victor Clark, *History of Manufactures in the United States* (Washington: Carnegie Institution, 1929). Basic descriptive source used by virtually every economist interested in manufacturing history.

***Paul David, "Labor Scarcity and the Problem of Technological Practice and Progress in 19th Century America," in *Technological Choice, Innovation and Economic Growth* (Cambridge University, 1975). Perhaps the last word on the labor scarcity controversy, with David's unique perspective.

‡***Paul David, "Learning by Doing and Tariff Protection: A Reconsideration of the Case of the Antebellum United States Cotton Textile Industry," *Journal of Economic History* 30 (Sept., 1970). Estimate of productivity change due to learning by doing, with exhaustive discussion of the justification for tariff protection.

‡***Paul David, "The Horndal Effect in Lowell, 1834–56: A Short-Run Learning Curve for Integrated Cotton Textile Mills," *Explorations in Economic History* 10 (Winter, 1973). Estimate of learning-by-doing where other factors influencing productivity change are stable.

**Lance Davis, "The New England Textile Mills and the Capital Markets: A Study of Industrial Borrowing 1840–60," *Journal of Economic History* 20 (March, 1960). How the textile industry financed expansion.

**Lance Davis and Louis Stettler, "The New England Textile Industry, 1825–60," in National Bureau for Economic Research, *Output, Employment and Productivity in the United States after 1800,* Studies in Income and Wealth Series, vol. 30 (Columbia University, 1966). Evaluation of technical change after 1825.

**Ian Drummand, "Labor Scarcity: A Comment," *Journal of Economic History* 27 (Sept., 1967). Attack on Temin's analysis.

**Alexander Field, "Sectoral Shift in Antebellum Massachusetts: A Reconsideration," *Explorations in Economic History* 15 (April, 1978). Explains the rapid industrialization of New England by the inability of redundant farmers to move to more productive western land.

**Robert Fogel, "The Specification Problem in Economic History," *Journal of Economic History* 27 (Sept., 1967). Uses Temin's labor scarcity analysis as an example of slippery logic in economic model-building.

‡***Robert Fogel and Stanley Engerman, "A Model for the Explanation of Industrial Expansion during the 19th Century: With an Application to the American Iron Industry," *Journal of Political Economy* 77 (May/June,

1969). Cleverly laid groundwork for estimating sources of output change with realitvely little data.

*H. J. Habbakuk, *American and British Technology in the 19th Century* (Cambridge University, Press, 1962). Historian's statement of the labor scarcity thesis.

**C. K. Harley, "Skilled Labor and the Choice of Technique in Edwardian Industry," *Explorations in Economic History* 11 (Summer, 1974). Argues that the relative abundance of skilled labor in Britain explains Britain's slower adoption of mechanization.

*Louis Hunter, "The Influence of the Market upon Technique in the Iron Industry in Western Pennsylvania up to 1860," *Journal of Economic and Business History* 1 (Feb., 1929). First careful analysis of change in the American iron industry.

‡***Paul Joskow and Edward McKelvey, "The Fogel-Engerman Iron Model: A Clarifying Note," *Journal of Political Economy* 81 (Sept./Oct., 1973). Analysis of the restrictive econometric assumptions implicit in the Fogel-Engerman model needed to justify its conclusions.

**Paul McGouldrick, *New England Textiles in the 19th Century, Profits and Investment* (Harvard, 1968). Detailed descriptive study of the industry; full of basic material needed for micro-analysis of textile production.

**Pamela Nickless, "Changing Labor Productivity and the Utilization of Native Women Workers in the Cotton Textile Industry 1825–60," *Journal of Economic History* 38 (March, 1978). Impact of women and immigrants on labor productivity during this period of very rapid change.

**William Parker, "Review of 'American and British Technology'," *Business History Review* 37 (Spring/Summer, 1963). Casts doubt on the veracity of the original observations showing that American technology was capital intensive.

*Nathan Rosenberg, "Anglo-American Wage Differences in the 1860's," *Journal of Economic History* 27 (June, 1967). Basic wage data central to the empirical resolution of the labor-scarcity question.

*Nathan Rosenberg, "Technology," in Lance Davis, Richard Easterlin, William Parker *et al.*, *American Economic Growth* (Harper and Row, 1972). Links well with Temin's chapter on manufacturing.

*Nathan Rosenberg, *Technology and American Economic Growth* (Harper and Row, 1972). Resource material and interpretation from the leading historian of technology.

**Edwin Rothbarth, "Causes of the Superior Efficiency of U.S.A. Industry as Compared to British Industry," *Economic Journal* 56 (Sept., 1946). First modern statement of labor scarcity hypothesis.

**Jacob Schmookler, *Invention and Economic Growth* (Harvard, 1966). Pioneering work in analyzing the determinants of inventive effort.

**Peter Temin, *Iron and Steel in 19th Century America: An Economic Inquiry* (M.I.T., 1964). Temin's Ph.D. thesis and masterful study of the evolution of the iron industry.

**Peter Temin, "Labor Scarcity: A Reply," *Journal of Economic History* 28 (March, 1968). Reply to Drummond's attack on Temin's original labor scarcity analysis.

**Peter Temin, "Labor Scarcity and the Problem of American Industrial Efficiency in the 1850's," *Journal of Economic History* 26 (Sept., 1966). Skeptical analysis of Habbakuk's labor-scarcity thesis in terms of a general equilibrium economic model.

**Peter Temin, "Labor Scarcity in America" *Journal of Interdisciplinary History* 1 (Winter, 1971). Careful review of the labor scarcity debate in which Temin recasts the issue to clarify it.

*Peter Temin, "Manufacturing," in Lance Davis, Richard Easterlin, William Parker, *et al., American Economic Growth* (Harper and Row, 1972). Basic descriptive material on early 19th-century manufacturing.

*Peter Temin, "Steam and Waterpower in the Early 19th Century," *Journal of Economic History* 26 (June, 1966). Description of early steam power technology and analysis of when and why it replaced water power.

‡**Paul Uselding, "Technical Progress in the Springfield Armoury," *Explorations in Economic History* 11 (Spring, 1974). Detailed industry study bearing on labor scarcity thesis.

‡***Paul Uselding and Bruce Juba, "Biased Technical Progress in American Manufacturing, 1839–99," *Explorations in Economic History* 11 (Fall, 1973). Econometric approach to evaluating Habbakuk.

***Jeffrey Williamson, "Embodiment, Disembodiment, Learning by Doing and Returns to Scale in 19th Century Cotton Textiles," *Journal of Economic History* 32 (Sept., 1972). Major work analyzing production process in leading 19th century industry.

**Robert Zevin, "The Growth of Cotton Production after 1815," in Robert Fogel and Stanley Engerman (eds.) *The Reinterpretation of American Economic History* (Harper and Row, 1972). Decomposition of factors explaining growth in cotton textile output.

Banks and money
before the civil war

6

Although the fact is unappreciated by initiates, no part of economics or economic history appears more impenetrable to outsiders than the role of money and banks. Textbook writers—who, after all, have to eat too—often deal with monetary issues by saying as little as possible about them. We are going to take the risk of saying a lot more than a little about antebellum money and banking, for a couple of reasons. First, the issues raised by monetary events in this period are very important, going to the core of basic issues in economic development. Second, the last two decades of research in this area have been remarkably productive. As a result, at least one durable historical myth has been laid to rest, and there is promise that others will soon depart, too.

What Do Banks Do?

Many of the arguments about banking and public finance in the antebellum years turn on the issue of whether private banks did do—or, indeed, could do—their jobs properly without government regulation. But there really is no way to assess these arguments without a yardstick of bank performance. Hence this digression.

First and foremost, banks are financial intermediaries. They link savers, who want to set aside part of their incomes for later use, with investors, who want to use that income to increase the quantity of capital goods devoted to production. In this role, bankers are brokers or market makers. Their standard of performance is how well they match buyers and sellers. They do a good job by minimizing the cost of the matching transaction.

Though simple in conception, intermediation is quite complicated in practice. Banks compete for depositors (savers) by offering them the highest return in the form of interest payments, security, and liquidity. They compete for borrowers (investors) by charging the lowest interest rate. The difference between what they pay depositors and what they charge investors is the banks' return for the matching service. The banks' profit also includes a return for bearing the risk of illiquidity: Depositors often wish the right to instant access to their deposits, while borrowers are rarely willing to repay their loans on demand. Banks intermediate by standing between short-term lenders (depositors) and long-term borrowers (investors).

If market making were the only function banks performed, we could measure their success or failure solely by their impact on the quality of the market for financial capital. Were savers and investors brought together, and at what price? Banks set out to maximize their profits by doing the most efficient possible matching job; competition keeps the fees they charge for their services to the cost of performing the service. Unlike other financial intermediaries, however, banks inadvertently perform a second function: They create money. The liabilities of banks—today checking and savings account deposits, before the Civil War, mostly bank notes—serve society as a liquid store of value and a medium of exchange.

There is nothing inherently wrong about allowing bank liabilities to serve as money; in fact there is something inherently right about it. Bank money is made of paper, or sometimes today merely magnetic blips on a computer tape. Paper, ink, and magnetic recording tape are cheap to produce, while traditional forms of "commodity" money like gold and silver, are extremely expensive. Commodities used as a medium of exchange reduce the amount of resources available for productive use—such as jewelry, electronics, and filling teeth—and thus represent a permanent drain on the economy.

But the ability to create money does put banks in a special position among private enterprises. The quantity of money in circulation has great impact on the economy as a whole by influencing interest rates and thus the demand for goods that are paid for with borrowed funds. It also indirectly affects the level of prices—and more important, the rate of change of prices. By changing the quantity of money in response to purely private profit motives and competitive pressures, banks have a collective power to influence the composition of output, the rate of growth and the inflation rate.

Today that power is controlled—a better word would be manipulated—by government regulators. One cannot fault or praise banks for changing the money supply, since their behavior is largely a response to regulations. In the first half of the 19th century, however, the federal government had no regular mechanism for regulating the money supply—and no particular understanding of what such regulation could accomplish. Hence another important standard for judging 19th century banks is how the private banking system affected the overall price level and the total demand for goods and services.

Defining the optimal role of banks in this regard is really quite difficult, since there are many goals to monetary policy and the goals themselves may be in conflict. Unexpectedly rapid expansion of the money supply, for example, may channel more physical resources into investment and thus raise the economic growth rate. But the monetary expansion may also generate unanticipated inflation, which, in arbitrary ways, reduces the wealth of people whose assets are fixed in terms of dollars and raises the wealth of those whose liabilities are similarly fixed. Assessing the performance of the banking system thus sometimes turns on judgments about the desirability of changing the distribution of wealth at some cost to efficient resource allocation—just the sort of judgment that economists schooled in modern welfare economics eschew.

Setting the Stage: The Bimetallic Standard

At the time the Constitution was ratified, the American financial system was, by modern standards, extremely rudimentary. The commodity—or "specie"—money supply consisted of foreign silver coins (largely Spanish dollars) and a small quantity of copper coins minted by the Confederation government. A small amount of private bank notes circulated as money—three commercial banks were chartered by the government in the 1780's. So, occasionally, did "bills of exchange"—IOUs written against the security of crops in transit between producers and buyers. But many exchanges of goods or sales of services were done by barter without the medium of money—one hog for two days' blacksmithing. Credit from commercial banks and international banking firms was used almost exclusively to finance the exchange of crops and consisted almost entirely of loans of a few months' duration.

Alexander Hamilton, then the first Secretary of the Treasury, was given the job of creating a national financial system almost from scratch. Hamilton opted for a bimetallic currency. Both gold and silver coins, fixed in relative value by law, would be minted and used as money. The Coinage Act of 1792 accepted both foreign and domestically minted coins as legal tender. Silver coins were valued by the benchmark of the silver content of the Spanish dollar, while the value of gold coins was set at exactly 15 times as much, by weight, as silver. Hamilton hoped that the use of two precious metals—the "bimetallic" standard—would increase the total money supply. With both gold and silver money around, he reasoned, commerce otherwise hampered by a lack of an exchange medium would be easier.

Economists today generally find Hamilton's logic naive. Bimetallism requires the government to fix the relative value of gold and silver and then freely exchange gold and silver coins at that fixed rate. But since the supply and demand for gold and silver were not fixed—both metals were continuously mined and both were used in ornamentation and jewelry—there was no reason to believe that the market value of the two metals would remain constant over time. If the relative price of the two diverged from the U.S. mint price by just a few percent, only one of the two metals would remain in circulation as money.

Here's why. Suppose the government offers to swap silver for gold (and vice-versa) at the ratio of 15 to 1. Suppose, too, that the rest of the world values gold more highly, requiring fully 16 times the weight in silver to relinquish a given amount of gold. Americans (or anyone else) can then collect 15 pounds of silver coins and buy a pound of gold coins with the silver from the government. They can then ship the pound of gold to London, where world prices prevail, and exchange it for 16 pounds of silver coins. After bringing the silver back home, our trader can once again visit the government mint, this time walking away with 1.067 pounds of gold (16 pounds of silver = 16/15ths pound of gold = 1.067 pounds of gold). This process will continue as long as it is possible to make a profit buying gold at the mint, or until the mint runs out of gold. The mint, after all, won't be able to get anyone to sell it more gold by offering less than the going rate. Thus only the metal which is "overvalued at the mint"—in this case silver—remains in circulation as money. Anyone lucky enough to be paid in gold coins would hoard them or sell them abroad.

Hamilton's 15:1 mint ratio left gold undervalued, and thus unlikely to stay in circulation; the coins that served as money were made of silver. And the composition of coinage remained a significant political issue, both because it was believed that a shortage of coins damaged commerce and because most of the coins used in domestic business were foreign. President Jackson's Gold Bill of 1834 attempted to restore gold as a medium of exchange by raising the mint ratio to 16:1. This left gold "overvalued" and, naturally, led to the importation of gold from abroad. But, at least in some parts of the country, the premium on gold was not sufficiently great to drive silver out of sight. In the 1850's, however, increased gold production shifted the relative value of gold downward, widening still further the difference between the U.S. mint ratio and the relative price of gold and silver in world markets. As a consequence, what silver remained in circulation finally disappeared.

Did bimetallism work? By the traditional standard, the answer must be "no". Gold and silver coins did not circulate together very frequently, since one metal or the other was officially overvalued. Hamilton thus failed in his objective. But Hamilton's standard doesn't seem very important from today's perspective. Most economists no longer work under the illusion that a large "commodity" money supply is necessary to the health of the economy. We are thus less willing to judge the success or failure of bimetallism by how much commodity money remained in circulation. A more interesting question would be whether the bimetallic standard affected the rate of growth or stability of the money supply. Here economists haven't had much to say; the debate over the pre–Civil War monetary system focuses on other issues. We shall return to the subject of bimetallism after the Civil War, however, when bimetallism again became a hot political issue.

Setting the Stage: The Banking System

Two kinds of commercial banks emerged in the new federal republic. The first kind, commercial banks chartered by state legislatures, generally followed the example of the first private commercial banks formed under the Confederation. A group of investors would set aside a reserve of specie from their own assets, the bank's capital, and then solicit deposits and make loans. The loans were generally in the form of engraved bank "notes"—bank obligations to redeem for specie on demand issues in exchange for borrowers' promises to pay back the loan with interest. Sometimes the bank notes found their way into the hands of people who exchanged them for specie at the issuing bank. But the banks hoped the notes would circulate as money. The more notes that remained in circulation, the larger the sum of interest-bearing loans the bank could maintain.

Sometimes the charters of the banks restricted the kinds of loans the banks could make and set minimum standards for the amount of specie that had to be kept on hand as security against outstanding bank notes. More often, such restrictions were self-imposed—not on grounds of altruism, but because it made good business sense. A balance sheet with a healthy amount of specie in the assets column increased the confidence of noteholders in the value of their "paper" assets.

The other kind of bank—of which there was just one—was the Bank of the United States. The B.U.S., modeled after the Bank of England, owed its existence to Alexander Hamilton. Chartered by Congress in 1791, the B.U.S. was a cross between a public and a private institution. It operated much like a private bank, printing notes and exchanging them for borrowers' interest-bearing promises to pay. But unlike a regular commercial bank, it had the federal government as a partner and number-one customer. One-fifth of the Bank's stock was owned by the nation, so one-fifth of the profits went to the Treasury. The Bank served as the fiscal agent for the government, holding government tax receipts, paying government bills, and performing various financial housekeeping tasks. In return, the B.U.S. had privileges unique among commercial banks. The government kept its cash as B.U.S. deposits, giving the B.U.S. a huge financial base. The government borrowed from the B.U.S., paying interest to the Bank for the use of its notes. The B.U.S.'s federal charter, moreover, allowed it to operate branches in all states, giving it a big competitive edge over regular state-chartered banks.

Because of its size, conservative note-issuing policies, and relationship with the federal government, the B.U.S. gradually evolved into a sort of banker's bank, gaining the power (if not necessarily the will) to police the function of lesser commercial banks. In general it was a net creditor to other banks—it held more notes issued by commercial banks as assets than commercial banks held B.U.S. notes. Thus, by using its branch system, the B.U.S. could speedily redeem commercial bank notes for specie hundreds of miles from where the note had originally been accepted. Though the B.U.S. rarely chose this course, its ability to demand specie for notes at will is thought to have deterred banks that would otherwise have stretched the size of their own note issues.

All this changed in 1811, when, by a razor-thin margin, Congress decided not to renew the B.U.S. charter. Why, one might ask, dump the Bank that had done well as both a commercial bank and financial housekeeper for the government? In part, opposition to renewal came from Antifederalists—notably Thomas Jefferson—who saw the Bank as a bulwark of big government, concentrated economic power, and foreign influence. English investors did own much of the Bank's stock, but, by law, were not permitted to serve as directors. The Bank's policies, no doubt, were influenced by "cosmopolitan" views. Yet it is hard to imagine that any bank run by upper-class city dwellers and dealing largely with the finance of international trade would have escaped such attitudes.

Probably as important as ideological objections to the bank were business objections. Many state-chartered banks resented the power—albeit discreetly exercised—the B.U.S. represented. And even bankers who might otherwise have supported the need for a conservative overseer of the private banking system, were eager to pick up a share of the profitable business the B.U.S. controlled.

In the five years following the demise of the B.U.S., the number of state banks more than doubled. The quantity of outstanding bank notes rose from $36 million to $76 million, while the specie held by the banking system actually declined. In 1814 a run on the banks forced most to renege on their obligations to exchange notes for specie—public distrust of the system had created a demand for specie that could not be met from the stock of coins held by banks. One might be tempted to explain these years of financial instability by the absence of the B.U.S. A strong national bank with a management devoted to conservative note-issuing practices could, with the support of the government, have prevented the rapid note expansion. But 1812–15 were war years, and there is no reason to believe that speculative opportunities were any less seductive during the War of 1812 than they were during other wars. The great increase in bank notes was probably due as much to the temptations of financing war-related schemes as to the cat's-away effect.

Whatever the explanation, financial instability and the accompanying difficulties of public finance did cause Congress to change its mind. The Second Bank of the United States was federally chartered in 1816, along the same lines as the first Bank. Four-fifth's of the capital (specie, government bonds) was private, one-fifth federal. Private directors once again controlled the Bank's day-to-day operations. After a rocky start— the first president, William Jones, was, apparently, an incompetent manager and a decidedly unconservative leader—the B.U.S. recaptured its special position in the banking community.

There followed more than a decade of national financial stability in which commodity prices, the money supply, and the stock of specie reserves in the banking system remained stable. A traditional school of thought on the period—what Richard Sylla calls the "quest for soundness" school—attributes this period of stability to the responsible policies of the Second B.U.S. and its president, Nicholas Biddle. The latest and perhaps the best of these Soundness School historians, Fritz Redlich and Bray Hammond, see the Second Bank as a precursor of modern central banks. The institution, they believe, was too little appreciated in its time and thus later casually abandoned to the great detriment of the economy.

We shall, soon enough, examine the destruction of the Second Bank and the effects of that destruction of the economy. Before we do, though, it is worth looking more closely at the B.U.S. to see how well it conformed to the role of a modern central bank. Our current central bank, the Federal Reserve (created in 1914), has two basic functions. It helps, along with other federal agencies, to assure the financial soundness of private banks. In part this is done by banning unsound banking practices. But the Fed's unique role here is as lender of last resort, protecting banks against the embarrassment of insufficient liquid assets to cover the withdrawal demands of their depositors.

The Fed's other task is to monitor and control the national money supply. It can order changes in the percentage of bank assets held as reserves, which in turn changes the ability of banks to create money by making loans. More important (at least in practice), the Federal Reserve can change the money supply directly by buying and selling government bonds in the open market.

Under Nicholas Biddle's direction, there is little question that the B.U.S. performed certain control functions. Like the First B.U.S., the Second limited the note issue of commercial banks by remaining a net creditor to the private banking system. On some occasions, it also lent money to commercial banks, in what some observers believe was a deliberate policy to preserve the liquidity of the banking system as a whole. And, by virtue of its size, the Second Bank could have changed the money supply by changing its own specie reserve policy.

In fact, the Second Bank did alter the money supply. But unlike the modern-day Federal Reserve, it was not really in the position to exercise this power in a constructive fashion when most needed. When financial crises threaten, the money supply tends to fall as individuals cash in their bank notes for specie and remove their deposits. A true central bank will stem the tide by trading its extremely liquid assets (in this case, specie) for less liquid assets (here, the paper liabilities of other banks). The Second Bank, however, had to worry about its own liquidity precisely when a true central bank would have been worrying only about the liquidity positions of other banks.

To expand the money supply, the Second Bank could deliberately hold the notes of private banks, rather than redeeming them for silver. But consider that this central banking practice would, in effect, have required that the Second Bank make interest-free loans to private banks because while the bank notes were the obligations of banks, they did not pay interest to their owners. Indeed, Biddle may have held back from cashing in other banks' notes. To the degree he did, however, he reduced the profitability of the B.U.S.

The B.U.S. could also expand (or control) the money supply by increasing its own note issue. Here too, though, the Bank's public and private goals were inconsistent. The expansion of its own note issue would have reduced its ability to police the lending policies of other banks; only as a net creditor to other banks could it threaten to punish unsound practices. Contracting its own note issue to counteract expansion by the rest of the banking system would have helped stabilize the money supply—but only at the sacrifice of profits to the B.U.S.

The Bank War

Like the First B.U.S., the second version had enemies. The commercial banks of New York and Boston were jealous of Biddle's special position and covetous of the huge, profitable banking business the B.U.S. attracted to its head office in Philadelphia. Banks in general resented the B.U.S. privilege of holding government deposits, funds they believed might as easily be part of their own reserve base. Most important, though, the B.U.S. had to contend with the bitter opposition of a re-markably effective politician—President Andrew Jackson.

Jackson, elected in 1828, detested the B.U.S. Just why remains a bit of a mystery and probably always will. Some historians see his opposition as part of an ideological opposition to antidemocratic, antifrontier, cen-trist forces in the nation. Biddle, the Bank's president, was, indeed, as close as Americans came to aristocracy—wealthy, established, suspicious of democratic levelers. Jackson was also opposed to the kind of expan-sionist banking practices that required a strong central banking author-ity to control.

However one explains Jackson's desire to torpedo the Second Bank, there is little doubt that he used his political skills extremely effectively to accomplish the task. He announced his goal in 1828, fully seven years before the Bank would need to be rechartered, and the Bank's existence became an important political issue in the election campaign of 1832. Biddle allowed congressional allies to pass a recharter bill in the summer of 1832, only to see Jackson's expected veto sustained and Jackson re-turned to office in the fall. Jackson—probably correctly—took the elec-tion victory as popular confirmation of his anti-Bank policy, and wasted no time in putting as much distance as was legally possible between the federal treasury and the national bank. He withdrew government de-posits from the B.U.S., placing them in various state-chartered banks around the country.

In spite of its federal charter, the B.U.S. was no stronger than its support from the Treasury. Biddle reacted—or was forced to react—to the withdrawal of federal funds by cutting down the volume of outstand-ing B.U.S. loans. It is possible that, as some historians contend, Biddle's loan contraction was unnecessarily large in order to convince Jackson to reconsider. The result was a national financial contraction—a mild con-traction, Peter Temin tells us, because inflows of British specie filled the gap left by the B.U.S.

After an estimated 6 percent drop in prices in 1834, however, an inflationary corner was turned. Commodity prices rose at an average rate of 13 percent a year in 1835 and 1836, and the country seemed gripped by a speculative boom psychology. Land sales—both urban and agricultural—increased enormously, as did the prices of slaves in the South. New canal construction commitments were made on the strength of a huge demand for state bond issues. Two changes in government policy were thought to have an impact on the boom. In June, 1836, Congress passed a measure (with President Jackson's support) authoriz-ing the distribution of federal revenue surpluses created by land sales revenues; distributions were to be made quarterly, beginning in Jan-uary, 1837. Then in August of 1836, President Jackson, in an apparent effort to check speculative purchases of public lands, ordered the Public Land Office to accept only specie as payment in land transactions.

In May, 1837, a financial panic forced banks to suspend redemption of their notes for gold. The Panic of 1837 was dramatic, though its impact was felt only briefly. In 1838 banks resumed specie payments and prices began to rise. But a year later, a second financial crisis forced bank specie payment suspension once again. And this time the crisis was followed by a prolonged period of falling prices. Numerous banks failed—including Biddle's own bank, the B.U.S., which had continued to operate with a Pennsylvania charter. Total economic recovery, at least in terms of prices, would take a decade.

Who Was to Blame?

Everyone agrees on the chronology of events beginning with Jackson's veto and ending with the financial contraction of the early 1840's. But interpretations of why the system failed differ dramatically. The Soundness School sees the events as the backbone of a morality play that goes like this. The Bank veto, and more important, the removal of federal funds from the B.U.S., eliminated a critical buttress to the stability of the banking system—the check on monetary creation. Without the B.U.S. to police them, state-chartered banks were free to expand note issue, increasing both the quantity of money in circulation and the vulnerability of the system to liquidity crises. The inflation of 1834–37 is attributed to this unchecked monetary expansion.

The Panic is thus seen as the inevitable product of accelerating money creation and inflation. Like an overfilled balloon, the financial structure gradually weakened until some minor event was sufficient to precipitate the bust. The Soundness School cites Andrew Jackson as the proximate cause of the panic: The Specie Circular, they claim, increased the public's demand for precious metal. This drained reserves from a banking system whose reserves were already insufficient to back the existing note issue. The distribution of the Treasury surplus, moreover, exacerbated the banking system's shortage of specie. Funds on deposit in federal accounts in commercial banks had to be reshuffled into state accounts, thus forcing a redistribution of specie from bank to bank and state to state. The strain of the Specie Circular and the distribution of the surplus proved too great, the reasoning goes, and banks were forced into suspension of specie payments.

The Soundness School interpretation endured for decades for two reasons. First, it was internally consistent—there are no obvious logical errors that would sink the theory on its own merits. Second, it appeals powerfully to preconceptions of the inherent instability of unregulated financial institutions. History—including recent history—is filled with examples of how the stupidity and/or the venality of those in charge have brought collective ruin to financial markets. A very close look at the evidence damning Jackson's policies, however, reveals the weakness of the Soundness School's case. And for just such an examination we are indebted to a number of scholars—in particular to Peter Temin.

From 1833 to 1836 prices rose 28 percent and the money in circulation—specie plus bank notes—increased by 64 percent, phenomena the Soundness School attributes to the unleashing of the commercial banks (see table 6.1). If this were true, however, we should be able to observe a decrease in the ratio of bank reserves to bank liabilities (notes and deposits). But, in fact, very little decrease occurred over the period; banks apparently did not react to the destruction of the B.U.S. by embarking on dangerous new loan schemes.

What, then, caused the increase in the money supply? We have ruled out a change in bank lending policies. That leaves two possibilities: (1) increased public willingness to use paper currency in lieu of coins, thereby leaving more specie on deposit in banks to serve as reserves; (2) an increase in the total amount of specie held by individuals and banks as reserves. Hugh Rockoff's computations, based on Temin's data, show that public willingness to use paper instead of coins actually *decreased*, leaving more than the total increase in the money supply attributable to an increase in the quantity of specie in the United States. Of the total 1833–36 money supply increase, 16 percent was due to decreased bank reserve ratios, 116 percent—more than the total change—was due to increased quantities of specie, and *-31 percent* was due to the substitution of bank notes for coins (see table 6.2).

The solution to this conundrum lies in looking beyond American shores. The money supply was in fact increased by new note issues built on new specie from abroad. The exact scenario of what happened is rather complicated, but, at the risk of losing subtleties, it can be summarized briefly. During the 1820's, the United States received substantial quantities of freshly mined specie from Mexico, sent in return for American commodity exports. This silver then made its way to China as payment for U.S. imports of tea and silk. The specie flow balance was disturbed in the 1830's by a shift in China's demand for a commodity produced outside China—namely, opium. Rather than hoarding silver, the Chinese spent it on opium sold by British merchants. So the Mexican silver eventually ended up as part of Britain's specie reserves, rather than buried in the backyards of rich Chinese.

During the same period British investors were buying American securities—this was the era of the canal boom, financed by foreign borrowing. If British overseas investments had caused a drop in the British domestic specie supply, the British government could have—and undoubtedly would have—taken steps to prevent flows of specie to New York. But coming at the same time as the inflows of Chinese silver to Britain, the specie outflows to America caused no alarm and were al-

TABLE 6.1

PRICES, MONEY, AND DETERMINANTS OF MONEY SUPPLY 1820–45

Year	Wholesale Price Index	Money (millions $)	Specie (millions $)	Bank Specie Reserves	Publicly Held Specie
				Bank Notes + Deposits	Total Money Supply
1820	106	85	41	.32	.24
1821	102	96	39	.30	.16
1822	106	81	32	.21	.23
1823	103	88	31	.25	.15
1824	98	88	32	.27	.13
1825	103	106	29	.19	.10
1826	99	108	32	.20	.12
1827	98	101	32	.20	.14
1828	97	114	31	.18	.11
1829	96	105	33	.22	.12
1830	91	114	32	.23	.06
1831	94	155	30	.15	.05
1832	95	150	31	.16	.05
1833	95	168	41	.18	.08
1834	90	172	51	.27	.04
1835	100	246	65	.18	.10
1836	114	276	73	.16	.13
1837	115	232	88	.20	.23
1838	110	240	87	.23	.18
1839	112	215	83	.20	.23
1840	95	186	80	.25	.24
1841	92	174	80	.23	.30
1842	82	158	90	.33	.35
1843	75	194	100	.35	.26
1844	77	214	96	.27	.24
1845	83	241	97	.23	.23

Sources: Prices: *Historical Statistics of the United States* (1975) E-52; all other data: Peter Temin, *The Jacksonian Economy* (Norton, 1969), pp. 71, 159.

TABLE 6.2

MONEY SUPPLY CHANGES 1820–43

	Mild Deflation 1820–29	Inflation 1829–39	Intense Inflation 1833–36	Deflation 1839–43
Average Annual Money Supply Change	2.3%	7.2%	16.5%	−2.6
Fraction of This Change Explainable by Changes in				
Quantity of Specie	−1.04	1.28	1.16	−1.81
Bank Reserve Ratio	.83	.08	.16	2.53
Public Currency Holding	.87	−0.33	−0.31	.58

Interpretation: Each entry shows what portion of the total money supply change in the period could be attributed to each potential source of change. For example, in the 1829–39 inflation, if other factors had remained constant, specie inflows alone would have explained more than the total increase in the money supply. Other factors, of course, were not constant—the large specie inflow was abetted by a greater willingness by banks to extend their note issue, and partially offset by a greater reluctance by the public to use bank notes instead of specie as money.

Source: Hugh Rockoff, "Money, Prices, and Banks in the Jacksonian Era" in Robert Fogel and Stanley Engerman, *The Reinterpretation of American Economic History* (Harper and Row, 1972), p. 452.

lowed to take place. Hence the American inflation was, through a long chain of events, caused not by Andrew Jackson but by the new Chinese taste for opium.

That explains the inflation, but what explains the Panic? Traditional interpretations pin the blame on the Specie Circular and the distribution, and Temin examines each in turn. If the Specie Circular had had much impact on the public's demand for coins, it should show up in flows of specie from East to West—land sales, after all, took place in the West. In fact, there is no evidence of a loss of bank specie reserves from the East following issuance of the Circular. Temin suggests that Jackson's avowed attempt to stop speculative land sales may have worked by dampening expectations of future demand for land. And *we* might speculate that falling land prices might have damaged the financial soundness of the holders of land mortgages. But, in itself, the Specie Circular did not trigger a run on the banks.

How about the distribution? On the order of $20 million was transferred from federal to state accounts in the first half of 1837. But, as Temin points out, this shuffle did not mean an equivalent amount of specie moved from bank to bank. Contemporary accounts suggest that, within states, public officials were generally willing to leave their newly acquired funds in the banks where the federal government had put them in the first place. Some specie did have to move interstate to reconcile federal obligations to the states. But an analysis of Treasury data shows that less than $3 million actually crossed state lines before the Panic began. Like the proverbial straw on the camel's back, this $3 million probably helped to break the system. However, in a banking community already capable of moving hundreds of millions of dollars annually between banks without breathing hard, it is sophistic to pick out this particular $3 million as the cause of the collapse.

Temin's villain—the agent most responsible for the Panic of 1837—is the British government. In 1836, British officials raised interest rates to stem the outward flow of specie, something they had not done in the previous few years. This led to an increase in interest rates on both sides of the Atlantic and, in combination with a fall in the price of the major American export crop, cotton, changed bank note holders' views on the security of their assets. The bank Panic, then, was largely the result of forces outside the control of Andrew Jackson or anyone else in the federal government. It is true that a stronger banking system might have better resisted the shock, but it is hard to see how Jackson's veto of the B.U.S. or his economic measures in 1836 weakened the system significantly. The plain fact is that a small economy operating in the context of open world trade and capital movements can exert only modest influence over its monetary system. Private finance was built from a base of specie that served as bank reserves and international money. That system didn't work as badly as some have inferred—more on that subject later—but it was obviously a helpless victim of rapid shifts in the demand for specie both at home and abroad.

Temin's research rewrote the drama of Jacksonian economic policy, demoting Jackson himself to a bit part. This need not, however, be the last word on the subject. The Soundness School is probably silenced forever, but the facts Temin unearthed can still be interpreted quite differently. Consider again what his research shows. From the observation that the ratio of private bank reserves to liabilities did not change with Jackson's destruction of the B.U.S., Jackson is exonerated from blame for the inflation of the 1830's and the subsequent deflation of the 1840's. In choosing the ratio of reserves to liabilities, however, banks were responding to multiple incentives—their own desire to issue more notes, customers' desire for security, each banker's personal perception of the stability of the whole system. The reserve ratio, then, is really an "endogenous" variable—the product of causal factors, not the moving force in events.

If changes in the bank reserve ratio provide an unsatisfactory measure of the impact of the bank war, the only satisfactory measure must come from a model that simultaneously explains the behavior of banks as suppliers of money and the public as demanders of money. Marie Sushka develops just such a model of the supply and demand for money—or to be more accurate, several variations of such a model. She then estimates the supply and demand equations separately for two periods—1823–35 and 1836–39—to see if either banks or the public changed their behavior in the absence of the B.U.S.

Sushka's conclusions are striking. After 1836 the public was far less willing to hold money in the form of bank notes, suggesting a basic loss of confidence in the banking system. And the banks were far less willing to "stretch" their available specie reserves to make additional loans, even where high interest rates made loans exceedingly profitable. This loss of confidence may have made the system more vulnerable to the shock of abrupt changes in specie flows by reducing the sanguinity of bank note holders in periods of financial stress. Edgy note holders might well provoke a run on the banks, even when there was little basis for believing that bank policies were fundamentally unsound or bank assets insufficient to cover liabilities. If one accepts Sushka's evidence, it is possible that Jackson's policies did have some impact on the financial system. But turning the tables on Temin hardly offers aid or comfort to the Soundness School. The destruction of the B.U.S. did not make the bankers more prone to take risks—just the opposite. And it is for the bankers' correctly perceived need to act more conservatively that Sushka ultimately faults Jackson.

Like much econometric work, Sushka's is potentially vulnerable to criticism on purely technical grounds. Her choice, for example, of 1835–36 as the break between two different banking regimes can be challenged; Jackson removed federal deposits from the B.U.S. years earlier. And it is entirely possible that factors other than the bank war caused the observed changes in banking practices. But even if Sushka's econometric model is open to challenge, her perspective has forced revision of the ground rules of the debate over the bank war. The Soundness School saw the dangers of banking purely in terms of temptations to excess. Sushka's work points out the additional dangers of government policies that independently cause rapid changes in the perceptions of the soundness of the system. Temin's central point stands: small, open economies, operating with a specie-based money are terribly vulnerable to economic events outside their control. Nonetheless, Jackson may still be held partially accountable for the Panic of 1837 *if* it can be shown that his policies reduced the stability of the mechanism that created paper money.

The Era of Free Banking

If, by traditional interpretation, the destruction of the Second B.U.S. was folly, then the price of that folly was several decades of financial instability. Left on its own, or to the spotty regulation of state authorities, the banking system was a failure. Unscrupulous entrepreneurs set up "wildcat" banks, nothing but legal con games and hardly different in principle from counterfeiting operations. According to historians of the Soundness School, a bank would set up shop with little or no capital, print bank notes, and exchange them for other assets, like specie. The owners would then pay themselves dividends and, when people attempted to redeem their bank notes, declare bankruptcy. It was no accident that such banks were typically located in the West, as far from civilization and intruding noteholders as possible. Wildcat banks, in view of the Soundness School, harmed the economy directly by victimizing unwary patrons and indirectly by reducing confidence in a financial structure dependent on public confidence.

In fact, a close look at what is called free banking presents a different picture than that drawn by traditional historians. Self-regulation and indirect state regulation surely did not work perfectly. But, as Rockoff's extensive work on the subject shows, the system didn't work all that badly, either.

The "free" in free banking refers to free entry into the banking business, not freedom to conduct business as the banker pleased. Between 1837 and 1860, the majority of states, particularly those in the West, experimented with some form of free banking. Typically, the law allowed anyone to set up a bank, provided they backed their note issue with securities kept on deposit with the state banking authority. If the bank failed to honor its liabilities, the state would sell the securities and compensate depositors and noteholders.

Some free banking states, like Louisiana, could boast of perfect success in protecting bank customers. Others—notably Michigan—became refuges for wildcatters. Rockoff pins this partial failure of free banking to the type of security required by the state. Michigan allowed banks to use land mortgages at face value, regardless of their true worth. Thus a wildcatter might deposit a $10,000 mortgage on land which the mortgagee had little chance of repaying, and then issue $10,000 worth of notes to unwary clients. In Minnesota, nearly worthless railroad bonds were accepted as security at 95 percent of their issue value. Much the same thing happened in New Jersey, where the law allowed the use of heavily depreciated bonds issued by other states as security at face value. The fault was thus not in the free banking concept, but in the way it was applied.

Actually the case against free banking is even weaker than the preceding paragraphs imply. When free banking did lead to failures, the

TABLE 6.3

**NOTEHOLDER LOSSES UNDER FREE BANKING,
CUMULATIVE THROUGH 1860**

State	Free Banking Years	Losses ($)
Vermont	1851–60	24,500
Massachusetts	1851–60	0
Connecticut	1852–60	0
New York	1838–60	394,700
New Jersey	1850–60	6,000
Pennsylvania	1860	0
Ohio	1851–60	77,600
Indiana	1852–60	227,900
Illinois	1851–60	21,300
Michigan	1837–60	1,000,000
Wisconsin	1852–60	0
Minnesota	1858–60	96,900
Iowa	1858–60	0
Georgia	1838–60	3,000
Florida	1853–60	0
Tennessee	1852–60	0
Alabama	1849–60	0
Louisiana	1853–60	0

Source: Hugh Rockoff, "The Free Banking Era: A Reexamination," *Journal of Money Credit and Banking* 6 (May, 1974), p. 150.

losses were less spectacular than historians have generally believed. Rockoff's computations show a total *cumulative* loss through 1860 from bank failures to be no more than $1.9 million, and perhaps a great deal less (see table 6.3). This redistribution of wealth from noteholder to wildcatter represents less than 1/100th of 1 percent of national income during the free banking era. It is true that losses were concentrated in just a few states—Michigan, Indiana, New York—but even so, they hardly represent a significant fraction of wealth.

In one sense, the "losses" discussed above weren't losses at all. The $1.9 million was not destroyed; it simply changed owners. But there were true efficiency losses from wildcatting, too. People hold money instead of other assets because of its convenience as a medium of exchange. If you don't believe that, try paying your dentist with a few square feet of land. The higher the risk of holding money—say, from inflation, or in this case the chance the issuing bank won't honor its obligation—the less money people will hold and the more inconvenience they will have to put up with in market transactions. Rockoff attempted to measure this true social cost to wildcatting—the inconvenience of not being able to use money—by econometrically estimating the determinants of the demand for money. His work suggests that in the states where wildcatting was common, per capita income was lowered by about a dollar a year. This loss is not trivial, but it is still less than one percent of annual per capita earnings.

Losses from (badly managed) free banking are clear. What about the gains, when and where the system worked well? At least in theory, the big advantage of free banking was increased competition among banks for business that would lower the cost of financial intermediation. Borrowers would pay lower interest rates, increasing the volume of loans and facilitating investment. Unfortunately, it is difficult to quantify the practical benefits of opening bank operations to all during this era. We are left instead with scraps of evidence: Philadelphia, a city with few banks and a tightly controlled chartering system, had less in loans outstanding per capita in the 1850's than it had in the 1840's. By contrast, New York, a highly competitive banking city, greatly increased its loans per capita over the same period. In Ohio, the introduction of free banking in 1851 substantially cut the profits of banks, suggesting (though hardly proving) that banking became more competitive.

The Impact of Banking: An Overview

How much did banks really matter to antebellum growth? As to their value as market makers—efficient allocators of capital to those who could use it most productively—we know relatively little. Prior to the Panic of 1837, there is evidence that commercial banks were expanding their business from short-term loans financing trade to longer-term loans to manufacturing and agriculture. After the Panic, banks were less eager to hold assets in such illiquid form, and state regulations often restricted them to short-term loans, anyway. The Louisiana free banking law even prohibited banks from renewing short-term commercial loans. It is difficult to know if this withdrawal to a narrow segment of the capital market mattered much, however. Other types of financial intermediaries, such as savings banks, life insurance companies, and investment banks made loans where commercial banks wouldn't or couldn't. And the public market for stocks and bonds—another means of channeling savings into investment—was becoming increasingly sophisticated.

Banks surely speeded development by increasing the use of money as an exchange medium and by substituting paper money and checks for commodity money that had alternative, productive uses. From this perspective, the system performed best in the heyday of Biddle's B.U.S. Stanley Engerman notes that the proportion of money held as specie was 15 percent or less during the entire 1823–37 period; from the Panic to the Civil War, specie holding was never below 23 percent. Whether one views the pre-Panic experience as exceptionally good or the post-Panic experience as disappointing, the fact remains that the banking system harbored considerable resources.

Engerman calculates just how much one part of this savings amounted to by comparing what actually happened to a counterfactual world in which the same amount of money would have been held entirely as specie. Every paper dollar that replaced a silver or gold dollar saved a dollar's investment in precious metals. Using contemporary rates of interest as the annual charge for holding precious metal, Engerman finds that the total interest costs of replacing paper money with specie would have averaged 0.46 percent of GNP in 1825–34, 0.35 percent in 1835–48, 0.43 percent in 1849–58.

Note that the savings as a fraction of national income declines after the Panic. That squares with the fact that people were more reluctant to hold paper money. Engerman and Sushka view their reluctance as a response to the destruction of the B.U.S., rather than to the experience of the Panic itself. If one accepts this inference, one might label the difference between the pre-B.U.S. social savings (0.46 percent of GNP) and the post-Bank social savings (0.35–0.45 percent) as one clear cost of the destruction of the B.U.S. The other cost—for which we have no measure—is the impact of the reduced use of money as a medium of exchange on the efficiency of commodity and factor markets. To the degree that a scarcity of exchange medium inhibited efficient resource allocation, it reduced income and growth. Many economists would infer that it is this cost, rather than the waste of using precious metals as money, that really added up.

Our preoccupation with the microeconomics of banking—the system's ability to allocate capital and conserve commodity money—might seem strange to anyone who reads the financial section of the newspaper. The banking system, after all, influences the size of the money supply, and today, the quantity of money is seen primarily as a macroeconomic issue—as an influence on prices, jobs, and income. Thus, economic historians casually inferred from the experience of the last half century that the size and rate of change of the money supply was equally important in the antebellum American economy: Witness the emphasis from the Soundness School on the failures of the banking system in the 1830's, which led to the deflation of the 1840's.

Peter Temin's examination of the 1840's questioned these casual inferences—and indeed questioned the impact of money supply changes on real economic activity. By modern criteria, the financial crisis was extremely severe, the money supply falling by 34 percent from 1838 to 1842 and the price level falling by 33 percent in 1839–43. By comparison, during the economic catastrophe of 1929–33 the money stock dipped just 27 percent, the price level just 31 percent. But the Great Depression of the 1930's also cut real GNP by 30 percent, while the latest estimates by Robert Gallman reveal that real GNP actually *grew* by 16 percent during the 1839–43 slump.

How can we reconcile the most acute price deflation in American history with what was, apparently, not a bad contemporary rate of economic growth? The answer lies in the relative simplicity and institutional flexibility of the early 19th-century economy. Economic theory tells us that the quantity of money in circulation (M) times the "velocity" (V), or rate of circulation of money, must be identical to the product of real output (Y) times the price level (P):

$$MV \equiv YP$$

Today, prices and wages are sticky—producers in oligopolistic markets, locked into long-term labor contracts and large fixed debts, are extremely reluctant to lower prices to attract customers. Money velocity, determined by how much cash businesses and individuals use to support their day-to-day operations, does adjust somewhat to business conditions, but not very rapidly. Hence, if the quantity of money falls dramatically today, the quantity equation regains balance partially through a drop in output. Money—or rather the stability of the money supply—matters all too much in determining national economic output.

By contrast, in the first half of the 19th century, markets rather quickly adjusted to a fall in demand by lowering prices. Most output, remember, was agricultural, and farmers went on planting and harvesting even when prices fell. Industry apparently reacted briskly to market conditions, too. There were no union contracts to contend with, and most manufacturers' debts consisted of short-term borrowings to finance current production. A rapid fall in the money supply was thus balanced primarily by a fall in the price level, not a fall in output.

This is not to say that the deflation of 1839–43 had no impact at all on the "real" economy. The rate of investment fell as foreign investors, alarmed by numerous bond defaults, lost their enthusiasm for canal and railroad building. Price deflation made foreign goods of all types more expensive, lowering the living standard of the relatively small percentage of the population that consumed large amounts of imports. But 20th-century experience provides a misleading perspective to what financial disruption in the 19th century could do to the economy.

Bibliography

**Lance Davis, "Savings Sources and Utilization" and "Banks and Their Economic Effects" in Lance Davis, Richard Easterlin, William Parker, et al., *American Economic Growth* (Harper and Row, 1972). Emphasis on theory.

**Stanley Engerman, "A Note on the Consequences of the Second Bank of the United States," *Journal of Political Economy* 78 (July/August, 1970). Shows the loss in real income associated with increased public demand for specie.

*Bray Hammond, *Banks and Politics in America from the Revolution to the Civil War* (Princeton, 1957). Political economy of the early banking system, from the view of a sophisticated central banker.

**Roger Hinterlinder and Hugh Rockoff, "The Management of Reserves by Banks in Antebellum Eastern Financial Center," *Explorations in Economic History* 11 (Fall, 1973). Econometric analysis of why eastern bankers chose to hold the level of reserves they held.

*David Martin, "Bimetallism in the United States before 1850," *Journal of Political Economy* 76 (May/June 1968). Description of (largely unsuccessful) attempts to maintain a bimetallic monetary standard.

*David Martin, "1853: The End of Bimetallism in the United States," *Journal of Economic History* 33 (Dec., 1973). Account of functional termination of bimetallism, 20 years before the Gold Standard was formalized as law.

**David Martin, "Metallism, Small Notes, and Jackson's War with the B.U.S.," *Explorations in Economic History* 11 (Spring, 1974). Account of Jackson's attempt to restore "sound" money by reducing the use of paper money.

*Fritz Redlich, *The Molding of American Banking: Men and Ideas* (Johnson Reprints, 1968). Reprint of classic banking history from the Soundness School viewpoint.

**Hugh Rockoff, "Money, Prices and Banks in the Jacksonian Era," in Fogel and Engerman (ed.), *The Reinterpretation of American Economic History*. Lucid summary of evidence supporting Temin's thesis on the cause of the panic of 1837.

**Hugh Rockoff, "The Free Banking Era: A Reexamination," *Journal of Money, Credit and Banking* 6 (May, 1974). Insightful analysis of how free banking worked and how it affected the efficiency of capital markets.

**Hugh Rockoff, "Varieties of Banking and Regional Economic Development in the United States: 1840–60," *Journal of Economic History* 35 (March, 1975). Assessment of the affect of free banking on economic development and the quality of capital markets.

**Harry Scheiber, "The Pet Banks in Jacksonian Politics and Finance 1833–41," *Journal of Economic History* 23 (June, 1963). Detailed description of Jackson's financial policies, with an emphasis on the Specie Circular as the proximate cause of the Panic.

*Arthur Schlesinger, *The Age of Jackson* (Little, Brown, 1945). Striking, pro-Jackson political analysis; naive economic interpretation of the bank war.

**Edward Stevens, "Composition of the Money Stock prior to the Civil War," *Journal of Money, Credit, and Banking* 3 (May, 1971). Estimates of the money supply and analysis of the impact of the California gold rush.

‡***Marie Sushka, "The Antebellum Money Market and the Economic Impact of the Bank War," *Journal of Economic History* 36 (Dec., 1976). Ambitious econometric analysis of the impact of Jacksonian policies. Puts blame on Jackson, but for unique reasons.

**Richard Sylla, "American Banking and Growth in the 19th Century: A Partial View of the Terrain," *Explorations in Economic History* 9 (Winter, 1971/72). Historiography of banking history and presentation of a nonnormative framework for judging bank function.

‡**Peter Temin, "The Anglo-American Business Cycle 1820–60," *Economic History Review* 27 (May, 1974). Mechanisms that caused business fluctuations and their relationships in the two countries.

**Peter Temin, "The Economic Consequences of the Bank War," *Journal of Political Economy* 76 (March/April, 1968). Brief, less complete analysis than contained in Temin's bank war book.

**Peter Temin, *The Jacksonian Economy* (Norton, 1969). Pathbreaking reinterpretation of the Bank War and its impact.

**Richard Timberlake, "The Specie Circular and the Distribution of the Surplus," *Journal of Political Economy* 68 (April, 1960). Jackson's role in precipitating the Panic.

**Thomas Willett, "International Specie Flows and American Monetary Stability, 1834–60," *Journal of Economic History* 28 (March, 1968). Attempt to sharpen the conceptual model working to change the money supply in the 1830's and 40's.

Northern agricultural expansion before the civil war

7

The economic history of the United States is the history of economic growth. And there is no more potent symbol of that growth process than the westward movement of family farming in the 19th century. After 1800, waves of settlers—first easterners, then a mix of easterners and newly arrived immigrants—poured across the Appalachians. Of the "western" states, Ohio was the first beneficiary, its population rising thirteenfold from 1800 to 1820. Other east north central states bordering the Great Lakes trailed in growth by only a decade or two. In 1810 only 4 percent of Americans lived in what we now call the midwest and northern plains; but by 1840 that figure had reached 17 percent—3 million people—and by 1860, 25 percent (see table 7.1).

Population growth is hardly a measure of economic success, however, as contemporary planners in overpopulated Asia, Africa, and Latin America are painfully aware. And, by current measures of prosperity and progress, the graining of America before the Civil War presents a series of economic contrasts that are, on first reflection, puzzling. The product of northern farms certainly grew at a healthy rate—the north central states yielded 13 percent of national output in 1840, 20 percent in 1860. In less than half a century wilderness was converted into one of the world's great agricultural regions—one able to keep pace with the food requirements of an emerging industrial power. On the other hand, western income per capita lagged far behind the national average. Richard Easterlin has calculated that in 1840, the average midwesterner earned barely half as much as the average resident of the northeast and

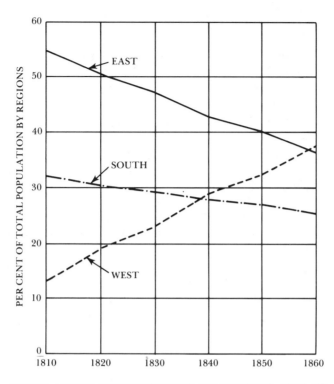

POPULATION DISTRIBUTION BY REGION, 1810–60

Source: Douglass North, *The Economic Growth of the United States* (Norton, 1966), p. 121.

TABLE 7.1

POPULATION CHANGE IN MIDWESTERN STATES 1800–1860
(thousands)

State	1800	1810	1820	1830	1840	1850	1860
Ohio	45	231	581	938	1,519	1,980	2,340
Indiana	6	25	147	343	686	988	1,350
Illinois	—	12	55	157	476	851	1,712
Michigan	—	5	9	32	212	398	749
Wisconsin	—	—	—	—	31	305	776
Iowa	—	—	—	—	43	192	675
Minnesota	—	—	—	—	—	6	172
Midwest as % of U.S. population	1.0%	3.8%	8.2%	11.4%	17.3%	20.3%	24.7%

Source: Bureau of the Census, *Historical Statistics of the United States* (Government Printing Office, 1975), Series A-7, A-195.

90 percent as much as the average southerner—the latter including deliberately impoverished slaves. On the eve of the Civil War, the region had lost still more ground to the northeast and only narrowed slightly the gap with the south.

The explanation for this wierd performance probably lies in the peculiar way in which the region grew. In the northeast, technical change and heavy capital investment in modern equipment lowered the labor input needed to produce a unit of manufactures at the same time that falling transportation costs widened the market for efficiently produced local and regional goods. Transportation did as much or more for northern agriculture, but farmers were slower to improve labor productivity through the use of new technology, and capital per worker grew little or not at all.

That is less an explanation than a description of what happened. Technical improvement and capital investment are not gifts from the gods. They are, rather, responses to incentives within the myriad constraints imposed by cultural attitudes, geography, engineering, and economic conditions. In this brief selective look at northern agriculture we will sketch out some of the issues raised by this development process.

Regional Specialization and the Growth of Markets

The first farmers of Ohio, Indiana, and Illinois followed the path of least economic resistance, populating the valleys formed by the Ohio and Mississippi rivers and their tributaries. They grew grain (mostly corn and wheat) and meat for home consumption and for shipment down the rivers to the seaport of New Orleans. The introduction of the steamboat on the western rivers—discussed in chapter 4—greatly reduced the costs of interregional trade. Douglass North points out that in 1818 pork cost $7.50 a barrel more in New Orleans than at the packing house in Cincinnati. Ten years later that figure had fallen to about $2.40, and by the late 1850's the differential was only about $1.25 (see table 7.2). The differential for wheat flour over the same period was cut by about 70 percent. Cost reductions for upstream transport were even greater. George Rogers Taylor estimates that upstream rates in 1860 were only 5–10 percent as high as they had been before the steamboat.

The effect of another transportation miracle—the canal system—was almost as startling. After 1825 the Erie Canal made it possible to ship grain and meat by water from lake ports in Ohio all the way to New York City. Western canal construction in the 1830's extended water routes into the interior of Ohio and Indiana. Pork, which may have cost as much as $10 a barrel to wrestle over the Appalachians from Cincinnati to New York in 1820, could be transported by water for about $3.50 in

TABLE 7.2

DIFFERENCE BETWEEN WHOLESALE COMMODITY PRICES IN CINCINNATI AND NEW ORLEANS

Period	Lard ($/lb.)	Pork ($/barrel)	Flour ($/barrel)	Corn ($/barrel)
1816–20	.051	7.57	2.16	NA
1821–25	.027	2.81	2.37	.59
1826–30	.024	2.41	1.75	.59
1831–35	.017	2.03	1.29	.64
1836–40	.014	2.67	1.66	.49
1841–45	.006	1.66	.61	.14
1846–50	.005	1.31	.60	.20
1851–55	.006	1.24	.59	.16
1856–60	.007	1.27	.63	.21
1856–60 difference as % of 1816–20 difference	14%	17%	29%	35%

Source: Thomas Berry, *Western Prices Before 1861* (Harvard University, 1943) cited in Douglass North, *Economic Growth of the United States 1790–1860* (Norton, 1966), p. 261.

the 1830's (see table 7.3). Over the same period, the differential in the price of flour was roughly cut in half.

Actually, the fall in transport costs was only one factor making western farming economically more attractive. Due both to lower transport costs and rapidly improving industrial technology, the western price of goods manufactured in the east fell sharply relative to the price of agricultural goods. Thomas Berry's computations show that the purchasing power of western output in interregional trade grew steadily over most of the antebellum years. A composite unit of western output (at a western market) would fetch twice as many eastern goods in the 1840's as it did in the 1820's, three times as many on the eve of the Civil War (see table 7.4).

The farmers' response to improved terms of trade—the price of the goods they sold relative to the price of the goods they bought—was predictable. Farming became more profitable, making it practicable to extend cultivation farther from the waterways. And the mix of farm output shifted away from goods for home consumption to goods intended for interregional markets. Douglass North illustrates this growing market orientation by following the change in population and output in four

TABLE 7.3

**DIFFERENCE BETWEEN WHOLESALE COMMODITY PRICES
IN CINCINNATI AND NEW YORK**

Period	Lard ($/lb.)	Pork ($/barrel)	Flour ($/barrel)	Corn ($/barrel)
1816–20	.048	9.53	2.48	.48
1821–25	.031	4.46	2.81	.39
1826–30	.026	4.18	1.78	.36
1831–35	.025	3.48	1.43	.38
1836–40	.020	3.11	1.02	.42
1841–45	.011	2.25	1.37	.30
1846–50	.010	1.06	1.68	.36
1851–55	.007	1.56	1.36	.31
1856–60	.004	1.18	.28	.27
1851–60 difference as a % of 1816–20 difference	11%	14%	33%	60%

Source: Thomas Berry, *Western Prices Before 1861* (Harvard, 1943) cited in Douglass North, *Economic Growth of the United States 1790–1860* (Norton, 1966), p. 261.

randomly selected counties in central Illinois. Between 1840 and 1850, the population of these counties increased by 60 percent, but the output of corn grew by 232 percent. The corn was, presumably, sold as feed for hogs raised for export down the Mississippi to New Orleans.

Between 1850 and 1860 the same four counties responded remarkably quickly once again to incentives. In the fifties, the rail link between Chicago and the east was completed. Some 2,700 miles of feeder rail lines crisscrossed Illinois, pulling traffic away from the Mississippi River toward Chicago and the east coast. Now the major crop of the four counties became wheat: While population increased by 178 percent, wheat production was raised by 655 percent.

As western grain and livestock began to compete for eastern markets, established northeastern farmers found themselves at a disadvantage. Thus, land in grain production declined, first on the thin rocky soils of upland New England and New York State, where land productivity was low, and then in the grain specializing regions of the mid-Atlantic. Railroads sharply reduced transport costs from upland areas of the rural northeast and cut the time it took to get food to market. This

TABLE 7.4

**WESTERN STATES TERMS OF
TRADE 1816–60**

Years	Five-Year Average
1816–20	58
1821–25	59
1826–30	75
1831–35	105
1836–40	125
1841–45	111
1846–50	130
1851–55	160
1856–60	162

Note: Western "Terms of Trade" is an index of prices received for western goods divided by prices paid by westerners for eastern goods.
100 = the average terms of trade for years 1824–46

Source: Thomas Berry, *Western Prices Before 1861: A Study of the Cincinnati Market* (Harvard University, 1943) cited in Douglass North, *The Economic Growth of the United States 1790–1860* (Norton, 1966), p. 255.

improved transport, combined with increased demand for luxury foods, encouraged the growth of the dairy industry, which had previously been limited to the fringes of urban areas. For the same reasons, Middle Atlantic farmers were induced to switch from their traditional grain crops to the production of fresh fruits and vegetables for urban consumption.

Along with the switch to crops that retained a location advantage over western land, there was also a movement in eastern farming toward capital-intensive, high-yield-per-acre farming. Some farmers experimented with fertilizer and crop rotation schemes as a means of saving land with declining fertility. One should not make too much of this movement, though. Relatively little was known before the Civil War about capital-intensive, scientific farming, and we have no strong basis for believing that it was profitable to use "land-saving" technology anyway as long as it was easy to open virgin lands in the west. Eastern adaptation to western agricultural expansion was largely based on shifts to crops in which the east had a "comparative advantage."

The Economics of Farm Making

Early 19th-century farmers pushed the frontier west at a stunning rate. Ohio, southern Indiana, and southern Illinois were thinly settled by 1820. Northern Indiana and Illinois, plus portions of Michigan, Wisconsin, and Iowa were opened by 1840. And with the railroad in the 1850's, the limits of settlement were extended into the rest of Iowa and portions of Minnesota, Kansas, and Nebraska.

The expansion may bring to mind images of endless lines of hardy pioneers waiting their turns for the ride downstream from Pittsburgh. Nothing so simple as deck space capacity on the steamboats, however, explains the pace of westward settlement. Settlement came in waves most probably associated with expectations of profit. As Douglass North has pointed out, the sale of federal public lands in the north central region is rather neatly tied to fluctuations in the price of wheat and corn, with peaks in the late teens, mid-thirties, and mid-fifties. Some of the land was purchased by speculators (rather than settlers who planned to farm what they bought), thereby putting a sort of statistical buffer between land sales and farm making. One might guess—there is no clear evidence—that speculation increased the elasticity of land sales with respect to crop prices. But there is little reason to believe that, without speculators, the timing of land sales would have been very different.

Virgin land purchased from the public land office was cheap. After 1820 it could be purchased at auction for as little as $1.25 per acre. And after 1841 squatters who had illegally settled and developed public land were guaranteed the right to purchase up to 160 acres at the $1.25 minimum. Actually, public lands changed title at even lower prices. Land warrants—the right to claim public land—were issued to veterans of the Mexican War and could often be purchased in the open market below $1.25 per acre. And under the Graduation Act of 1854, public lands that had been surveyed and opened to auction were gradually reduced in price if they remained unsold. The Graduation price fell as low as 12.5¢ an acre for land available for 30 years.

Not all unimproved farmland cost $1.25 or less, of course. Settlers who wanted to be close to water or rail transport or within hailing distance of a market town paid much more. But there is little question that land costs represented only a minor barrier for those who wanted to become farmers. Although the availability and cheapness of western land has long fascinated social historians—the West has been characterized as a safety valve, offering the landless discontented an opportunity to become established farmers—the seminal studies of Clarence Danhof demonstrate that the cost of virgin land was just a fraction of the cost of making a farm.

Farm making meant much more than acquiring title of 80 or 160

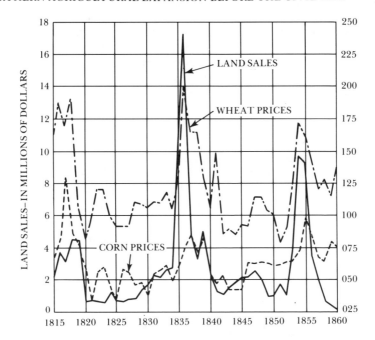

LAND SALES IN SEVEN WESTERN STATES, 1815–60
(Ohio, Illinois, Indiana, Michigan, Iowa, Wisconsin, Missouri)

As Douglass North points out, the irregular pattern of public land sales in the family farming regions of the Northwest appears to follow the price trends of corn and wheat.

Source: Douglass North, *The Economic Growth of the United States 1790–1860* (Norton, 1966), p. 137.

acres of arable land. To begin, the land had to be cleared, and in the forests of Ohio, Michigan, Wisconsin, and Minnesota, clearing was an extremely arduous task. First, trees had to be cut down and burned or hauled away. Then the stumps and any large rocks had to be removed, usually by brute animal force. Martin Primack estimates that about a month's labor, plus the services of a team of oxen, was required to clear an acre. The fact that the farmer would do the work on his or her own time doesn't eliminate the cost of the operation—a month of farm labor devoted to land clearing was a month in which the family still had to be fed, sheltered, and clothed. Substantial additional labor, moreover, was required to build fences capable of keeping livestock out of the fields.

Thus a farmer had two choices, each of which involved considerable investment. The usual course was for the family to clear five or ten acres each year, planting crops on land as it became available. This meant that it took five or ten years to build a complete farm, five to ten years in which the farmer would be forced to draw down savings (or moonlight as a farm laborer) in order to survive. The alternative was to hire outside labor, a practice that was increasingly common by the 1840's. With outside help, the required investment—about $10–12 per acre for clearing alone—was essentially the same, but the farmer had to have the cash up front.

Land clearing thus represented a vast hidden economic investment, one which at least in part explains the relatively low western commodity output figures we mentioned earlier. Martin Primack estimates that in the forested areas of the midwest, an average of 1,330,000 acres were cleared per year in the 1850's (see table 7.5). At $10–12 implicit (or explicit) cost per acre, the clearing of forested land thus meant an average annual investment of $13–16 million, diverting an equivalent amount of resources from commodity production. To put it another way, roughly one-sixth of total midwestern labor force time was engaged in land clearing. This eventually paid off in terms of higher output. But in the pre-Civil War era, it was clearly a serious drain on productive labor resources.

Land, with improvement, was the largest single investment needed to make a family farm, but by no means the only investment. Danhof offers a western New York State farmer's 1821 itemized list of farm making costs as a benchmark. This (very small) hypothetical farm comprises 50 acres, of which 15 are devoted to crops, 15 to a house, pasture, orchard and garden, and 20 are left wooded:

Clearing 30 acres @ $10 per acre	300
Fencing	70
Log House and Frame Barn	200
Outhouse, Well, Orchard	150
1 pair oxen	50
1 horse	50
2 cows	40
2 hogs	10
10 sheep	50
plow, harness, tools	50
purchase 50 acres @ $2 per acre	100
essentials for family consumption before first crop	75
Total	$1,145

Note that the cost of raw land at $2 per acre is only 9 percent of the farm's cost. The first four items, totaling $720, might be "self-financed" over time with the family's own labor. And the land might be used as collateral for a loan—for purposes of argument, let us assume that the land could be mortgaged for the full $100, with no down payment required.

TABLE 7.5

INVESTMENT IN CLEARING FARMLAND, THE 1850'S

Region	Average Annual Acres Cleared (thousand acres)	% Forested	Average Labor Years Invested (thousands)	% Total Farm Labor Devoted to Clearing
Northeast	570	100	66	7.3
South	1610	99	175	9.9
Midwest	1480	90	147	17.7
West	1230	39	56	16.8
total	4890	81	445	11.6

Source: Martin Primack, "Land Clearing Under 19th Century Techniques, *Journal of Economic History* 22 (Dec., 1962), p. 492.

But the remaining $325, three year's wage for the average American in 1840, would have to be paid in cash. Thus the prospective farm family would have to save $325 and then endure a long period of backbreaking work and subsistence living in order to own a tiny farm that would barely be self-sustaining. These figures suggest that farm makers had either big rainy day savings or powerful motivations or some combination thereof. By contrast, farm making on the western prairie offered welcome freedom from the task of clearing trees and stumps. All one needed to do to get the soil ready for grain was to break up the heavy, grass-covered sod with a plow, and then build fences. Starting from scratch, however, still required a large investment beyond the land purchase price. Sodbreaking demanded extremely heavy plows powered by teams of three to eight oxen. Typically, a farmer would contract out the task to specialists at a not inconsiderable cost of $2–5 per acre. Unlike with the forests of Ohio, moreover, fencing materials on the barren prairie were costly. Danhof estimates that the cost of bringing 60 acres of prairie from virgin soil to the first finished crop was about $600. Add to that the cost of a rudimentary house ($150), the purchase price of the land (say, 80 acres at $2 per acre), and the requisite draught animals and livestock ($200–400), and again, we discover that prairie farming was not for the impecunious.[1]

If these numbers do represent the minimum investment in a going farm, what was the typical investment? The Census shows that the average Illinois farm in 1850 was worth over $1,650 (including livestock,

[1] Some economic historians believe that Danhof's minimum may be too high, as Census records do show farms with a smaller declared net worth. Still, it is hard to interpret the evidence as support for the notion that farm-making was open to the poor.

equipment and structures), the average Iowa farm over $1,450. A farmer who wanted to buy an average working farm would have had to pay $19 an acre in 1850, $32 an acre in 1860. Since the market value of a successful farm represents what it could produce, not what it cost to create, we can assume that part of the $19 per acre was capitalized "economic rent." But the weight of evidence leaves little doubt that antebellum farming for food—on prairie or forest land—was a substantial financial undertaking.

Farm Technology

The machinery and techniques employed by typical northern farmers in the first third of the 19th century were remarkably crude by modern standards. The process of growing wheat and other small grains—the most important antebellum crops—is illustrative. First the soil had to be loosened sufficiently to bury the seed and provide adequate drainage and space for root development. This was done with a simple wooden or metal sheathed wooden plow pulled by a horse or an ox. Then the seeds were scattered by hand and buried under a shallow cover of soil by a light, animal-drawn plow or harrow. When the plants matured, they were cut by a hand-swung scythe and bound together in shocks. The gathered shocks of grain were stored in a barn until the farmer had time to separate the grain from the straw and then remove the remaining chaff and dirt by screening.

Labor productivity—the amount of grain produced by a worker—was limited by (1) by the number of acres each worker could plow and harvest, (2) the number of bushels of grain each acre could yield, and (3) the number of bushels each worker could thresh. Little progress was made in raising acreage yields before the Civil War, because, in large measure, yields can be manipulated only by biochemical techniques. Basic understanding of genetic principles was insufficient to make seed selection very productive. And seat-of-the-pants experimentation with seeds, fertilizers, and other yield-increasing techniques were frustrated by the enormous range of soil and weather conditions farmers faced. Yields might, of course, be raised by farming more productive soil regions. William Parker and Judith Klein show that just such a change did take place after the Civil War, largely because the share in total output of low productivity southern grain acreage fell. But the shift of grain production from northeast to north central states before the war left yield levels virtually unchanged.

By contrast, techniques for reducing the amount of labor needed per acre and for reducing the labor requirement in threshing were developed in the pre–Civil War period. Technical improvements came fairly easily, as mechanics adapted techniques invented for the construction of industrial machinery. Wooden plows gave way to cast-iron plows of superior durability, and much more important, superior design requiring less animal power. Steel plows gradually replaced cast iron, particularly in the West, where they were better suited for moving heavy prairie soil. In the 1830's and 1840's, mechanical threshers greatly reduced labor inputs in removing the grain from the stalk. Threshers were very expensive, and the capacity of a single machine was much greater than that needed by an average farm with fifty or sixty acres in small grains. But the market place adapted easily to this economic "indivisibility": Entrepreneurs rented out threshing services to neighboring farmers as their needs required. Prior to mechanization, it took between one and two hours to thresh a bushel of wheat. Mechanical threshing could cut the cost of the operation down to 3 or 4 cents per bushel, a saving of perhaps half over hand threshing.

The single most demanding task in the grain production cycle was harvesting. Until the 1830's harvesting placed a clear constraint on overall labor productivity. Hand harvesting took a great deal of time. Yet the task had to be started and completed in a very limited season. Temporary harvest labor might be used to break the constraint for an individual farmer. However, since everyone's wheat needed to be harvested in the same period, there was a real risk that outside help would be unavailable, or only available at very high wages. Hence the importance of the mechanical, horse-drawn harvester. The first harvesters were patented by Obed Hussey in 1833 and Cyrus McCormick in 1834. At first, the machines sold poorly—only 3,400 were manufactured in the years through 1850. But in the early 1850's, sales took off: over 70,000 of the labor saving devices were purchased between 1850 and 1858.

Why the long lag between the invention of the "reaper" and its general adoption on American farms? The conventional explanation is that high wheat prices in the 1850's raised the profitability of wheat farming, while the use of traditional hand harvesting methods became impractical because of the general shortage of labor. This explanation may well be correct. However it is unnecessarily ambiguous in meaning. In a famous article—one of the first of the New Economic History—Paul David restated the hypothesis in more testable language.

Figure 7.1 shows the average cost curve for a grain farmer, relating output in the cost per bushel of producing wheat. C_H is the farmer's cost if he or she chooses to harvest by hand. It is shown here as perfectly flat up to a certain point to emphasize the idea that, within the constraints of the family labor supply, an individual farmer could use labor at roughly constant cost per bushel harvested. The curve C_M shows the alternative average cost of producing wheat using a mechanical harvester. For low outputs, costs are very high, but C_M falls rapidly. This reflects the fact

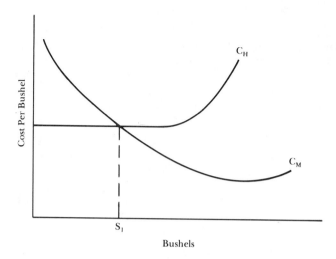

FIGURE 7.1

that much of the cost of operation of a harvesting machine is fixed regardless of output—the farmer has to buy the same piece of equipment whether five acres or fifty acres are to be harvested.

A farmer planting relatively few acres in wheat would naturally prefer to harvest by hand. But now suppose that wheat prices rise and individual farmers wish to plant more land in wheat. Even if the cost of the additional labor remains the same per unit, the more a farmer expands grain output, the less the advantage of using hand labor. When output S_1 is reached, it pays the farmer to buy a mechanical harvester. Actually, by the traditional historical explanation, it may pay to switch at an output below S_1. If the wages needed to hire extra labor rise (or sacrificed by family members who might moonlight), reflecting a general upward shift in the demand for labor, the C_H curve shifts upward to C_H', as shown in figure 7.2. The average cost of hand harvesting now exceeds mechanical harvesting at S_2.

This scenario—connecting the switch to the rising cost of labor and the increased demand for wheat—makes sense. But sense isn't proof. David set out to test the explanation by estimating the acreage threshold (S) at which it would pay to switch to mechanical reaping, and then comparing the threshold with actual acreage in grain on Illinois farms. In the 1849–53 period, David finds that the delivered purchase price of a standard McCormick reaper was equivalent to 97.6 laborer-days' wages. Using estimates of the labor per acre the reaper saved, and the annual cost of keeping a reaper, it is easy to show that the hand-machine threshold was 46.5 acres. This was far above the typical Illinois farmer's acreage in small grains, which at the time of the 1850 Census averaged

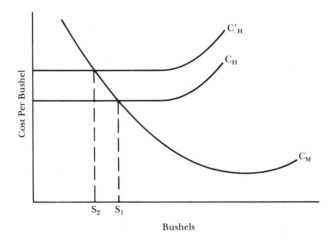

FIGURE 7.2

just 15–16 acres statewide and 37 acres in the northern Illinois wheat belt.

The threshold declined shortly thereafter, however; wages rose faster than the price of reapers, pushing the threshold down to 35 acres. David can't be certain of a parallel increase in grain acreage per farm due to increasing profits in wheat production. The Census does not provide enough information to identify what parts of the state showed increases in wheat acreage per farm. But we do know that small grain output per farm for the state as a whole rose by 19 percent over the decade, suggesting that average farm acreage in the wheat counties could easily have pushed across the (reduced) threshold.

Tidy though David's explanation of the rapid transition to mechanical reaping may be, it is not invulnerable to criticism. Alan Olmstead attacks both David's assumptions and inferences, and offers his own explanation of the long lag between invention and rapid adoption of the reaper. Olmstead's first target is the threshold calculation. David based his estimate of the annual cost of owning a reaper on the assumption that loans to finance the machines could be had at 6 percent interest and that reapers had a useful life of ten years. There is reason to believe, however, the credit charges for time purchases of reapers were closer to 10 percent and that the reapers may have lasted as little as five years. These alternative assumptions raise the cost of mechanical harvesting relative to hand harvesting, and naturally, raise the threshold. David's 1848–53 46.5-acre threshold becomes 89.4 acres, and his 1854–57 35-acre threshold jumps to 67.6 acres. By this reckoning, mechanical reaping should have remained out of favor even in the later period.

Olmstead's interpretation of the threshold computation can be chal-

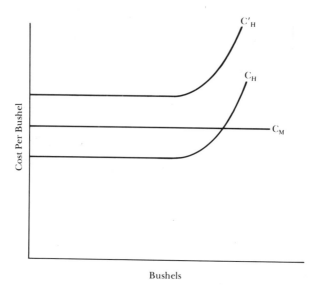

FIGURE 7.3

lenged—as we shall see shortly. But his other criticism goes to the very heart of David's analysis. David must assume that reapers are "indivisible"—that a farmer can't buy the services of a fourth or a half of a reaper. Otherwise, the threshold argument becomes meaningless. Mechanized technology would either be cheaper on all farms or none, depending on the relative cost of hand labor and reapers. To see why, check figure 7.3.

The cost curve for hand harvesting (C_H) remains the same. But if a farmer need not buy any fixed amount of a reaper, the mechanical harvesting cost curve (C_M) loses its downward slope. Now if C_M lies above C_H, hand harvesting is cheaper, regardless of the farm acreage planted in grain. If hand harvesting is more expensive (C_H^1), all farms, whatever their grain acreage, will use mechanical harvesters. Since David argues that large farms (over 46 acres) could profit from the use of McCormick's reaper in 1849, by this same logic all farms could have profited from renting the services of a reaper. Hence nothing in David's analysis explains why just a few farms used reapers in 1849, while many used them in 1856.

Was it really possible to buy less than a whole reaper? David claims it wasn't, citing the problems of cooperative ownership or rental arrangements. This argument seems a bit strained in view of the thriving contemporary market for less than 100 percent of the services of threshing machines. And, in fact, Olmstead unearths some direct evidence that neighboring farmers and related farmers often pooled their resources to buy reapers jointly. So much for tidy explanations.

Olmstead's somewhat untidy alternative explanation is based on the notion that, over time, reaper design changed substantially. The job the machines were intended to perform remained the same, but the machines themselves were constantly being improved. At a certain point, presumably in the 1850's, technical refinements had sufficiently improved the quality, versatility, and durability of reapers such that they were generally recognized as superior to hand harvesting. Using figure 7.3, Olmstead argues that the transition took place when C_M shifted down below C_H. Olmstead does not refer to the rising cost of labor as a factor in the transition, but it is not inconsistent with the rest of his story that C_H shifted upward as C_M shifted downward.

If one accepts the view that cooperative ownership of reapers was a practical alternative in the 1840's, it is difficult to give much weight to David's technical argument about threshold changes. If one remains agnostic about the assumption, however, Lewis Jones's defense of David becomes relevant. Jones notes that both David and Olmstead erred in using *average* acreage in small grains as the threshold factor in the choice of harvesting technology. In both periods examined by David, small grain planting ranged from just a few acres on some farms to more than a hundred acres on others. What we really need then to test David's hypothesis is an estimate of the *number* or percentage of farms in each period that exceeded the hand-machine threshold.

Jones used the manuscript of the Illinois Census to make just this calculation. He discovered that 3,420 farms exceeded David's 46-acre threshold in 1849 and 836 exceeded Olmstead's recomputed 89-acre threshold. Ten years later he found that, as a result of increasing farm specialization, the number of farms meeting David's threshold specification rose 730 percent. That is no surprise. But it is surprising that the

TABLE 7.6

FARM SIZE THRESHOLD AND USE OF REAPER

Year	National Reaper Stock, Est. A*	National Reaper Stock, Est. B*	Illinois Farms over David's Threshold	Illinois Farms over Olmstead's Threshold
1849	3,862	3,821	3,420	836
1859	56,026	44,428	28,080	8,550

*Estimate A is based on the assumption that reapers lasted ten years, while estimate B is based on Olmstead's assumption of a five-year useful life.

Sources: Lewis Jones, "The Mechanization of Reaping and Mowing in American Agriculture: A Comment," *Journal of Economic History* 37 (June, 1977), p. 454. Hugh Knox, "The Mechanization of Harvesting 1839–79," unpublished paper presented to the University of Pennsylvania Economic History Seminar, 1966. Cited in Jones, p. 452.

number of farms meeting Olmstead's threshold requirement went up even more—930 percent (see table 7.6).

How does that compare with the growth in the use of mechanical reapers? Assuming, as Olmstead did, that reapers had an effective life of five years, reapers in service rose by 1,062 percent. Thus, if it weren't for the separate issue of cooperative ownership, Olmstead's own data and assumptions would tend to confirm David's basic hypothesis. So much, once again, for tidy explanations in economic history.

Growth and Interregional Dependence

In ways that vary from crude to subtle, most explanations of the remarkable rate of growth and the rate of expansion westward during the pre–Civil War era are "supply" oriented. Mechanization reduced the quantity of labor needed to make manufactured goods. New transportation technology—the steamboat, the canal, the railroad—increased the size of markets serviceable from one location. Fertile land in the midwest (and, as we shall see, in the South) allowed virtually unlimited extension of agriculture without a significant reduction in labor productivity.

By contrast, one school of thought is boldly and unashamedly "demand" oriented, emphasizing the role of international demand for basic American staples—more specifically, for southern cotton. This school has been around for some time: Historiographers can trace the idea back to Guy Callender (1902) and Louis Schmidt (1939). It is generally associated, though, with one of the first New Economic Historians, Douglass North.

North's thesis is both simple to state and satisfyingly rich in explanatory power. Why was the United States able to enjoy rapid sustained economic growth for the first six decades of the 19th century? Supply factors can't be ignored. But the driving force, North tells us, was the demand for King Cotton. British demand for raw cotton to feed its booming mills allowed the South to specialize in the production of this one export crop. Southern specialization in cotton created a regional food deficit, which, in turn, created a demand for western grain and livestock. Farmers from Ohio, Indiana, and Illinois were encouraged to produce less for themselves and more for the market towns on the Ohio and Mississippi rivers. From there, the food was sent south to New Orleans for sale within the Cotton South. Cotton income stimulated economic growth in the Northeast both directly through sales of manufactures to the South, and indirectly, by providing purchasing power to the food-exporting West.

Attractive though the North thesis may be, critics have been successful in burying it under a mountain of contrary evidence. The first serious blow to export-led growth was struck by Albert Fishlow, who argued

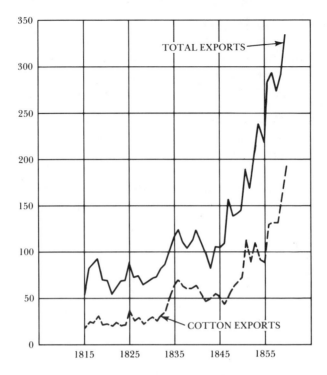

TOTAL EXPORTS AND COTTON EXPORTS, 1815–60
(millions of dollars)

After 1815, cotton accounted for roughly half of all American export value. Hence, in any export-led theory of economic development, cotton must play a major role.

Source: Douglass North, *The Economic Growth of the United States* (Norton, 1966), p. 76.

that Mississippi River traffic in food was largely destined for northeastern cities, foreign markets, and the urban population around New Orleans. Less than one-fifth of the West's exports, Fishlow allowed, ended up on the dining tables of cotton plantations.

Fishlow's work has been confirmed in two separate ways. Diane Lindstrom approached the problem directly, tracing the disposition of western food from trade statistics. The South, Lindstrom notes, was not one section, but three fairly distinct economic subsections. The upper South—Kentucky, Tennessee, Virginia, and North Carolina—was a major producer of grain, exporting much of its product to other parts of the South. The middle South—interior portions of Louisiana, Mississippi, Alabama, South Carolina, and Georgia—rarely imported food. In fact the middle South actually exported wheat and corn to Atlantic and Gulf Coast cities after the construction of rail lines. Only the lower

South—the dense cotton and sugar regions around New Orleans, plus a strip of Atlantic and Gulf Coast from the Carolinas south—were net food importers.

In the early 1840's, Lindstrom calculates, only about half of the corn and flour sent down river to New Orleans remained in the South (see table 7.7). About two-thirds of the corn plus one-third of the flour received at New Orleans, moreover, came from the upper South rather than the West. By the late 1840's, New Orleans receipts of corn and flour had roughly tripled, but almost all of the additional shipments were exported to foreign countries. It is the poor harvests in Europe (in particular, the Irish potato famine), not the needs of the cotton economy that produced the surge of western grain exports.

TABLE 7.7A

DISPOSITION OF CORN TRAFFIC THROUGH NEW ORLEANS

Year	Annual Average Traffic (1,000 sacks)	% Exported East	% Exported Abroad	% Consumed in South
1842–45	529	36	16	48
1846–49	1920	20	55	25
1850–53	1309	17	21	62
1854–57	1592	9	43	48
1858–61	1831	3	20	78

TABLE 7.7B

DISPOSITION OF FLOUR TRAFFIC THROUGH NEW ORLEANS

Year	Annual Average Traffic (1,000 barrels)	% Exported East	% Exported Abroad	% Consumed in South
1842–45	499	31	21	48
1846–49	1044	29	41	30
1850–53	817	15	23	63
1854–57	991	24	30	47
1858–61	1146	17	20	63

Source: Diane Lindstrom, "Interregional Trade Flows . . ." in William Parker (ed.), *The Structure of the Cotton Economy of the Antebellum South* (Washington: Agricultural History Society, 1970), p. 104.

Trends reversed sharply in the 1850's. More of the Mississippi grain traffic originated in the West, and more of the grain that made it down to New Orleans remained within the South. In the last few years before the Civil War 78 percent was either consumed in the New Orleans area or shipped to other southern ports. This looks like confirmation of the North thesis, albeit a bit late in coming as an explanation of a half century's growth. Not so. Western grain shipments to the South grew in the last peacetime decade, but at a rate far slower than total western production. Most of the increased western output went to meet the demands of the growing western population, and to rail and lake shipments direct to the east coast (see Table 7.8).

TABLE 7.8

WESTERN AND UPPER SOUTHERN GRAIN EXPORTS

| Year | Flour | | Corn | |
	Million Barrels	% Shipped East	Million Bushels	% Shipped East
1835	0.4	30	1.0	2
1839	0.8	47	1.0	2
1844	1.5	70	1.5	10
1849	3.0	69	6.0	61
1853	3.0	73	8.0	63
1857	4.0	66	12.0	68
1860	5.0	78	24.0	81

Sources: A. L. Kohlmeier, *The Old Northwest as the Keystone of the Arch to the Federal Union* (Bloomington: Principia Press, 1938) and Albert Fishlow, *American Railroads and the Transformation of the Antebellum Economy* (Harvard, 1965). Both cited in Diane Lindstrom, "Interregional Trade Flows . . . in William Parker (ed.), *The Structure of the Cotton Economy of the Antebellum South* (Washington: Agricultural History Society, 1970), p. 112.

If the modest statistical holes in Lindstrom's study leave any room for doubt, Robert Gallman's alternative approach closes them tight. If the South was an important customer for western grain, one should surely find evidence that the regions specializing in cotton production were unable to feed themselves from local production. To test this hypothesis, Gallman used data on grain output and food requirements from a Census sample of some 5,000 farms and plantations in southern countries producing 1,000 or more bales of cotton in 1859. He found that, on average, these farms generated 53 bushels of grain (mostly corn) per capita, compared to national per capita output of 38 bushels. Only the smallest classes of farms, those under nineteen acres in the sample, slipped below the thirty-eight-bushel national norm.

Were he a less conservative scholar, Gallman might have rested his case. But, it was possible, at least in theory, that enough of his grain was siphoned off as seed or as food for animals to create a farm food deficit. In fact, accounting for seed and for consumption by slaves, free people, work animals, and sheep, he found that southern farms of 100 acres and above generated substantial surpluses (see table 7.9). This excess grain must have been used to fatten hogs, the staple southern meat.

Gallman estimated the amount of meat the grain surplus could have yielded and then used evidence of meat consumption allowed slaves to see how much meat would be left over for the free population. If the grain surplus was utilized entirely for pork production, southern cotton farms produced well over 300 pounds annually per person (see table 7.10). Since national per capital consumption of all meats was less than 230 pounds, it is clear that the cotton plantations as a group were self-sufficient in food. In fact, Gallman estimates, the Cotton South's food *surplus* would have been sufficient to supply all the slaves and one-sixth of the free people living in non-cotton-producing southern counties, many of which presumably had their own food surpluses.

The implications of Gallman's findings are striking. By 1860, the cotton economy had moved west into the fertile soils of Louisiana, Mississippi, Arkansas, and Texas. Cotton prices were high and transportation costs to food-exporting regions were historically low, factors that should

TABLE 7.9

COTTON FARM FOOD CONSUMPTION AS PERCENT OF FOOD OUTPUT 1859

Consumption by	Farm Size (acres)				
	100–199	200–299	300–499	500–999	1000+
Slaves	10	14	14	17	21
Free Persons	6	4	2	2	1
Seed	6	6	6	6	6
Work Animals	38	36	39	32	33
Milk Cows	7	5	5	4	4
Cattle	6	5	3	3	3
Sheep	1	1	1	—	1
Young Animals	4	3	2	2	2
	77	74	73	65	69
Residual Available for Pork Production	23	26	27	35	31

Source: Robert Gallman "Self-Sufficiency in the Cotton Economy of the Cotton South" in William Parker (ed.), *The Structure of the Cotton Economy of the Antebellum South* (Washington: Agricultural History Society, 1970), p. 11.

TABLE 7.10

COTTON FARM PORK AND BEEF CONSUMPTION BY SLAVES AND MEAT RESIDUAL, 1859

Farm Size (improved Acres)	Per Capita Slave Consumption (pounds)	Residual Meat Production Per Free Person (lbs.)	% Residual Exceeds Estimated Free Person Consumption
100–199	144	300	33
200–299	146	357	59
300–499	146	392	74
500–999	146	658	192
1000+	150	350	56

Source: Robert Gallman "Self-Sufficiency in the Cotton Economy of the Cotton South" in William Parker (ed.), *The Structure of the Cotton Economy of the Antebellum South* (Washington: Agricultural History Society, 1970), p. 19.

have induced specialization in cotton. Yet Gallman shows that the Cotton South was still more than self-sufficient in food. Perhaps the real question, then, is how the South was able to absorb even the modest amounts of western food that Fishlow and Lindstrom believe ended up in southern homes.

Hence, the most direct version of North's thesis offered here does not hold water: Western growth could not have been dependent on nonexistent southern demand for western food. This does not mean that western economic expansion was independent of economic activities in the rest of the country. Richard Easterlin cites data showing that, as early as 1840, the East was in substantial food deficit, producing only 88 percent as much wheat per capita, 29 percent as much corn, 43 percent as much pork, and 80 percent as much beef as the national average. Clarence Danhof's calculations suggest that somewhat less than 40 percent of western farm products left rural areas in the late antebellum period. Some of that ended up in western cities like Chicago, Cincinnati, and Akron. And some was exported to Europe and the Caribbean. But a growing portion fed the factory and urban service workers of the East. To put it another way, without industrialization and rapid population growth in the Northeast, specialized grain farming would have progressed less rapidly. Just how much less rapidly we cannot say.

Note that the dependence of the East on western foodstuffs does offer some indirect confirmation of the North thesis. Southern cotton production generated export revenues used by the East to purchase foreign capital, and thereby to specialize in nonagricultural production. It also generated a market for manufactured goods produced in the

Northeast, speeding industrialization. Thus refutation of the West-South food link does not preclude a major role for cotton in the drama of national economic development, to which we now turn.

Bibliography

*Percy Bidwell and John Falconer, *History of Agriculture in the Northern United States 1620–1860* (Washington: Carnegie Institution, 1925). Classic text, still useful.

*Alan Bogue, "Farming in the Prairie Peninsula, 1830–90," *Journal of Economic History* 23 (March, 1963). Careful research on farm making and farm operation in Iowa and Illinois.

*Alan and Margaret Bogue, "Profits and the Frontier Land Speculator," *Journal of Economic History* 17 (March, 1957). Estimates of the return to speculative holdings in Illinois and Nebraska.

*Clarence Danhof, *Change in Agriculture: The Northern United States, 1820–70* (Harvard, 1969). Distinguished historian's description of institutional change.

*Clarence Danhof, "Farm Making Costs and the Safety Valve: 1855–60," in Vernon Carstenson (ed.), *The Public Lands* (University of Wisconsin, 1963). Classic accounting of the high cost of starting a family-size farm.

**Paul David, "The Mechanization of Reaping in the Antebellum Midwest" in *Technical Choice, Innovation and Economic Growth* (Cambridge University, 1975). Explanation of why reaping machines suddenly caught on in the midwest in the 1850's.

*Richard Easterlin, "Review of 'The Economic Growth of the United States 1790–1860'," *Journal of Economic History* 22 (March, 1962). Early critique of the North thesis, emphasizing the importance of the east-west food link.

**Albert Fishlow, *American Railroads and the Transformation of the Ante-Bellum Economy* (Harvard, 1965). Among other tasks this major work sorts out interregional trade flows to the detriment of Douglass North's cotton-led development theory.

*Albert Fishlow, "Antebellum Interregional Trade Reconsidered" in Ralph Andreano (ed.), *New Views in American Economic Development* (Harvard, 1965). Disputes North's theory of interregional dependence in early growth.

*Robert Gallman, "Self-sufficiency of the Cotton Economy of the Antebellum South" in William Parker (ed.), *The Structure of the Cotton Economy of the Antebellum South* (Washington: Agricultural History Society, 1970). Computation of the food surplus generated by the cotton south.

**Lawrence Herbst, "Interregional Commodity Trade from the North to the South and American Economic Development in the Antebellum Period," *Journal of Economic History* 35 (March, 1975). Summary of University of Pennsylvania Ph.D. dissertation. Shows relatively minor impact of cotton exports on Northern growth.

**Lewis Jones, "The Mechanization of Reaping and Mowing in American Agriculture, 1833–70,: A Comment," *Journal of Economic History* 37 (June, 1977). Critique of Olmstead, generally supporting David.

*Diane Lindstrom, "Demand, Market, and Eastern Economic Development: Philadelphia 1815–40," *Journal of Economic History* (March, 1975). Summary of University of Delaware Ph.D. dissertation. Shows relative independence of Philadelphia's growth.

*Diane Lindstrom, "Southern Dependence upon Interregional Grain Supplies," in William Parker (ed.), *The Structure of the Cotton Economy of the Antebellum South* (Washington: Agricultural History Society, 1970). Computation of interregional grain shipments. Shows lack of southern dependence on western food.

*Douglass North, *Growth and Welfare in the American Past,* 2nd ed., (Prentice-Hall, 1974.) Chapter 6 explains North's theory of export led growth.

**Douglass North, *The Economic Growth of the United States* (Norton, 1966). Chapter 12 and the statistical appendix explain the pattern of farm development in the midwest.

**Alan Olmstead, "The Mechanization of Reaping and Mowing in American Agriculture 1833–70," *Journal of Economic History* 35 (June, 1975). Refutation of David's "threshold" thesis, substituting more conventional explanation.

*William Parker, "Agriculture" in Lance Davis, Richard Easterlin, and William Parker, *et al., American Economic Growth* (Harper and Row, 1972). Overview of agricultural expansion and sources of productivity change.

**William Parker and Judith Klein, "Productivity Growth in Grain Production in the United States 1840–60 and 1900–10" in Dorothy Brady (ed.), *Output, Employment and Productivity in the United States after 1800,* Studies in Income and Wealth, vol. 30 (National Bureau for Economic Research, 1966). Analysis of sources of productivity change in grain agriculture.

**Richard Pomfret, "The Mechanization of Reaping in 19th Century Ontario," *Journal of Economic History* 36 (June, 1976). Parallel study to David's, with conclusions halfway between David and Olmstead.

*Martin Primack, "Land Clearing under 19th Century Techniques" *Journal of Economic History* 22 (Dec., 1962). Estimates of labor requirement in land clearing.

*Louis Schmidt, "Internal Commerce and the Development of the National Economy Before 1860," *Journal of Political Economy* 47 (Dec., 1939). Early exposition on the importance of interregional demand.

**Paul Uselding, "A Note on Interregional Trade in Manufactures in 1840," *Journal of Economic History* 36 (June, 1976). Evidence confirming minor role of interregional trade in U.S. development.

*Melville Watkins, "A Staple Theory of Economic Growth," *Canadian Journal of Economics and Political Science* 29 (May, 1963). Theoretical framework used by North to explain export-led growth.

Slavery and the
southern economy

8

Slavery—and its moral, political, and economic consequences—
dominates American history. The shameful institution of human
bondage was first the rock upon which a modern economy was built,
and then the catalyst for a great civil war. One hundred and twenty
years after its abolition the ugly residue of the institution—racism—
lingers, complicating the solution to virtually every social problem we
face.

It is no coincidence, then, that, page for page, slavery has generated
the most interesting and the most controversial research by economic
historians. Though it was not the first application of modern economics
to economic history, the 1958 article on the economics of slavery by
Alfred Conrad and John Meyer is commonly viewed as the first shot in a
continuing war between "old" and "new" economic historians. Sixteen
years and millions of words later, Robert Fogel and Stanley Engerman's
reinterpretation of the economics of slavery, *Time on the Cross,* touched
off another intellectual conflagration, one that split the ranks of the New
Economic Historians. We cannot hope to do justice to every issue raised
by the combatants, but the next five chapters discuss a good number of
them. We begin with a look at how the antebellum southern economy
worked, and the role slavery played in its development.

The Growth of the Cotton Economy

It was tobacco, not cotton, that made the South hum in the 18th century.
Tobacco had been the primary crop of the Upper South—Maryland,
Virginia, North Carolina—since early colonial times. But as intensive

cultivation of the noxious weed began to deplete the soil of critical minerals and to leave it fit mostly for feed grains and pasture, the tobacco economy gradually receded from northern and coastal areas (where it had begun) into the hills of the Appalachian Piedmont. Adding to tobacco's economic woes was a decline in export demand after 1790.

Even early on, tobacco was not the only cash crop grown in the South. Down the Atlantic coast, in South Carolina and Georgia, the sandy lowland coastal areas were dominated by rice cultivation. And in southern Louisiana, climate and soil made sugar production competitive with the cane fields of the Caribbean sugar islands.

In fact, in the 18th century, cotton could hardly be considered a serious competitor for land or labor in the South. A variety of cotton was grown along the southern Atlantic coast and in the Sea Islands offshore Georgia; but though this Sea Island cotton was much in demand after 1785, the plant did not adapt well to soil and climate inland. And the alternative, short-staple, green seed variety that did grow well away from the coast had one serious drawback: The seeds could not be removed from the picked cotton with the simple roller gin employed in the Sea Islands. With English cotton mills begging for raw cotton, the prospective returns to new gin technology were enormous. Eli Whitney was the first to respond successfully to this incentive, producing a practical gin for short staple, upland cotton in 1793.

Whitney's gin removed the highest technical barrier to cotton expansion. But it was the unique combination of southern climate, soil and transportation that made it possible to grow cotton virtually anywhere in the United States south of Virginia and Kentucky. Not surprisingly, cotton thrived in the deep alluvial topsoil of the Mississippi River valley and its tributaries. But upland cotton also did very nicely in a variety of other southern soil-climate conditions: The hillsides of the Appalachian Piedmont, the relatively infertile central plain stretching from Southern Carolina around to Mississippi, the distinctive "black prairie" soil of Alabama, Mississippi, and Tennessee, and the hills of east Texas, northern Louisiana, and Arkansas. The pattern of cultivation, moreover, was less markedly tied to transport innovation than it was in the Midwest. Navigable rivers served the region well. Equally important, cotton by weight and bulk was a far more valuable crop than midwestern grain. This made it practicable to grow cotton considerable distances from the rivers.

Cotton took hold in the Piedmont and the western river valleys in the first fifteen years of the century. There followed in the 1820's and 1830's an almost explosive rush into Alabama, Tennessee, and Mississippi. And then, after the decade-long pause following the Panic of 1837, rapid growth of cotton cultivation in Texas and Arkansas. Meanwhile, some of the land in Georgia, the Carolinas, and Virginia which

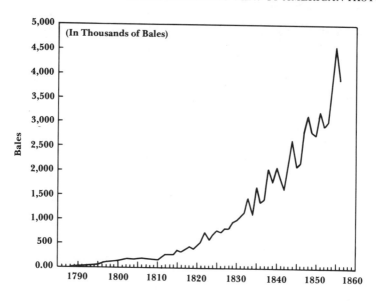

COTTON PRODUCTION IN THE AMERICAN SOUTH
1971–1861
(thousands of bales)

Source: Robert Fogel and Stanley Engerman, *Time on the Cross* (Little, Brown, 1974), p. 90.

was opened to cotton in the first two decades of the century had been returned to subsistence food farming, or even abandoned, by the 1850's. The specter of these abandoned, eroded hillsides shocked agricultural reformers of the era, who took it as evidence of poor land management and the destructive impact of cotton culture.

Today, however, economists view that historical phenomena quite differently. Unlike tobacco, cotton was not pushed west by soil depletion. It was *pulled* west by the attraction of high yields not attainable on the central plain or on the Piedmont. Sometimes farmers just walked away from still adequate farmland because they could make a far better profit exploiting western soils. More typically, farmers failed to make the necessary costly effort to maintain soil fertility on marginal land because they knew better opportunities awaited them elsewhere.

Actually, cotton is one of the least depleting crops. When the discarded stalks (and in the antebellum period, the seeds, too) are ploughed under, virtually no change in the chemical composition of the soil is evident. Cultivation of cotton, or most any other crop, does, however, make the soil vulnerable to wind and water erosion by removing the natural vegetation cover. The thinner the topsoil and the steeper the slope of the land, the faster the yields deteriorate. But it is probable that even the minimal precautions against soil erosion advocated by contemporary reformers were too expensive to be economically justifiable.

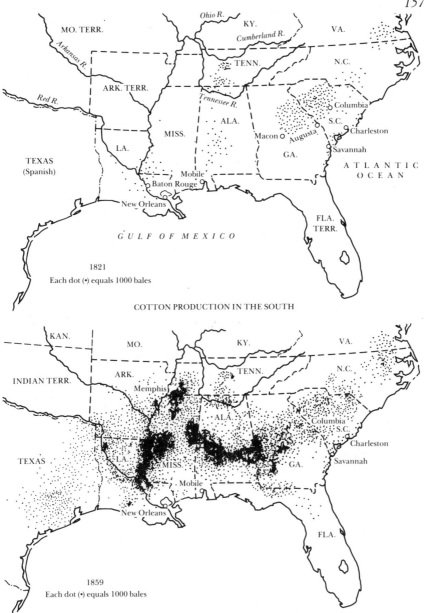

SOUTHERN COTTON PRODUCTION 1821–59

In the 1820's the cotton economy centered in the Georgia-Carolina Piedmont, with smaller concentrations in Tennessee, Alabama, and the lower Mississippi. By the Civil War, the cotton economy had moved far to the West, exploiting the new lands of the rich, alluvial valleys and eastern Texas.

Source: Gavin Wright, *The Political Economy of the Cotton South* (Norton, 1978), p. 16.
Source: Adapted from United States Department of Agriculture, *Atlas of Agriculture*, Part V, Advance Sheets (December 15, 1915).

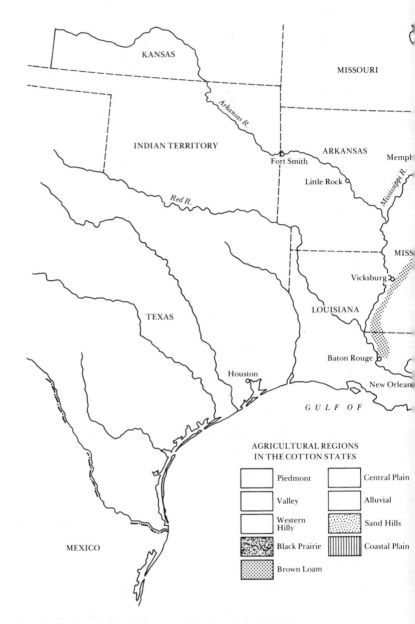

AGRICULTURAL REGIONS IN COTTON STATES

Source: Gavin Wright, *The Political Economy of the Cotton South* (Norton, 1978), p. 20.
Source: Adapted from U.S. Bureau of Census, U.S. Census of Population: 1880, Volume V.

Ohio R.

KENTUCKY

VIRGINIA

Cumberland R.

TENNESSEE

NORTH CAROLINA

Raleigh

Chattanooga

Columbia

SOUTH CAROLINA

Atlanta

Augusta

Charleston

ALABAMA

GEORGIA

Montgomery

Savannah

ATLANTIC OCEAN

FLORIDA

XICO

As we shall see in sections following, the existence of slavery changed the character of the cotton economy in ways both subtle and gross. But in no way did slavery drive out family farmers. The research of Frank Owsley and his students shows that small family farms coexisted with medium and large plantations run with large slave forces in all parts of the Cotton South. According to Gavin Wright's estimates, 50 percent of all farms in the cotton belt had no slaves at all in 1860. Even in the fertile western alluvial valleys, the region with the highest concentration of big commercial plantations, 36 percent of all farms were slaveless.

With or without slaves, economics and botany determined the rhythm of work life on cotton farms. As might be expected, plantations devoted a higher percentage of available land and labor to the production of the market crop—cotton. But less intuitively, even the largest, most commercially oriented plantations failed to specialize, aiming instead for self-sufficiency in food by producing substantial quantities of corn, beans, pork, and sweet potatoes. Roger Ransom and Richard Sutch's analysis shows that roughly forty percent of the value created by cotton plantations with more than fifty slaves was food, while on plantations of sixteen to fifty slaves, the comparable figure was fifty percent.

If cotton was more profitable to grow than food, why grow both? The answer, Robert Gallman suggests, lies in the uneven seasonal demands cotton cultivation placed on labor. Assuming plenty of land was available, a farm that grew cotton alone would be constrained in its total output by the amount of labor available in the fall for harvesting the crop. In other seasons, as little as one-eighth the work force could attend to the crop. So, rather than let the labor remain idle, farmers looked for ways to utilize it without reducing the farms' capacity to grow cotton. Corn was the natural candidate. Though not particularly suited to southern soils or climate—yields per acre were much higher in the Midwest—it was extremely well suited to the seasonal cotton cycle. Corn placed little demand on workers during the cotton-picking season but kept them busy at times when the cotton plants needed little attention.

Note that corn was not "free" to cotton farmers in the sense that no additional resources need be expended to generate a corn crop. Land was needed to raise the corn—thus requiring an initial investment in clearing—and some labor was needed year 'round also. This meant that a plantation growing corn would, in fact, sacrifice some potential cotton output. But while not free, home-grown corn was made uniquely cheap by the special economics of cotton—cheaper, surely, than corn bought at market for cash.

Men and women do not live by corn alone—though southerners could come close when pressed. Corn was converted into meat by using it to fatten pigs. Various types of peas and beans, moreover, could be planted between the corn rows without reducing corn yields, and then harvested as food or left for the farm animals to graze. Some foodstuffs still had to be bought from the outside. But as Gallman's work shows (see chapter 7), virtually all working cotton farms were nearly self-sufficient in food.

The Viability of Slavery

In the 18th century, slavery in North American was largely confined to tobacco, sugar, and rice plantations of the South. In the 19th century, the vast majority of slaves were employed in the plantation cultivation of cotton. This has led historians to stress the special link between southern plantation agriculture and slavery. Without the dramatic appearance of cotton, they argue, slavery might have become unviable and withered away on its own. Moreover, the case had been made that the continued expansion of the cotton economy in the 19th century was critical to the viability of slavery. That once put into motion, the southern slave economy had to be fed from an ongoing menu of fresh lands—a diet that was economically necessary in the short run to keep up demand for slaves but an economic disaster in the long run. Hence the seeds of self-destruction were deeply rooted in what appeared to contemporary observers to be a thriving economic system based on forced labor. This argument cannot be dismissed out of hand. But stated in its boldest, most uncompromising form—that is, that slavery was an economic contradiction on the verge of destroying itself—the assertion has little merit.

Early concentration of slaves in southern staple crop production cannot be explained by the peculiar social outlook of southern landowners, nor by the peculiar nature of tobacco, rice, and sugar cultivation. There is no convincing evidence that the majority of northerners had a special distaste for the enslavement of blacks that could not have been overcome by profit incentives. Indeed, when the prospects for the profitable use of slaves in grain production seemed promising, the free citizen farmers of Illinois fought to enter the union as a slave state. As to the second part of the argument—that slavery and plantation agriculture were tied by the unique labor requirements of southern staple production—evidence is also lacking. Tobacco, rice, and sugar did all take vast amounts of backbreaking labor to produce, but so, too, did grains cultivated in the North.

Economists generally reckon that slaves ended up on southern plantations rather than northern farms because (1) plantation owners gradually lost access to alternative source of labor and (2) among American crops, only southern staples were sufficiently lucrative to justify bidding away scarce slave labor from employment in the Caribbean sugar islands. Planters turned to black slaves in the late 18th century because they could no longer meet their needs with white labor. Tobacco and rice had originally been cultivated by indentured laborers from Europe. In return for passage, impoverished workers would agree to a few years of contractual obligation to farm owners. However, as ocean transportation costs fell and prospects for immigrants as free workers rose, the supply of those willing to submit to indenture dried up. Free labor could—and did—grow tobacco on family farms. But for reasons discussed later, it was extremely difficult to induce free workers to labor as hired hands. That left black slaves as the most promising labor source for any farmer who wanted to expand operations beyond the farm size serviceable by family members only.

Many farmers in both the North and South dreamed of expanding beyond the confines of family farm scale. But in the 18th century, only southern export staple producers could afford to buy the slaves needed to accomplish the job. Before the slave trade was outlawed in 1808, the international market for slaves was competitive. Thus the market price of a slave imported from Africa (or born in America) was determined by the most productive use of unskilled labor. It is highly likely that only plantation owners could make sufficiently intensive use of slaves to match high Caribbean slave productivity during this period.

By this logic, slavery was never in danger of withering away in the late 18th century. High productivity outside the United States, not low productivity in America, kept slavery confined to southern plantations; the rise of cotton was simply a new twist. Opportunities in tobacco, rice and sugar, and later, in cotton, did give southerners the incentive to import slaves who otherwise might have been sold to Caribbean planters. But then too, it is also possible that without cotton as competition, American slaves would have ended up on wheat plantations in Illinois.

Most economic historians now accept the notion that slavery constituted no actual or potential economic burden on slave owners. But this consensus has not been won easily, nor has the controversy over slave profitability and viability been entirely laid to rest. The notion that the slave economy was paving its own road to ruin is often—though incorrectly—credited to the Yale historian, U. B. Phillips. Phillips believed that African Negroes were inferior in intelligence to whites; thus they were fit only for work on southern plantations, where tasks were extremely simple (though arduous) and supervision was close. As long as land was plentiful and demand conditions made for high profits, slaves could earn their keep. But after the close of the slave trade, the price of slaves was bid up to levels at which, Phillips believed, owners could not justify the investment as a sound business practice. Phillips attributed the price increase to (1) a speculative boom based on the unavailability of imported slaves and (2) the desire of individual plantation owners for more slaves as a form of conspicuous consumption.

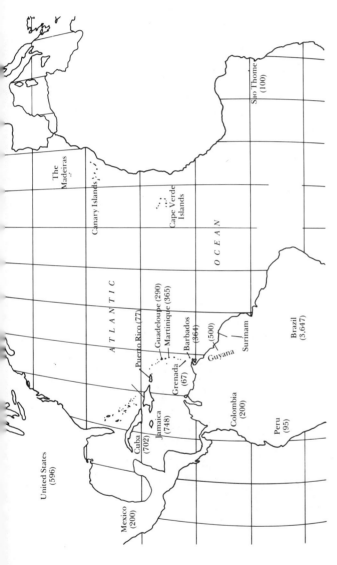

SLAVE IMPORTS TO THE NEW WORLD 1451–1870
(thousands of slaves)

Note the relatively small number of slaves imported into the United States, by comparison with the Caribbean and Latin America. In many parts of the slave-using world, imports were the primary source of slaves, as slaves were not encouraged to reproduce and their offspring were unlikely to survive to adulthood.

Source: Robert Fogel and Stanley Engerman, *Time on the Cross* (Little, Brown, 1974), p. 18.

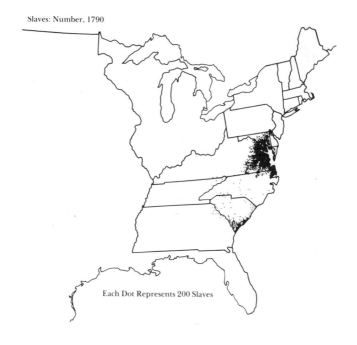

Slaves: Number, 1790

Each Dot Represents 200 Slaves

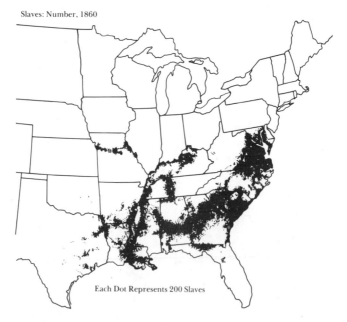

Slaves: Number, 1860

Each Dot Represents 200 Slaves

DISTRIBUTION OF SLAVE POPULATION, 1790 AND 1860

Slaves followed the westward movement of the cotton economy.

Source: Robert Fogel and Stanley Engerman, *Time on the Cross* (Little, Brown, 1974), p. 45.

Phillips never actually argued that slavery would collapse of its own weight, merely that antebellum slave buyers were paying too high a price to be able to make a profit. The distinction is vital. Today stock market investors might bid up the price of, say, IBM stock to a level at which they had no rational hope of making a return on their financial investment comparable to returns available elsewhere. But this doesn't mean that IBM itself would cease to make a profit selling computers, or that the company would eventually close up shop. Rather, at some point, the speculative bubble would burst, the price of the stock would fall, and investors who had made imprudent purchases would take a loss. By analogy, Phillips only asserted that market overvaluation of slaves would at some point make slave owners sorry they had paid so much. Those who were sorry would not, however, have an incentive to abandon their property.

Unfortunately the concept of private profitability and economic viability were often confused by historians writing in the "Phillips tradition". And the historical battle over viability was often fought on the false ground of profitability. Among the works of these traditional historians, Charles Sydnor's is probably the most cited. Sydnor examined the account books of large Mississippi plantations in the 1850's and reconstructed a typical profit and loss statement. His figures show average net earnings after expenses of just $880 on an investment of $36,000 ($30,000 for 50 slaves, plus $6,000 for 600 acres of cleared land). That leaves a yield of just 2.4 percent (880/36,000) on capital, well below the return obtainable by investing in secure private bonds. Thus, Sydnor concluded, slave labor was not a profitable investment.

A careful look at Sydnor's figures (table 8.1), however, seems to show just the opposite of what Sydnor thought he had demonstrated. As Kenneth Stampp first noted, at least two of the expense items—the implicit interest cost of the slaves and of the land investment—really belong as part of the return to the total investment. Shuffling the numbers accordingly, the profit becomes $3,040 ($1,800, plus $360, plus $880), for a return on investment of 8.4 percent (3,040/36,000). That return compares favorably with the 5 to 6 percent yield in comparably risky enterprises. In fact, the true return to slave investments might have been considerably higher. Sydnor included a depreciation cost for slaves but failed to include the symmetric profit from slave reproduction. Sydnor, moreover, probably overcounted true plantation expenditures by adding in some of the owner's expenditures for food and clothing.

A more rigorous attempt to arrive at a rate of return on an investment in slaves was made years later by Conrad and Meyer. As two microeconomists foraying into economic history, they approached the issue as an analytically simple problem in business economics. For computation purposes, slaves could be treated like any other productive asset that generated income, required maintenance, and eventually wore out.

TABLE 8.1

SYDNOR'S MISSISSIPPI PLANTATION ACCOUNT

Income:

63,200 lbs. of cotton @ 10¢ per pound		$6,320

Less Expenses:

Interest cost on $30,000 slave investment @ 6%	$1,800	
Depreciation (death, injury) of slave investment @ 6%	1,800	
Interest cost on $6,000 land investment @ 6%	360	
Depreciation on land investment @ 3%	180	
Overseer's wages	300	
Plantation supplies	1,000	
		−$5,440
profit		$ 880

Source: Charles Sydnor, *Slavery in Mississippi* (Appleton-Century, 1933), cited in Robert Fogel and Stanley Engerman (ed.), *The Reinterpretation of American Economic History* (Harper and Row, 1971), p. 321.

Gross slave income consisted of the market value of the cotton they produced plus, in the case of women, the market value at birth of their offspring. Maintenance costs consisted of the expenditures to keep slaves alive and healthy—food, clothing, shelter, medical care—plus supervision. The durability of slave assets depended on the length of their working lives.

Conrad and Meyer used traditional sources to make estimates of the cost of purchasing a slave, the average amount of cotton produced per field hand, the price of cotton, out-of-pocket maintenance, and life expectancy. In the case of female slaves, they also estimated the expected number of successful pregnancies and the net cost of raising children to productive age. Then they separately computed the expected yield on hypothetical investments in male and female slaves on lands of differing productivity. Returns for males varied from 2.2–5.4 percent (depending on cotton prices and yields) on poor quality eastern seaboard land, to returns of 10–13 percent on fertile western land. The average return to investors, Conrad and Meyer reckoned, was about 6 percent. For females working on average quality land, the return varied from 7.1 percent for those having five children to 8.1 percent for those bearing ten.

What do these figures signify? They don't tell much about what a slave owner actually earned in the late antebellum years. Consider, for example, the plantation owner who bought young adult slaves in 1850 in anticipation of getting thirty years of labor from them. Just eleven years after the purchase date, the gross income from slave labor would have fallen drastically—during the Civil War, the blockade of southern ports made it almost impossible to sell cotton abroad. And fifteen years after the purchase date, the slave owner would have seen his or her capital confiscated—that is, liberated. But—assuming Conrad and Meyer plugged in the right numbers into the formulas—their estimated rates of return can tell us what a plantation owner might have expected to earn in a stable economic environment. With an average expected return on male slaves of six percent and on female slaves of between seven and eight percent, slave owners could quite reasonably justify their investment in slaves at current market prices.

The initial opposition to Conrad and Meyer came from those who were appalled by the cold, analytic treatment of human beings as just another kind of capital good. Comparing slaves to machines was immoral; hence no significant historical issue could be resolved by the exercise. Twenty years later, this attack appears a little silly. Measuring the profitability of slavery is no more immoral than analyzing Hitler's military success at the battle of Arnhem, or studying a devastating smallpox epidemic. More significant criticism came from economists and historians, who either doubted the reliability of Conrad and Meyer's data and assumptions or challenged the specific historical relevance of profitability computations.

The numbers skeptics have scored a few direct hits. Using Census data, Edward Saraydar argued that the average amount of cotton produced per slave was 15 percent less than Conrad and Meyer estimated, while the market price of the average slave was 15 percent more. These adjustments reduce the average rate of return on male slaves from 6 percent to 1.5 percent. Noel Butlin concentrated an attack on the demographic assumptions employed by Conrad and Meyer. Conrad and Meyer's thirty-year average prime working life may be reasonable, Butlin notes, but that does not imply that the lost product of slaves who died prematurely is exactly offset by the unexpected output from slaves with longer than average working lives. The bale of cotton lost when a slave dies today at age thirty is worth more than the bale gained from a slave's labor thirty years from today: The income derived from the latter bale must be discounted to reflect the opportunity cost of the initial financial investment.

Butlin also claims that Conrad and Meyer's estimates of life expectancy and fertility were exceedingly optimistic. Implicit in Conrad and Meyers calculation is a 4 percent annual growth rate of the slave population—twice the rate actually recorded in the Census. To more closely approximate the American slave experience, Butlin uses life tables from Jamaica and reproduction data from the Hutterites. The Hutterites, an economically prosperous religious sect living communally in the American grain belt, believe in maximizing their collective birth rate. Their reproduction record surely represents an upper bound on possible slave birth rates under ideal conditions since the Hutterites have access to the best medical services. Reworking Conrad and Meyer's figures with the alternative demographic data pushes the average rate of return on slaves below 5 percent.

Were Conrad and Meyer wrong? No, not according to other research to date. Other studies—those in particular by Battalio and Kagel and by Robert Evans—conclude that Conrad and Meyer underestimated the average rate of return on slave investments. The wide variations in results in these studies suggest that the issue can't be resolved easily because rate of return estimates are so sensitive to unreliable data and assumptions.

Luckily, though, we need not be agnostic about the more important issue—the viability of slavery. Fairly early in the profitability debate, three economists, Yasukichi Yasuba, Richard Sutch, and Robert Evans, independently identified the viability issue and, for practical purposes, settled it. Yasuba argued that the contemporary rate of return on market investments in slaves isn't really relevant to the long-term viability of the system. Slavery will continue as long as owners have an incentive (1) to keep the slaves they already own and (2) to allow the slave population to reproduce.

As to the first criterion, it is almost self-evident that as long as the productivity of labor is greater than subsistence, it will pay to keep slaves of working age. Given the fact that labor productivity in America in the 19th century was far above the true subsistence level, it is hard to believe that slave owners, who had almost absolute power over their chattels, would have been unable to capture some portion of the difference. There is always the theoretical possibility, of course, that passive slave resistance (feigned incompetence, abuse of machinery and work animals, malingering) or active slave resistance (slave rebellion) might one day have pushed the surplus to zero. But every profitability study, from Sydnor to Butlin, provides indirect evidence that antebellum slave owners had no difficulty whatever in getting more out of an adult slave than they put in.

The second criterion is not quite so easy to meet. If owners are to have an incentive to allow their slaves to reproduce, the market value of a working slave must exceed the cumulative investment in reproduction and child-rearing costs—that is, the mother's lost work during pregnancy and nursing, plus subsistence during childhood. Yasuba very conservatively calculated the difference between market value at maturity

TABLE 8.2

CAPITALIZED RENT IN AN 18-YEAR OLD MALE SLAVE

Years	Average Price	Gross Rearing Costs	Income From Child Labor	Capitalized* Rent	Capitalized Rent as % of Price
1821–25	736	657	349	428	58
1826–30	792	614	286	464	59
1831–35	974	671	431	734	75
1836–40	1,206	848	497	855	71
1841–45	744	591	379	532	72
1846–50	936	737	546	745	80
1851–55	1,252	807	600	1,045	83
1856–60	1,596	938	922	1,580	99

Interpretation: As long as the capitalized rent—the portion of a slave's value above the investment needed to raise a slave to working age—is positive, it pays to raise more slaves. Note that the capitalized rent per slave was large, and generally rising across the decades.

*Average slave price, less rearing costs, plus child labor income.

Source: Yasukichi Yasuba, "The Profitability and Viability of Plantation Slavery in the United States" reprinted in Robert Fogel and Stanley Engerman (ed.), *The Reinterpretation of American Economic History* (Harper and Row, 1971), p. 367.

and rearing costs, and discovered that at no time between 1820 and 1860 did this "capitalized economic rent" in a young adult slave fall below 50 percent of a slave's market value (see table 8.2). Even Butlin's work, which is the single most pessimistic on viability, can be used to confirm Yasuba's conclusion.

Everything we know, then, about the returns to antebellum slavery points toward the conclusion that slavery was viable in Yasuba's sense of the term. We do not know how the system would have stood up under extreme stress—say, during a long depression in cotton prices or perhaps to a liberation movement funded and armed from outside. But the numbers give us every reason to believe that slavery would have been around for a long while.

One footnote before leaving the subject: It is at least conceivable that, in the long term, slavery was unviable in the sense that a fundamental change in the formal master-slave relationship might have left both parties better off. Under slavery, owners profited by confiscating the difference between what a slave produced and what a slave consumed; Yasuba and others leave little doubt that this surplus was substantial. But it is is also possible that the surplus could have been even larger if slaves had had incentives to work as hard and productively as they were capable. Slaves, of course, did have incentives—the threat of punishment and, not unusually, the promise of special treatment for good service. As Kenneth Stampp and Eugene Genovese point out, though, these incentives did not always work; passive resistance, which cut labor productivity, was probably not uncommon.

Hence, at least in theory, there was the possibility of a rearrangement of the slave-master "contract," leaving workers with more income and privilege and plantation owners with a greater return. For example, an arrangement where slaves bought their freedom over a period of many years by working as independent contractors would have meant that the harder the slave worked the faster the slave would have gained freedom. If the traditional forced labor relationship was very wasteful— that is, if slaves worked substantially less productively than they might otherwise have—the arrangement might have dominated traditional slavery and eventually led to voluntary emancipation.

How practical might such an arrangement have been? It is difficult to say. Fogel and Engerman note that in a small number of recorded cases slaves were able to buy their freedom and that the price they paid was typically above the market value. It is difficult to infer from this scrap of evidence that self-purchase would have been mutually attractive for the average field hand and master, however. Most cases of self-purchase involved skilled artisans working in cities rather than agricultural laborers. And even if individual masters and slaves had seen opportunities in alternative arrangements, society as a whole might not have accepted the change. It is hard to imagine, for example, that the presence of a large number of free blacks working alongside blacks still in bondage would have been tenable.

We are still free to speculate, of course, and one other scenario does seem plausible. Suppose slaveowners decided—under pressure from abolitionists—that there was no way to guarantee absolutely their property rights in the future. Some combination of political threat from without and increasing resistance from slaves within might have led owners to accept—even welcome—a general program of compensated abolition. Under such circumstances, slavery might have remained viable in Yasuba's sense, but the attractiveness of alternative arrangements might have been sufficient incentive to abolish the institution.

The Efficiency of the Slave Economy

One need not doubt the viability of slavery as a labor system to question the impact of slavery on the efficiency of southern agriculture and the long-term growth prospects of the region. Indeed, it is commonplace to attribute the relative economic backwardness of the South today to the heritage of the Peculiar Institution. Some of these hypothesized links are perfectly plausible, but difficult to test or quantify. For example, plantation agriculture might have been uneconomical without slavery such that southern enterpreneurs might have better developed the commercial and industrial sectors of the South. But there are other possible relationships more amenable to empirical analysis. And, with occasional exceptions, it is these we shall take a look at.

SLAVERY AND ECONOMIES OF SCALE

Did the use of slave (as opposed to free wage) labor affect the productivity of the cotton economy? Common sense would argue that it did, that the coercive nature of slavery would tend to reduce the output available from a given set of inputs. Slaves were reluctant workers since they were not working for themselves; it is hard to imagine that owners could fully overcome that reluctance with force or persuasion. There is one possible way, however, in which slavery might have actually increased productivity, and it is on this possibility that a number of economists have focused their attention.

Much of the agricultural labor force of the antebellum South consisted of free whites. But as noted before, few of these free whites worked as hired hands on other peoples' farms, and none worked in the labor gangs common to large plantations. Historians generally explain this pattern by the strong taste of 19th-century Americans for owning land. Those who could afford to buy and improve land became farmers; those who could not remained in urban areas. An elaboration of this view has been offered by Gavin Wright. Wright argues that the family farm provided a degree of income security otherwise difficult to obtain in the 19th century. Growing one's own food gave protection against market price fluctuations and against the threat of unemployment. In an era in which few savings vehicles were safe, moreover, the investment in land and improvements was a relatively secure means of amassing a nest egg. And the family structure built on the farm enterprise protected the aged and disabled against hardship.

As a consequence, southerners who ran big farms either had to have a lot of children or buy slaves. Some casual farm laborers might be found on occasion, but their presence was hard to guarantee during the critical picking season, and their performance at any time was likely to be lackluster. Slaves, on the other hand, offered a certain means of extending operations to any desired scale—some plantations were operated with hundreds of slaves. Slavery thus gave the South a potential efficiency advantage over free areas by giving entrepreneurs the opportunity to exploit potential economies of scale.

Fogel and Engerman assert that this advantage was critical. It al-

lowed a division of tasks and a degree of teamwork that more than overcame any inherent inefficiency in using involuntary labor. As evidence,
the two economists offer their calculation of total factor productivity by
farm size in the South in 1860 (see table 8.3). They found that, on
average, farms with slaves were 29 percent more productive than farms
without slaves. There were clear efficiency gains as scale increased, at
least to the 16–50-slave range. Fogel and Engerman argue, moreover,
that the very big plantations were probably the most efficient of all; and
that the observed decline in productivity on large plantations in the
newer lands of the South was likely due to an incomplete accounting of
output, rather than to inefficiency.

Gavin Wright challenges these findings. The key to interpreting
these total factor productivity comparison, Wright notes, lies in systematic differences in the mix of crops grown on large and small farms.
Family farms devoted a much higher proportion of their land and labor
to food production than plantations, a decision Wright attributes to family farmers' unwillingness to bear the risk of unanticipated changes in
cotton prices or yields. By taking a "safety-first" approach—growing
enough food to keep the family alive—they avoided the chance of losing
their farms and becoming landless laborers. In years like 1860 when cotton prices and yields were very high, this meant a loss of income and, of
course, a loss in measured labor productivity and total factor productivity.

TABLE 8.3

TOTAL FACTOR PRODUCTIVITY INDICES*
FOR COTTON FARMS 1860

Slaves per Farm	Old South States	New South States	All Cotton States
0	100	100	100
1–15	105.0	112.9	107.7
16–50	126.9	156.3	144.7
51+	137.3	137.3	133.5
All Slave Farms	120.8	135.8	128.5

Interpretation: On large cotton farms (those with more than fifteen
slaves) the value of output generated per unit of input was substantially
larger than on smaller farms.

Source: Robert Fogel and Stanley Engerman, *Time on the Cross II: Evidence and Methods*
(Little, Brown, 1974), p. 140.

*See the appendix to chapter 4 for a discussion of total factor productivity.

If gang labor offered opportunities for scale economies, these economies should be observable when the impact of random year-to-year price or yield variations are eliminated. Wright tried to do exactly that by limiting his statistical analysis to groups of farms that grew cotton and corn in constant proportions. He found that there was no measured increase in output per worker (or per acre) as farm size increases.

Can we come to a verdict about scale economies in antebellum cotton? The jury is still out. The fact that small farms coexisted with large farms—and that no clear trend over time toward bigness or smallness is discernible—is consistent with either view. Fogel and Engerman argue that family farmers accepted lower returns to their labor so that they could avoid unpleasant gang labor. Wright argues that they accepted lower expected returns so that they could avoid the risk of enormous fluctuations in income. The mix of farm sizes, says Wright, was largely determined by the distribution of wealth in the society. Rich people ran big farms; the less rich could only run small ones.

Note, however, that Fogel and Engerman establish a case here for the efficiency of farming with slaves, if not exactly a case for the efficiency of gang labor. Wright's risk-averse family farmers might well choose to grow more cotton and less corn if they could cut the inherent risks. In modern economies, efficient market mechanisms make this possible: Farmers can easily borrow money to tide them over bad periods, or they can use forward sales contracts to nail down the price they will receive for crops months from market. Small antebellum farmers had no such alternatives, so they sensibly avoided risk at the sacrifice of expected profit. By contrast, slave-using farmers did not have to worry about not eating or losing their property if they risked all in cotton and lost; their wealth protected them. This doesn't mean that big farms were inherently more efficient than little farms, but it does mean that wealthy entrepreneurs, by virtue of their willingness to take risks and their access to labor beyond the family unit, were able to generate more output value from a given quantity of land and labor.

SLAVERY AND TOTAL FACTOR PRODUCTIVITY

Fogel and Engerman compared indices of total factor productivity to distinguish the relative efficiency of large and small farms within the Cotton South. As we noted, while the proper interpretation of the productivity difference is not clear, the application of the technique is not really in dispute. The same cannot be said for Fogel and Engerman's analysis of the relative efficiency of northern agriculture and southern agriculture.

Prior to the publication of Fogel and Engerman's *Time on the Cross* in 1974 the dominant middle ground on the issue of the efficiency of the cotton-slave economy went roughly like this: Slavery was surely efficient enough to make the labor system viable. Involuntary labor, combined with plentiful, fertile land and strong world demand for cotton, allowed free white southerners to enjoy a high standard of living—about the same standard as that of easterners, and higher than that of midwesterners. But there is reason to believe that slavery itself was a hindrance to allocative efficiency, keeping total income below the level that the south might have enjoyed in its absence.

Fogel and Engerman did not attempt to test this counterfactual hypothesis directly. They did, however, challenge the conventional view by comparing total factor productivity[1] in agriculture in the North and South in 1860. Using Census data, they estimated that the South used 93 percent as much labor as the North, 51 percent as much land, and 53 percent as much capital, in order to generate output worth 3 percent more. Weighting the inputs by factor shares of output to obtain a geometric index of factor productivity, Fogel and Engerman estimated that southern agriculture was 41 percent more efficient than northern. Restricting the comparison to the cotton economy and northern agriculture changes the results very little: Total factor productivity on 5,000 Cotton South farms sampled by William Parker and Robert Gallman was 35 percent higher than on northern farms.

Basically Fogel and Engerman attribute these findings to the economies possible only on farms bigger than family size. Their critics offer other explanations. First and foremost, these critics do not accept the idea that Fogel and Engerman really measured efficiency in the usual sense of the term. Total factor productivity indices have generally been used to compare the efficiency of a single economy at two points in time or to compare the efficiency of two economies with similar product mix alternatives. The comparison of northern and southern agriculture is conceptually quite different, since the North had no means of producing cotton, the single largest source of southern agricultural income. Climate gave the South an advantage, which shows up in the greater revenue producing capability of southern farms.

To put the issue another way, suppose southern farms—complete with soil, labor, and capital—had been moved a thousand miles north. In spite of the fact that the farms were physically unchanged, their "efficiency" would plummet because climate would bar the use of any portion of their land and labor to grow cotton. There is no way, then, that comparisons of total factor productivity can really yield the desired insight into the relative efficiency of the southern, slave-based labor system.

"Big think" objections aside, there are plenty of "little think" ones that raise important questions about how to interpret Fogel and Enger-

---

[1] See appendix of chapter 4 for an explanation of this term.

man's exercise. The first is possible measurement biases in the numerator of the productivity index, output. Total factor productivity is a ratio of the value of crops produced, to a weighted average of inputs used to grow them. There is reason to believe that in the year Fogel and Engerman's estimated northern and southern productivity, crop values were unusually high in the South and unusually low in the North—biasing upward, of course, the relative productivity of the South. Cotton made up much of the southern crop by value. And 1860 is remembered for its bumper crop, which, thanks to strong world demand, was salable at very good prices.

There are no accurate statistics on crop output or price that would provide comparable information about harvest results for the North. But the indirect evidence points to a poor crop year in 1860. Wright notes that exports of wheat, flour, and corn were all below previous years' averages and well below the upward trend expected of a growing export economy. The output loss was apparently not made up in higher prices, which were no better than average by historical standards. Another confirming indicator is public land sales. Land demand generally followed profit expectations, and, in 1859, sales were extremely slow in the midwestern grain belt. In the South, by contrast, land sales were reaching an historical peak.

According to Paul David and Peter Temin, biases in input measurement also distort the relative efficiency computation. Fogel and Engerman counted units of labor, worker-years, in the North and South identically. But the amount of labor inputs per worker may have been quite different in the two sections. Climate allowed southerners to work in the fields about 60 additional days each year. The number of hours slaves worked per day, moreover, may have been much greater than that of their free northern counterparts. In fact, Roger Ransom and Richard Sutch estimate that given the chance to allocate their own time after the war, ex-slaves cut their average work day by 16 to 22 percent.

Actually the antebellum free-slave differential may have been even greater than the numbers suggest, since free whites before the war were much richer than free blacks after the war and could thus more easily afford the luxury of leisure. David and Temin estimate that, taken together, these factors led Fogel and Engerman to underestimate southern labor inputs by 28–34 percent, and thereby to overestimate relative southern productivity by 15–18 percent.

Potential biases built into Fogel and Engerman's measure of land inputs are much more difficult to analyze. Land measurement problems stem from the fact that there is no way of directly estimating land quantity. Figures on acreage are available, but they mask the reality of vast differences in land quality. Fogel and Engerman attempt to finesse this problem by substituting land *value* for land *quantity*, assuming that price

differences accurately reflect quality differences. But, say David and
Temin, this adjustment procedure invites error. Land values reflect not
only quality differences in land, but location advantages as well.

To illustrate the argument, they provide a not-so-hypothetical example. Consider the case in which rail and canal transport greatly increased the amount of land in the North that could be farmed at a profit.
This transportation base increased the value of nonmarginal land as
well, and thus, by the method used by Fogel and Engerman, raised the
"quantity" of land inputs used to create crops and spuriously reduced estimated total factor productivity. The magnitude of the error introduced by using land value as an input measure isn't known, but it
could be large. If Fogel and Engerman had simply used acreage—not a
recommended procedure either, since land quality varies—relative
southern efficiency would have been cut by 25 percent, or more than
two-thirds of the identified efficiency advantage.

Taken as a whole, it is hard to make much one way or the other from
these total factor productivity comparisons. At best, we end up with a
measure, in one unusual year, of the relative ability of northern and
southern farms to turn productive resources into cash output. This is an
efficiency measure of sorts, but not the usual one. And as Gavin Wright
argues, it tells more about how lucky southern land and slave owners
were to have exclusive access to a commodity (cotton) much in demand
than it does about how effective southerners were in wringing physical
output from productive resources. At worst, the techniques for estimating land and labor inputs generate biases of such great magnitude that
nothing whatever can be said about relative efficiency, no matter how
the concept is defined.

SLAVERY AND INDUSTRIALIZATION

Slavery is generally conceded to have been a factor retarding industrialization and the growth of urban areas in the antebellum South. It
does not necessarily follow, however, that slavery blocked efficient division of resources between agriculture and industry. Quite the contrary:
Slavery may simply have made it possible for the South to exploit more
fully its inherent economic advantage in cotton agriculture. Indeed, efficiency questions hinge on just such distinctions.

There is no doubt that industrialization and urbanization preceded
relatively slowly in the South. Tables 8.4 and 8.5 clearly reveal the
large—and growing—differences between North and South. In 1860,
the South produced less than one-third the value of manufactures per
capita as the nation taken as a whole. Less than one southerner in ten
lived in a city, compared to one New Englander in three. The most reasonable explanation for the failure to industrialize and urbanize is the
enormous pull of cotton agriculture created by the environment, foreign

TABLE 8.4

MANUFACTURING INVESTMENT AND OUTPUT
($/capita)

Region	Manufacturing Capital 1850	1860	Manufacturing Value 1850	1860
New England	57.96	82.13	100.71	149.47
Middle States	33.50	52.21	71.24	96.28
South	7.60	10.54	10.88	17.09
Cotton South	5.11	7.20	6.83	10.47
United States	22.73	32.12	43.69	59.98

Source: 8th and 9th Census of Manufactures, cited in Gavin Wright, *The Political Economy of the Cotton South* (Norton, 1978), p. 110.

TABLE 8.5

PERCENTAGE OF POPULATION LIVING IN URBAN AREAS

Region	1820	1830	1840	1850	1860
New England	10.5	14.0	19.4	28.8	36.6
Mid-Atlantic	11.3	14.2	18.1	25.5	35.4
East North Central	1.2	2.5	3.9	9.0	14.1
West North Central	—	3.5	3.9	10.3	13.4
South	5.5	6.2	7.7	9.8	11.5
East South Central	0.8	1.5	2.1	4.2	5.9

Source: Douglass North, *The Economic Growth of the United States 1790–1860* (Norton, 1966), p. 258.

demand—and, of course, slavery. Persons of wealth were able to make enormous profits by investing in plantations and devoting much of the land to cotton. As discussed before, slavery was the key to large scale operations concentrating efforts on cotton. Hence, in an important sense, slavery was a necessary though not sufficient condition for the huge southern commitment to cotton.

Cotton's attraction dampened southern industrial growth for reasons both obvious and subtle. It is possible, as Heywood Fleisig argues, that the limited number of entrepreneurs desirous and capable of running factories were lured away to the big plantations where such managerial talents were in demand. It is also likely, as Gavin Wright suggests, that slavery was indirectly responsible for the sluggish demand for machines to aid southern farmers. In the North the constraint of family labor made mechanization necessary for farmers who wanted to expand their profits and acreage. By the 1850's, a variety of tools to reduce labor requirements in threshing and harvesting grains were being sold on a wide scale; and much of midwestern urban expansion during the late antebellum years was related to the farm implement industry. Southern cotton planters, on the other hand, faced no comparable constraints; farms could expand merely by adding slaves and acreage. And only the simplest tools need be purchased by cotton farmers.

A third (complementary) explanation for slow southern indus- trialization is that slavery reduced the demand for manufactured goods by increasing inequalities in the distribution of income. Eugene Geno- vese was probably wrong in his assertion that such skewed income dis- tribution reduced total southern demand for mass market produced manufactures like inexpensive textiles—slaves, too, had to be clothed. But as William Parker points out, slavery may have dampened demand for small-scale manufactures that family farmers in the midwest bought in nearby towns rather than making for themselves.

Suppose we accept one or more of the above explanations. Does this mean that slavery inhibited efficient resource allocation? Not necessarily. Efficiency is only lost if the resources devoted to agriculture would have had a higher value to society if they had been devoted to industry. But our explanations are not based on the failure of individuals to use their resources to the greatest profit. Nor are they based on clear-cut instances of market failure to match resources to their highest value demanders. To be sure, Bateman, Foust, and Weiss have unearthed some evidence that the return to southern manufacturing was higher than the return to agricultural capital. But, as they acknowledge, this does not necessarily demonstrate quantitatively significant market failure. Hence to make a convincing case for inefficiency, it must be argued that society's eco- nomic interests differed from the interests of the individuals who made the decisions.

This sort of "externalities" argument, in fact, does make some sense, though it is difficult to measure the actual deviation between social and individual interests. Industrialization may generate benefits greater than those captured by resource owners by increasing the average skill level of the work force through "learning-by-doing" (see chapter 4), or by reducing the cost of inventive activity. It may also diversify the fortunes of the economy, protecting it from the rapid income fluctuations that are common when many are dependent on a single export crop.

Note, though, that the case for externalities here is far from self- evident. To the degree that northern manufacturing substituted for southern manufacturing, the external benefits were not lost, only trans- ferred to another region of the country. That represents a cost to society only if "society" is narrowly defined to mean the South. Slavery, more- over, made it possible to capture one important external benefit—investment in human skills—that evades manufacturers operating in a free labor market. A trained crafts worker gets to keep the payoff from the invested skills when he or she changes jobs—unless, that is, the worker is a slave.

A very different argument about slavery and urbanization hits directly at the efficiency question without requiring a detour via the externalities route. This argument, popularized by Richard Wade, claims that slavery was incompatible with urban life. Wade argues that it was more expensive to secure the free population against slave revolt in cities because it was harder to isolate slaves and shield them from abolitionist propaganda. Slaves also upset the free workers with whom they associated by lowering the self-perceived status of the white working class. Thus, urban fears of slaves and the concomitant increased cost of slave security, Wade theorizes, explains the relative decline of urban slavery after the 1830's, and the absolute decline during the 1850's.

If Wade is correct, the slave labor system was an artificial (and increasingly important) constraint on the allocation of black labor to industry. If free white labor could not substitute perfectly for black slave labor, the cost of manufacturing was raised in the South, and the division of resources between industry and agriculture was inefficient. Wade's evidence—the decline in the urban slave population—does not, however, in itself prove Wade's case. Claudia Goldin has offered an alternative explanation for the fall in urban slave population based on the efficiency, not the inefficiency, of the southern labor market.

Goldin argues that the demand for both free and slave labor was growing in southern cities. The slaves left because their owners were pulled by opportunities for profit in the cotton fields, not because they were pushed by increasing reluctance to use slaves in manufacturing. Goldin's argument works like this: Slave and free labor were fairly close substitutes in cities; they performed the same tasks in the same ways. Hence the urban demand for slave labor was elastic with respect to price: A small increase in slave hire rates, other factors equal, would lead urbanities to switch to free labor. On cotton plantations, however, slave "willingness" to be driven in labor gangs made slave labor unique. Since there were no close substitutes for their services, the rural demand elasticity for slaves was low. The slave exodus from cities in the 1850's, Goldin claims, was caused by an increase in slave prices associated with the cotton boom. Urban areas did not compete for slave services at higher prices because they did not need to compete.

What is the bottom line to these conflicting arguments? Surely the burden of proof still rests on those who see the concentration of southern resources as a less than efficient response to profit incentives. Undoubtedly, it was possible to find examples in which slavery inhibited the growth of industry, whose product, properly defined, was greater than

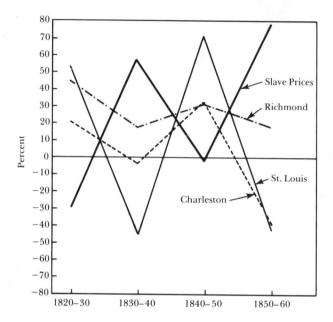

**SLAVE PRICES AND SLAVE POPULATION CHANGES
IN THREE SOUTHERN CITIES**

When slave prices rose, the growth of urban slave populations slowed or reversed. This gives weight to Goldin's theory that slaves were taken from the cities
because of their high productivity in agriculture.

Source: Robert Fogel and Stanley Engerman, *Time on the Cross* (Little, Brown, 1974), p. 99.

the opportunity cost of the labor and capital it would have employed.
But it is also likely that slavery made possible the exploitation of profitable opportunities in agriculture. A more substantial conclusion is left to
the next section.

SLAVERY AND ECONOMIC GROWTH

If the debate over cotton, slavery, and the efficiency of the antebellum slave economy has a satisfactory outcome, it must be measur-
able as economic growth. The standard test for efficiency, at least from
the luxurious position of historical perspective, is the ability of an economy to raise per capita income. Strictly speaking, growth rates reveal
very little about allocative efficiency. Rapid growth does not necessarily
indicate efficiency—opportunities might be so great that a better growth
rate might have been possible. Rapid growth based on high savings and
investment rates, moreover, is efficient only if it is consistent with individual desires to postpone current consumption in return for future income.

Nonetheless, this latter objection is typically assumed away on the premise that individual savings-consumption preferences are rarely critical obstacles to rapid growth. Given some assurance about the security of the investment vehicles, all but the very poor are usually willing to sacrifice for a better future. And economic historians are not prepared to quibble in the case of 19th-century America. That is why impressions of the antebellum southern economy have been so influenced by the research on regional income growth of Richard Easterlin (see table 8.6).

As might be expected, northerners had higher per capita incomes in both 1840 and 1860. But it may surprise those who think of the South as backward that the region was substantially better off at both dates than the predominantly rural north central states (Ohio and west). The South, moreover, grew one-fifth faster than the North and at a rate that ranks it well up with the growth experience of successfully industrializing countries. Fogel and Engerman see these figures as macroeconomic icing on the microeconomic cake of plantation efficiency. How else, they ask, can we interpret such a long period of sustained growth that compares favorably with the American North and with European economies?

TABLE 8.6

**PER CAPITA INCOME AND REGIONAL ECONOMIC GROWTH,
1840 AND 1860
(1860 dollars)**

Region	1840	1860	% Average Annual Growth
United States	$ 96	128	1.4
North	109	141	1.3
Northeast	129	181	1.7
North Central	65	89	1.6
South	74	103	1.7
South Atlantic	66	84	1.2
East South Central	69	89	1.3
West South Central	151	184	1.0

Interpretation: Southern incomes were, on average, lower than northern incomes before the Civil War. But note that most parts of the South had a higher living standard than the predominantly rural north central (midwest) states. And most important, southern income was growing substantially faster than northern during the two decades before the Civil War.

Source: Robert Fogel and Stanley Engerman, *Time on the Cross I* (Little, Brown, 1974), p. 248.

Well, in fact there are other interpretations. One researcher, Gerald Gunderson, simply disputes the quality of Easterlin's original estimates. But a more persuasive overview is offered by Gavin Wright. The good fortunes of the South, he argues, were dependent on factors outside the control of southerners. The relentless increase in the demand for raw cotton (at an average rate of 5 percent annually from 1830 to 1860) provided opportunities for southerners to extend the cotton economy westward without experiencing a long-term decline in cotton prices. The enormously high quality of land in the New South (Alabama, Mississippi, Texas, Louisiana, Arkansas), moreover, made it possible to raise labor productivity with no apparent change in technology or farm organization. High-quality land raised output per worker by effectively changing factor proportions. More land per worker allowed risk-averse farmers to shift a higher percentage of their output into profitable cotton without sacrificing the benefits of self-sufficiency in food.

The southern response to growing foreign demand and to the availability of fertile land was surely efficient—cotton was where the profit lay. But the resulting per capita growth must be looked at somewhat differently than, say, the growth record of the North. The South was a modern extractive economy capable of growth because it possessed abundant resources and was blessed by expanding demand from the outside. Growth did take place, but the resulting specialization may have left it unprepared to cope with the changes wrought by decelerating demand for cotton in the late 19th century.

But does that mean slavery was an economic as well as a moral error? Slavery made extremely rapid economic expansion possible by allowing plantations to achieve economies of scale—or as Wright claims, by allowing greater market orientation by farmers. The attraction of cotton-slave agriculture (naturally) retarded industrial development, leaving the South vulnerable to the long-term vicissitudes of the world cotton market.

The critical issue, then, is how well the Slave South would have coped with demand changes that reduced the return to cotton farming. If southerners had succeeded in transferring resources to industry, the transition from cotton agriculture would have been cheap in economic terms. The slave society of the antebellum South might have become a sort of precursor to South Africa, operating a diversified economy off the backs of an exploited underclass of workers. If, on the other hand, the commitment to cotton had been difficult to reverse under slavery, losses of late 19th-century growth opportunities might have outweighed the gains from early growth opportunities. It would be comforting to be able to argue with confidence that profit follows morality, that slavery would have eventually done in the enslavers. The state of the debate, alas, does not allow such comforting conclusions.

Bibliography

**Hugh Aitkin (ed.), *Did Slavery Pay?* (Houghton-Mifflin, 1971). Useful collection of articles on the profitability controversy, including some very old ones.

**Fred Bateman, James Foust, and Thomas Weiss, "Profitability in Southern Manufacturing: Estimates for 1860," *Explorations in Economic History* 12 (July, 1975). Evidence showing that the return to southern manufacturing was higher than the return to alternative investments.

**Fred Bateman and Thomas Weiss, "Comparative Regional Development in Antebellum Manufacturing," *Journal of Economic History* 35 (March, 1975). Why southern manufacturing lagged.

**Raymond Battalio and John Kagel, "The Structure of Antebellum Southern Agriculture: South Carolina, A Case Study," *Agricultural History* 44 (Jan., 1970). Estimated productivity of slave labor.

**Noel Butlin, *Antebellum Slavery* (Australian National University Press, Canberra, 1971). Extraordinarily painstaking recalculation of slave profits, suggesting that Conrad and Meyer's numbers cannot be trusted.

*Alfred Conrad, Douglas Dowd, *et al.*, "Slavery as an Obstacle to Economic Growth in the United States," *Journal of Economic History* 27 (Dec., 1967). Bitter panel discussion revealing the deep split between traditional and revisionist views on the economics of slavery.

**Alfred Conrad and John Meyer, "The Economics of Slavery in the Antebellum South," *Journal of Political Economy* 66 (April, 1958). Classic article estimating profitability of antebellum slavery and the allocative efficiency of slave labor.

**Paul David, Herbert Gutman, Richard Sutch, and Gavin Wright, *Reckoning With Slavery* (Oxford University, 1976). Critical essays examining *Time on the Cross*.

**Richard Easterlin, "Farm Production and Income in Old and New Areas at Mid Century" in David Klingaman and Richard Vedder (eds.), *Essays in 19th Century Economic History: The Old Northwest* (Ohio University, 1975). Updates classic estimates of sectional income.

**Richard Esterlin, "Interregional Differences in Per Capita Income, Population and Total Income 1840–1950" in National Bureau for Economic Research, *Trends in the American Economy in the 19th Century*, Studies in Income and Wealth, vol. 24 (Princeton, 1960). Basic estimates needed to compare antebellum growth rates.

**Robert Evans, Jr. "The Economics of American Negro Slavery" in National Bureau for Economic Research, *Aspects of Labor Economics* (Princeton, 1962). Uses rental rates for slaves to measure profitability.

**Heywood Fleisig, "Slavery, the Supply of Agricultural Labor, and the Industrialization of the South," *Journal of Economic History* 36 (Sept., 1976). How slavery influenced the allocation of labor.

**Robert Fogel and Stanley Engerman, "The Relative Efficiency of Slavery: A Comparison of Northern and Southern Agriculture in 1860," *Explora-*

tions in Economic History 8 (Spring, 1971). Controversial estimate showing that the South used productive resources more efficiently than the North.

**Robert Fogel and Stanley Engerman, "Exploring the Relative Efficiency of Slave Agriculture in the Antebellum South," *American Economic Review* (June, 1977). Revised calculations attempting to show that high southern productivity was not critically dependent on unrepresentative 1860 data.

‡***Robert Fogel and Stanley Engerman, "The Economics of Slavery" in Fogel and Engerman (ed.), *The Reinterpretation of American Economic History* (Harper and Row, 1971). Review essay on the economics of slavery, sharpening the arguments by putting them in mathematical terms.

*Robert Fogel and Stanley Engerman, *Time on the Cross* (Little, Brown, 1974). Immensely controversial interpretation of the evidence on slavery.

‡***Robert Fogel and Stanley Engerman, *Time on the Cross Volume II: Evidence and Methods* (Little, Brown, 1974). Technical appendix keyed to the arguments presented in volume one.

**James Foust and Dale Swan, "Productivity and Profitability of Antebellum Slave Labor: A Micro Approach," *Agricultural History* 44 (Jan., 1970). Disaggregation of profitability calculations by region and farm size.

**Robert Gallman, "Southern Antebellum Income Reconsidered," *Explorations in Economic History* 12 (Jan., 1975). Defense of Easterlin's estimates of sectional income.

*Eugene Genovese, *The Political Economy of Slavery* (Vintage, 1967). Marxist historian's treatise on why slavery was inefficient.

‡**Claudia Goldin, *Urban Slavery in the American South* (University of Chicago, 1976). Attributes decline of slavery in cities to increased demand for rural labor.

*Lewis Gray, *History of Agriculture in the Southern United States to 1860* (Washington: Carnegie Institution, 1933). Standard reference work on southern agriculture; still not dated.

*Ralph Gray and Betty Wood, "The Transition from Indentured to Involuntary Servitude in Colonial Georgia," *Explorations in Economic History* 13 (Oct., 1976). Argument that the economic cost advantages of slave labor made its introduction in Georgia inevitable.

**Gerald Gunderson, "Southern Antebellum Income Reconsidered," *Explorations in Economic History* 10 (Winter, 1973). Attack on Easterlin's sectional income estimates.

**Jacob Metzer, "Rational Management, Modern Business Practice, and Economies of Scale in the Antebellum Plantations," *Explorations in Economic History* 12 (April, 1975). Close view of the incentives facing managers of southern plantations using slave labor.

**John Moes, "The Absorption of Capital in Slave Labor in the Antebellum South and Economic Growth," *American Journal of Economics and Sociology* 20 (Oct., 1961). Ingenious attempt to resurrect the notion that slavery absorbed capital.

*Frank Owsley, *Plain Folk in the Old South* (Louisiana State University, 1949). Pioneering work revealing the economic importance of a large middle group of slaveless farmers in the South.

*William Parker, "Slavery and Southern Economic Development," *Agricultural History* 44 (Jan., 1970). Speculation on how slavery affected distribution of income, farm size and industrialization.

*Ulrich Phillips, "The Economic Cost of Slaveholding in the Cotton Belt," *Political Science Quarterly* (June, 1905). Classic view that slavery was a burden to southern development; set tone of historical interpretation for decades.

*Charles Ramsdell, "The Natural Limits of Slavery Expansion," *Mississippi Valley Historical Review* 16 (Sept., 1929). Argues that slavery was ready to self-destruct on the eve of the Civil War; bears on the historical "inevitability" of the war.

**Edward Saraydar, "A Note on the Profitability of Antebellum Slavery," *Southern Economic Journal* 30 (April, 1964). Attack on Conrad and Meyer's empirical work.

*Kenneth Stampp, *The Peculiar Institution* (Knopf, 1956). Lucid overview of the economics of slavery before Conrad and Meyer.

*Robert Starobin, *Industrial Slavery in the Old South* (Oxford University, 1970). Seminal work on the use of slaves in industry.

**Richard Sutch, "The Profitability of Antebellum Slavery-Revisited," *Southern Economic Journal* 31 (April, 1965). "Second generation" economics of slavery article, pointing to the critical historical importance of the viability issue.

*Charles Sydnor, *Slavery in Mississippi* (Appleton-Century, 1933). Attempt to measure profitability from plantation records.

‡**Peter Temin, "The Causes of Cotton Price Fluctuations in the 1830's," *Review of Economics and Statistics* 49 (Nov., 1967). A simpler model of the cotton market than Wright's, which generates very different conclusions.

**Robert Thomas and Richard Bean, "The Fishers of Men: The Profits of the Slave Trade," *Journal of Economic History* 34 (Dec., 1974). Hypothesis that slave trade was a competitive industry, limiting the opportunities for economic profit.

*Richard Wade, *Slavery in the Cities: The South 1820–60* (Oxford University, 1964). Argues that slavery held back southern urbanization.

‡**Gavin Wright, "An Econometric Study of Cotton Production and Trade 1830–60," *Review of Economics and Statistics* 53 (May, 1971). Neatly crafted statistical model of the relative impact of supply and demand factors on cotton price and output.

**Gavin Wright, "Economic Democracy and the Concentration of Agricultural Wealth in the Cotton South, 1850–60," *Agricultural History* 44, (Jan., 1970). Careful measurement of the distribution of wealth, with comparisons to the North.

**Gavin Wright, "New and Old Views on the Economics of Slavery," *Journal of Economic History* 33 (June, 1973). Insightful essay on the relevance of profitability research to historical issues.

**Gavin Wright, "Slavery and the Cotton Boom," *Explorations in Economic History* 12 (Oct., 1975). Refutation of Fogel and Engerman's case for the relative efficiency of southern agriculture.

**Gavin Wright, "The Efficiency of Slavery; Another Interpretation," *American Economic Review* 69 (1979). Rebuttal to the Fogel-Engerman defense of their efficiency estimates.

‡**Gavin Wright, *The Political Economy of the Cotton South* (Norton, 1978). Relevant to this chapter for analysis of the economics of plantation agriculture.

**Yasukichi Yasuba, "The Profitability and Viability of Plantation Slavery in the United States" in Robert Fogel and Stanley Engerman (eds.), *The Reinterpretation of American Economic History* (Harper and Row, 1971). Introduces viability concept, effectively answering the important question about the economics of slavery.

‡***Thomas Zepp, "On Returns to Scale and Input Substitutability in Slave Agriculture," *Explorations in Economic History* 13 (April, 1976). Econometric confirmation of economies of scale on large plantations.

Slavery and society

9

The last chapter answered a very limited sort of question about the antebellum slave economy—the kind of question economists like best. Investments in slaves were probably profitable . . . Slavery was indeed viable, since owners had a financial incentive to keep and breed slaves . . . The slave economy worked well, in the sense that per capita output was large and growing rapidly . . . Slavery most likely created long-term economic weakness by encouraging specialization in a single export crop . . .

Non-economists find the games economists play with slavery frustrating and perhaps even morally tainted. The premier question about the slave economy—how much did those in bondage suffer as a consequence of slavery—is never posed. One reason economists have avoided this issue is that modern "welfare economics" (the study of how production and distribution influence social well-being) is poorly equipped to provide satisfactory answers. Welfare economics achieves a sort of scientific neutrality by refusing to judge the desirability of acts in which some benefit at the expense of others, no matter how large the benefit or how small the loss. Thus we can only say the world is a better place when Joe has more to eat if Sally has no less.

This leads economists to very narrow welfare judgments indeed, implicitly accepting the distribution of wealth and privilege as given and then asking how changes in resource allocation can make everyone better off. For example, Country A's economy is operating inefficiently even though everyone is well fed and apparently content, if some rearrangement of resources could make everyone even better fed. Country B's economy, on the other hand, is operating efficiently because, even though half the population eats sirloin three times a day and the other half is starving, there is no way to make the malnourished better off without discommoding the steak eaters.

The tension inherent in analyzing economic behavior in such a rigid framework is one reason why Robert Fogel and Stanley Engerman's *Time on the Cross* is so controversial. For here Fogel and Engerman walk a fine intellectual line between moral neutrality and implicit apology for slavery. The issues raised by Fogel and Engerman are dealt with briefly below. Readers are advised, though, to consult the book and its critics before making judgments.

Controlling Slaves: The Sweet Potato and the Whip

No one who writes about slavery today doubts that its imposition was an outrage and that the value of the freedom lost by those in bondage is incalculable. But there is still substantial disagreement over how well blacks fared under slavery. The popular contemporary view—one, incidentally, not shared by historians old or new—has its origins in the propaganda of the 19th-century abolitionist movement. The abolitionists, morally offended by slavery, sought allies among people with no special distaste for the coercion of labor by emphasizing the physical deprivation of black slaves. Simon Legree, and Liza on the ice floe, are the enduring creations of a campaign to discredit the slaveocracy among middle-class northerners.

But a moment's thought suggests the internal contradictions of a world in which slaveholders paid vast sums for slaves—as much as ten times the average annual product of a worker—only to drive them to early graves. For slaveholders whose primary interest in slaves was the cash surplus that could be extracted from slave labor, the issue of how to treat slaves was complex. It would never pay to deny slaves basic subsistence; that much is obvious. On the other hand, the optimal balance of force and material rewards needed to maximize the difference between slave production and slave maintenance is not at all obvious.

Force—physical coercion, restriction of freedom of movement—usually has the advantage of being cheap. It will not be effective, however, if slaves resist passively, taking opportunities to vandalize equipment and avoid work. Material incentives—better food, clothing, additional leisure, promotion within the slave hierarchy—are expensive in the sense that they raise maintenance costs. If used effectively, though, they might induce the slave to identify with his or her owner's interests and thus raise labor productivity.

Two economists, Giorgio Cannarella and John Tomaske, have formally analyzed the conditions leading to "optimal" slave utilization. As they are the first to admit, their mathematical analysis has no inherent meaning without specific information about slaves' psychological responses to the carrot and stick. Still, they argue, the internal logic of slavery should bias owners toward the use of force. First, they cite an asymmetry in slave response to positive and negative incentives. Force always works (if applied carefully) up to the point where slaves can do no more. Material reward, by contrast, works only up to the point where the additional income to the slave outweighs the unpleasantness of additional effort. Second, there are positive "externalities" in the use of force which are missing in the use of reward incentives. Punish one slave harshly, and the threat of punishment may suffice to keep the others in line. Providing a Christmas ham for a hard worker, on the other hand, has no impact on slaves who don't get hams.

These specific arguments seem less than overwhelming. As suggested originally, force does not always work if resistance is passive or secretive: How does one punish a slave who convincingly feigns stupidity? As to the externalities argument, it is not difficult to turn it on its head. A reward to one slave can surely induce others to work harder in hope of receiving similar benefits; punishing one slave may act as a deterrent to others—or, it may generate sympathy and slave community solidarity against the oppressor.

Then, too, there is a more general argument against guestimating slave owners' behavior. If both force and reward work reasonably well in getting labor out of slaves, the advantages of one over the other may be too subtle for all slave owners to agree upon. Thus some may take the force route, some the reward route, and some may switch back and forth. Of course, in a perfectly competitive marketplace, where information is obtained costlessly and all slaves respond identically to incentives, only the best technique would survive; non-optimizing owners would not be able to cover their opportunity costs. But the slave labor market was not so perfectly competitive, nor was information cheap. Perhaps more important, plantation agriculture was so lucrative that owners could typically afford to use less than optimal techniques. They might earn less than maximum profits this way, but with economic rents on slaves so high, they would be unlikely to go out of business.

The Physical Treatment of Slaves

How well did slaves actually live? Strikingly well, compared to free people, in the view of Fogel and Engerman. Their argument and rebuttal by their critics is summarized here.

DIET
Corn and pork constituted the core of the slave diet, and there is little question that the energy value of the basic ration described in documented instructions to overseers was adequate to keep slaves going.

Fogel and Engerman argue, moreover, that the corn-pork ration obscured the substantial variety and nutritional balance provided by slave masters—presumably as an incentive to good work.

They base their claim not on plantation records but on indirect evidence provided by the Census on food production on large plantations. After making allowances for food consumed by free whites and for meat sold by the plantation in local markets, Fogel and Engerman compute the slave diet as a residual from the food committed to other uses. The result is a numerical breakdown for eleven foodstuffs, including sweet potatoes, beans, beef, wheat, and dairy products; these, along with corn and pork, formed the bulk of slave consumption (see table 9.1). Foods other than corn and pork provide one-third the calories, and a degree of variety in diet not very different from that enjoyed by contemporary free persons. The average slave diet computed was high in protein, iron, calcium, vitamins A and C—high enough in fact to meet modern recommended daily consumption requirements.

Richard Sutch's exhaustive analysis of the Fogel and Engerman food study casts doubt on these findings. Sutch is unpersuaded that the sample of large plantations used by Fogel and Engerman is representative of

TABLE 9.1

SLAVE DIET

Food	Fogel and Engerman lbs/day	Calories	Sutch lbs/day	Calories	Standard Ration[a] lbs/day	Calories
Pork	.24	543	.41	685	.39	653[b]
Corn	1.39	2265	1.74	2805	1.56	2516[b]
Beef	.12	108	.08	96		
Mutton	.01	5	—	—		
Milk	.47	144	.29			
Butter	.01	30	.01			
Sweet Potatoes	.87	424	.56	233		
White Potatoes	.06	19	.05	14		
Cow Peas	.28	427	.10	149		
Wheat	.09	156	.09	138		
Other Grains	.04	64	—	—		
Total		4185		4206		3169[b]

[a]The simple corn-pork diet that most historians have concluded was the lot of slaves.
[b]These calorie conversions are consistent with Sutch's estimates, not Fogel and Engerman's.

Source: Richard Sutch, "The Care and Feeding of Slaves" in Paul David et al., *Reckoning with Slavery* (Oxford University, 1976), p. 262.

southern cotton agriculture as a whole. He notes, moreover, that the residual technique employed is sensitive to assumptions about other ways in which food may have been used, particularly in the amount of beef sold off the farm, and the amounts of specific foods consumed by resident whites.

Sutch's most significant argument strikes at the heart of Fogel and Engerman's conclusion. While everyone agrees that slaves ate a lot of food, the issue is its quality and variety. The Census data used by Fogel and Engerman give only information on crop output and livestock inventories. It is up to the researcher to convert these into food on the dinner table, and Fogel and Engerman must therefore apply conversion factors—corn into corn meal, livestock into meat, and so on. Mistaken conversions, Sutch contends, explain why Fogel and Engerman found so much variety in the slave diet. To make his point clear, Sutch used the identical data from the (disputed) sample of large farms, merely reworking the conversions to match antebellum practices.

The Sutch revision (shown in table 9.1) suggests energy consumption almost identical to Fogel and Engerman's estimates, but fully 83 percent of these calories are derived from corn and pork. Sutch's milk, sweet potato, and beef consumption figures are all smaller by about a third, while cowpea consumption is smaller by two-thirds. Corn consumption, on the other hand, is up by about 80 percent, while pork is up 25 percent.

Sutch's revisions are surely adequate to cast doubt on the exact cowpea count in the Fogel and Engerman finding. Sutch does not, however, bury forever their basic claim regarding the relative quality of slave diets: by either set of figures slaves consumed substantial quantities of beef, sweet potatoes, milk, wheat flour, and beans. Slaves may not have eaten well by present standards, or by the standard of employed rural whites of the era, but they surely ate much better than the minimum dictated by physiological need.

HOUSING AND CLOTHING

Fogel and Engerman's typical slave was housed and clothed in much the fashion he or she was fed—simply but not badly. Five adults lived in an 18 x 20 foot cabin with one or two rooms, a plank floor, fireplace, and shuttered windows—more space per person than New York's free poor could expect in the late 19th century. They each received four sets of cotton shirts and pants, or dresses, one or two pairs of leather shoes, plus coats and blankets as needed. Not much perhaps, but more than unskilled white urban dwellers. And in many cases, slaves were able to earn money from crops cultivated in small gardens which could be used to supplement the standard clothing issue.

Once again, Sutch is skeptical of the statistical support for Fogel and

Engerman's generalizations. Only anecdotal evidence is available on cabin size, and from a rereading of the same anecdotes Sutch argues that 15 x 15 (225 square feet) was more typical than 18 x 20 (360 square feet). He also believes that Fogel and Engerman underestimated the number of occupants per cabin, thereby exaggerating the total space available per slave by 50 percent. Sutch considers inappropriate the comparison between antebellum rural slave quarters and the housing available to very poor people in crowded urban slums. Measured against typical housing for yeoman farmers or working class city dwellers, neither the space nor the amenities granted to slaves was up to par.

MEDICAL CARE, LIFE EXPECTANCY,
AND INFANT MORTALITY

Medical care—access to physicians and hospitals—was almost irrelevant to the well-being of antebellum Americans, white or black. Medical knowledge was so primitive that a physician was as likely to hurt as help, and hospitals were merely sinks for communicable diseases. General environmental factors—adequate sewage, clean water, diet—thus largely explained differences in successful pregnancy rates, infant mortality, and life expectancy, the key measures of general health. And here Fogel and Engerman argue, the record for slaves is reasonably good.

Among slave women in 1850, only 6 out of 1,000 pregnancies ended in the death of the mother, a figure lower than that of white southern women. However, 183 slave infants out of each 1,000 failed to reach one year of age, as opposed to 146 deaths per 1,000 among white babies. The paradox of relatively low maternal mortality and high infant mortality estimates, Fogel and Engerman believe, stems from statistical biases and possible genetic differences between whites and blacks. "The ultimate test of wellbeing"—as Fogel and Engerman put it— is life expectancy at birth. Slaves do not do as well as whites in 1850 by this test (36 years versus 40 years), but viewed in world perspective, they don't do so badly. Life expectancy for Holland, France, and Italy were roughly the same, while 19th-century Austrians and city dwellers in England and the United States fared much worse.

Sutch, for the most part, does not buy the argument. He notes that Fogel and Engerman accept Robert Evans's estimate of slave infant mortality (186/1,000), but arbitrarily reject Evans's estimate of white infant mortality (104/1,000) in favor of their own much higher calculation (146/1,000). In fact, Sutch claims, a case can be made for even greater black-white disparities than those found by Evans, a case that would leave a two-to-one black-white differential for Fogel and Engerman to explain away. As for the life expectancy estimates, Sutch again accuses Fogel and Engerman of selectively choosing the one estimate most favorable to their case from a wide range of estimates. If one plays the game on the opposite side, it is possible to conclude that black life expectancy was even lower than 28 years.

PUNISHMENT

Whipping, public humiliation, and loss of privileges were the primary means of punishment on plantations—long-term imprisonment or execution, after all, reduced labor productivity. Fogel and Engerman remind the readers that whipping was not viewed in the early 19th century as cruel or unusual. And it could be argued that the typical means used to discipline free wage labor—firing them—was far crueler, since it left the workers and their families without income.

Fogel and Engerman assert, moreover, that plantation owners with no particular scruples about corporal punishment still used whipping with discretion. As evidence, they cite the diary of Louisiana planter Bennett Barrow. Over a two-year period 45 percent of the slaves were never whipped and another 19 percent were whipped just once. The average number of whippings per hand was 0.7 per year.

Herbert Gutman and Richard Sutch take exception to both the Barrow data and the implied benevolence of plantation discipline. The frequency of whippings was actually much higher, they note, because the number of field slaves on the Barrow plantation was lower and the recorded number of whippings higher than Fogel and Engerman report. By the Gutman-Sutch reckoning, only 22 percent of Barrow's slaves escaped the lash, and whippings per hand per year was 1.2, not 0.7.

More important than the numbers revision is the revision in how they should be interpreted. Gutman and Sutch argue that successful punishment systems operate through deterrence and that the cruelty of the system depends upon the terror and rage it engendered among obedient slaves as well as the beatings actually absorbed by the undisciplined. Obviously, there is no measure of this cruelty, but one might wonder about the quality of life in a slave quarters in which, on average, one public whipping was administered every fourth day. During the two-year period, Gutman and Sutch point out, Barrow also "jailed, beat with a stick, threatened with death, shot with a gun, raked the heads of, and humiliated" his slaves.

GIFTS AND NON-APPROPRIATED INCOME AS REWARD

Fogel and Engerman argue that rewards were used systematically as an incentive to work. Good performance in the fields might mean extra days off, luxury goods, or prizes. Barrow distributed substantial gifts at Christmas to this end. On a Texas plantation owned by Julian Devereux, slaves cultivated cotton on special plots in their spare time. In a good year, Fogel and Engerman report, Devereux's slaves earned $100 per family this way.

Another planter, William Jemison of Alabama, was even more clearly oriented toward material rewards as incentives. Jemison's slaves were, in effect, sharecroppers with lifetime, unbreakable contracts. They were obliged to set aside one-third of the crop for their owner, but were allowed to keep the proceeds from the rest after netting out the cost of services provided by Jemison.

Gutman and Sutch's reading of the record is—no surprise—different. Barrow's gift giving was no regular thing. Of the ten years' experience recorded in his diary, Barrow made major gifts in only three; the other seven years the slaves had to settle for holiday parties. Even accepting the fact that gifts were sometimes given, Gutman and Sutch challenge the economic rationality of the motives of the givers. Jemison's scheme is explicable only as an incentive program. But should Barrow's gifts be interpreted as incentives for hard work from a capitalist employer, or were they a matter of custom in which paternalism was the dominant motive? It is very hard to say.

As for the separate land plots, the evidence can be read either way. By setting aside a small amount of land for slaves, owners might be rewarding their chattels for services rendered. Or they might simply be sharing the market and risks associated with farming in a convenient and socially acceptable manner. In good years, master and slave ate well; in bad years they suffered together. Unless evidence surfaces showing that the plots were increased or decreased in size according to specific actions by slaves, there is no obvious way of interpreting masters' motives.

OCCUPATION AS REWARD

For free men and women, occupational choice is a matter of personal motivation, aptitude, family wealth, and kinship ties. For slaves, occupation could (if the master wished) be a matter of rational income maximization. On first thought, this would suggest that some kind of "human capital" model would be appropriate: An owner might single out bright, young, willing workers and train them in crafts or as managers. The earlier they gained skills, the greater the return on the investment to the owner.

In fact, Fogel and Engerman found, younger workers were underrepresented among the skilled, whereas male slaves in their 30's and 40's and 50's were overrepresented. They believe the explanation for this seemingly irrational choice on the owners' part lies in the use of occupation as a reward for service. Field hands could get away from the labor gangs only by hard work and docility for a decade or two. Those lucky enough to succeed would have a chance at less monotonous work, greater control over their daily lives, and status within slave society.

Skilled labor also offered the chance at an income many times greater than basic subsistence and the remote possibility of buying freedom.

In operation, Fogel and Engerman argue, this system created substantial opportunities for patient males. Slaves were virtually excluded from the professions and from top managerial posts. But, judging by the mix of skilled and unskilled workers among all Americans in 1870, they did about as well as the population in other occupations: Fogel and Engerman report that seven percent were managers, twelve percent were crafts-persons, and seven percent had semi-skilled jobs as personal servants, gardners, and teamsters.

As Gutman and Sutch see it, however, the evidence used by Fogel and Engerman just does not support their startling conclusion. The overrepresentation of older workers in skilled jobs may be explained by a reward system. But it is also consistent with two plausible older hypotheses. First, skilled older workers may have been less fit to work as field hands; at least on occasion crafts jobs were assigned to those maimed or herniated by strenuous labor. Then too, there is the possibility that the observed age structure reflects a "disequilibrium" in which it had ceased to pay to train young or old slaves in crafts. Free workers may have filled new skilled jobs created by economic growth, with slaves doing skilled work only if they had been trained in an earlier era.

This second alternative appeals because it meshes with Fogel and Engerman's own views, developed elsewhere in *Time on the Cross,* on the relative inelasticity of demand for gang labor. Skilled work could be done by whites or blacks—they were close substitutes as productive factors. But only slaves could grow cotton on plantations—only workers, that is, who could be forced to grow cotton on other people's land. As a result, it is reasonable to expect white workers to replace slaves in skilled positions when the returns to growing cotton were high. More important, this expectation could be borne out in underrepresentation in skilled job categories for those slaves beginning their work years during cotton booms.

Appealing though the "disequilibrium" explanation is, it falters a bit in the face of the numbers. Fogel and Engerman look at the occupation profile in 1850. If the underrepresentation of workers under thirty is to be explained by demand factors, the decade prior to 1850 should be characterized by strong profit opportunities in cotton. In fact, the 1840's was a period of mild depression for cotton, years in which no particular premium would have been placed on field labor.

Gutman and Sutch take their lumps on that argument, but they do better attacking the evidence on which the occupation-as-reward theory is based. Occupation data were obtained from a sample of thirty plantations, all in Plaquemines Parish, Louisiana, with adjustments to measure the number of black overseers and drivers whom Fogel and Engerman believe were statistically underrepresented in the group. Gutman and Sutch argue, however, that findings from this sample of medium to large *sugar* plantations (adjusted for drivers and overseers) dramatically over-states the percentage of male slaves in privileged positions. First, Sutch and Gutman expand the sample to include 65 (rather than 30) Plaque-mines Parish holdings and then weight the results to reflect farm size in the cotton South as a whole. They then readjust Fogel and Engerman's adjustments for black overseers and drivers. The result: 11.5 percent of adult male blacks, rather than 26.3 percent, held non-field jobs (see table 9.2). If Gutman and Sutch are correct, the slave occupation hierarchy was clearly skewed toward less skilled and less responsible jobs.

The Rate of Exploitation and the Paradox of Forced Labor

Evidence on material well-being, presented above, does offer some in-sight as to the benevolence of slavery in practice. Another approach is to measure the degree to which the product of black labor was diverted to slave owners. If slaves were able to retain most of the value of their out-put, slavery could be viewed as relatively benevolent. If they were not, the opposite conclusion might be drawn. There are, however, a number of problems with the rate-of-exploitation approach—including which concept of exploitation is appropriate to use, and what quantitative benchmark of "benevolence" makes sense. More troubling still, the rela-tionship between exploitation and benevolence is suspect; the subject is an intellectual snare specially set to trap unwary practitioners of "scien-tific" welfare economics.

Exploitation means different things to different people, and Fogel and Engerman take some pain to justify what it does and does not mean to them. For Karl Marx, exploitation was based on a specific ethical framework: Labor was ultimately responsible for all output. Thus the difference between total output and the portion of output paid to work-ers was exploited "surplus value." The ratio of this surplus value to ac-tual worker income was an index of the rate of exploitation. If, for ex-ample, U.S. Steel produces $8 billion worth of steel and pays the workers who mine the raw materials, transport them to mills, operate the fur-naces, and so on, just $5 billion, surplus value is $3 billion ($8 billion − $5 billion) and the exploitation rate is 60 percent ($3 billion/$5 billion).

Modern economists whose reasoning follows the traditions of 18th and 19th century classical economics, favor another common sense defi-nition of exploitation. In a competitive economy, workers are paid the value added by the last worker, not the average product of labor.[1] Hence a worker is exploited only when he or she fails to get that competitive re-

---

[1] See the appendix to chapter 15 for an explanation of this theory of "marginal productiv-ity" income distribution.

TABLE 9.2

PERCENTAGE OF ADULT MALE SLAVES IN NON-FIELD OCCUPATIONS

Fogel and Engerman Estimate:

Overseers	7.0
Skilled Crafts	11.9
Semi-Skilled	7.4
Total	26.3%

Gutman and Sutch Adjustments:

Large Plantation Sample Bias	−5.2
Barrel Makers Only on Sugar Plantations	−2.0
Overestimate of Drivers (sample bias)	−4.5
Overestimate of Overseers (Census Misintrepretation)	−0.5
Total	14.8%

Gutman and Sutch Estimate:

Drivers and Assistant Drivers	8.2
Skilled Workers, Overseers, Other Semi-Skilled	3.3
Total	11.5%

Source: Herbert Gutman and Richard Sutch, "Were Slaves Imbued with the Protestant Ethic?" in Paul David et al., *Reckoning with Slavery* (Oxford University, 1976), p. 87.

turn. It then follows that the neoclassical rate of exploitation is the percentage of the competitive wage that the employer (or in this case, the slave owner) expropriates. This is known as the "Robinsonian" (after the English economist Joan Robinson) rate of exploitation. Suppose, for example, the competitive wage for steel workers is $10 an hour, but U.S. Steel somehow gets away with paying only $8. The Robinson exploitation rate is 20 percent $[(10-8)/10]$.

Fogel and Engerman buy the neoclassical approach but modify it to account for the special properties of slave economics. A regular employer, they note, hires and fires labor at will. A slave owner, by contrast, finds it in his or her interest to assume the costs of maintaining slaves even when they are too young or too old or too sick to earn as much as they cost to maintain. Thus, during early childhood and old age, the neoclassical rate of exploitation is negative. Fogel and Engerman define the expropriated portion of a slave's product as the difference, at birth, between discounted lifetime earnings and discounted lifetime slave income (that is, maintenance costs). The rate of exploitation, they then argue, is the ratio of that difference (or "birthright") to the present value at birth of the slave's gross lifetime earnings. If, for example, a baby slave has a market value of $50 and is expected to generate a lifetime income (discounted to the present) of $300, the exploitation rate is $50/300, or one-sixth.

Note that if slavery is viable by Yasuba's test, the rate of exploitation must be positive. Should the present value of the expected lifetime earnings of a baby slave fail to exceed the present value of the expected lifetime costs, the slaveholder has no motive to raise slaves from birth. As Fogel and Engerman calculate it, the expropriation rate is indeed positive, but it is much smaller than one might intuitively expect. Until age 9, the annual value of a slave's earnings was less than maintenance (see figure 9.1). From that point on, the neoclassical exploitation rate is positive, but it takes another 18 years for a typical slave to pay back the debt accumulated in those years of burden on the owner. From age 27 to death (say at age 70) the surplus is substantial, but in terms of present value at birth in 1850, the surplus barely tops $32. Since the calculated present value of lifetime earnings at birth is about $265 for the same slave, the rate of exploitation (by Fogel and Engerman's definition) is just 12 percent ($32/$265). In fact, argue Fogel and Engerman, it may be closer to 10 percent, since some of the income imputed to slaves is valued at wholesale rather than the more appropriate retail market cost.

Why is this rate of exploitation so low? Two factors tend to depress the figure. First, slaves who live full lifetimes must, in effect, pay for the 40 percent who do not survive to become adults. Second, the costs of slave rearing come "up front," while the years of high productivity are decades down the road. When one uses a high (but not unreasonable) rate of discount to find the present value of the owner's future costs and income, the upfront costs weigh heavily in the calculation while the more distant income does not. To put it another way, the $32 birthright estimate is consistent with the fact that young adult slaves already earning surpluses were worth about fully $800 and that good field hands could often generate $100 a year more in earnings than they cost to maintain.

Two sorts of criticism have been leveled at the Fogel-Engerman expropriation calculation. The first accepts the spirit of Fogel and Engerman's definition, but contests important details of the calculation. Paul David and Peter Temin argue that the maintenance costs imputed to young slaves are too high, thereby exaggerating the deficit accumulated by slaves before they began to work in the fields. David and Temin also argue that the birthright (and hence the expropriation rate) is biased downward due to a shortcut employed by Fogel and Engerman in their calculation. In essence, the computational shortcut ignores the impact of owners' risk-avoidance behavior on slave prices, leading to undervaluation of the birthright.

The second, and more important, class of criticism is directed at the

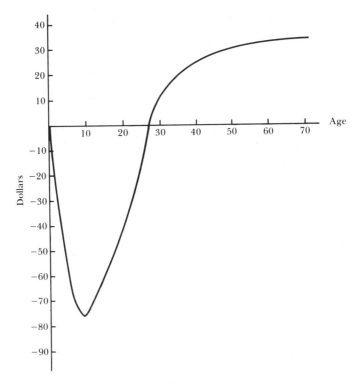

FIGURE 9.1

**AVERAGE ACCUMULATED VALUE (DISCOUNTED TO BIRTH)
OF INCOME APPROPRIATED FROM SLAVES**
(1850 dollars)

The chart shows the cumulative value of the surplus an average slave earned over his or her lifetime. Note that at about age nine, owners begin to get back more than they put into a slave. Sometime in the slave's early twenties the owner breaks even on the investment, as the slave's earnings discounted back to birth equal the slave's discounted rearing cost. Fogel and Engerman guess that around age 50 slave earnings again fall to about the level of maintenance costs. By this point, the cumulative value, discounted back to birth, of net slave earnings equals a little more than $30. Hence the argument that, at birth, a slave is worth about $30.

Source: Robert Fogel and Stanley Engerman, *Time on the Cross* (Little, Brown, 1974), p. 154.

definition of exploitation. By linking it closely to the viability issue, Fogel and Engerman are measuring exploitation from the viewpoint of the slave owner. That is fine if you are interested in how much better off slavery makes owners but has limited relevance to the question of how much worse off slavery makes the enslaved.

In large part the Fogel and Engerman exploitation rate is low because, across their lives, slaves are expected to pay back with interest their own rearing costs and the rearing costs of those who die prematurely. In a free society, people have no legal obligation to return these rearing costs to their parents or to the next generation. Most people do, of course, accept this burden voluntarily; otherwise the stock of capital per person inherited by each succeeding generation from the last would tend to fall. But as a matter of definition, it is questionable to include the entire sum used to rear the next generation of slaves as part of the consumption of this generation of slaves. Some slaves might wish progeny raised as slaves. Others, however, we would speculate might not, so it is unfair to "charge" them for the rearing costs.

There is a much larger point here too, one which Fogel and Engerman acknowledge but do not connect directly to their measure of exploitation. A good portion of the research effort in *Time on the Cross* is devoted to showing that the food, housing, medical care, and clothing provided slaves were substantially above the subsistence level—not, presumably, because of paternalism, but because it paid masters to give slaves positive incentives to work hard. In fact, Fogel and Engerman estimate, a prime field hand received consumption goods worth approximately 15 percent more than the wage imputed to free farmers tilling their own land. It was possible to sustain this relatively high material living standard for slaves and still reap a tidy return from their labors, Fogel and Engerman reason, because plantation agriculture was so much more productive than small scale family farming. Slaves got to keep roughly one-fifth of the extra value made possible by large-scale farm organization.

Assume Fogel and Engerman are right (an assumption not universally shared). Does that mean slavery left everyone—slaves and owners—better off than they would otherwise have been? "No," Fogel an Engerman respond; the peculiarly productive farm organization made possible by slavery was so repugnant to slaves that the intangible "non-pecuniary" losses they suffered more than offset their tangible material gains. The arithmetic of gains and losses attributable to forced productive labor can be inferred from experience with black gang labor after the Civil War. To induce free people to work in labor gangs on sugar plantations in Louisiana, landowners had to pay wages $75 a year above the going rate for non-gang labor. It is understandable that, once the plantation owner lost the right to compel gang labor, the arrangement became a rare one. The implicit non-pecuniary loss to workers ($75) was far greater than the potential material gain attributable to gang labor scale economies ($23 per year).

With this in mind, return to the concept of exploitation. Under slavery, Fogel and Engerman calculate that the average annual per capita income of slaves was $42.99, while adult males received goods worth $60.62. This was more than the return to free labor, though it still allowed owners a margin of exploitation of about 10–12 percent over the slave's lifetime. But from the slave's viewpoint, the huge unmeasured personal cost of gang labor renders this rate of exploitation calculation meaningless. Slaves would have felt exploited receiving incomes up to $67 a year higher (that is, $75, less the extra $8 owners actually gave to slaves in return for gang labor). It is possible, then, to recalculate the exploitation rate from a slave's perspective by looking at the difference between what slaves actually got and the enormous sum needed to get them to work voluntarily in gangs. But even this procedure would grossly underestimate the slave's subjective rate of exploitation since it would not account for the additional hypothetical payment needed to compensate slaves for their loss of freedom in their non-work lives.

The alert reader may have noticed one striking implication of the asymmetry of the exploitation rates from the master's and slave's view. If slaves lost more from being slaves than owners gained from enslaving them, why couldn't they work out a deal in which slaves traded some of their material income for the intangible benefits of freedom? The answer is deceptively simple. It would take an average of $15 (the $23 productivity advantage to gang labor, less the $8 returned to slaves as incentives to work) to compensate slave owners for their annual net loss of income. But slaves couldn't afford to make the deal: They just weren't rich enough to give up an additional $15 a year and still have enough income to survive.

Modern welfare economics is not capable of comparing the gain to slave owners with the loss to slaves because any exchange would have been impossible without a prior redistribution of wealth to slaves. Was freedom less valuable to slaves than their bondage was to masters? Only in the sense that food is less valuable to a starving person with no money than it is to those who are both well fed and affluent. And that sense is virtually irrelevant to any analysis of the cost of slavery to those who were slaves.

Slavery and the Family

Economists have always felt free to poach on the territory of other social scientists, happily raiding the domains of sociology, government, psychology, demography, and anthropology. Hence Fogel and Engerman make no break with tradition in their foray into what has been generally labeled social history. While investigating the economic condition of blacks under slavery, they also examined the impact of slavery on family life. Their conclusions are, arguably, more controversial and more important than their findings on slave economics. For it is here, in the destruction of family ties, that some scholars see the most lasting damage of slavery to black Americans.

FORCED SEPARATION

Under ordinary circumstances families are vulnerable to involuntary separation created by death, military conscription, and so on. But slave families were faced with an additional threat: separation through sale. And it has long been assumed that the great westward movement of the cotton economy meant the separation of a high percentage of families living in less productive parts of the South.

Fogel and Engerman challenge the economic logic of casual separation and use their own and other statistical sources as evidence that they have good reason to be skeptical. Fogel and Engerman believe that the family was a valuable tool exploited by owners in maintaining the productivity and fertility of slaves. The natural family hierarchy could be used to discipline the young and to ensure fair distribution of food and clothing. Kinship ties, moreover, helped ensure proper care for the young, sick, and old and prevent run-aways. Thus planters had economic incentives to encourage marriage, discourage adultery, and avoid relocation that would separate husbands from wives or parents from children.

How might it have been possible for the cotton economy to move west without massive family disruption? The key, Fogel and Engerman argue, was the relative rarity of slave movement through sale: 84 percent of slaves who moved west, moved with their owners. Extrapolating data from one slave-exporting state, Maryland, Fogel and Engerman estimate that the total slave sales (inter and intra-state) averaged only 1.92 percent of the slave population per year. Of slave sales, data from the New Orleans slave market suggest that only 13 percent resulted in the separation of mates. And since 16 percent of slaves moving west changed owners, they figure that just 2 percent (.13 x .16) of the marriages of displaced slaves were destroyed in the process.

Herbert Gutman and Richard Sutch retrace Fogel and Engerman's steps in order to attack both their data manipulation and interpretation. What if, they ask, Fogel and Engerman are correct? Can we then assume that migration posed no serious threat to the stability of the slave family? An annual sale rate of 1.92 percent implies that, over a thirty-five-year lifetime, the average slave would have faced a 49.3 percent chance of being sold. A slave with sixteen close ralatives (two parents, six siblings, seven children, one spouse) could expect to live to see eleven of them sold.

Actually, Gutman and Sutch believe the best reading of the data paints a much more depressing portrait of separations. The percentage of slaves sold rather than moved with their masters may have been as high as 70 percent, as opposed to Fogel and Engerman's 16 percent. And the marriage destruction rate in migration might have been as high as 63 percent.

SEXUAL MORES

Another threat to the slave family, it has been asserted, was interference, motivated by lust or desire for profit, in the sex lives of slaves. Slaves might be sexually abused by masters. Or more likely, owners might encourage early sexual activity by slave women as a means of maximizing the number of children they bore.

Fogel and Engerman do not deny the economic interest of owners in promoting slave fecundity. But they believe that owners typically understood that their long-term interests lay in the high morale and discipline engendered by tight family structures. Hence owners discouraged sex activity among young unmarried slaves—the average age for first births was twenty-two. And they even discouraged early marriage—men, Fogel and Engerman calculate, averaged twenty-four years at their nuptials, while women averaged twenty years.

As for sexual abuse of slave women by whites, the indirect evidence suggests that, while the incidence was not negligible, it was probably not very different than the abuse white women suffered from white men. Based on the Census estimates of the percentage of the slave population born of mixed parentage, Fogel and Engerman calculate that the percentage of slaves fathered by whites was extremely unlikely to have been above 14 percent. Interviews with ex-slaves put the percentage at 4.5 percent, while genetic data from rural black Georgians suggest a figure as low as 1 to 2 percent. There is no hard evidence on the number of black women used as prostitutes. But, Fogel and Engerman maintain, racial prejudice probably kept the demand for black prostitutes low, while the high opportunity cost of taking blacks away from the plantations kept the supply low.

Once again, Gutman and Sutch take issue with the quality of Fogel and Engerman's evidence. And even conditionally accepting their evidence, they have little sympathy for the inferences Fogel and Engerman draw. First, they note that the estimate of first births at age twenty-two is based on estate probate records of the average age differential between mothers and their oldest children. Miscarried fetuses, children who died young, and children who were separated from their parents are thus left out of the calculation.

Reworking the data to allow for these possibilities lowers the *median* age of mothers at first birth to 19.3 years—a figure, incidentally, that matches direct evidence from the records of four plantations examined by Gutman. This age would still be considered rather high in a sexually promiscuous society in which women began menstruating at age twelve or thirteen. But, Gutman and Sutch argue, the age of menarch probably came much later during this era; contemporary evidence from Europe puts it between 16 and 17. Hence Gutman and Sutch conclude that Fogel and Engerman's probate data is actually consistent with the notion that slave women had lost their virginity as young teenagers and became pregnant as early as they were physiologically capable.

Unlike Fogel and Engerman, Gutman and Sutch are prone to accept the 4.5 percent miscegenation rate reported by ex-slaves as a *lower bound* to the actual rate. The simulation model for gene transmission rates offered by Fogel and Engerman as evidence has also been used to estimate that 7.16 percent of black children had white fathers. If the miscegenation rate had been just 4 percent, an average slave mother of seven children would have had one chance in four of bearing the child of a white man. To put the 4 percent rate in another light, suppose that one pregnancy resulted from every four incidents of owner-slave intercourse. Then, on the assumption that only women between fifteen and thirty were vulnerable,[2] the average slave women stood a 58 percent chance of being victimized over the fifteen-year period.

Is it now possible to draw conclusions about the physical or mental condition of blacks in bondage? Not really. Fogel and Engerman effectively challenge our *a priori* convictions that, because owners had the legal right to brutalize their slaves, they also had the incentive to do so, or, in fact, did so. If most slave owners treated chattels as they treated other earning assets—an assumption that has not been proved or disproved—it follows that consideration would be given to constructing positive incentives for hard work and obedience. Thus purely economic considerations might have protected slaves from condemnation to a short, brutish existence.

Economic theory alone, even theory based on strong assumptions about the rationality of slave owners, can take the debate only so far. For rational profit maximizing might also have led planters to emphasize the stick over the carrot. It might have paid, moreover, to encourage sexual promiscuity and to sell slaves at will. Each owner would have had to balance the potential financial gain against the potential cost in terms of lost family cohesiveness and general loss of morale.

Fogel and Engerman, of course, argue that evidence from a variety of sources adds weight to their rational benevolence theory, while their critics believe just the opposite. We remain agnostic. *Time on the Cross* is flawed by overstatements and errors of inference and fact, but it is also true that the bits and pieces of historical record used by both sides are rarely sufficient to dismiss the case for rational benevolence.

---

[2] Note the apparent inconsistency between the age of menarch agreed above, and the implied age here.

Anyone trying to substantiate a theory about slavery is working at a disadvantage. Data samples are small and often unreliable, making inferences drawn from them vulnerable to reinterpretations.

Perhaps the deepest insight generated by the *Time on the Cross* controversy is the subtle shift away from slavery itself as the sole explanation for the plight of black Americans today. It surely is convenient to blame the deep social and economic divisions between blacks and whites on a bunch of morally degenerate and long-gone slave owners. But convenience, like tidiness and other such qualities appealing to textbook writers, can be misleading. Fogel and Engerman's conclusion that blame belongs more to modern racism than to the Peculiar Institution is arresting and deserves to be taken seriously.

Appendix: An Alternative Measure of Exploitation

Fogel and Engerman attempt to measure the slave exploitation rate in the Robinsonian tradition by calculating the ratio of the present value, at birth, of the net slave income capturable by slave owners to the present value of the total income gained through slave labor. This roundabout calculation provides the exploiter's view of labor exploitation in the special historical case of slavery. Equally interesting, perhaps, is the actual Robinsonian exploitation rate: the percentage of the competitive market wage that owners are able to extract from the average slave. What this definition lacks in subtlety, it makes up in simplicity. The Fogel-Engerman variant, unlike the Robinsonian definition, has no intuitive meaning beyond providing a benchmark for the economic viability of slavery.

Richard Vedder, and Ransom and Sutch, have independently calculated the Robinsonian rate; their findings are shown in table 9.3, along with comparable estimates by Fogel and Engerman. Given differences in their estimation procedure, it is striking how similar their results are. Vedder and Fogel-Engerman derive labor's competitive share of income from the estimated coefficients of the production function for southern farms. Ransom and Sutch, leery of using production function estimates, arrive at their more conservative numbers via an accounting route. They take total income and subtract from it the cost of capital, implicit interest costs and depreciation on land, and supervisory costs. The remaining value is then attributed to labor.

Vedder makes no pretense of a detailed computation of slave consumption, the portion of slave earnings the average slave actually got to keep. He simply takes an estimate in the general range employed by Conrad and Meyer and others. Fogel and Engerman use the relatively rough computations prepared for *Time on the Cross*, while Ransom and Sutch rely on the exhaustive critique of the Fogel and Engerman numbers developed by Sutch.

TABLE 9.2

ROBINSONIAN EXPLOITATION RATE

	Vedder	Ransom-Sutch		Fogel-Engerman	
		All Slave Farms	Large Plant	All Slave	Large Plant
Labor Share (%)		49.0	53.3	58	58
Labor Share ($)	85.76	62.46	78.78	73.98	85.80
Slave Consumption ($)	30	28.95	32.12	34.13	42.99
Exploited Income ($)	55.76	33.51	46.66	39.85	42.81
Rate of Exploitation (%)	65	54	59	54	50

Sources: Richard Vedder, "The Slave Exploitation Rate," *Explorations in Economic History* 12 (Oct., 1975), p. 455; Roger Ransom and Richard Sutch, *One Kind of Freedom* (Cambridge University, 1978), p. 203–12; Robert Fogel and Stanley Engerman, *Time on the Cross* (Little, Brown, 1974), vol. II., p. 159.

What should we make of the results? It is obvious that slave owners were able to skim off a very substantial portion of the product of slave labor. Beyond that, however, there is not a lot one can say.

Robinsonian exploitation is not a measure of the misery of slavery. A hopelessly "benevolent" owner who allowed his or her slaves to consume the full value of their product (that is, set the exploitation rate equal to zero) could not fully compensate slaves for their condition of servitude. Nor is it an accurate index of the viability of slavery, unless the age profile of slaves were in equilibrium. A relatively immature slave population might be viable even if the average slave consumed more than he or she earned, while a population with an unnaturally high proportion of slaves of working age might show a positive exploitation rate yet still be unviable in the long run.

One interesting use of the exploitation index is to compare the exploitation of slaves with the exploitation of individuals in a free labor market who are exploited by monopoly consumer goods sellers or labor market imperfections, or monopsony buyers of labor services. Vedder notes that monopsonistic labor markets may have lowered antebellum textile workers' wages in the North by 20–30 percent. DeCanio and Mokyr estimate that northern civilian workers during the Civil War lost at least 47 percent of their wages due to unanticipated inflation (see chapter 11). Ransom and Sutch argue that postbellum southern country stores may have expropriated about 13 percent of sharecropper income by charging monopoly interest on small loans.

Bibliography

*John Blassingame, *The Slave Community: Plantation Life in the Antebellum South* (Oxford University Press, 1972). Social history of slave life, largely reconstructed from slave narratives.

**Giorgio Cannarella and John Tomaske, "The Optimal Utilization of Slaves," *Journal of Economic History* 35 (Sept., 1975). Theoretical model of incentives inherent in master-slave relationship.

**Paul David, Herbert Gutman, Richard Sutch, and Gavin Wright, *Reckoning With Slavery* (Oxford University Press, 1976). Non-technical essays critically analyzing each major argument in *Time on the Cross*. Summarizes much material presented elsewhere in more technical form.

**Paul David and Peter Temin, "Slavery: The Progressive Institution," *Journal of Economic History* 34 (Sept., 1974). Attack on the evidence and conclusions of *Time on the Cross*.

*Stanley Elkins, *Slavery* (Grosset and Dunlap, 1963). Examines the psychology of slavery and why American slavery was pecularily damaging to those affected.

*Robert Fogel and Stanley Engerman, *Time on the Cross* (Little, Brown, 1974). Dramatic reinterpretation of the economics of American slavery.

‡***Robert Fogel and Stanley Engerman, *Time on the Cross, Volume II: Evidence and Methods* (Little, Brown, 1974). Technical appendix.

*Eugene Genovese, *The Political Economy of Slavery* (Vintage, 1967). Modern Marxist historian argues that slavery was incompatible with capitalist economic development.

*Eugene Genovese, *Roll Jordan Roll: The World the Slaves Made* (Pantheon, 1974). Massive research effort on the sociology of slave life.

**Herbert Gutman, "The World Two Cliometricians Made: A Review Essay," *Journal of Negro History* (Jan., 1975). Critical evidence on *Time on the Cross* from a leading social historian.

*William Scarborough, *The Overseer: Plantation Management in the Old South* (Louisiana State University, 1966). Qualitative assessment of the role of the overseer.

*Kenneth Stampp, *The Peculiar Institution* (Knopf, 1956). Masterful description of the economics of slavery by an historian anticipating much of the revisionist view offered by economists.

*Richard Sutch, "The Treatment Received by American Slaves," *Explorations in Economic History* 12 (Oct. 1975). Exhaustive analysis of Fogel and Engerman's evidence on the relatively benevolent treatment of slaves.

**Richard Vedder, "The Slave Exploitation (Expropriation) Rate," *Explorations in Economic History* 12 (Oct., 1975). Using one definition of the concept, Vedder finds a higher exploitation rate than Fogel and Engerman.

Economics and the coming of the civil war

10

Writing about economic interpretations of the Civil War is like walking through a minefield. All the usual problems of analyzing the causes of a complex historical event are here, but made especially sensitive by the importance of the war as an ideological touchstone for historians. Economists are particularly apt to look foolish on this dangerous ground by virtue of their affection for models of "rational" behavior in which the actors understand the consequences of their actions. War is generally an imperfectly foreseen turn of events for at least one side, and typically both.

No one gains, after all, from the loss of life or property. The winning side might, after the fact, decide that the spoils of victory were worth fighting for. But from the perspective of military defeat, losers almost certainly had better alternatives than battle. Hence sensible economic models of conflict resolved only by combat must generally incorporate a special sort of "rational" irrationality: "We must risk war to maximize national interests, even though war itself is rarely worth the cost.

Sensible though this may be, such models are intellectually very unsatisfying. By focusing on the dynamics of conflict rather than on the sources of conflict, they ignore the "big picture." Thus not only is there a compelling case for avoiding a close analysis of the motives of Union and Confederate leaders in the final months before Fort Sumter, but there are equally solid reasons to back away from expansions of the Civil War as an exercise in cost-benefit calculus. Instead, our goal here is to examine the underlying forces that made war likely.

Were there inherent sources of conflict between the North and the

South? One traditional view, going back to Charles Beard in the 1920's, interprets the war as a struggle between competing forms of economic organization: industrial capitalism versus feudal agrarianism. By this account, the political power of the South had to be broken to prevent tradition-bound agricultural interests from holding back the development of modern capitalist institutions. A somewhat different, but not really uncomplementary, view held by many Republican partisans in the 1850's, was nicely stated by the British economist J. E. Cairnes late in the 19th century. Cairnes saw the slave-cotton economy as one that had to expand or die; only by wresting control of the West from free family farmers could the enormous investment in slave labor be rationalized. A closer look, though, shows these analyses to be less than convincing.

The Tariff

Press a Beardian to expand upon the industrialism vs. agrarianism theme and, chances are, the first words will be about tariffs. In the first few decades after the signing of the Constitution, tariffs were used principally as a revenue device. They were set high enough (5–15 percent) to pay a good portion of the federal government's bills, but not so high as to discourage imports significantly and thereby kill the revenue-producing goose. After the War of 1812, however, the nation's struggling manufacturers—notably cotton textile producers—were threatened by competition from British exports. And the first tariff meant specially as a protective device was passed by Congress in 1816.

That act set tariff rates on cotton cloth at 25 percent of value, but a rider was attached allowing rates to go much, much, higher. Cloth priced below 25¢ a yard was to be taxed as if it were worth 25¢, leaving an effective minimum duty of 6¼¢ a yard, regardless of the actual selling price. This minimum was raised in 1824 and again in 1828, leaving the United States with the highest overall tariff rates on manufactured goods that it would ever experience: The ratio of tariffs collected to the value of imports at the dock exceeded 60 percent. Cotton textile imports were hit particularly hard because world competition and enormous productivity gains drove prices sharply downward; Bennett Baack and Edward Ray note that from 1830 to 1832 the effective rate was 71 percent. In In 1833 the tariff per yard of cloth was cut sharply (from 8.75¢ to 8.4¢), but the price of simple cotton sheeting fell much more, leaving the tariff rate at an average of 82 percent!

That was, by no means, the high water mark for cotton tariffs. The duty per yard was pared to 7.53 cents in 1842, but sheeting prices slipped below 7 cents. Only after 1846 did tariffs on cotton textiles fall. The minimum valuation provision was dropped, thereby equalizing the effective and nominal, ad valorem rate at 25 percent. And in 1857 the rate was cut to 24 percent, in line with general manufactured goods duties.

Elementary economics suggests that the North and South had divergent interests on the issue of protective tariffs. Owners of northern factories and skilled manufacturing workers would presumably benefit from protection since the higher prices the tariff would allow manufacturers to charge would be partially reflected in higher profits and higher wages. Producers of nonprotected goods—including virtually all southerners—would foot the bill by getting less manufactures for each unit of exported and nontraded goods they sold.

This is how northerners and southerners perceived the tariff issue, and the division of economic interest is usually cited as a major source of political friction between the two regions. The southern champion of states' rights John C. Calhoun went so far as to estimate the redistributive impact of the tariff between sections. He calculated that southerners lost $15,000,000, or almost $4 per person annually in the form of higher prices. Calhoun's method was hopelessly inaccurate, but there is little doubt that in the 1830's southerners, typically perceived themselves victims of a northern conspiracy.

A New Economic Historian, Clayne Pope, points out that the impact of the tariff on the distribution of income by region is, as a matter of economic theory, ambiguous. Several decades ago the economist Lloyd Metzler proved that, under certain conditions, tariffs may have a perverse effect, actually raising the income of the unprotected industry—in this case raw cotton producers.

Here is how the "Metzler effect" might work: Higher tariffs raise the profitability of textile production, drawing labor away from raw cotton production. As a consequence, the raw cotton supply is reduced, raising the world price for the commodity. If this price effect is sufficiently large, cotton farmers more than make up for the fact that the price of protected manufactured goods has also risen. Total national income could thus go up—the foreign cotton buyers bearing the burden—and the share of income going to cotton farmers could also go up.

Is this, in fact, what happened in the antebellum American economy? Metzler guessed that it did, since the United States held a virtual monopoly on cotton production. With 80 percent of Britain's raw cotton supply coming from the American South, British textile manufacturers would bid up the price sharply when cotton output declined. Actually the problem of analyzing the case is not quite that simple. More than demand insensitivity to price is needed to make the Metzler effect work; and Metzler's model does not really apply directly anyway, since raw cotton was an input in the protected American manufacturing sector as well as an export good.

Pope demonstrates, though, that in a complex model designed to show the tariff's impact on income distribution, the unintuitive result is quite possible. And, strikingly, Pope argues that it is plausible as well. Making reasonable assumptions about the way productive factors and industries will respond to price changes, he simulates the impact of an increase in the textile tariff. While the results can prove nothing—they are no better than assumptions used to generate them—Pope's exercise does suggest that southern land and slave owners could have benefited.

Since Pope published his simulation study, two independent estimates of the relationship between antebellum tariffs and southern income have been made. John James was able to elaborate on Pope's complex but rigid simulation model of the American economy by applying a powerful mathematical tool, the Scarf algorithim. This tool cannot cut to the heart of Pope's dilemma—a lack of solid evidence about how the economy worked—but it does enable James to make his own simulation model somewhat more realistic and to apply some direct estimates of production relationships to the simulation procedure. The tariff, he concludes, probably did injure southern slaveholders and landowners. Free laborers in the North were the big winners, while owners of industrial capital benefited slightly.

Baack and Ray attacked the tariff incidence problem directly: If the Metzler effect is to function, they argue, one should be able to identify statistically a positive relationship between the relative price of raw cotton to cotton textiles on the one hand, and the textile tariff rate on the other. In other words, higher textile tariffs should raise the number of yards of cloth a plantation owner could buy with the proceeds from selling a bale of cotton. Baack and Ray find no such relationship, however. Their statistical analysis supports the conventional view that textile tariffs reduced the terms of trade for cotton farmers.

Economists, then, offer support, albeit weak, for the conventional view that the tariff created a clear division of interest between the north and south. But, taken in perspective, it is hard to hang the Civil War on such slender threads. After the reform of 1846 the odious minimum valuation provision was stricken from the tariff law, reducing duties as a percentage of import value. In pushing this reform through Congress, moreover, the South showed that it was capable of defending its interests effectively within the union. Why, then, should the South see in the tariff a source of conflict irresolvable except through secession?

It could be argued, of course, that while dormant as a popular issue, the tariff conflict was perceived by both sides as fundamental. And southerners understood that if the North ever consolidated its political power, the tariff would go back up agian. The point is reasonably taken, but it hardly constitutes proof that many southerners were willing to risk Civil War over a hypothetical conflict over future tariffs.

Competition for Land

After the tariff, the most frequently mentioned source of regional conflict was land policy. The dramatic growth of cotton output in the four decades before the war was made possible by the availability of fertile land west of the Appalachians. And in the 1850's southern politicians echoed the fears of some of their constituents that restrictions on the right to use slave labor would close the frontier to cotton planters. It does not take intricate reasoning to make economic sense of this political threat; indeed, scholars who agree on little else have viewed land expansion as a vital southern interest.

The argument goes like this: The more good land available to slave owners, the higher the productivity of slave labor. Since the value of slaves is, in part, dependent on expected future labor productivity, securing western land for the slaveocracy helped secure property rights in slaves. Conrad and Meyer, among others, suggested that land expansion was the key to profitability for eastern plantations, whose major cash crop was young slaves. To put it in starker terms, by closing the West to slavery the South would be faced with declining land per worker, and inevitably, declining cotton output per slave. Eventually the quarantining of slavery in the Old South could reduce labor productivity sufficiently to threaten the viability of the institution and thus the entire southern investment in slave labor.

There are numerous problems with this hypothesis. The most obvious is that anyone who looked beyond the rhetoric of "land shortage" would have seen a vast inventory of virgin land suitable for cotton already secured for slave owners. The westward rush of the cotton economy had left much of the good land in the south central region untouched, and the annexation of Texas as a slave state guaranteed to several future generations fertile soil on which to expand. There is nothing hypothetical about this abundance of land: Improved acreage per capita grew in *every* state in the south prior to the Civil War. And Fogel and Engerman estimate that the quantity of land planted in cotton in former slave states *doubled* between 1860 and 1890.

Then, too, there is a confusion between slave productivity and the revenues generated by slave labor. Raising the land-to-slave ratio may increase the amount of cotton a slave can produce, but the productivity increase may be partially or wholly offset in revenue terms by the decline in cotton prices associated with increased cotton supply. Passell and Wright estimate that for each 10 percent addition of land, the value of the marginal product of a slave declined between 1.19 and 1.75 percent. Since the maintenance cost of a slave did not vary much with slave productivity, the surplus left over from the output per slave changed more rapidly than the value of the slave's product. Passell and Wright infer that the corresponding fall in slave prices would thus have been between 1.31 and 1.93 percent.

Actually, the impact on southern wealth as a whole is much greater. As Susan Lee points out, there is no ambiguity in the impact of westward expansion on the revenues derived from land already in use. More land lowers the price of cotton by expanding cotton production, and it lowers the productivity of each acre by reducing the intensity with which land could be worked with a given labor force. Plantation owners lose a small portion of the value of their slaves as the cotton economy expands; at the same time, they lose a substantial portion of the value of their land investment. Note, too, that the great mass of farmers in the South who worked their own land were in essentially the same boat. More land in the West meant lower prices for the crops these slaveless farmers sent to market.

This grim economic reality does not count for much, of course, if southerners did not understand on which side their biscuit was buttered. But if some southerners misperceived their economic interest, Wright notes that many others did not. One South Carolina senator was roundly criticized by the state's press for supporting liberal land expansion policies in 1829. And southern states representatives regularly split on Congressional votes over public land policy through the 1830's, 40's, and early 50's. Research by Dean Yarwood shows that, in 1850, North-South divisions had little to do with Congressional land votes. This conclusion is supported by Lee's analysis of land votes in 1846 and 1852—years before the imperatives of secessionist politics drove the South into a solid front on every national issue.

Competition Between Economic Systems

Those who see the origins of the Civil War in inherent economic conflict—but admit the weakness of the tariff and land arguments—fall back to less specific complaints. The economies of the North and South were remarkably different in the late antebellum years. The North was gradually specializing into an eastern industrial sector powered by immigrant labor and a western sector of family farms, each sector becoming increasingly dependent on one another for markets. The South was culturally independent of the North and economically oriented toward Europe, both as a place to sell cotton and a place to buy manufactures. Economics might provide the North and South little to fight about. But neither did it give them much reason to cooperate as a nation. Hence, the reasoning goes, minor conflicts over the tariff, or over the largely symbolic issue of the legality of slavery in the great plains territories, could easily become foci for sectional paranoia.

The trouble with this argument is that, in spite of differing cultural orientation, the North was in fact economically dependent on the Cotton South and it even had a stake in the continuation of slavery. The free farmers of the western territories might fear direct competition from slave labor, but more generally, northern labor and capital had something to gain and very little to lose from the expansion of the cotton economy and the enslavement of blacks.

The bigger the cotton economy, the larger the output of cotton—and the lower the price of this important raw material for northern textile mills and the better the terms of trade received by northern sellers of manufactures. The institution of slavery, moreover, independently contributed to northern living standards by breaking the natural constraint on labor supply imposed by the family unit in cotton farming, thereby lowering the competitive market price of raw cotton.

Possibly a larger—and certainly a more visible—gain to the North from slavery was the resulting reduction of competition for industrial jobs and markets. As noted in the last chapter, there is virtually a consensus among economic historians that slavery retarded southern industrialization. Perhaps the reason was the incompatibility between factory work and slavery suggested by Wade and Genovese; more likely it was the relative attraction of using forced labor and scarce entrepreneurial talent to grow cotton. Either way, though, the net result was underdeveloped industrial and commercial sectors in the South, leaving much of southern market for manufactured goods, and banking transportation, and insurance services to be filled by northerners.

Free labor in the North had a stake in the continuation of slavery for the very reason that free farmers wanted to keep slaves out of the West. Slavery was an impenetrable barrier for blacks who might otherwise have migrated north to the cities and competed for jobs with whites. Thus northern workers could—and some did—see emancipation as a threat to their livelihoods. In the relatively competitive, rapidly growing economy of the antebellum North, it is unlikely that emancipation would have created chronic white unemployment, but it is likely that it would have meant lower competitive wages and living standards for white workers.

Sectionalism and the Instability of Property Rights

The preceding arguments are rather unsettling. After all, the Civil War was the greatest catastrophe the United States has ever experienced. A far higher percentage of American lives were lost and American property destroyed in the Civil War than in the Revolution or World War I or World War II. Why then would the North and South have risked so much when so very little was at stake?

A possible answer is that a great deal was actually at stake: southern property rights in slaves. This is not to say that the Civil War should be viewed as the logical consequence of the abolitionists' moral crusade against slavery. As we have seen, the North had no economic reason to oppose slavery, and most important, most northerners knew it. They might, in theory, have had moral objections to slavery that overrode narrow economic interest. But the evidence is unpersuasive that this was in fact the situation. Neither public opinion nor the policy-making political elite of the North showed a marked inclination to force abolitionist views on the South.

How then is it possible to argue that slavery was at the root of the conflict between North and South? Barrington Moore sees slavery as a source of inherent instability in the same way that a new weapons technology today, making both sides vulnerable to a devastating first strike, might create military instability. Sectional politics flourished in antebellum America, reflecting cultural differences and the psychological need for group identity more than regional economic differences. This ill-defined political competition might have gone on indefinitely without precipitating a war, were it not for one special perceived vulnerability of the South: Much of the wealth of the South was tied to slave property rights. Claudia Goldin estimates the capital value of slaves in 1860 at $2.7 billion, while Louis Rose puts the figure about a billion higher. Had slavery been abolished in 1860 without compensation to slave owners, white per capita income in eleven cotton states, Gerald Gunderson estimates, would have been 23 percent smaller (see table 10.1). And although most northerners were indifferent to the plight of slaves, a small vocal minority—the abolitionists—were not.

As noted previously, these agitators hardly represented a direct, immediate threat to the South in 1860. But they sharpened southern fears about the long-term security of their property rights. Even though the compromises over tariffs, land policy, and slavery in the territories suggested the South was holding its own in intersectional political scraps, time, geography, and demography were on the side of the North. Looking twenty years down the road, it is possible to envision a Congress dominated by the representatives of family farmers and urbanities whose attachment to slavery was weak and whose votes were potentially available to the abolitionists. Industrialists and the urban working class had a stake in keeping slaves out of cities and on the farms. But from the slave owner's viewpoint, that stake did not offer the sort of absolute protection—the sort of protection the law affords property rights in land—they craved. Why take a chance on the North's common sense and good will when secession offered a permanent solution to the problem?

Gavin Wright sharpens this "cold war" scenario by elaborating on the vulnerability of slave property. In 1860, it would not have been necessary to abolish slavery to render slaves less valuable to their owners.

TABLE 10.1

POTENTIAL INCOME LOSS TO WHITE SOUTHERNERS FROM ABOLITION IN 1860

State	Per Capita Income (all persons)	Per Capita Income (free persons)	% Population Enslaved	% Potential Income Loss to Whites Post-Abolition
Alabama	75	120	45	42
South Carolina	80	159	57	36
Florida	89	143	44	34
Georgia	84	136	44	29
Mississippi	125	253	55	29
Louisiana	131	229	47	24
Texas	100	134	30	24
North Carolina	79	108	33	19
Tennessee	75	93	25	18
Arkansas	95	121	26	17
Virginia	88	120	32	17
Total	91	135	38	23

Source: Gerald Gunderson, "The Origin of the American Civil War," *Journal of Economic History* 34 (Dec., 1974), p. 922.

For as the profitability of slavery debate has brought out, the value of a slave was tied to expectations of future revenues from slave services. During the 1840–60 period, all who owned slaves of working age or below (and had the sense and luck to treat the slaves well enough to keep them alive) earned huge capital gains on their property. Yasuba's estimates show that the average price of an eighteen-year-old male slave rose by 115 percent between 1841–45 and 1856–60. But future increases in value—or even the maintenance of current value—depended upon continued buoyant expectations about both the price of cotton and the security of investments in slave property.

This link to expectations, Wright observes, explains the extreme, almost paranoid, reaction of slave owners to the menace of abolition, their escalating demands for reassurance from the North, their intolerance for dissent on slavery-related issues within the South, and—finally—their decision to risk all in secession. Wright compares owning a slave in 1860 to owning a house in a racially segregated neighborhood today. Individual white homeowners may be entirely free of racial prejudice, not caring whether a black person moves in down the block. But they do care about the resale value of their houses, and thus must worry whether or not others will object to integration.

A slave owner, by analogy, may understand how irrelevant the issue of the legality of slavery in New Mexico or the sanctity of the fugitive slave law in Massachusetts is to the profitability of slave labor in Alabama. Our rational slave owner knows that cotton will not be grown on the desert and that the number of slaves who actually manage to escape to the North will be trivial. But he or she does not know how other slave owners will react to symbolic changes in the legal status of slavery and thus presses vigorously for slavery in the territories and for vigorous enforcement of fugitive slave statutes.

To buttress his argument, Wright examines the attitude of belligerent, seemingly paranoid, secession-minded slaveholders to the question of reopening the slave trade. As part of a general emotional defense of the legitimacy of slavery, some southerners actively participated in a movement to permit international trafficking in slaves. In part, they saw it as a gesture, a direct challenge to the charge that slavery was immoral. In part, too, slave importation was seen as a way to protect the political power of the South: More slaves would mean greater representation in the House—each slave counted as five-ninths of a person for voting purposes—and more rapid westward expansion.

But when the issue was actually voted upon, slave owners rationally perceived their primary interest in the value of existing slave property, not in some metaphysical defense of the system. Additional slaves, they understood, would undoubtedly lower the market price of slaves. No southern state voted to reopen the slave trade, and the Confederate Constitution of 1861 actually left to Congress the right to prohibit the entry of slaves into the Confederacy from slave states that remained in the Union. This may have been only a bluff designed to press wavering states into joining the secession. But it should not be dismissed entirely as evidence of Southern rationality about slave property values.

A most plausible connection, then, between economics and the coming of the Civil War is through expectations. The South had no serious economic grievances with the North, and the North was surely not injured by the expansion of the cotton economy or by the existence of slavery. But southerners held a large proportion of their wealth in property rights under attack by a vocal minority in the North. And even though the South had no good reason to believe that their property would ever be confiscated by Congress, they did have reason to fear that, without solid guarantees, the value of their property could be subject to considerable fluctuation.

Secession was a means of obtaining the sort of iron-clad guarantee that a democratically elected Congress was not about to extend. It was a bold political move and one hardly justifiable if the price was to be a long, bloody Civil War. But it is unfair to burden the decision to secede with the demand that it look rational with hindsight. We know how costly the war would be, and how the South would eventually lose precisely the property it was attempting to protect through secession. Southerners did not know this, and, in fact, had some reason to expect that the North would not fight. From the perspective of slave-owning southerners, secession appeared to be a prudent means of assuring property rights.

Postscript: The Economics of Compensated Emancipation

The emancipation of slaves in the American South was never discussed as a practical issue before the Civil War. Southern slave owners had no desire to free their chattels, with or without compensation; nor did northern political leaders have much motive for tackling the issue. When the war came, Congress appropriated funds to compensate slave owners in the District of Columbia and the border states who had stayed loyal to the Union. But Lincoln's Emancipation Proclamation, the 1863 executive decree abolishing slavery in enemy territory, as well as the postwar 13th amendment to the Constitution (1865) outlawing slavery in the nation, provided no compensation.

Few today question the appropriateness of uncompensated abolition. Slavery is (and was) immoral, and those who profited from its existence had no more right to compensation that do people today who knowingly purchase stolen merchandise. This was not the way most property-owning citizens looked at the issue in the 19th century, however. In countries that abolished slavery it was generally accepted that free society as a whole should bear the burden of the loss. Northern states that abolished slavery long before the Civil War allowed compensation by various means—though as Fogel and Engerman point out, a primary consideration here appeared to be minimizing the cost of emancipation to taxpayers. For that matter, Lincoln and the conservative majority in Congress during the war probably did believe in compensation as a practical and as an ethical matter. Hence it is an interesting, and in a sense a relevant, historical inquiry to ask how slavery might have been abolished in the south without a war.

IMMEDIATE EMANCIPATION WITH
FULL COMPENSATION

Had all slaves in America been purchased by the federal government in 1860 at market price and then freed, the total cost, Goldin estimates, would have been $2.7 billion. Raising that amount all at once from taxes in a country with a GNP of only $4.2 billion would obviously have been impossible. Thus compensation would have necessarily been financed with government bonds, refundable over a long period.

Goldin guesses that slave owners could have been fully compensated

TABLE 10.2

THE COST OF EMANCIPATION IN 1860

		Annual Per Capita Cost		
Plan	Total Cost (million $)	All Free Persons	North-erners	All Persons
Immediate Emancipation	2,700	7.25	9.66	6.30
Immediate Emancipation + Resettlement in Africa	3,084	8.00	10.70	6.90
Emancipation in Next Generation	210	.56	.75	.49
Abolition in 30 Years	550	1.50	2.00	1.30

Source: Claudia Goldin, "The Economics of Emancipation," *Journal of Economic History* 33 (March, 1973), p. 85.

with government obligations paying 6 percent. This interest rate is lower than many estimates of the rate of return on slave investments. But Goldin figures that a lower rate makes sense since slave property was inherently riskier than government obligations. Had Congress issued $2.7 billion worth of thirty-year bonds at six percent, an annual tax of $7.25 per person (excluding former slaves) would have sufficed to meet interest and principle payments (see table 10.2). The annual tax rate would have amounted to about five percent of national income at the beginning of the period, and much less by the time the bonds were fully refunded in 1890. That is a lot of money; no more, though, than the burden assumed by British taxpayers during the decade of the 1830's to pay off former slaveowners in the British West Indies. If Congress had had sufficient foresight to emancipate the slaves in 1850 rather than 1860, taxpayers would have avoided the cost of the enormous capital gains earned on slaves during that decade. The total debt would have been only $1.3 billion, fundable over thirty years at a bargain rate of only $4.80 per person, per year.

Would this scheme have fully compensated slave owners—that is, left them indifferent between keeping their slaves and emancipating them? Not if they shared in the added tax burden placed on the economy by the bond interest and principle payments. Had southerners as a group, as well as former slaves, been forgiven the tax obligation, the annual per capita cost in 1860 would have gone up to $9.66, or about seven percent of GNP the first year. Actually, Goldin notes, it isn't clear that the $2.7 billion market value represents the entire burden of emancipation to white Americans. Once freed, blacks represented an enormous potential problem for a racist society loath to integrate, and many who favored emancipation also believed that it would have to be tied to recolonization in Africa. Had Congress allocated $100 per ex-slave in resettlement costs—a figure well below the actual cost of voluntary resettlements earlier in the century—the total 1860 emancipation bill would have topped $3 billion, or $10.70 annually per northerner.

GRADUAL EMANCIPATION WITH FULL OR PARTIAL COMPENSATION

Morality might have dictated immediate emancipation; precedent, and the practical cost considerations outlined above, did not. The northern states with significant numbers of slaves—New York, Pennsylvania, and New Jersey—opted for gradual emancipation early in the 19th century by freeing the children of slaves after a specified term of service. The point of requiring some years of obligation from the next generation was to eliminate owners' incentives to abandon infants. As discussed in chapter 9, maintenance costs exceeded revenues from slaves until they reached the age of 8 or 9. And an additional decade or more of positive cash flow from slave earnings was needed to offset this accumulated rearing debt. Goldin estimates that the northern state legislatures chose emancipation ages remarkably close to the break-even point, where discounted slave earnings could just compensate for rearing costs.

Gradual abolition, on this model, had much to commend it to practical-minded northerners. The system eliminated slavery in 1½ generations at relatively little cost to owners and no cost to taxpayers. Owners were fully compensated, save for that portion of female slave value attributable to potential gains from reproduction. It did have two drawbacks—apart from the big drawback of consigning all current slaves to life sentences. Owners were encouraged to work young slaves more intensively, since their continuing productivity after the age of emancipation was a matter of economic indifference to the profit-maximizing owner. And owners were also given an incentive to break the law and smuggle their young slaves to the South, where northern emancipation laws had no effect.

Elsewhere in the hemisphere, emancipation schemes were less gradual, and thus more costly either to taxpayers or to owners. Slaves in the British colonies were only forced to work an extra four to six years for their freedom, while owners were compensated with a total of 20 million pounds sterling. Goldin reckons that this sum was not quite sufficient to compensate owners fully. So, in effect, the British plan split the cost of emancipation three ways, forcing slave, owner, and taxpayer alike to share the burden. Venezuela started with a gardual abolition scheme much like the ones first used in the American North. And like the northern states, events overtook the gradual process. An immediate abolition law was passed thirty-three years after the gradual emancipation statute was enacted. Here, however, owners were granted very substantial compensation.

How might gradual emancipation have worked in the American South? Goldin computes the cost of two schemes. If only the children of slaves had been freed, and only at the age when they would have fully returned their rearing costs, the total cost to owners (or taxpayers) would have been the value of female reproduction. This portion of property rights in female slaves was worth about $210 million in 1860. A more liberal emancipation plan would have freed all slaves in 1890, at an 1860 present value cost of $340 million. Combining this with the proviso that children be freed when they had repaid their rearing costs, the total cost comes to $550 million.

Bibliography

‡***Bennett Baack and Edward Ray, "Tariff Policy and Income Distribution: The Case of the United States 1830–60," *Explorations in Economic History* (Winter, 1973/74). Empirical test of the impact of the tariff on the south; supports conventional, intuitive view of the tariff.

** Richard Edwards, "Economic Sophistication in 19th Century Congressional Tariff Debates," *Journal of Economic History* 30 (Dec., 1970). Analysis, from the record of Congressional debates, of how intellectual concepts influenced votes.

** Heywood Fleisig, "Slavery, the Supply of Agricultural Labor and the Industrialization of the South," *Journal of Economic History* 36 (Sept., 1976). Basic case that slavery retarded southern industrialization by making large-scale cotton farming practical.

** Robert Fogel and Stanley Engerman, "Philanthropy at Bargain Prices," *Journal of Legal Studies* 3 (June, 1974). A model for measuring the cost of gradual emancipation and estimates for the northern states and the British West Indies.

** Claudia Goldin, "The Economics of Emancipation," *Journal of Economic History* 33 (March, 1973). Estimates cost of various emancipation schemes and speculates about why they weren't tried.

** Gerald Gunderson, "The Origin of the American Civil War," *Journal of Economic History* 34 (Dec., 1974). Attempts to quantify the incentives to defend slavery by means of war.

‡***John James, "The Welfare Effects of the Antebellum Tariff," *Explorations in Economic History* 15 (July, 1978). General equilibrium analysis of the impact of the tariff on national income and regional income distribution. Finds South was probably injured by the tariff.

*** Laurence Kotlikoff and Sebastian Pinera, "The Old South's Stake in the Interregional Movement of Slaves," *Journal of Economic History* 30 (June, 1977). Examines the impact of hypothetical restrictions on interstate slave movements on slave income.

‡**Susan Lee, "Antebellum Southern Land Expansion: A Second View," *Agricultural History* 52 (Oct., 1978). Subregional impact of westward movement on southern wealth.

**Lloyd Metzler, "Tariffs, the Terms of Trade, and the Distribution of National Income," *Journal of Economic History* 57 (Feb., 1949). Shows the conditions under which a tariff will have the opposite of the intended protective effect and nominates the antebellum American economy as a possible example.

*Barrington Moore, *Social Origins of Dictatorship and Democracy* (Beacon Press, 1967). Chapter 3 explores the classic sources of North-South economic conflict.

***Peter Passell, "The Impact of Cotton Land Distribution on the Antebellum Economy," *Journal of Economic History* 31 (Dec., 1971). Measures the perverse impact of cotton expansion on southern income.

‡***Peter Passell and Gavin Wright, "The Effects of Pre-Civil War Territorial Expansion on the Price of Slaves," *Journal of Political Economy* 80 (Nov., 1972). Argues that depression in cotton prices from the westward movement outweighed higher productivity in determining the income from slaves.

***Clayne Pope, "The Impact of the Antebellum Tariff on Distribution," *Explorations in Economic History* 9(Summer, 1972). Simulation model suggesting the possibility that the textile tariff actually increased southern income.

**Louis Rose, "Capital Losses of Southern Slaveholders due to Emancipation," *Western Economic Journal* 3 (Fall, 1964). Estimate, from Phillips's data, of the capital value of slave assets.

‡**Gavin Wright, *The Political Economy of the Cotton South* (Norton, 1978). Chapter 5 offers Wright's explanation of the role of slavery as a cause of the Civil War.

**Dean Yarwood, "Legislative Persistance: A Comparison of the U.S. Senate in 1850 and 1860," *Midwest Journal of Political Science* 11 (May, 1967). Useful here because it shows the relative lack of importance of land policy in the North-South split.

The economic impact
of the civil war

11

For four long years civil war dominated the fortunes of Americans as no other armed conflict in history. More than 600,000 died—quadruple the United States' casualty rate in World War II—and another 500,000 were wounded. Civil War scars run deep: even at the remove of more than a century, many of us still count it important as to whether our great great grandfathers wore the blue uniform or the gray.

Hence, the war is treated as a watershed in American history—not merely a convenient place to end the first semester, but a social and political revolution of far greater import than the war for independence four score and seven years earlier. Economic historians are no exception; the civil-war-as-watershed fits the notion that American economic history divides neatly into agrarian and industrial periods, with the dividing line sometime between Fort Sumter and Appomattox. This chapter assesses the economic impact of the war, both direct and indirect, and then focuses on the hypothesis that the war signaled the triumph of industrial capitalism.

The Cost of the War

For all the tens of thousands of pages written describing the destruction and trauma caused by the Civil War, economic historians have been diffident about actually totaling up the bill. In part this may be attributed to a sensitivity to the problem of how to place a monetary value on human life, a problem as trying for bloodless economists as it is for everyday individuals. For the underlying body of economic theory, known as welfare economics, tells only how markets value resources, not how much satisfaction people derive from their own existence.

Still, it is interesting to ask a more limited question related to the cost of the war. If the Civil War had not been fought, how much more material resources, valued at market prices, would have been available to the non-military economy? Claudia Goldin and Frank Lewis attempt an answer; their results are shown in table 11.1.

The table's first entry, government expenditures, is reasonably straightforward. The numbers reflect the price of war equipment and supplies, plus the wages and bonuses paid to the military. Since Goldin and Lewis assume that a standing army would have been maintained for national defense even if there had been no war, they net out the estimated cost of a peacetime military budget.

The next item is included to adjust for the fact that the draft was used to coerce service at below the pay scale needed to obtain volunteers. Today there is no way of knowing what it would take to hire a wartime army. But in the 1860's, those drafted could (if they had the money) buy substitutes. Goldin and Lewis use an estimate of the typical payment—$150—as the hidden cost of conscription for those who bought substitutes as well as for those who could not afford to or did not want to. Casualty costs consist of the lost potential earned income of those killed and wounded as a result of the war. Obviously, there are problems in translating this lost income into an objective measure of lost human welfare. It is worth noting, though, that the figure overstates the financial impact

TABLE 11.1

DIRECT COSTS OF THE CIVIL WAR
(in millions of 1860 dollars, discounted at 6% back to June, 1861)

	North	South
Government Expenditures	2,291	1,011
Undercounted Labor Costs Associated with the Draft	11	20
Destruction of Physical Capital	—	1,487
Human Capital Loss		
Killed	955	684
Wounded	365	261
Less the "Risk Premium" Component in Soldiers' pay	−256	−178
	3,366	3,286

Source: Claudia Goldin and Frank Lewis, "The Economic Cost of the American Civil War," *Journal of Economic History* 35 (June, 1975), pp. 304–9.

on the survivors, since much of the lost lifetime wages of those who were killed would have been spent on their own consumption.

Most of the damage to capital was done in the South, where most of the fighting took place, and where the Union Army deliberately pursued a policy of destroying the Confederacy's economic capacity to sustain its military. Data on buildings and implements destroyed, however, are not available. James Sellers has noted that a Senate report estimated the southern war loss in property (exclusive of slave property) at $1.1 billion. But the figure is not reliable because it includes changes in property values related to changes in expectations of future earnings as well as physical damage. Goldin and Lewis resort to extrapolating backward from the 1880 Census to arrive at an estimated 1865 capital stock and then compare that number with the capital valuation in the 1860 Census. Their result, they argue, is probably unrealistically high—a conclusion shared by most other economic researchers interested in this period.

The last item—"risk premiums" on soldiers' wages to be *subtracted* from the war's cost—requires some explanation. Including all pay as a cost of the war would lead to "double-counting," Goldin and Lewis reckon, since a portion of high military wages compensated soldiers in advance for the risk of death or injury. The same cost would be counted once as special combat wages and a second time as lost lifetime earnings for the unlucky 600,000. Goldin and Lewis assume that the entire difference between civilian and military wages consisted of this risk pay, and thus must be subtracted from the actual human capital loss.

Why, by this logic, did the members of the Union Army settle for premium pay of only $256 million as compensation for $1,320 million ($955 million + $365 million) in lost future wages? Perhaps they systematically underestimated the risks, a common error apparently for those who voluntarily go to war. Or perhaps the difference between the actual human capital loss and the required risk premium paid reflected unmeasured non-material benefits the soldiers received in fighting for their cause(s). Even the most cold-blooded economist should be unwilling to put a price on patriotism.

Although the shaky empirical structure behind the Goldin-Lewis estimates makes it difficult to infer very much from them, some kind of reckoning is surely appropriate, if only to get an idea of the magnitude of the war's cost in terms of contemporary productive capacity. The $6.6 billion estimated direct cost is $206 for every American in 1861, and almost twice the average amount consumed by individuals in the last year before the war. Had the same amount been invested in productive resources at a safe 6 percent return, it could have provided each of the 32 million living Americans with an annual bonus forever equal to about 10 percent of 1860 consumption expenditures.

If that does not impress, consider the following scenario: $6.6 billion would have been enough to buy the freedom of all the slaves (at 1860 market value), present each slave family with a 40-acre farm and a mule, and still leave $3.5 billion for reparations payments in lieu of 100 years of back wages. The South's losses alone ($3.3 billion) would have been plenty to cover compensated emancipation, land, and even the mules. Of course no one was sufficiently prescient in 1860 to understand how expensive the war would be.

The Beard-Hacker Thesis: Civil War as Semester Break

For Charles and Mary Beard (and later for Louis Hacker), the Civil War had a grand purpose. By destroying not only slavery but the slaveocracy and thereby transferring political power from landowning southerners to northern industrialists, the war allowed American industrialization to proceed unhindered by rigid anticapitalist interests. Never again would those who pursued profit through industrial capital be thwarted by traditional agrarian attitudes. This is the big picture, the view of the Civil War forest so appealing to those who want to explain how the agrarian land of Jefferson and Jackson awoke one morning to find itself run by Andrew Mellon and Henry Ford. Unfortunately, the perspective from down among the trees offers more complicated insights on the impact of the war.

Perhaps the most troubling aspect of the Beard-Hacker thesis is its attempt to explain the existence of a turning point in economic growth and industrialization that is difficult to identify from historical data (see table 11.2). Stanley Engerman points out that growth in commodity out-

TABLE 11.2

AVERAGE ANNUAL RATE OF GROWTH OF COMMODITY OUTPUT

Year	U.S. Economy	Manufacturing Sector
1840–59	4.6	7.8
1860–69	2.0	2.3
1870–99	4.4	6.0

Interpretation: Manufacturing growth was as rapid from 1840 to 1859 as it was from 1870 to 1899.

Source: Robert Gallman, "Commodity Output 1839–99" in National Bureau of Economic Research, *Trends in the American Economy in the 19th Century*, vol. 24, Series on Income and Wealth, (Princeton, 1960).

put was as rapid in the twenty years before the war (4.6 percent average annual rate) as it was in the 30 years following economic recovery (1870–1900 average annual growth rate = 4.4 percent). Value added by the manufacturing sector grew at an average rate of 7.8 percent from 1840 to 1860, and only 6 percent from 1870 to 1900. It is true that these figures are somewhat misleading since aggregate output growth is partially dependent on population growth, and the declining rate of the latter partially offset the former. Output in per capita terms grew at an annual rate of 2.1 percent from 1870 to 1900, as opposed to just 1.45 percent from 1840 to 1860. But as Engerman notes, the most reasonable explanation of the higher rate in the postbellum decades is the "catch-up" induced by war losses. When the 1860–69 decade is lumped with 1870–1900, the per capita growth rate is virtually the same as the 1840–60 experience.

There is a more conservative interpretation of Beard-Hacker: Growth may not have accelerated for the country as a whole, but the war put the winners in a better position. If growth rates were a competitive matter, if the South's losses counted somehow as the North's gain, this would no doubt be true. According to Robert Gallman's estimates, southern per capita income fell from 72 percent of the national average in 1860 to 51 percent in 1880 and 1900. The share of total personal income going to southerners slipped from 26 percent on the eve of the war to 15 percent 20 years later, while in the same period the share going to the North and Midwest climbed from 70 to 78 percent.

Surely though, the more relevant test is the North's absolute growth performance rather than its relative performance. And here there is some modest tangible evidence of postwar acceleration. The North grew at an average annual per capita rate of 1.3 percent from 1840 to 1860. From 1860 to 1879, however, that rate rose to 1.75 percent, and from 1880 to 1900, it rose again to 1.9 percent. The percentage of income devoted to new capital formation—land improvements, factories, buildings, and so on—shows a similar discontinuity. From 1850 to 1860, the share was 19.4 percent; from 1869 to 1878 it rose to 27.4 percent. These numbers do not *prove*, however, that the Beard-Hacker thesis is correct, since it has yet to be shown that the war generated the political and economic preconditions for growth. The mere temporal coincidence of war in the 1860's, and growth in the 1870's doesn't necessarily mean that the war made the growth possible. Proper evaluation of the Beard-Hacker thesis turns on a close look at the specifics of their case.

WAR AS STIMULUS TO MANUFACTURING

Historians' thoughts about the past are often influenced by perceptions about the present. And the Beards' prove no exception. Writing in the 1920's, they were inspired by the clear impact of mobilization during the First World War on industry to hypothesize a similar experience a half century earlier. In fact, there is little direct evidence of demand stimulus to the manufacturing sector during the Civil War and, on reflection, little reason to believe *a priori* that the war put much constructive demand on industry.

Twentieth-century wars are fought with iron and petroleum; 19th-century wars were foughts with mules and salt pork. Cannons and rifles and ironclad ships were indeed used in the Civil War, but in quantities too small to have much impact on these basic heavy manufacturing industries. Engerman estimates that small arms production used just one percent of total U.S. iron output from 1861 to 1865. The war, moreover, disrupted construction in the most iron-intensive industry of all—the railroads. Projecting from 1855–60 track-laying rates, small arms demand made up just one-seventh of the 1861–65 shortfall resulting from the suspension of rail projects.

That still leaves open the possibility that the war stimulated production and mechanization in other industries—boots, clothing, and agricultural implements are the prime candidates. The data between Census years are sketchy and thus cannot provide conclusive proof one way or the other, but what evidence is available hardly supports the Beard-Hacker thesis. Engerman notes that Massachusetts boot and shoe production (one-half the national capacity) slipped from 45 million pairs in 1855 to 32 million in 1865. Military demand apparently fell well short of replacing lost markets in the South and declining demand from urban dwellers suffering the impact of war inflation (more on this later). Nor is there evidence of mechanization induced by labor shortages raising labor productivity; shoes produced per worker remained virtually unchanged from Census to Census.

The wool textile industry, by contrast, did boom, probably doubling output during the war. And labor productivity—value added per worker in the Massachusetts woolen industry—also rose by twelve percent. But this gain was largely due to the decline in the availability of raw cotton, whose sale was, of course, embargoed by the Union military. Growth in the woolen industry, moreover, less than fully offset the thirty percent production decline in cotton textiles.

Armchair theorizing would suggest that agricultural machinery sales might do very well under the pressure of war demand. Unlike clothing manufacturers, midwestern grain farmers did not depend upon the South for raw materials or markets. The war probably stimulated demand—armies eat a lot of food and waste even more. And there is evidence of increased European demand for North American grain in the early 1860's that would have put further pressure on production. With grain demand high and labor scarce—about one-fourth of the northern adult male population was in uniform—a surge in demand for labor-saving agricultural machinery might follow.

The numbers, however, show no clear deviation during the war from the prewar trend. Sales of mowers and reapers did take off in the decade of the 1850's and manufacturers continued to do well throughout the war. But there is anecdotal evidence that after an extraordinary year in 1861, sales figures slipped: The unsold inventory of reapers held by the McCormick Company after the 1864 harvest is reported to have been unusually high. Perhaps the only really satisfactory way to measure how much the war influenced grain mechanization would be to construct a statistical model of supply and demand and infer from it the degree to which the war shifted the demand function outward. If indeed the war had any positive impact on reaper and mower sales, it was not so great as to be obvious from any casual reading of the figures.

The closer the look for evidence of direct war-related stimulus to industry and/or capital-intensive production methods the larger the disappointment. Manufacturing value added in the two industrial states with five-year census reports—New York and Massachusetts—show declines for the war years. On reflection, this should not really be surprising. No shock was needed to bump the 1860's economy out of a rut—rapid industrialization and the mechanization of grain agriculture were well under way before the fighting was contemplated. Given the fact that the war placed enormous stresses on an economy already going full tilt, that the services of perhaps one-fifth of the labor force was withdrawn from production, and that normal channels of raw material supply and foreign exchange earnings were broken, it would, in retrospect, be surprising if the war did not disrupt industrial growth.

THE CIVIL WAR AND PROFIT INFLATION

In free enterprise economies, unanticipated inflation tends to redistribute income from laborers to owners of land and capital. This follows from the fact that, in the near term, the return to enterprise is a "residual"—what is left over after the bills have been paid. During inflation, most firms' revenues keep pace with market prices. But wages, determined by custom and by infrequent negotiation, tend to lag behind. The real income of the wage labor force slips, and the "slippage" ends up in the profit residual.

This sort of redistribution process figures prominently in the Beard-Hacker explanation of how capitalists managed to gain from the war. Real civilian wages fell sharply, apparently because workers failed to anticipate the decline of the dollar's purchasing power generated by President Lincoln's inflationary war finance policies. The extra resources ended up in the pockets of capitalists who, the argument goes, were predisposed to invest it in additional industrial capacity.

Does the wage lag thesis stand scrutiny? There is no doubt that real wages fell during the war; Wesley Mitchell's 1903 research has never been challenged on this point. Average annual wages in 1860 purchasing power fell from $363 in 1860 to $261 five years later. But there is a question of whether or not they fell because of unanticipated inflation, as the wage lag process suggests. Until recently, the tide of historical interpretation had been running strongly against the Beard-Hacker wage lag hypothesis. But recent research by Steven DeCanio and Joel Mokyr has again put the issue in doubt.

First a look at alternatives to the wage lag hypothesis. One possibility, cited by Engerman, is that reduced labor incomes resulted not from inflation but from deterioration in the quality of the labor force. If the military drew heavily from the pool of skilled wage workers, and if wartime demands brought marginal workers into the labor force, the result might be lower real wages, unadjusted for skill levels. Unfortunately there are no solid data on labor force quality with which to confirm or refute this argument. It does seem logical that wartime labor scarcity would suck unskilled and undisciplined workers into the labor market. But it also seems logical that workers with substantial skills and earning power would be more likely to avoid military service. If skill levels did decline, a precipitous drop would have been required to overcome the positive potential impact of labor shortages on real wage rates. As Engerman points out, it is just this upward pressure on wages that the Beardians somewhat inconsistently use to explain the hypothesized increase in the rate of mechanization.

A more satisfying alternative is offered by Reuben Kessel and Armen Alchian. They too believe that it is unnecessary to resort to the wage lag theory to explain the decline in the purchasing power of wages. Half of the observed fall, the two economists argue, can be attributed to the sharp drop in the international terms of trade caused by export disruption. Before the war, southern cotton generated two-thirds of the nation's export revenues and was a major source of raw materials for northern factories as well. The blockade effectively eliminated cotton exports and actually created northern demand for foreign raw cotton; both phenomena helped to generate a huge balance of payments deficit for the Union.

Exchange deficits can often be financed by loans from foreigners—that, for example, is how in 1973–74 the oil-importing nations managed to adjust in the face of the overnight tripling of petroleum prices. But in 1862 no one was very eager to loan money to the Union; on the contrary, foreigners were eager to repatriate loans to Americans in view of the uncertainties caused by the war. Hence the United States effectively had to do what countries do today in similar circumstances: They devalued their currency.

In the Civil War era this meant going off the gold, or specie, standard, the system whereby exchange rates were automatically fixed by the relative precious metal content of their coins. The Treasury printed paper money—greenbacks—that were not freely exchangeable for gold coins with the same face value. The greenbacks served as a national currency, while, predictably, coins were hoarded for their gold value.

By effectively "floating" its currency against others, the United States allowed international supply and demand to determine the exchange value of the paper dollar. As a result, gold (and foreign currency) prices rose relative to the dollar, and imported goods became far more expensive for Americans who paid their bills in dollars. This reduced the real purchasing power of anyone—wage earner, farmer, capitalist—whose product was sold abroad or who consumed goods made abroad. Kessel and Alchian estimate that, even if wages had been explicitly tied to the cost of goods made in America, higher foreign prices would explain fully half of the observed decline in wage purchasing power from 1860 to 1864.

Most of the remaining deterioration in real wages Kessel and Alchian attribute to changes in taxes. Federal expenditures rose from $63 million in 1861 to $674 million in 1865. A big chunk of these expenditures were financed through the sale of war bonds and by payment with freshly minted greenbacks, but taxes were also raised. The nation's first income levy, imposed in 1862, had relatively little effect on wage earners; most of them were too poor to be affected by the progressive rate structure.

Import duties, so-called turnover taxes, and excise taxes, however, were another matter. With tariff hikes in 1862 and 1864, the downward trend in antebellum tariff rates (see chapter 10) was reversed. By the last year of the war they had again reached an average level of 47 percent. Total customs receipts rose from $39.6 million in 1861 to $102.3 in 1864. The total cost to consumers was probably much greater because added tariff protection also allowed domestic manufacturers to raise prices. In addition, a 5–6 percent tax on manufactured goods instituted in 1864 was often collected at more than one stage of production, doubling or tripling the final rate passed on to consumers. Last but not least, specific excise taxes were placed on many goods in 1862, with rates raised in 1864. Total federal internal tax revenues peaked in 1865 at $209 million, of which, Kessel and Alchian estimate, 85 percent came from sales and excise taxes directly affecting wage purchasing power.

Although Kessel and Alchian cannot quite prove their point because they lack adequate information either on the incidence of the war taxes or on the precise impact of international terms-of-trade deterioration on wage earners' cost of living, they do shift the burden of proof back to the wage lag advocates. Why resort to a theory, they argue, that depends upon the failure of labor markets to determine wages according to productivity, when there are perfectly reasonable explanations that require no such market imperfection?

Two economic historians, Stephen DeCanio and Joel Mokyr, may yet save the last laugh for the Beards-Hacker; their recent research supports the wage lag hypothesis and provides estimates of its magnitude. To separate the effect of unanticipated inflation (the wage lag) from other forces acting on wages, they statistically estimate the determinants of real wages for the 1861–1900 period. "Real" factors—technology, taxes, labor force quality, international terms of trade, labor force size, industrial capacity—can affect the purchasing power of wages in the DeCanio-Mokyr model. But so, too, might unanticipated changes in the general price level. The estimated wage lag is the difference between actual wages paid and the wages the model predicts would have been paid in the absence of inflation. Since neither economic theory nor the estimated equations themselves give the researchers much reason to choose one mathematical specification of the timing of the wage lag over any other, DeCanio and Mokyr offer a range of alternatives. High and low statistical estimates of the lag are shown in table 11.3.

In 1861 they find no evidence of a wage gap—in fact, real wages were slightly higher than would be expected without unanticipated infla-

TABLE 11.3

ANNUAL WAGE GAP FOR AVERAGE
NORTHERN NON-FARM WORKER
(1860 dollars)

Year	Low Estimate	High Estimate	Total Loss in Real Wages from 1860 (million 1860 $)	Low Estimate as % of Total Loss
1861	−15.27	−1.86	14.07	—
1862	16.43	31.21	46.49	35.3%
1863	44.92	66.00	59.17	75.9%
1864	53.75	78.14	95.36	56.4%
1865	48.63	85.50	101.91	44.7%
Total	148.46	258.99	317.00	46.8%

Interpretation: The estimate separates the impact of unanticipated inflation on real wages from other factors reducing wage purchasing power. As column 4 shows, inflation seems to explain a substantial portion of the loss (35–76 percent) in each of the Civil War years after 1861.

Note: Column 4 equals the low estimate (column 1) times the total labor force, divided by the total loss in real wages since 1860 (column 3)

Source: Stephen DeCanio and Joel Mokyr, "Inflation and the Wage Lag During the Civil War," *Explorations in Economic History* 14 (Oct. 1977), p. 324.

TABLE 11.4

THE WAGE GAP AS A MEANS OF FINANCING THE CIVIL WAR

Year	Total Wage Gap Low Estimate ($ millions)	Total Wage Gap High Estimate ($ millions)	High Estimate as % of Federal Expend.	High Estimate as % of Federal Deficit
1861	−31.2	−3.8	—	—
1862	32.5	61.8	16.2	18.2
1863	88.0	129.4	25.7	31.8
1864	107.6	156.4	30.6	46.1
1865	99.9	175.7	26.0	36.9
Total	328.1	523.3	24.5	33.0

Interpretation: Unanticipated inflation may well have cost workers heavily during the war, but their lost wages covered only an estimated 24.5 percent of government expenditures and only 33 percent of the federal war deficit.

Source: Stephen DeCanio and Joel Mokyr, "Inflation and the Wage Lag During the American Civil War," *Explorations in Economic History* 14 (Oct. 1977), pp. 315 and 324.

tion. Thereafter, however, a gap opens up, explaining at least 47 percent of the actual decline in real wages during the war years. But even the highest estimate of the wage gap doesn't fully account for the deterioration in worker living standards. The explanations Kessel and Alchian offer may well account for the rest.

As remarkable a phenomenon as the wage lag may have been, it is difficult to argue that it can fill the very large shoes in which the Beardians have placed it. At the time of the Civil War, a relatively modest proportion of the northern labor force worked for wages—DeCanio and Mokyr put the figure at 28 percent. Hence even a major "inflation tax" on this small, poorly paid group doesn't add up to much. The highest DeCanio-Mokyr estimate of the average annual wage gap ($103.7 million) is less than one-fourth of average northern capital formation in the late antebellum period. And as table 11.4 shows, it accounts for (at most) 25 percent of total federal expenditures during the war, and only 33 percent of the difference between government expenditures and tax revenues.

CIVIL WAR FINANCE

The limited impact of the wage lag does not necessarily rule out the possibility that financial policies stemming from the problems of war finance were good for industrial growth. Jeffrey Williamson argues persuasively that, while Civil War finance sharply reduced industrial growth during the war, the government's handling of the war debt and biased tariff policies in postbellum years enabled the North to quickly catch up to its long-term growth path.

As noted before, taxes played a relatively minor role in paying for the war. The lion's share of the federal war effort (74 percent) was financed through the sale of interest-bearing bonds. This made it possible to pay for the war without cutting very deeply into the resources available for personal private consumption. To use a term now in vogue, the federal government "crowded out" private investment expenditures by exchanging its bonds for the financial resources private investors would otherwise have made available for purchases of farm machinery, factory construction, housing, and so on. There is no estimate of the quantitative importance of this crowding out. Williamson notes, though, that increases in the federal debt during the war represented 15.5 percent of northern GNP, and according to Robert Gallman, gross investment in the last decade before the war was 19.4 percent of GNP.

Hence if just one-fourth of gross investment went toward the replacement of depreciated capital equipment—a good ballpark guess—federal deficit spending financed by bond sales may have equaled more than 100 percent of expected net investment! To put it another way, the private non-war-related capital stock of the North may have actually shrunk during the Civil War, as scarce investment resources were channeled into the war machine. Zero (or negative) civilian net investment during the war is not a certainty; the DeCanio-Mokyr estimated wage lag suggests that a piece of the deficit was absorbed out of reduced consumption by wage laborers. There seems little doubt, though, that the direct impact of the Civil War finance on private investment was substantial.

Were this the end of the tale, the Beardians would come up short again. But there is little doubt that postwar government financial policies were almost perfectly tailored to allow the private investment sector to recoup. The initial response of the government was to use the large federal tax revenue surpluses earned after the war to retire the greenbacks printed during the conflict. Congress soon rejected the greenback retirement strategy, however, in favor of a policy of first reducing the interest-bearing debt outstanding. Between 1866 and 1893, Williamson reports, the stock of greenbacks was only pared from $429 million to $374 million. During the same period, debt retirement was pursued relentlessly: Government bonds held by the private sector declined from $2.33 billion in 1866 to $587 million in 1893.

The decision to dump the federal debt instead of lowering taxes or retiring government paper money produced the opposite effect of "crowding out." Wealthy investors exchanged their accumulated war bonds for money, which, it is reasonable to assume, was reinvested in private capital. Assuming a dollar-for-dollar shuffle from government bonds to private investment, Williamson calculates that one percent of GNP per year extra was thereby made available to the private capital market between 1866 and 1872. Between 1872 and 1878 the comparable figure is 0.8 percent of GNP.

To this must be added the extra money available for investment due to the government's decision to maintain a regressive postwar tax structure. Taxes were collected from the low end of the income scale to pay war debt interest to those at the high end. Since the wealthy saved a higher proportion of their income than the poor, this regressive redistribution increased the national savings rate. Following Engerman, Williamson guesses that high-income interest recipients saved 40 percent more of their added income than the poor. He is thus able to estimate that the net impact of interest payment redistribution from poor to rich was to raise investment by 1.8 percent of northern GNP immediately after the war. A full accounting of his numbers is shown in table 11.5.

As can be seen from the last column, government borrowing, minus

TABLE 11.5

FEDERAL DEBT MANAGEMENT AND NORTHERN CAPITAL FORMATION

Years	Federal Bond Change as % of GNP	Net Interest Redistribution Available for Reinvestment as % of GNP	Bonds + Interest as % of GNP
1849–59	0	0	0
1861–66	−15.5	0.7	−14.8
1866–72	1.8	1.0	2.8
1872–78	0.1	0.8	0.9
1869–78	0.8	0.9	1.7

Interpretation: Column 1 shows the change in federal debt as a percentage of national income. A positive percentage indicates that the government was retiring bonds, freeing capital for use in the private sector.

Column 2 shows the impact on savings associated with taxing poor people to pay government bond interest to rich people.

Column 3 shows the combined impact on the percentage of income available for private investment.

Source: Jeffrey Williamson, "Watersheds and Turning Points: Conjectures on the Long Term Impact of Civil War Financing," *Journal of Economic History* 34 (Sept., 1974), p. 651.

payment of interest to the wealthy, set back private capital formation by about 14.8 percent of northern GNP during the war. In the immediate postwar years (1866–72), however, debt repayment plus regressive interest transfers allowed a 2.8 percent catch-up in investment. Over the 1869–78 period, the catch-up rate is 1.7 percent of GNP.

These numbers constitute a substantial portion of the savings spurt in the postwar decades, and as Williamson notes, they probably are an underestimate of the overall impact of conservative federal debt management. After the war, substantial quantities of government securities were purchased from Americans by European investors who were once again confident that the federal government would honor its debts. These foreign purchases—at least in part attributable to the clear policy of the government to refund the national debt quickly—had a complementary "uncrowding" impact, freeing domestic funds for capital goods purchases. Hence, Williamson argues, the decision to retire the debt may explain as much as half of the postwar bulge in capital formation.

Not only did federal policies free funds for investment, they also may have reduced the relative cost of capital goods like machinery and transport equipment, thereby increasing the expected profitability of postwar investment expenditures. Table 11.6 shows the abrupt decline in relative capital goods prices during the Civil War decade and the enduring price edge capital goods buyers maintained over consumption goods buyers thereafter. This shift is perhaps the most dramatic evidence yet of a Civil War "watershed" favoring industrial capitalism in the Beard-Hacker sense. Williamson argues that the change was not a statistical accident, nor a result of invisible economic forces. Rather it was a function of tariff policies instituted during the war and then maintained in the postwar decades. The war tariffs protected most internationally traded goods, but their relative price impact on consumer goods was much greater than on capital goods. Assessing the incidence of tariffs is a complex task, as the unintuitive results of Clayne Pope's pre–Civil War simulations demonstrate (see chapter 10). Still, there is reason to believe that the postwar tariff was made to order for the Beardians: A tariff model constructed by Williamson generates the relative price effects shown in the data (see table 11.6).

ECONOMIC LEGISLATION

Once the South seceded, the log jam on economic legislation stalemated by southern Congress people was easily broken. Hacker makes much of this shift in political power, seeing in it the legislative mandate for an industrial revolution. Tariff policy figures prominently here, as we have just seen. But Beard-Hacker defenders had more in mind; to wit: the Homestead Act, railroad subsidies and land grants, contract labor laws permitting overseas recruitment of workers, the creation of a national banking system, and land grant subsidies to colleges.

TABLE 11.6

RATIO OF CAPITAL GOODS PRICES TO THE OVERALL PRICE LEVEL
(index 1929 = 100)

Year	Price Index (Capital Goods/ All Goods)	Year	Price Index (Capital Goods/ All Goods)
1839	111.9	1899–1908	77.2
1849	109.4	1909–18	94.8
1859	103.4	1919–28	100.3
1869–78	86.6	1929–38	107.3
1879–88	89.3	1939–48	108.5
1889–98	81.2	1944–53	111.6

Interpretation: The table shows a strong, continuous price trend favoring buyers of investment goods over all goods through 1909. Williamson associates this trend favoring investment in part to tariffs.

Source: Jeffrey Williamson, "Watersheds and Turning Points: Conjectures on the Long Term Impact of Civil War Financing," *Journal of Economic History* 34 (Sept. 1974), p. 654.

Evaluating the overall impact of these major legislative initiatives is difficult, Engerman concludes; the connections between industrial growth and institutional change are not very well defined. Contract labor was rarely used after it was legalized. Rail construction subsidies, though justifiable in terms of their rate of return on investment, are now thought to have had little effect on national income. There is not much evidence, one way or the other, about the effect of national banking or the distribution of free land to Homesteaders. But enough is known about 19th-century banking to be skeptical that centralized regulation would have much impact on capital markets. And there is no clear break in tradition associated with giving away public land to small farmers. Land had been getting progressively cheaper and easier to finance ever since 1800. Moreover, land cost, as we have seen, was a relatively minor portion of farmmaking costs, so it is doubtful that the promise of free land would "democratize" land ownership or hasten the westward movement to any significant degree.

What, then, is the bottom line on the Beard-Hacker thesis? Surely we are suspicious of the grand theme. The Civil War did not eliminate fundamental impediments to industrial growth since it is hard to find impediments to be eliminated. The war cost the North dearly, setting back the process of industrialization and retarding the rate of economic growth during the years of struggle. On the other hand, the war proved to be less of a hindrance to northern growth than it might have been. Evidence of an industrial wage lag and regressive war taxation suggests that the urban working class absorbed more than its share of the war burden. And the decision to refund the federal debt, and to continue to protect northern consumer goods producers from foreign competition, made a rapid northern catch-up possible after the war.

The last word on Beard-Hacker simply cannot be written today. It is true that Beard-Hacker advocates have left themselves extremely vulnerable to criticism, both on their evidence and their logic. But from the current perspective, early attacks by New Economic Historians seem somewhat unbalanced. The fact that Beard-Hacker partisans lose the paragraph-by-paragraph debates on points doesn't necessarily mean that the thesis itself is wrong. We just do not know enough about the impact of postwar institutional changes or the impact of political realignments caused by the war on those changing institutions to make a judgment. Call it the eighth round of a fifteen-round bout—Beard-Hacker are behind, but there is no K.O. in sight.

Bibliography

*Charles and Mary Beard, *The Rise of American Civilization* (Macmillan, 1927). Seminal (though probably misleading) essay on the Civil War as a source of industrial stimulus.

*Thomas Cochran, "Did the Civil War Retard Industrialization?" in Ralph Andreano (ed.) *The Economic Impact of the Civil War* (Cambridge, Mass.: Schenkman, 1967). Debunks the Beard thesis on the Civil War as industrial watershed.

‡***Stephen DeCanio and Joel Mokyr, "Inflation and the Wage Lag During the American Civil War," *Explorations in Economic History* (Oct., 1977). Estimates the impact of inflation on northern wage income; partial support for Mitchell.

**Stanley Engerman, "The Economic Impact of the Civil War," *Explorations in Economic History* 3 (Spring/Summer, 1966). Lucid critique of Beard-Hacker thesis; rebuts the argument that Civil War fundamentally altered the economy.

**Claudia Goldin and Frank Lewis, "The Economic Cost of the American Civil War: Estimates and Implications," *Journal of Economic History* 35 (June, 1975), Two approaches to measuring the dollar cost of the war.

*Louis Hacker, *The Triumph of American Capitalism* (Columbia University Press, 1940). Classic statement of Beard-Hacker thesis.

**Reuben Kessel and Armen Alchian, "Real Wages in the North During the Civil War: Mitchell's Data Reinterpreted" in Ralph Andreano (ed.), *The Economic Impact of the Civil War* (Cambridge, Mass.: Schenkman, 1967). Attributes fall in wages during the Civil War to deterioration in the international terms of trade, rather than to income redistribution.

*Wesley Mitchell, "The Greenbacks and the Cost of the Civil War" in Ralph Andreano (ed.), *The Economic Impact of the Civil War* (Cambridge, Mass.: Schenkman, 1967). Excerpt from his 1903 book, propounding thesis that labor paid for the northern war effort in reduced real wages.

**James Sellers, "The Economic Incidence of the Civil War on the South," in Ralph Andreano (ed.), *The Economic Impact of the Civil War* (Cambridge, Mass.: Schenkman 1967). Assessment of economic losses, largely based on census data.

**Jeffrey Williamson, "Watersheds and Turning Points: Conjectures on the Long Term Impact of Civil War Financing," *Journal of Economic History* 34 (Sept. 1974). Assesses the positive impact on growth of postwar financial policies.

The south after the
civil war

12

For the northern economy, the Civil War emergency resulted in a brief pause in long-term expansion. Northern per capita commodity output held its own, growing at a somewhat retarded, though historically not unhealthy, average annual rate of one percent from 1860 to 1870. And economic acceleration after 1870 was sufficient to keep the growth rate for the 1860–80 period above the achieved from 1840 to 1860. For the South, however, the war appears to have been a great economic as well as military trauma.

In 1860, southern per capita commodity output was slightly higher than the North's, thanks largely to the splendid returns of cotton agriculture in the fertile lands west of the Appalachians. But while the North was recording an overall per capita gain of 9 percent in commodity output during the Civil War decade, southern per capita output slipped by 39 percent. For the last thirty years of the century, although the South did grow at about the same average pace as the North, the huge income gap opened during the war decade began to close for good only around World War II.

It is not difficult to come up with an explanation for this long-term southern distress. In fact, the real problem is choosing among an abundant variety of plausible theories. Here, we survey competing explanations for the South's dismal economic performance and then consider a closely related issue—the bitter experience of ex-slaves in the hostile postwar world.

The Southern Economy in Decline

It is hardly remarkable that the Civil War's losing side took a greater economic beating than the winning side. With just half of the population, and less than half the capacity to feed, clothe, arm, and transport its military, demands on the private economy associated with the fighting effort were naturally far greater in the South. Then, too, much of the war was fought on southern territory. Major cities, including Charleston, Richmond, and Atlanta were destroyed by the Union army. Whatever livestock and food supplies in the path of the fighting that were not requisitioned by Confederate forces were confiscated by the boys in blue. The Goldin-Lewis extrapolation of $1.5 billion in war-related capital destruction, and Seller's estimate of $1.1 billion in property loss (40 percent of the total property value) may somewhat overstate the actual physical damage. There is no doubt, however, that the damage was extensive.

Historians have generally accepted this damage as the primary source of the southern economic decline. This interpretation also suited succeeding generations of southerners, who blamed the long postwar malaise on the Yankees-who-stole-the-silver-tea-set. Roger Ransom and Richard Sutch, however, are skeptical that so great and lasting a decline can be explained so easily. After all, rapid recovery after appalling levels of war destruction appears to be the rule rather than the exception in modern history. Ransom and Sutch cannot literally prove that the capital loss was unimportant in explaining the South's relatively slow recovery. But they can, and do, offer some contradictory evidence.

Contemporary accounts suggest that damage to rail lines and rolling stock was quickly repaired, and that southern transportation was virtually restored to prewar capacity by 1870. Manufacturing establishments in the towns and cities of the cotton belt—presumably a prime target of the Union forces—were producing about 5 percent more output (with about 5 percent more invested capital) in 1870 than they had in 1860.

Manufacturing, of course, generated a trivial percentage of southern income in both 1860 and 1870; agricultural commodity production remained the key to the economic fortunes of the South. But here, the indirect evidence suggests no shortage of capital. If the loss of work animals—the Census records a one-third decline between 1860 and 1870—was a serious constraint on output, the result might be an increase in the price of the remaining stock as farmers bid for the scarce resource. Yet, Ransom and Sutch report, the inflation-adjusted price for mules was lower in 1870 than it had been at any time during the 1850's. In terms of the relative price of mules and cotton, the decline was dramatic—a mule colt that would have fetched 1.03 bales of cotton in 1859 was worth only .54 bales in 1870.

Why, then, was southern per capita commodity output in 1880 still 20 percent below 1860 levels? The list of competing explanations is long. An early favorite, expounded by Conrad and Meyer, cites the South's loss of its export monopoly position during the war, as European factories replaced lost American supplies with Indian, Brazilian, and Egyptian cotton. Once other growers were induced to clear and plant new cotton land for the European market, the argument goes, they were reluctant to switch back to other crops, and America's lost market share became doubly difficult to recapture. As table 12.1 illustrates, the South's share in the huge British cotton market dipped to 10 percent during the war blocade, and total share recovery took more than a decade after hostilities ended.

TABLE 12.1

AVERAGE ANNUAL BRITISH COTTON IMPORTS
(in 1,000's of bales)

Years	U.S.A.	India	Brazil	Egypt	U.S. Percentage Share
1850's	1638	406	132	103	72
1860	2581	563	103	110	77
1861	1842	987	100	98	61
1862–65	216	1418	206	282	10
1866	1163	1867	408	200	31
1867	1226	1511	437	198	35
1868	1269	1452	637	201	35
1869	1040	1496	514	227	31
1870–71	1957	1150	459	246	50
1872–73	1651	1179	595	317	42
1874–75	1909	1048	461	291	50
1876–77	2041	649	324	313	60
1878–79	2330	469	102	220	73
1880–81	2688	544	176	256	72
1882–83	2670	870	291	249	65

Interpretation: The U.S. prewar share of the cotton market was not recovered until the late 1870's. India and Brazil, which had picked up the market during the Civil War gradually lost it again—but the regression took over 15 years.

Source: Thomas Ellison, *The Cotton Trade of Great Britain* (Augustus Kelley, 1968) cited in Gavin Wright, "Cotton Competition and the Post Bellum Recovery of the American South" *Journal of Economic History* 34 (Sept., 1974), p. 611.

Mark Aldrich offers an alternative reason why, once lost, the market recovery was so slow. By abandoning the fixed international exchange rate based on the gold content of the dollar, dollar exchange rates "floated" on world money markets until rates were again fixed in 1879. This effectively depreciated the dollar in world trade during the war. At one point, it cost 2.5 paper dollars to buy one gold dollar or its equivalent in foreign gold-backed currency; in 1866, the ratio was still 1.4:1. However, after the war, Aldrich argues, a combination of deflationary federal policies, increased world demand for midwestern grain, and inflows of capital from Europe whittled away this market-determined international gold premium more rapidly than gains in the domestic purchasing power of the dollar would have dictated. The underlying changes in the structure of world trade and capital movements that caused the dollar's gains were not necessarily bad for the United States. Nor did they result from some conscious northern plot against the South. However, rapid postwar dollar appreciation did have the effect of reducing foreign demand for American cotton sold in dollars by making dollars more expensive in terms of foreign currency.

Gavin Wright asserts that these "market displacement" theories alone cannot explain why the southern economy never recovered its prewar growth path. Market share doesn't determine the profitability of growing cotton; it is the price of cotton in terms of what it will buy producers that really counts. Only if changes in the international economy [Conrad and Meyer's foreign competition in production, or Aldrich's dollar appreciation] reduced the purchasing power of American cotton producers from prewar levels can the decline in market share be tied to the South's problems. Yet as table 12.2 indicates, the real price of cotton remained consistently above the level that had allowed the South to thrive in the 1850's.

There is still a sense, though, in which the Conrad-Meyer-Aldrich notion is relevant to the South's postwar problems. If the Civil War had never happened, it might be argued that foreign competitors would not have been induced into expanding cotton production in the first place, and the South would have been able to sell any given quantity of cotton it produced for a higher price. Similarly, if federal policies had not been so firmly directed toward the restoration of the international gold standard in the 1870's, foreign demand for American cotton would have been greater, and the South's income would have been greater, too.

These counterfactual hypotheses can be restated in formal terms: The war and subsequent economic policies tended to shift forward the foreign supply function for cotton (increasing the amount of cotton offered for sale at any given price) and shift backward the foreign demand curve for American cotton (reducing the amount of American cotton foreigners would buy at any given price). Wright tests their validity by

TABLE 12.2

COTTON PRICES IN NEW YORK
(cents per pound)

Year	Nominal Price	Real Price (1880 $)	Year	Nominal Price	Real Price (1880 $)
1850's	11.45	11.76	1872	20.48	15.06
1860	11.00	11.83	1873	18.15	13.65
1861	13.01	14.62	1874	17.00	13.49
1862	31.29	30.09	1875	15.00	12.71
1863	67.21	50.53	1876	13.00	11.82
1864	101.50	52.59	1877	11.73	11.07
1865	83.88	45.07	1878	11.28	12.40
1866	43.20	24.83	1879	10.38	11.53
1867	31.59	19.50	1880	12.02	12.02
1868	24.85	15.73	1881	11.34	11.01
1869	29.01	19.21	1882	12.16	11.26
1970	23.98	17.76	1883	10.63	10.52
1871	16.95	13.04	1884	10.64	11.44

Interpretation: The price of cotton fell sharply and continuously between 1864 and 1879. But this masks the fact that the purchasing power of a pound of cotton was about the same in the 1870's and 1880's as it had been in the boom years of the 1850's.

Source: M. B. Hammond, *The Cotton Industry* (Macmillan, 1897), reproduced in Gavin Wright, "Cotton Competition and the Post Bellum Recovery of the American South" *Journal of Economic History* 34 (Sept., 1974), p. 611.

statistically estimating the supply and demand function for cotton, and then inferring from the estimates whether market conditions were changed fundamentally by the war.

Wright discovers that Indian, Brazilian, and Egyptian cotton supply curves were indeed shifting outward, suggesting that competition from these countries was growing over time. But his estimates offer no comfort to the Conrad-Meyer view that the war experience was at the root of the supply shift. The supply curve of the South's largest competitor, India, grew as fast before the war as it did during and immediately after. In years subsequent to 1870, Wright notes, Indian cotton exports were below 1860 levels in spite of relatively high cotton prices and years of Indian commitment to cotton marketing.

The decline, Wright speculates, was probably related to Indian food shortages (which induced farmers to return to subsistence crops), to problems with cotton plant diseases, and to changing tastes and technology, which made Indian short-staple cotton less attractive as a substitute for American medium-staple varieties. Speculation aside, there is nothing in the numbers to suggest that the Civil War made India a tougher competitor for foreign cotton markets.

Brazil and Egypt were much smaller producers than India. Hence shifts in their supply functions had less impact on the demand for American cotton. Even so, they too offer little support to Conrad and Meyer. There is no way to differentiate statistically the causes of prewar and postwar Egyptian supply expansion. In the five years following the Civil War, growth actually slowed below the statistically predicted rate. Brazil, on the other hand, may have shifted its supply function outward in response to American supply disruptions. However the observed shift is small, and quite possibly related to factors other than the American conflict. The evidence, thus, is too meager to provide a satisfying explanation of southern economic retardation.

Evaluating Aldrich's theory, Wright argues, is more difficult—largely because the relationship between exchange rates and American cotton prices was simultaneous in nature: Certainly, as Aldrich argues, exchange rates caused changes in cotton prices. But so, too, did the price of this key export good cause shifts in exchange rates. We don't know which end is the tail and which end is the dog.

Wright points the way out of the measurement dilemma. He offers a direct statistical test of the impact of the "adjusted price ratio"—the extent to which the dollar price of gold was out of line with dollar purchasing power—on the demand for American cotton. Wright estimates the determinants of cotton demand, including in his model the adjusted price ratio as an explanatory variable. He discovers a positive statistical relationship, suggesting that Aldrich has the equation reversed: High cotton prices probably affected exchange rates more than the other way 'round. This statistical exercise doesn't prove that Aldrich is wrong. But it does show that statistics provide no particular support for arguing that postwar federal policies were wrecking the world market for American cotton.

Wright's own interpretation of southern retardation relegates the Civil War to a minor role. The trauma of war, he argues, camouflages the fundamental dependence of the southern economy on world demand for cotton. It is in the changing character of demand that Wright identifies the real culprit. In the three decades before the Civil War, the demand for cotton expanded at roughly 5 percent a year—that is, on average, the amount of cotton that textile producers would buy at a given price increased annually by 5 percent. Prices fluctuated from year to year because crop size varied with the weather. But in the long run, Wright notes, cotton suppliers responded as textbooks expect a competitive economy to respond, expanding output at constant cost to maintain the real price of cotton at about 11¢ a pound (1880 prices). Five percent cotton output growth at a stable price meant rapid extensive economic growth for the South throughout the antebellum years.

Now consider the impact of demand changes on the postwar cotton market. Wright's estimate of the world demand curve for cotton reveals a minor change in the demand response to price, making price some-what more sensitive to year-to-year fluctuation in crop size, and a major change in the average annual growth in demand. Where demand had been growing at 5 percent (1820–60), it slowed to 1.3 percent per year for the period 1866–95. Even when extended through the cotton boom years prior to World War I, the 1866–1913 estimated growth rate is only 2.7 percent, or about half the antebellum average.

Hence, with or without the war, it would have been impossible for the South to continue along the path that had led to economic success before 1860. The long boom in cotton textiles was sagging, presumably because the world market for inexpensive cotton clothing was finally sat-urated. Wright concludes that the American South felt the pinch in the counterfactual sense that any suppliers' attempt to expand output faster than sluggish demand growth would have led to price declines for raw cotton. Cotton, the foundation for an agricultural empire, could support only a finite amount of weight.

Ransom and Sutch concentrate their explanation on an entirely dif-ferent change in the southern economy: the reduction in labor supply associated with Emancipation. Under slavery, they find, blacks started working earlier in life, worked more days each year, and worked more hours each day than poor whites. Hence it is reasonable to expect that, with freedom, they would spend some of their potentially greater in-come on time off. Indeed, Ransom and Sutch estimate that freed black children (ages 10–15) and freed women put in only about half as many hours of work per year, while freed men cut their annual hours of work by about one-fifth. As table 12.3 shows, the net effect of emancipation was to reduce average rural black work effort per capita between 28 and 37 percent.

Such a drastic reduction in labor supply plausibly explains much of the shortfall in postwar output. Blacks had supplied about 70 percent of southern labor before the war, so a 37 percent reduction in black labor could indeed cut total southern labor per capita by as much as 26 per-cent. Since 1859 crop yields were 25 to 50 percent above what might be considered normal in antebellum times, the combined effect of a return to expected output per laborer and the reduction in hours worked due to emancipation probably reduced per capita output by 57–59 percent. In fact, physical productivity actually fell to 52 percent of the 1859 level. The sharp decline in southern economic fortunes can thus be entirely ascribed to factors other than the war itself.

TABLE 12.3

DECLINE IN WORK HOURS PER CAPITA
BY EMANCIPATED BLACKS

Source	Percent Change	
	Low Estimate	High Estimate
Fraction of Rural Population Employed	−17	−24
Number of Days Worked per Year	−8	−11
Hours Worked per Day	−9	−10
Cumulative Impact	−28.3	−37.2

Source: Roger Ransom and Richard Sutch, "The Impact of the Civil War and of Emancipation on Southern Agriculture," *Explorations in Economic History* 12 (Jan., 1975), p. 14.

Note the contrast between Wright, on the one hand, and Ransom-Sutch on the other. Wright's explanation centers on demand factors, Ransom-Sutch's on supply factors. Can they be reconciled? Yes; in fact, Peter Temin manages precisely this task.

Suppose, Temin asks, southern cotton output had followed the observed postwar pattern, but (counterfactually) demand had continued to grow at the healthy 5 percent prewar rate? Then cotton prices, and income from cotton sales, would have been about 80 percent higher in 1877–84 than they actually turned out to be. Since agriculture accounted for about 80 percent of income in the major cotton-producing states and cotton created about half of agricultural income, a continuation of demand growth at the prewar rate, superimposed on postwar supply conditions, would have raised income per capita by about 32 percent (.80 × .80 × .50 = .32). Conveniently, any supply response to such hypothetically higher prices that raised cotton output (without reducing other crop outputs) would have little effect of total southern income since the demand elasticity for cotton was about equal to one. Any greater volume of cotton would be just offset by lower cotton prices.

Suppose, instead, postwar demand had slowed on schedule, but emancipation had somehow left per capita crop output on the prewar growth path. Total cotton output would have been one-third to one-half greater, and (using an estimated demand elasticity of 1.5) total cotton revenues would have been 15–25 percent greater. The increase in cotton revenues would have raised southern per capita income, Temin estimates, between 5 and 10 percent. That is not the entire gain, however, since the output of other commodities also would have increased roughly in proportion to cotton. Assuming that the national demand curve for these other southern commodities—largely food—was very responsive to change in southern prices, a one-third to one-half increase in output would have raised revenues proportionately, and total southern income would have been augmented by 15–20 percent. Hence the total increase of revenues on all commodities due to an outward shift in labor supply would have been 20–30 percent (5–10 percent from cotton, the rest from other crops).

This analysis suggests that the impact of Wright's demand stagnation and Ransom-Sutch's labor force withdrawal are on the same order of magnitude. Demand changes, other factors remaining constant, reduced 1880 per capita income by about 30 percent. Supply changes, other factors constant, reduced per capita income 20–30 percent. Note one important difference, though. Cotton demand stagnation generated a real loss of welfare to the South, while the withdrawal of black labor due to emancipation merely transformed measured income into unmeasured nonpecuniary income for the blacks who worked less.

The Efficiency of Postbellum Agriculture

The fact that the sharp drop in southern per capita income following the war can be explained by external demand forces and the emancipation of the slaves does not necessarily mean that the postwar economy operated efficiently. Most economic historians remain convinced that the South's growth performance was well below the rate achievable in a more flexible, competitive economy. Why, for example, was the South apparently unable to switch from cotton to more productive economic activity? They focus their critique of southern economic institutions on three areas: labor organization, "debt peonage," and racism. We deal with each in turn.

SHARECROPPING AND SMALL-SCALE FARM EFFICIENCY

In the wake of military defeat, southern planters attempted to retain the basic features of the plantation system by hiring former slaves on annual wage contracts. Blacks continued to work the fields in gangs and to be subjected to discipline by overseers; the only major difference in their work lives was the take-home pay. This wage system broke down within a few years, however, in part because blacks fiercely resisted the idea of continuing to work as gang labor on plantations. Courts and legislatures did try to restrict black movement and to block open competition for their labor services, but the general shortage of labor created by the voluntary withdrawal of women and children from the labor force probably made it difficult to stop landowners from competitively offering labor arrangements more pleasing to their former chattels.

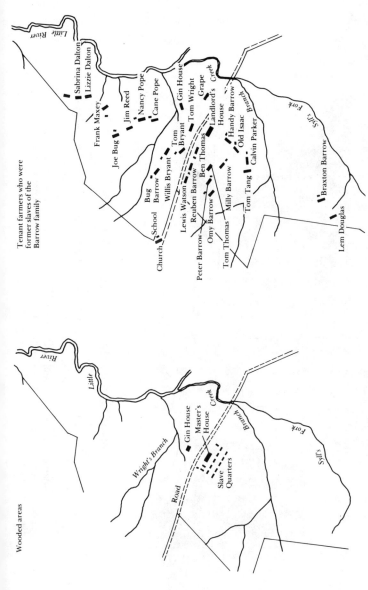

THE TRANSITION TO TENANT FARMING: THE BARROW PLANTATION IN 1860 AND 1881

For many plantations the transition from slave labor to tenant farming meant that the available farmland was divided into small parcels and let to the plantation's former slaves.

Source: Adapted by Roger Ransom and Richard Sutch, *One Kind of Freedom* (Cambridge University, 1977), p. 72; from *Scribner's Monthly* 21 (April, 1881), pp. 832–33.

Counties are grouped into five equal sized categories
defined by percentage of farms sharecropped

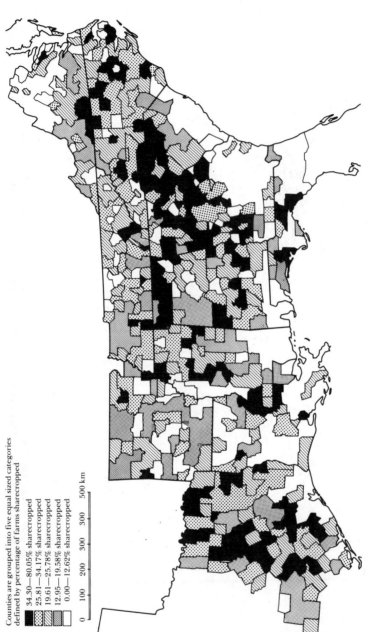

- 34.30—80.05% sharecropped
- 25.81—34.17% sharecropped
- 19.61—25.78% sharecropped
- 12.95—19.58% sharecropped
- 0.00—12.62% sharecropped

0   100   200   300   500 km

SHARECROPPING IN THE SOUTH IN 1880

The most heavily sharecropped counties were in the Piedmont and East Texas. Relatively little land was sharecropped in the rice and sugar regions.

Source: Adapted by Roger Ransom and Richard Sutch, *One Kind of Freedom* (Cambridge University, 1977), p. 93; from U.S. Census Office, Tenth Census, 1880, *Report of the Production of Agriculture* (Government Printing Office, 1883), Table 5.

Virtually all large plantations were broken into 20–50-acre plots suitable for farming by a single black family. By 1880, Ransom and Sutch estimate, only 9 percent of southern cropland was cultivated by wage laborers on large farms. About two-fifths of all land was worked by tenant farmers, black and white, while the remaining acreage was mostly owned and worked by white family farmers. Far and away the most important form of tenancy was sharecropping, in which the landlord provided land, equipment, and supervision in return for half the output.

It is not completely clear why sharecropping dominated other possible tenant-landlord arrangements. As a means of apportioning risk to the party who could bear it at minimum cost, a straight wage system—in which property owners rather than impoverished blacks received any unanticipated gains and losses from unusually good or bad harvests—would be superior.

Ransom and Sutch describe sharecropping as a sort of compromise. Blacks detested wage work, obviously preferring to bear some risk rather than work like slaves. Owners, on the other hand, disliked the idea of arms-length, cash-rental agreements because they did not trust blacks to work hard or to maintain property carefully on their own. Sharecropping involved a mix of the two systems, providing some independence to blacks, but not so much that landowners could not supervise the day-to-day activities of their tenants.

Was the sharecropping arrangement efficient? The classic argument against sharing (as opposed to renting) is that it reduces production incentives. Consider, for example, a worker who knows that one more pass through the cotton fields harvesting the remnants will increase total crop output by $5 worth. For, say, $3, the worker would be willing to put in the long day's effort, but his or her half-share of the crop will come to only $2.50. The worker thus lets $5 worth of cotton rot in the fields, even though the labor needed to save it is worth just $3.

There is a potential flaw in this analysis of sharecropping inefficiency, however. Sharecropping agreements were not lifetime arrangements; they were renegotiated annually. And if the landlord suspected that tenants might have produced greater yields, the landlord could always look for a new tenant. Competition among tenants thus might force sharecroppers to work as hard as renters.

There is a parallel potential for inefficiency rooted in the landlord's incentive to have the land worked as labor-intensively as possible. With the landowner receiving a fixed share of the total crop, the more intensively the land is worked, the more money the landlord will make. It was thus the strategy of landowners to induce intensive cultivation by limiting the acreage worked by a single tenant family. This land constraint presumably reduced tenant productivity and forced the tenant family to put in more hours of labor simply to survive. In economists' jargon, with less land per tenant, it took more hours of labor for each tenant to equalize the marginal value of additional output retained to the marginal value of leisure.

Again, though, competition comes to the rescue. If the labor market was competitive, market forces would prevent landlords from reducing labor productivity: Tenants and landlords rarely bargained over shares—the 50/50 arrangement was the rule—but Ransom and Sutch report that they did often bargain over the quantity of land to be worked by a single family. If there were idle farmland, there would be market pressure to bid up the land allotment per worker because with farms below the efficient size, there would not be enough labor to go around. Hence, unless landlords colluded to hold land off the market, each would have a powerful incentive to entice away the neighbors' tenants with promises of more or better acreage.

The real question—one that cannot be answered by appeals to economic theory—is how efficient sharecropping actually was in practice. The potential pressures that push labor and land toward their highest value use were present in sharecropping. However, competitive pressures could have been blocked by legal restrictions on labor mobility, or by lack of information, or by landlord collusion. One would expect, in fact, that the roundabout path toward efficiency in sharecropping described above might be harder to follow than simple bargaining arrangements over wages or straight cash rentals.

Joseph Reid suggests, however, that just the opposite may have been true. Under a wage contract, the worker's duties must be laid out in great detail, and then fixed for the year. Reid claims that such rigid contractual obligations made it difficult for owners and laborers to adapt quickly to changing expectations across the crop year. It might pay, for example, to plant fewer sweet potatoes and more corn, if, after the contract were signed, corn prices looked particularly high. But in a wage contract or straight land rental contract, one of the two parties has a guaranteed income, and thus no direct stake in maximizing the value of output. Under a sharecropping arrangement, by contrast, both parties have a clear stake in rapid adjustment to changes in weather or price expectations, and no barrier stands in the way of adjusting work schedules.

Ransom and Sutch believe that the direct allocative inefficiencies created by sharecropping were probably minor. They are not sanguine, however, about the impact of tenant farming on incentives for long-term investment in land improvements. Tenants have a short-term objective: maximizing this season's crop. For them, effort expended preventing soil erosion, repairing fences, improving breeding stock, and so on was effort wasted. The fruits of any significant productivity improvement could be captured by the landowner who would be able to bargain down the tenant's land allotment for the following year.

Economic theory can be invoked once again, of course, to suggest why tenants would in fact feel pressure to maintain or improve land. Tenants who shirked on maintenance could always be thrown off the land at the end of the contract year, to be replaced by laborers who would offer a competitive level of service. Cash side payments, moreover, could be made to get tenants to finish specific tasks. Ransom and Sutch believe, though, that this incentive structure did not work very well, presumably because the costs of overseeing investment activity were too high to make the expenditure worthwhile to owners. They have no evidence other than anecdotes about the failure to invest or to use sophisticated yield-raising devices like crop rotation, however. And it is difficult to devise a statistical test of the proposition that tenancy led to serious underinvestment in southern land.

The prevalence of tenant farming is not the only distinguishing feature of postwar southern agriculture: Economic historians searching for an explanation of relatively low labor productivity are also tempted to pin the rap on the reduced size of landholdings. As table 12.4 makes clear, there is no question that the abandonment of plantation organization had a dramatic effect on average farm size by 1870.

Small is not necessarily bad, of course. As noted in another chapter, the evidence for scale economies in the antebellum South is not irrefutably established. Gavin Wright was not able to identify a relationship between average labor productivity and farm size for any part of the South in 1860 other than the lower Mississippi Valley. Although Robert Fogel and Stanley Engerman do report efficiency advantages for large plantations, it is possible that these results were biased by extremely high cotton yields in 1860. Plantations devoted a higher percentage of their acreage to cotton than smaller farms, and thus stood to gain when cotton crops were especially large and cotton prices especially high.

TABLE 12.4

FARM SIZE DISTRIBUTION IN FIVE MAJOR COTTON STATES

Improved Acres	Percentage in Size Class		Percentage of Land in Size Class	
	1860	1870	1860	1870
3–49	36.9	60.9	7.4	20.2
50–99	24.2	19.8	12.0	19.6
100–499	32.0	17.2	47.6	49.1
500+	6.9	2.1	33.0	11.0

Source: Roger Ransom and Richard Sutch, *One Kind of Freedom* (Cambridge University, 1977), p. 71.

If there were indeed scale economies for plantations, many would argue that they were attributable to increased work intensity achievable only through the use of gang labor. The other possible sources of productivity differences—specialization of tasks, mechanization—may have existed but are not likely to have had much quantitative importance. This makes it important to distinguish between the failure to utilize work routines that maximize output per worker and economic inefficiency. Gang labor prevailed in antebellum agriculture because slaves had no say in the labor system. It probably disappeared after the war because the productivity advantages were more than offset by the high wages necessary to compensate ex-slaves for the unpleasantness and humiliation of the gang labor system.

Thus in an important sense, plantation agriculture was never efficient: The nonpecuniary disadvantages of gang labor outweighed the pecuniary advantages. By another interpretation of the same facts, plantations were efficient, but ceased to be efficient when slave property—the capitalized value of slave labor—was transferred from slave owners to slaves themselves. With the new distribution of wealth, blacks ceased to make the sacrifices necessary to obtain the fruits of gang labor.

In neither sense, then, was small-scale postbellum southern agriculture inefficient for reasons of scale alone. It is possible, nonetheless, that observed low levels of labor productivity in the South were indirectly due to reduced farm scale, and that the South's recovery in crude terms of commodity output was slowed by the demise of gang labor used on large plantations.

DEBT PEONAGE AND COTTON OVERPRODUCTION

Before the Civil War, the South had relatively few banks. However, since the average loanable assets of southern banks were quite large, there is no particular reason to suspect that the system was unprepared for the task of providing short-term credit for cotton and other staple crop producers. This credit system was shattered by the Civil War: In 1865, Ransom and Sutch estimate, the quarter of the American population living in the South was served by just 2 percent of the banks. By 1880 the system had partially recovered, but growth in the number of banks masks the reduction in total bank assets from prewar levels. And nowhere was the resulting lack of bank credit felt more strongly than among small farmers.

Family farmers had neither the time nor the skills to travel twenty or thirty miles to the county seat to negotiate a $100 loan against next autumn's crop. Thus local merchants became bankers by default, lending food, clothing, and agricultural inputs (rather than cash) to farmers who pledged their crops as security. These merchants were able to exercise some monopoly power, Ransom and Sutch argue, because of (1) location advantages—farmers were naturally reluctant to travel beyond the nearest town to do their provisioning, and (2) high market entry and contract enforcement costs—merchants had to know their credit customers well.

Interest rates charged by Georgia merchants in the 1880's on credit purchases averaged 57 percent a year—a rate of return, one might note, that could be earned only for the fraction of the year in which the credit was outstanding. But in spite of the high interest rates, these merchants rarely became wealthy; Ransom and Sutch report that few had a net worth over $5,000. This was probably due to the small number of customers per store rather than any failure to extract monopoly profits in the form of exorbitant interest.

Under ordinary circumstances, monopoly power distorts resource allocation by reducing the output of the product or service monopolized—in this case agricultural credit. It is generally assumed, however, that the demand for country store credit was not very sensitive to the price (interest rate) and that most small farmers had no choice but to go into debt at the local store. Country store credit, however, is widely believed to have created or at least exacerbated a very different sort of allocative inefficiency—overspecialization in cotton production. Merchants insisted that debtors grow cotton to secure their debts, most probably because this tended to lock-in debtors, reducing farm self-sufficiency in food and thereby insuring that the farmer would be back next year needing food on credit.

TABLE 12.5

FOOD PRODUCTION PER CAPITA IN FIVE MAJOR COTTON STATES

Food	1850	1860	1870	1880	1890
Corn (bushels)	31.1	29.6	14.7	15.6	16.3
Other Crops (Corn-Equivalent Bushels)*	6.7	6.3	2.6	3.9	2.7
Total Food Crops (Corn-Equivalent Bushels)*	37.7	35.8	17.3	19.5	18.9
Pigs (Head)	2.11	1.64	0.73	0.88	0.73
Cattle (Head)	0.73	0.51	0.29	0.31	0.30
Sheep (Head)	0.49	0.31	0.26	0.24	0.22

Interpretation: Food production per person declined dramatically from prewar levels, turning the Cotton South from a food-surplus region to a food-deficit region.

*Other food crops are converted into the caloric equivalent of bushels of corn.

Source: Roger Ransom and Richard Sutch, *One Kind of Freedom* (Cambridge University, 1977), p. 152.

The impact of this "debt peonage," it is argued, was a marked decline in southern food production (see table 12.5). With per capita food output at barely 50 percent of prewar levels, the South turned from a net exporter of food into a net importer. More striking still, the old relationship between cotton-corn output mix and farm size was reversed. Before the war, small farmers tended to grow a lot of corn and relatively little cotton, presumably because they had self-sufficiency in food as their primary goal. But after the war, small farmers devoted a relatively high percentage of their acreage to cotton, and the poorest farmers—those who rented or sharecropped—devoted an even larger share to cotton (see table 12.6).

Gavin Wright and Howard Kunreuther offer an alternative explanation of the dramatic decline in southern farm self-sufficiency. Farming without much equity in the land, they argue, forced small farmers to abandon their traditional self-sufficiency-in-food strategy, which served as a defense against unanticipated market price changes. A farmer with a potential income above subsistence would plant enough corn to survive on, and then plant the remaining acreage in profitable market crops. But a small tenant farmer living at the edge of subsistence could not afford not to gamble. The tenant's share on a small plot simply would not be sufficient to live on unless the tenant concentrated on growing the most lucrative crop—cotton. Hence the crop choice dictated by economic necessity for tenants pushed the South toward specialization.

TABLE 12.6

CROP ACREAGE BY FARM SIZE, COTTON SOUTH, 1880

Farm Size	Average % in Cotton	Average Number of Crops Grown
Less than 50 Acres	50.9	4.2
Owner-Operated	45.7	4.8
Rented	58.1	3.7
Sharecropped	53.6	3.8
50–100 Acres	46.2	5.4
Owner-Operated	43.1	5.7
Rented	56.1	4.7
Sharecropped	50.0	5.1
100+ Acres	52.4	5.6

Interpretation: In both the small and medium farm categories rented and share-cropped land was more concentrated in cotton production. This fits either the Ransom-Sutch or the Wright interpretation.

Source: Roger Ransom and Richard Sutch, *One Kind of Freedom* (Cambridge University, 1977), p. 157.

From the viewpoint of world economic efficiency, specialization induced by credit market monopoly—the Ransom-Sutch position—meant that more cotton and less food was grown by southern farmers than they would otherwise have chosen. Specialization due to the Wright-Kunreuther hypothesis wasn't necessarily inefficient, but it did reduce the income of the South as a whole.

Wright's argument that specialization reduced southern income follows from the fact that the demand for cotton was not very sensitive to the price of cotton. Hence resources devoted to cotton production (at the expense of food production) generated little or no additional revenues for the South; the gain in cotton volume was offset (or nearly offset) by the fall in cotton prices. Cotton specialization was thus a trap. The failure to limit cotton production had always cost the South income in the sense that output below the level dictated by competitive markets would have raised cotton prices sufficiently to raise total export revenues. Greater cotton specialization—producing more than the prewar competitive output for any given price—only deepened the wound.

Both the Ransom-Sutch lock-in to cotton, based on indebtedness, and the Wright-Kunreuther hapless-victim theory have provoked vigorous criticism. William Brown and Morgan Reynolds are skeptical of the potential monopoly power of country store creditors when entry into the country store business was so easy. High interest rates, they suggest, indicate the high risk of default and high transactions costs for very small loans, rather than monopoly power. Robert McGuire and Robert Higgs dispute the underlying theory that attitude toward risk changed self-sufficient antebellum farmers into "gamblers" dependent on the marketplace. Stephen DeCanio's statistical research suggests that southern farmers were as responsive to changes in relative crop prices in making planting decisions as were midwestern grain farmers. And all three sets of critics agree that the burden of proof must rest on those who argue that the South's postwar movement toward crop specialization needs some explanation other than classical "comparative advantage."

The case hasn't actually been proved one way or the other, though it is difficult to explain—without some kind of Ransom-Sutch or Wright-Kunreuther theory—why it was small renters and tenant farmers rather than medium-size owner-operators who so abruptly abandoned self-sufficiency. And in any case, the argument stands that increasing specialization in a crop whose demand was insensitive to price cost the South dearly, at least partially explaining the lag in antebellum southern income growth.

ECONOMIC EFFICIENCY AND RACISM

The social cost of racism is usually calculated by the "distributive" rather than the "allocative" impact of discrimination. Most aspects of discrimination—the right to sit at the front of the bus or buy a house in a white neighborhood, for example—are largely distributive in the sense that the distribution of personal happiness, rather than the creation of value, is affected. This discrimination allows blacks less, and, presumably, whites more. Since, by this reasoning, there is no clear means of making some people better off by reducing discrimination without making others worse off, discrimination in this strict sense does not reduce economic efficiency. There were, however, ways in which the South's denial of equal rights to former slaves may explain allocative waste and reduced growth rates.

The most obvious potential source of inefficiency was racially based access to nonmenial jobs and to agricultural credit markets. Even if there had been no discrimination in the postwar era, it is reasonable that most blacks who remained in the South worked in unskilled agricultural jobs, since few were literate or possessed marketable skills. But by 1890, the barriers to occupational mobility built by racism can be distinguished.

Ransom and Sutch show how skewed occupational entry was (see table 12.7). In 1890, 61 percent of black men and 91 percent of black women in the southern labor force were employed in menial jobs, as opposed to just 31 percent and 54 percent for whites whose parents were born in the United States. Menial labor among first generation and immigrant whites was even lower, but the comparison with blacks is probably not relevant since new arrivals in the South were unrepresentative of Americans in general.

The potential impact of racism is thus clear, though quantifying the cost in terms of lost output is very difficult. Because responsible positions were filled almost solely on the basis of race, many jobs were not done as well as they might otherwise have been. Probably more important in the rural South where output was largely farm crops, racism blocked the natural path of personal advancement: land ownership. Blacks could rarely borrow money to buy land, and when they did amass the necessary cash, whites were generally reluctant to sell to black buyers.

The observation that a far smaller percentage of blacks managed to obtain their own land does not in itself prove discrimination. Land, after all, is an asset that represents many generations' accumulated savings, and typically, ex-slaves started from the position of owning nothing. But Ransom and Sutch offer indirect evidence of systematic discrimination. For whites in the Midwest, tenancy was thought of as a stepping stone to personal independence; one worked other people's land while saving for one's own. Table 12.8 shows a sixteen-year average age difference between tenants and owners among eastern Iowa farmers in 1880, and an eight-year age difference for Cotton South whites. By contrast, black tenants were just five years younger on average than black owners. Just how one should interpret these numbers remains open to debate. Joseph Reid, for one, notes that at later dates the differences melt away. Yet few would argue that the South was less racist in 1910 than it was in 1880.

TABLE 12.7

PERCENTAGE DISTRIBUTION OF WORKERS BY OCCUPATION IN FIVE MAJOR COTTON STATES, 1890
Males (over Age 10)

Occupation	Nonwhite	Whites			Total
		Native Parents	Foreign Parents	Foreign Born	
Agriculture	73.6	70.3	14.5	14.3	69.1
Laborer	41.9	22.1	4.3	5.5	31.5
Farm Operator	31.7	48.2	10.2	8.8	37.6
Non-Agriculture	26.4	29.7	85.5	85.6	30.9
Low Skill	19.2	8.4	23.0	25.0	14.8
High Skill	7.3	21.3	62.5	60.6	16.1
Ag. Labor + Low Skill Non-Ag.	61.0	30.5	27.3	30.5	46.3

Females (over Age 10)

Occupation	Nonwhite	Whites			Total
		Native Parents	Foreign Parents	Foreign Born	
Agriculture	62.2	51.4	6.1	6.2	58.8
Laborer	56.3	30.7	2.8	3.0	50.2
Farm Operator	5.9	20.7	3.3	3.2	8.6
Non-Agriculture	37.8	48.6	93.9	93.8	41.2
Low Skill	34.8	23.0	30.7	42.0	32.6
High Skill	3.0	25.6	63.3	51.9	8.5
Ag. Labor + Low Skill Non-Ag.	91.1	53.7	33.5	45.0	82.9

Interpretation: 25 years after the abolition of slavery, blacks remained trapped in low-skilled agricultural jobs, with relatively few working their own land.

Source: Roger Ransom and Richard Sutch, *One Kind of Freedom* (Cambridge University, 1977), pp. 226–27.

In cases where black farmers were able to obtain land, there is some evidence that they were still unable to acquire necessary capital with which to work the land at competitive rates. Ransom and Sutch report that on small farms operated by whites, the value of farm implements per acre in crops was $2.25 in 1879, while on black farms it was only $1.28. Of small white-run farms, 36.8 percent purchased fertilizer, compared to 21 percent of black-owned farms. Blacks, moreover, had less opportunity to raise productivity by means of land-intensive farming methods. Owner-operated white farms used nearly twice the acreage per worker, allowing them to rest about double the acreage each year.

Compounding the "static" allocative inefficiency in the current use-productive factors, created by occupation and credit discrimination, was the "dynamic", long-term inefficiency created by racial barriers to invest-ment in education and skill acquisition. The ability to read, write, and do simple arithmetic gave farmers access to information useful in raising productivity. But white-dominated governments were loath to provide schools for blacks. And when they did, the strictly segregated schools were generally greatly inferior to white schools. According to the 1880 Census, four out of five white farm operators in the Cotton South could read and write, but only one black farm operator in five was literate.

Nonfarm occupational skills were even more difficult for blacks to acquire, since training usually came through apprenticeship. The major-ity of white artisans were, it is presumed, prejudiced against using black helpers. Those who might otherwise have been attracted to hiring black apprentices because they could be had for less pay than whites were de-terred by the general racial climate. If customers would not patronize a shop with black labor because they thought black work was inferior or job integration was wrong, it did not pay to hire blacks no matter how competent they might be.

The Plight of the Ex-Slave

In spite of the social and legal discrimination, the economic status of blacks surely improved with the end of slavery. By assuming that ex-slaves were able to obtain the equivalent of a competitive wage—that is, that ex-slaves were not exploited in the Robinsonian[1] sense—Ransom and Sutch calculate that the typical per capita income for a black share-cropping family was 43 percent higher than that for slaves. Slaves on large plantations enjoyed more material benefits; hence the gain from the transition to freedom—some 30 percent—was smaller (see table 12.9). Note, however, that the use of Fogel and Engerman's computation of typical slave incomes would generate somewhat different results. Their more generous estimates, particularly for plantation slaves, put the material gains to freedom at a much lower level.

Any possible ambiguity in the direction of change in income—Fogel and Engerman's large plantation slaves actually appear to lose a bit with freedom—disappears by imputing a value to the increase in leisure time freed slaves chose to consume (see table 12.10). The low estimate, assum-

[1] See chapter 9 for an explanation of this term.

TABLE 12.8

AVERAGE FARM OPERATORS' AGE BY TYPE OF LAND TENURE, 1880

	Eastern Iowa		Cotton South	
Tenure Form	Native Born	Foreign Born	White	Black
Owner-Operated	46.9	48.0	43.6	45.5
Tenant	32.9	38.6	35.7	40.7
All Operators	43.5	45.1	40.9	41.7

Source: Roger Ransom and Richard Sutch, *One Kind of Freedom* (Cambridge University, 1977), p. 181.

TABLE 12.9

BLACK PER CAPITA INCOME (1859 dollars)

	Fogel-Engerman (1859)	Ransom-Sutch (1859)	Black Sharecroppers (1879)
Large Plantations	42.99	32.12	41.39
Average	34.13	28.95	

Sources: Robert Fogel and Stanley Engerman, *Time on the Cross, Volume II* (Little, Brown, 1974), p. 159; Roger Ransom and Richard Sutch, *One Kind of Freedom* (Cambridge University, 1977), pp. 3, 5.

TABLE 12.10

BLACK PER CAPITA INCOME-EQUIVALENT WELFARE (1859 dollars)

	Large Plantations	Sharecroppers (1879)	% Change 1859–79
Material Income	32.12	41.39	29
Value of Additional Leisure Time			
Low Estimate		16.34	
High Estimate		24.52	
Total			
Low Estimate	32.12	57.75	80
High Estimate	32.12	65.91	105

Source: Roger Ransom and Richard Sutch, *One Kind of Freedom* (Cambridge University, 1977), p. 7.

ing blacks reduced their average work input by 28 percent, brings per capita income equivalence to $57.73; the high estimate, based on a 37 percent labor time reduction, puts the figure at $65.91. The narrowest margin—the one between Fogel-Engerman's plantation slave and an ex-slave with an income equivalent to $57.73—suggests a gain of at least 34 percent.

Output per black slave in cotton south plantations fell from $147.93 in 1859 to just $74.03 per black sharecropper in 1879, a decline of 50 percent. That does not mean expected physical output per labor hour fell anywhere near this amount, however. The comparison year, 1859, was an unusually productive one; Ransom and Sutch argue that the bumper crop accounts for 25–30 percent of the difference. The decline in labor hours supplied accounts for almost all the rest (or more than all, if one uses the high range of the Ransom-Sutch estimate). Thus the reorganization of agriculture had little direct impact on productivity. By Ransom and Sutch's numbers, labor productivity changed somewhere between −8 percent and +9 percent.

Did, in fact, freedom mean the end of economic exploitation for blacks? Ransom and Sutch simply assume that black sharecroppers received the full competitive wage. But there is little doubt that land-owners made an effort to strangle competition for labor, barring black entry into some occupations and passing vagrancy laws that restricted blacks from searching for alternative employment. If landowners limited the opportunities for landless blacks, they might have been able to cut real wages below that dictated by labor productivity. Stephen De-Canio tests the assumption of zero exploitation by landowners by estimating the share of output that would accrue to southern agricultural labor in a competitive market and then comparing it to sharecroppers' allotments.

DeCanio's results cannot be considered definitive because the needed estimation of the underlying production relationships must be based on a set of unverifiable assumptions. Still, the results are interesting. The share going to labor that is predicted by the statistical analysis varies from 21 percent (Texas) to 36 percent (Alabama), with an average predicted share of 31 percent for the South as a whole. These shares are well below the 50 percent specified in most sharecropping contracts, and are typically below estimates of the net return to labor after subtracting possible capital inputs by the tenants. This evidence can be interpreted in two ways. DeCanio argues that it shows that landlords were unable to exploit their tenants by paying an implicit wage below the competitive market wage. Gavin Wright suggests, however, that exploitation may still have been possible if tenants were forced to farm very small plots of land. By this reckoning, exploitation follows from constraints on labor productivity, rather than from wage payments below the competitive level otherwise expected.

TABLE 12.11

FOOD PRICES FOR SOUTHERN FARMERS 1879–80

Food	Cash	Credit	% Difference
Shelled Corn ($/bushel)	.765	.998	30
Bacon ($/lb.)	.080	.102	28
Food Index (1859 = 100)	79.1	101.5	28
Overall Cost of Living			
(1859 = 100)	86.2	99.6*	13

*If 60 percent of family purchases are made on credit.

Source: Roger Ransom and Richard Sutch, *One Kind of Freedom* (Cambridge University, 1977), p. 218.

Small farmers were potential prey to creditors, as well as employers. And Ransom and Sutch believe that debt peonage created very serious exploitation. By lending food and other necessities at prices above market levels (see table 12.11), the country stores were able to appropriate a good fraction of the income surplus above subsistence that slaves received with their freedom. Assuming that three-fifths of family purchases were made on credit, per capita real income falls to an estimated $35.82, thirteen percent less than the gross output earned by sharecroppers of $41.39. Thus by one definition of the term, the average rate of exploitation of black sharecroppers was thirteen percent.

This number cannot be compared directly to Fogel and Engerman's controversial 10–12 percent estimated rate of exploitation under slavery; that figure is derived from a comparison of the present value at birth of the slave's expected surplus accruing to owners with the present value at birth of lifetime slave earnings (see chapter 9). A more relevant comparison would be to the ratio of the annual surplus earned by an average slave (the slave's product, less slave consumption) divided by the slave's product. Fogel and Engerman estimate the product attributable to the average slave on large plantations at $85.80 in 1859. Since Fogel and Engerman also estimate per capita slave consumption at $42.99, the comparable slave exploitation rate is 50 percent ($85.80–$42.99)/($85.80).

Ransom and Sutch, incidentally, put the large plantation slave exploitation rate even higher (59 percent), because they believe that slave consumption was well below the $43 rate calculated by Fogel and Engerman (see chapter 9 appendix). By either calculation, one fact is clear: As exploitative as post–Civil War economic institutions may have been, they did not compare in harshness with the economic penalties of slavery.

From the perspective of a century, a few modest conclusions seem apparent. In the transition from slavery, free markets performed reasonably well, at least when they were given a chance. The South's unimpressive economic performance in the first few postwar decades was almost inevitable: Free blacks could not be expected to work like slaves. Nor could the South control the declining fortunes of cotton in the world economy. The real failing of the southern economic system was its lack of flexibility. Land and labor remained locked into staple production when per capita economic growth depended upon diversification and, most probably, substantial movement of labor into manufacturing or out of the region entirely.

In part, the continuing misery of blacks after Emancipation is attributable to economic exploitation and to racial discrimination in everyday life. But the great portion of blame must go to the failure to provide ex-slaves with property comparable to landed whites, or to provide access to the education and jobs vital to social mobility.

Bibliography

**Mark Aldrich, "Flexible Exchange Rates, Northern Expansion and the Market for Southern Cotton," *Journal of Economic History* 33 (June, 1973). Argues that slow cotton recovery after the war was due to inability of Americans to compete because of appreciation of the dollar.

**Yoram Barzel, "An Economic Analysis of Slavery," *Journal of Law and Economics* 20 (Jan., 1977). Useful here because it shows the parallel impact of slavery and debt peonage on labor allocation.

**William Brown and Morgan Reynolds, "Debt Peonage Reexamined," *Journal of Economic History* 33 (Dec., 1973). Questions Ransom and Sutch's conclusion that southern country stores exerted monopoly power and interprets concentration in cotton as a response to comparative advantage.

*Alfred Conrad and John Meyer, "Slavery as an Obstacle to Economic Growth in the United States," *Journal of Economic History* 27 (Dec., 1967). Comments in a panel discussion useful here as they relate to the explanation of postwar southern recovery.

‡***Stephen DeCanio, "Cotton Overproduction in Late 19th Century Agriculture," *Journal of Economic History* 33 (Sept., 1973). Argues that southern concentration in cotton was consistent with underlying economic flexibility in the choice of crops.

‡***Stephen DeCanio, "Productivity and Income Distribution in the Postbellum South," *Journal of Economic History* 34 (June, 1974). Explores hypothesis that black poverty was due to labor market exploitation.

‡***Robert Fogel and Stanley Engerman, *Time on the Cross, Volume II: Evidence and Methods* (Little, Brown, 1974). Useful here for computation of the exploitation rate.

**Robert Gallman and R. Anderson, "Slaves as Fixed Capital," *Journal of American History* 64 (Jan., 1977). Insightful essay on the difference emancipation made on the allocation of labor in the South.

**Robert Higgs, "Patterns of Farm Rental in the Georgia Cotton Belt, 1880–1900," *Journal of Economic History* 34 (June, 1974). Division between wage labor and land rental systems shown to depend on farm size.

***Robert Higgs, "Race, Tenure and Resource Allocation in Southern Agriculture, 1910," *Journal of Economic History* 33 (March, 1973). Argues that ability to bear risk, rather than racism, determined the type of contract between landowner and tenant.

*Jay Mandle, "The Plantation States as a Subregion of the Postbellum South," *Journal of Economic History* 34 (Sept., 1974). Notes that the Cotton South should not be indiscriminately used as a surrogate for the South as a whole.

‡***Robert McGuire and Robert Higgs, "Cotton, Corn and Risk in the 19th Century: Another View," *Explorations in Economic History* 14 (April, 1977). Critique of Wright-Kunreuther argument that extreme poverty forced southern tenant farmers to abandon diversified agriculture.

**Roger Ransom and Richard Sutch, "Debt Peonage in the Cotton South After the Civil War," *Journal of Economic History* 32 (Sept., 1972). Documents monopoly power of southern country stores and explains concentration in cotton as a response to store owners' demands.

**Roger Ransom and Richard Sutch, *One Kind of Freedom: The Economic Consequences of Emancipation* (Cambridge University Press, 1977). Survey summarizing several years of research on Emancipation; the single most useful reference on the subject.

**Roger Ransom and Richard Sutch, "The Ex-Slave in the Postbellum South: A Study of the Impact of Racism in a Market Environment," *Journal of Economic History* 33 (March, 1973). Argues that racism reduced economic opportunity for blacks.

**Joseph Reid, "Sharecropping as an Understandable Market Response: The Post Bellum South," *Journal of Economic History* 33 (March, 1973). Argues that sharecropping permitted low-cost renegotiation of contracts across the year, allowing maximum efficiency.

**Peter Temin, "The PostBellum Recovery of the South and the Cost of the Civil War," *Journal of Economic History* 36 (Dec., 1976). Apportions the relative impact of supply and demand factors on the retardation of southern growth.

‡**Gavin Wright, "Cotton Competition and the Post Bellum Recovery of the American South," *Journal of Economic History* 34 (Sept., 1974). Attributes slow recovery largely to the reduced rate of growth of foreign demand for raw cotton.

**Gavin Wright, "Freedom and the Southern Economy," *Explorations in Economic History* (forthcoming, 1979). Analytical review of *One Kind of Freedom,* suggesting that Ransom and Sutch came at some of the issues from the wrong perspective.

‡***Gavin Wright and Howard Kunreuther, "Cotton, Corn and Risk in the 19th Century," *Journal of Economic History* 35 (Sept., 1975). Explains shift away from subsistence agriculture by the desperate plight of small tenant farmers.

Economic growth
and institutional
change after the
civil war

13

Thus far, the search for "turning points" in American economic history has proved unrewarding. As chapter 3 suggests, the view of the 1840's as a transition decade from agrarian stagnation to market-oriented growth is not supported by the available—albeit fragmentary—evidence. The acceleration process was gradual, with no marked discontinuity early in the 19th century, no Rostovian "take-off." Nor have proponents satisfactorily demonstrated that the Civil War was an economic watershed. War and the emancipation of the slaves surely disrupted growth; but, given the remarkable amount of resources poured into the conflict and the social and political changes of the postwar era, it is, actually, striking how little the long-term growth process seems to have been affected.

This does not mean, of course, that the economy of the 1820's looked much like the economy of the 1850's, or that the pre–Civil War economy much resembled the national economic machinery in place before World War I. But the search for discontinuities, ironically, obscures miraculous changes in structure and productivity that characterized late 19th and 20th century growth. This chapter first surveys the growth record from the Civil War to the first decade of the 20th century. (The choice of dates reflects convenience rather than some more profound theory of economic transition.) The chapter closes with a look at current research on the impact of one of the major sources of change—the railroad—and at the economics of a related phenomenon, the epidemic of farm protest late in the 19th century.

Postwar Growth: A Statistical Overview

In 1870 net national product (that is, total output less an allowance for replacement of worn out capital goods) was about $6.2 billion. Forty years later it would be nearly five times greater—some $30.1 billion in 1870 prices. That record of growth, an average of 4 percent annually, is quite impressive. It was roughly one-third greater than Germany's growth rate during the same period, almost double the rate of Great Britain, and more than double that of France. Before the spirit of self-congratulation overwhelms, however, some details are needed to put the American experience in better perspective.

Extensive growth surely matters less than intensive growth. Total output may reflect some sense of national power—Belgium would be no match for the Soviet Union in a tank-production contest—but per capita output is a better benchmark of success where individual welfare is the primary social goal. Hence it makes sense to net out the effect of population growth before making international comparisons.[1]

Post–Civil War America still does pretty well; net national product per capita grew at a 1.9 percent annual rate from 1870 to 1910. That compares nicely with the 1.6 percent annual pace recorded by the United States between 1840 and 1860, and looks good when matched against Germany, the United Kingdom, or France. Remember that, over long periods, small differences in growth rates add up to big differences in living standards: 1.9 percent average annual growth increased per capita income by 110 percent between 1870 and 1910, while a 1 percent per annum rate would have increased real per capita income just 49 percent.

America's special economic success in the late 19th and early 20th century does not, however, necessarily mean that the American character—some uniquely American spirit of enterprise—was at work. Direct comparisons with Europe, especially with Britain during this period, load the dice in favor of the U.S. The United States was blessed with abundant natural resources—in particular, arable land. Coupled with transport improvements (canals, steamboats, railroads), this resource base augmented the productivity of both capital and labor, raising the return on investment and ensuring that natural population growth and immigration would exert no drag on the growth of per capita income.

One telling way of dissecting the American growth performance is to

---

[1] Actually, in these periods of heavy migration, two alternative measures—both of which would show greater growth—would be superior measures of the change in welfare: (1) the rate of growth of income for those living in the United States when the period began and (2) the per capita income growth for all residents using the pre-migration income of immigrants in the base year per capita income computation. Neither alternative is practicable, due to data limitations, however.

TABLE 13.1

INDEXES OF FACTOR INPUTS AND NET NATIONAL PRODUCT 1840–1910

Year	Labor	Land	Capital	N.N.P.
1840	100	100	100	100
1850	146	135	181	161
1860	196	208	357	253
1870	228	240	512	324
1880	313	307	785	520
1890	412	415	1,159	765
1900	514	566	2,343	1,037
1910	662	761	3,683	1,573

Explanation: The table shows how changes in the quantity of factor inputs changed the quantity of outputs. For example, in 1870, 2.28 times as much labor, 2.40 times as much land, and 5.12 times as much capital (by comparison with 1840) were used to make 3.24 times as much national product.

Source: Lance Davis et al., *American Economic Growth* (Harper and Row, 1972), p. 34.

look at the relative contribution of various factor inputs and of changes in total factor productivity across the period. If we use data on factor inputs prepared by Gallman, Lebergott, and others (see table 13.1), this is a simple exercise. A 10 percent increase in factor X, other things equal, can be expected to increase output by 10 percent, times the elasticity of output with respect to factor X. Unfortunately, we have no direct measure of the three elasticities (those for land, labor, and capital). But the economic theory of marginal productivity distribution allows us to infer these elasticities from the relative distributive shares of income. For example, if capital owners in a competitive economy receive 15 percent of output as payment, we expect that the elasticity of output with respect to additional capital inputs equals 0.15. Gallman's ballpark estimates of the three factor shares are given in table 13.2, making it possible to apportion the sources of growth.

Table 13.3 shows that slightly more than half (54 percent) of economic growth between 1870 and 1910 can be attributed to sources other than labor force growth. Land had some impact on the growth rate, but it is capital and otherwise unaccounted-for sources that contributed the lion's share of the rest. The effect of investment in land improvements, factories, buildings, transport systems can be inferred. But how can re-

TABLE 13.2

FACTOR GROWTH AND OUTPUT ELASTICITIES

Average Annual Growth (%)	1840–60	1870–1910	Output Elasticity
Net National Product	4.75	4.03	—
Labor	3.42	2.70	.68
Land	3.73	2.79	.13
Capital	6.57	4.81	.19

Explanation: The table, showing average rates of growth in the quantity of factor inputs available to the economy, allows some perspective on the growth process. Note the tremendous growth of capital, relative to land and labor, in both periods. Its contribution to the rate of change of NNP is somewhat vitiated, though, by the low elasticity of output with respect to capital (see table 13.3).

Source: Lance Davis et al., *American Economic Growth* (Harper and Row, 1971), pp. 34, 39.

TABLE 13.3

SOURCE OF ECONOMIC GROWTH

Contribution of:	1840–60 Ave. Annual Growth (%)	1840–60 Relative Impact (%)	1870–1910 Ave. Annual Growth (%)	1870–1910 Relative Impact (%)
Labor	2.33	49	1.84	46
Land	0.48	10	0.36	9
Capital	1.25	26	0.91	23
Residual Productivity	0.69	15	0.92	23
Net National Product Growth	4.75	100	4.03	100

Interpretation: Observed increases in capital, all other sources of growth held equal, would have increased NNP by 1.25 percent annually between 1840 and 1860. Each factor entry equals the factor growth rate (see table 13.2) times the factor's output elasticity. Growth not explained by increased factor inputs is attributed to residual productivity change.

Source: Table 13.2.

sidual sources account for nearly one-fourth of late 19th-century economic expansion?

The computation itself tells nothing about this residual source except that it is there. In part we believe that the residual reflects organizational improvements that increased the efficiency of resource allocation, raising the value of output derived, on average, from a given amount of inputs. Capital markets—stock and bond exchanges, banks, insurance companies—better allocated savings to high-return investments. Improved transport (railroads, steamboats) and communications—newspapers' want ads, for example—channeled workers to where they were most needed; large urban agglomerations reduced the unit cost of distributing goods to consumers. In part, too, the residual can be explained by more intensive use of capital, as entrepreneurs devised new means of running their machines more hours each day and more days each year.

But it is generally believed that the most important sources of productivity change were technical improvements embodied in new capital and increased worker skill levels. Labor skills are a sort of "human capital," which many economists prefer to measure as a distinct factor of production, like land or machines or structures. The potential impact of technical education—this was the era in which formal training of engineers began in earnest—is obvious. Not as obvious, but possibly more important, were more fundamental labor skills like literacy, the ability to follow schematic diagrams, and facility in arithmetic.

The role of residual productivity change is particularly notable when its impact on per-worker output is isolated. Our computations suggest that, from 1870 to 1910, increased capital and land accounted for about 60 percent of real growth per worker, while residual productivity increases explain fully 40 percent. Note, too, the increased importance of residual productivity as a contributor to growth. Table 13.3 reveals that the residual accounted for 15 percent of aggregate growth from 1840 to 1860, compared to 23 percent from 1870 to 1910. In per-worker terms, the comparison is equally clear: The residual generated 42 percent of productivity change in the latter period, only 28 percent in the earlier.

Greater reliance on the residual as a source of growth is characteristic of modern economies. Though we won't take the space here to reproduce comparable calculations for the 1910–60 period, it is interesting that the trend continued. During those 50 years, changes other than additions to the capital and land stock accounted for 69 percent of the increase in output per worker. It should not be surprising, then, that many economists are disturbed by the virtual disappearance of the residual as a source of growth in the 1970's.

Some attribute this remarkable about-face to costly hidden adjustments associated with rapid changes in the cost of energy and environmental regulation. Others associate it with decreased investment in basic research by business and government or argue that confiscatory tax rates act as deterrents to highly productive but extremely risky investment. And still others feel the change is caused by a shift in the opportunities for productive investment. This last explanation is the most depressing because it suggests that no institutional change—tax reduction, government investment in research, deregulation—can bring productivity growth back to its historic growth path. Whatever the cause of current problems, however, there is little doubt about the importance of the intangible productivity factor in 19th-century economic maturation.

The massive accumulation of productive capacity after the Civil War was, of course, accompanied by great shifts in the kinds of goods produced and in the location and income of the people who made them. The shift in the labor force from agriculture to manufacturing took place before the Civil War (see table 13.4). Thereafter, the manufacturing sector absorbed a proportional share of labor force growth. The very substantial continuing relative losses from agriculture were paralleled by enormous employment gains in transportation, commercial services, and growth in the professions (the last is not shown in the table). This *relative* decline of farm employment was tracked by a roughly equal decline in the contribution of agricultural output to national income (see table 13.5).[2]

The reasons for the shift away from agriculture are not difficult to pinpoint. The income elasticity of demand for food is generally believed to be below one. Hence every ten percent increase in per capita income results in less than a ten percent increase in food demand. With per capita income growing at about two percent a year and no compensatory reduction in the relative price of food, a slow shift in the share of resources devoted to food production is reasonable. Foreign demand for grain temporarily buoyed agricultural demand growth after the Civil War; but this gain must be balanced against the clear decline in the rate of growth of foreign cotton demand.

Economic theory suggests that population follows economic opportunity, moving from regions with low labor productivity (and low wages) to regions with high productivity. There are no regional breakdowns on marginal labor productivity. However, Richard Easterlin's work does provide estimates of a substitute—per capita income—and for the most part theory seems to be vindicated. Per capita income fell sharply in the South after the war; the percentage gap did not begin to narrow until well into the 20th century (see table 13.6). And accomodatingly, the South's population and total income share fell too (see tables 13.7 and 13.8).

[2] Note the emphasis on *relative;* both farm employment and farm output continued to grow in absolute terms until World War I.

TABLE 13.4

DISTRIBUTION OF LABOR FORCE BY SECTOR
(1,000's of workers)

Year	Total	Manufacturing	Agriculture	Transport	Mining & Construction	Trade
1840	5,660	500(8.8%)	3,570(63.1%)	102(1.8%)	322(5.7%)	350(6.2%)
1870	12,930	2,470(19.1%)	6,790(52.5%)	295(2.3%)	960(7.4%)	1,310(10.1%)
1880	17,390	3,290(18.9%)	8,920(51.3%)	541(3.1%)	1,180(6.8%)	1,930(11.1%)
1890	23,320	4,390(18.8%)	9,960(42.7%)	870(3.7%)	1,950(8.4%)	2,960(12.7%)
1900	29,070	5,895(20.3%)	11,680(40.2%)	1,145(3.9%)	2,302(7.9%)	3,970(13.7%)
1910	37,480	8,332(22.2%)	11,770(31.4%)	2,005(5.3%)	3,017(8.0%)	5,320(14.2%)

Note that the big jump in manufacturing labor use (relative to other sectors) took place before 1870. Thereafter the labor drained from agriculture was spread fairly evenly across other sectors.

Source: U.S. Bureau of the Census, *Historical Statistics of the United States* (Government Printing Office, 1975) Series D167–181, p. 139.

TABLE 13.5

UNITED STATES INCOME BY SECTOR
(percentage division)

Sector	1839–59	1869–79	1889–99	1919–40
Agriculture	25.8	21.6	15.2	10.4
Mining and Manufacturing	14.0	17.5	24.7	26.2
All Other	60.2	60.9	60.1	63.4

Source: Lance Davis *et al., American Economic Growth* (Harper & Row, 1971), p. 55.

TABLE 13.6

RELATIVE PER CAPITA INCOME 1840–1920
(U.S. average = 100)

Region	1840	1860	1880	1900	1920
Northwest	135	139	141	137	132
Midwest	68	68	98	103	100
South	76	72	51	51	62
West	—	—	190	163	122

Source: Richard Easterlin, "Regional Income Trends 1840–1950," in Robert Fogel and Stanley Engerman (eds.), *The Reinterpretation of American Economic History* (Harper & Row, 1971), p. 40.

TABLE 13.7

TOTAL PERSONAL INCOME BY REGION 1840–1920
(percentage distribution)

Region	1840	1860	1880	1900	1920
Northeast	58	50	44	41	39
Midwest	13	20	34	36	32
South	29	26	15	15	18
West	—	4	7	8	10

Source: Richard Easterlin, "Regional Income Trends 1840–1950" in Robert Fogel and Stanley Engerman (eds.), *The Reinterpretation of American Economic History* (Harper & Row, 1971), p. 44.

TABLE 13.8

POPULATION DISTRIBUTION BY REGION 1840–1910

Year	Total (1,000's)	Northeast (%)	Midwest (%)	South (%)	West (%)
1840	17,120	39.5	19.6	40.6	—
1870	38,559	31.9	33.7	31.9	2.6
1880	50,189	28.9	34.6	32.9	3.6
1890	62,979	27.6	35.6	31.8	5.0
1900	76,213	27.6	34.6	32.2	5.7
1910	92,229	28.0	32.4	31.9	7.7

Source: U.S. Bureau of the Census, *Historical Statistics of the United States* (Government Printing Office, 1975), Series A172.

The big population winners in the postwar world were the Midwest and the West. Western population growth follows from the obvious economic opportunities for labor, but the Midwest's surge requires some more *ad hoc* explanation. Some of the new residents were probably drawn by the availability of inexpensive farmland. Hence it is at least plausible that a good portion of their income was nonpecuniary. They may have accepted low nominal returns to their labor in order to have the independence and security of farming their own acreage. It is also likely that emigrants to the region expected to do better than they actually did. The existence of widespread farm discontent is explored later in this chapter.

The Role of the Railroads

For Walter Rostow, the railroads have a special place in the explanation of American economic growth. His "take-off" dates from the 1840's, when the direct and indirect effects of steam powered rail transport were first felt. Rostow is not the only economic historian to pay homage to the railroad; nor was he the first. Leland Jenks's classic 1944 article (summarizing the views of many others) talks of the railroad "revolution" and covers much of the same ground as Rostow. Louis Hacker, writing in 1940, cites subsidies to railroads as a crucial government initiative in the emergence of industrial capitalism. In fact, for decades, railroads had been one historical issue enjoying widespread agreement from the experts.

All that changed abruptly in the early 1960's with the publication of research results on the quantitative impact of the railroads, both before

and after the Civil War. While the independent studies by Albert Fishlow and Robert Fogel arrive at somewhat different conclusions, both
have been interpreted as debunking the old consensus conclusion.
Fogel's work, in particular, created a controversy startlingly like the slavery contretemps of the early 1970's. This section offers some back-
ground material on the rise of the railroads and then looks at the historical and methodological battle over the impact of railroads on American
growth.

RAILROAD DEVELOPMENT

As noted in chapter 4, the first major rail projects in the 1830's which
connected eastern seaboard cities with the interior were built as a commercial defense against diversion of traffic by barges. The city of Baltimore, for example, promoted its line to the Ohio River in order to lure
shipping from the Chesapeake and Ohio Canal, which had its terminus
at Alexandria, Virginia. In general, these ambitious east-west rail projects were financial failures; they cost too much to construct and were extremely vulnerable to the business depression of the early 1840's. So,
too, were the short feeder railroads built largely with public funds to
connect market towns with water transport networks. Of the 3,000 miles
of track built in the 1830's, only the less ambitious north-south lines that
relied on passenger, rather than freight, traffic were clear successes.

Thus, rail development proceeded cautiously thereafter, with more
than half the track laid in the 1840's designed to serve densely populated
parts of New England and New York. Fishlow argues, however, that the
impetus for construction was still frequently collective rather than private: Boston, for example, pushed hard for its own route to the Great
Lakes in order to save commerce that would otherwise have been fun-
neled off to New York. By the early 1850's, Boston, New York, Philadelphia, and Baltimore had rail connections across the mountains to the
Midwest.

The big push awaited the 1850's. When Chicago was linked to the
East Coast, virtually every productive farm market area in the Midwest
was tied into the East Coast trade. The South held its own in construction during this second rail boom. Cotton marketing centers in the interior of Mississippi and Alabama were connected by rail to New Orleans
and Mobile, and an all-southern east-west railroad hooked Memphis and
Nashville to the east coast. Some 30,000 miles of track—half the world
total—were in place in America on the eve of the Civil War (see table
13.9).

Postwar rail expansion, like prewar expansion, came in waves. The
first surge—Fishlow dates it between 1868 and 1873—again doubled
total track in place. A good portion of the growth, oddly enough, came
in the Northeast and Midwest, where service was already relatively good.

TABLE 13.9

STATE RAILROAD MILEAGE 1840–60

Region/State	1840	1850	1860
New England	436 (13%)	2,633 (30%)	3,660 (12%)
Maine	10	257	472
New Hampshire	15	471	661
Vermont	—	366	554
Massachusetts	270	1,042	1,264
Rhode Island	47	61	108
Connecticut	94	436	601
Mid-Atlantic	1,510 (45%)	2,972 (33%)	6,353 (21%)
New York	453	1,409	2,682
New Jersey	192	332	560
Pennsylvania	576	900	2,598
Delaware	16	16	127
Maryland	273	315	386
Midwest	199 (6%)	1,307 (15%)	11,064 (36%)
Ohio	39	590	2,946
Indiana	20	226	2,163
Illinois	26	118	2,799
Michigan	114	349	799
Wisconsin	—	20	905
Iowa	—	—	655
Missouri	—	4	817
Old South	988 (30%)	1,578 (18%)	5,463 (18%)
Virginia	341	341	1,731
North Carolina	247	249	937
South Carolina	136	270	973
Georgia	212	666	1,420
Florida	52	52	402
New South	195 (6%)	389 (4%)	4,072 (13%)
Kentucky	32	80	534
Tennessee	—	48	1,253
Alabama	51	112	743
Mississippi	50	60	862
Arkansas	—	—	38
Louisiana	62	89	335
Texas	—	—	307
Total	3,328	8,879	30,613

Source: George Rogers Taylor, *The Transportation Revolution* (Holt, Rinehart, and Winston, 1951), p. 79.

But the enormous northeastern regional economy easily absorbed the growth. And land grants offered by Congress spurred construction in the Plains and Far West (see chapter 14). Clearly the most impressive accomplishment of this wave of construction was the completion of the first transcontinental line in 1869.

Rapid western expansion was built on a fragile financial structure that collapsed during the cyclical decline of the national economy in the mid-70's. With nearly one-fifth of the nation's track in bankruptcy, construction paused for a few years before climbing back up to the rates set in the early 1880's. Some 8,000 miles a year, on average, were built between 1879 and 1883, including the Southern Pacific and Northern Pacific and Santa Fe transcontinentals. Another short cyclic pause in the mid-80's is recorded by Fishlow, followed by a last surge (1886–92) that finished off the basic American rail system. The big holes in the southern and Gulf Coast systems were filled in, and a final transcontinental rail line was laid to the Pacific Northwest. Traffic density also made practicable secondary connections in much of the country. Aggregate statistics show strong, continuing growth into the 20th century; but this growth was virtually all intensive, raising the capacity of existing lines and providing service to less important trade centers.

CONSTRUCTION AHEAD OF DEMAND?

The rapid extension of the railroad between the 1850's and the 1880's has led many observers, including the great political economist Joseph Schumpeter, to argue that railroads literally pulled the economy west. By building "ahead of demand" across the Midwest, Great Plains, and Rockies, the railroads led the growth of the country. This view fits nicely too, at least in a casual sense, with Rostow's special endorsement of the railroads as the "leading" sector in the growth process.

This notion of "building ahead of demand" has assumed an honored position in the history of the American economy. But it is difficult to pin down exactly what is meant. Building ahead of demand might imply that the service created its own demand. This is a fuzzy concept indeed— every new product—frozen yogurt, autos, electric generators, frisbees— must create its own demand in the sense that no one had asked for the product before it was invented. This is probably not what people generally have in mind.

Building ahead of demand might mean investing in production facilities that will, at first, be utilized at less than capacity. This seems closer to the mark. Does such investment promote economic growth? If the returns are entirely captured by the investors, the test should be whether the present value of the discounted future income is greater than the opportunity cost of the resources invested. Sometimes building "ahead of demand" is extremely productive—a power utility, for example, might profitably begin construction of a new nuclear power plant eight years before it is really needed, provided that the discounted income is sufficiently great. Sometimes, of course, it is not. But the focus on lead time between construction and full utilization can only obscure the real issue: Was rail construction the most valuable use of investment resources at the time of the investment?

Society's gains from a major investment like a railroad may be greater than the gains to the investors. Some of the benefits may be classically defined "externalities"—increased knowledge applicable to production in other sectors, for example. Others may derive from the non-marginal aspect of a major innovation like the railroad; since market prices are determined by the value of services to users who value it least, benefits may flow to those lucky consumers who would have been willing to pay more, but don't need to. A wealthy tourist from New York, for example, might happily pay $500 for a safe, comfortable ride to San Francisco. But the price is set much lower to accommodate travelers who might otherwise forgo the trip or use alternate transportation.

In this case, the "building ahead of demand" notion takes on a different shading. It is possible that the private return to a rail project may come so far in the future that the discounted returns are insufficient to attract private investors but that the total gains to society are still well above the investment cost. It is also possible that private investors' aversion to risk is greater than society's as a whole, leading private investors to discount future returns at too high a rate and thereby to undervalue the income stream from a rail project.

In either of these cases the long lag between construction and profitable operation—building ahead of demand, so to speak—might make the private market reluctant to proceed with rail investments that, nonetheless, raised the rate of economic growth. In these circumstances the government would be justified in providing subsidies; and precisely this justification has been offered for the post–Civil War program of land grant subsidies to railroads (see chapter 14).

Fishlow finds that the antebellum railroads do not fit the description. He argues that midwestern rail construction was conservative, revealing no propensity to build ahead of demand. Most routes were profitable almost immediately. Average current returns on these routes were not spectacularly high (see table 13.10), but they hardly suggest that railroads were draining enterprises in which the payoff—if any—would come decades later. Rail lines were typically built to serve established farm regions. Of the total track mileage completed in Illinois by 1853, for example, sixty percent was located in the leading wheat and corn counties that made up just twenty-five percent of the state's area. In Wisconsin, seven wheat-producing counties (plus Milwaukee), comprising ten percent of the state's area, had sixty percent of the track in 1856. In

TABLE 13.10

**AVERAGE CURRENT NET EARNINGS OF
WESTERN RAILROADS**

	(percentage of construction costs)		
State	1849	1855–56	1859
Ohio	7.5	6.4	3.7
Indiana	6.1	6.2	5.2
Michigan	4.2	10.2	4.6
Illinois	8.7	6.8	3.5
Wisconsin	—	12.5	3.1
Iowa	—	—	3.0
Average	5.6	7.2	3.7

Source: Albert Fishlow, *Railroads and the Transformation of the AnteBellum Economy* (Harvard, 1965), p. 178.

Iowa, Fishlow demonstrates that virtually no rail construction took place until well after the first wave of settlement had begun.

Fogel's investigation of the Union Pacific Railroad paints a somewhat different picture. Judging by investors' behavior before construction, the transcontinental railroad was indeed built ahead of demand in the sense that the expected private return to capital was insufficient to attract capital at competitive rates. This justified the investment of public subsidies in the project since Congress was convinced that the total social returns—including the "binding" of the continent—were very large. In fact, both the private and social returns estimated by Fogel (see table 13.11) turned out to be very high (see table 13.12).

RAILROAD PRODUCTIVITY AND RATES

Often neglected in discussions of the railroads' impact on national productivity are the productivity gains made within the rail sector itself. Fishlow argues that technical improvements accounted for a major portion of the change. The very first lines in the 1830's were carbon copies of English railroads. But, in short order, less capital-intensive techniques were substituted. Road beds were built to avoid topographic obstacles rather than leveling them, bridging them, or tunneling through them. Iron/wood combinations replaced all-iron tracks and ties. Fishlow also notes that American railroads improved on European designs, as well as adjusting to relative factor scarcity. The "T" profile rail was adopted to increase the strength-to-weight ratio, for example. And domestically manufactured locomotives incorporated flexible trucks, which made them capable of riding tighter curves at higher speeds.

TABLE 13.11

RETURN ON CONSTRUCTION COSTS FOR UNION PACIFIC RAILROAD

Year	Accumulated Cost (millions$)	Net Earnings	Benefits Not Captured by Investors (millions$)	Private Return (%)	Social Return (%)
1870	53.1	2.2	5.9	4.2	15.3
1871	54.0	3.6	6.8	6.7	19.4
1872	54.8	3.7	7.8	6.7	20.9
1873	55.2	5.0	8.8	9.1	25.0
1874	55.5	5.5	9.8	9.9	27.5
1875	55.6	7.0	10.7	12.6	31.9
1876	55.6	8.8	11.7	15.7	36.8
1877	59.2	8.7	12.7	14.7	36.1
1878	59.2	10.5	13.7	17.8	40.9
1879	59.2	10.4	14.7	17.5	42.2
Average	—	—	—	11.6	29.9

Source: Robert Fogel, *The Union Pacific Railroad: A Case of Premature Enterprise* (Johns Hopkins, 1960), p. 106.

To minimize maintenance and increase load capacity, steel gradually replaced iron in rails after the 1860's. Locomotives increased in power without proportional cost increases, which then allowed the use of larger boxcars and longer trains. Automatic couplers, air brakes, and a new signaling system, all reduced labor requirements and permitted operation at higher speed.

Fishlow estimates that technical innovation explains about half of the increase in total factor productivity between 1870 and 1910. The rest he attributes to economies of scale, organization changes that maximized equipment operating time and reduced transhipment of freight. All this added up to an average annual increase in productivity of 2.6 percent for 1839–1910, and 1.9 percent for 1870–1910 (see table 13.12). For purposes of comparison, remember that total factor productivity change for the economy as a whole was below one percent annually for both time spans.

Who received the benefits of increased productivity? In terms of 1910 prices, the average cost of hauling a ton of freight one mile dropped from 1.65 cents to .75 cents from 1870 to 1910. This works out to an average annual savings of 2 percent, slightly more than the industry's 1.9 percent productivity improvement. Productivity change need not precisely mirror cost changes, of course. Factor prices were also changing. But when considered in light of the substantial competition between railroads in most places, the statistics strongly suggest that consumers and shippers received much of the benefits.

DIRECT RAILROAD BENEFITS

Rostow and other development economists have concentrated their attention on the indirect benefit of railroads, a subject considered shortly. But common sense suggests that the direct benefits, as measured by the reduced real cost of moving freight and passengers around the country, should be the central source of the railroads' contribution to growth.

Fishlow computed the direct benefits for both passenger and rail service in 1859, and then extrapolated to generate a rough guess about the magnitude of savings in 1890. The initial calculations procedure was enormously detailed, so no attempt will be made to reproduce the process. Instead, here is a summary of the method behind the numbers derivation and Fishlow's basic conclusions.

TABLE 13.12

INDEX OF RAILROAD PRODUCTIVITY

Year	Output	Labor	Capital	Fuel	Total Factor Productivity
1839	.08	.3	.8	.07	16.0
1849	.46	1.1	2.2	.20	32.8
1859	2.21	5.0	10.1	1.5	33.5
1870	6.57	13.5	16.6	5.4	47.3
1880	13.87	24.5	31.5	11.7	53.6
1890	32.82	44.1	61.9	28.7	66.6
1900	54.84	59.9	72.3	45.9	86.7
1910	100	100	100	100	100

Interpretation: Total factor productivity is explained in the appendix to chapter 4. The table shows inputs, outputs, and productivity relative to the levels existing in 1910. For example, in 1880 (by comparison with 1910) roughly 12 percent as much fuel, 32 percent as much capital, and 25 percent as much labor were used to yield 14 percent as much rail service. This implies a total factor productivity of about 54 percent of the 1910 level.

Source: Albert Fishlow, "Productivity and Technological Change in the Railroad Sector 1840–1910" in National Bureau of Economic Research, *Output Employment and Productivity in the United States After 1800*, vol. 30, Studies on Income and Wealth (Columbia University, 1966), p. 626.

The social savings per ton of freight equals the difference between rail and water transport charges, plus an allowance to account for the speed, freedom from seasonal restrictions, and safety advantages of railroads. For passengers, the social savings calculation is based on the per-mile price difference between rail, and either water or stagecoach, whichever was relevant to the particular route. No allowance is made for the sharp improvement in comfort that railroads provided over land transport. Fishlow's initial 1859 social savings estimates are $155 million for freight and $70 million for passengers. After much consideration of possible biases and alternative formulations, he concludes that the total 1859 social savings—passenger and freight—was probably a minimum of $150 to $175 million.

That figure represents about 4 percent of GNP, a not inconsiderable sum, but less than many would have expected. Fishlow attempts no ambitious analysis of rail social savings at later dates. He argues, though, that if the ton-mile and passenger-mile rate differences between railroad and the alternatives were the same in 1890 as they had been in 1859, the social savings would have been much larger. A reduction in freight costs of roughly three-quarters would yield $1.5 billion annually, while the passenger gain would total $300 million. Together they would account for about 15 percent of GNP in the late 19th century.

Robert Fogel attempts a more explicit measure of rail social savings for freight traffic in 1890. He divides the problem into two parts: interregional traffic savings and intraregional traffic savings. The first component is measured in roughly the same way as Fishlow derives his estimates; east-west water and rail rates are compared and the differences multiplied by the actual tonnage hauled for the four major agricultural commodities: pork, beef, wheat, and corn. His first approximation is *negative*—rail costs more than water. But the superior service provided by railroads—reduced cargo losses, lower inventory costs, simplified handling—generates a net positive savings of about $73 million.

Fogel's estimation procedure for intraregional savings, the reduced cost of moving commodities from farm to distribution center, is more complex. A first approximation is needed to estimate the net cost difference in hauling the goods actually produced in 1890 by wagon and by existing water routes. The total, amended to account for service quality differences, is $337 million. But this obviously exaggerates the real social savings because many farms were able to operate far from canals and rivers only because of the availability of low-cost rail service. In some cases, the hypothetical cost of getting the crop from farm to city by alternative means would have exceeded the total market value of the crop. And in many others it surely would have exceeded the difference between a farmer's variable costs—seed, labor, wear on animals and machinery—and the market price, ensuring that under no circumstance would the shipment have actually been made.

AREAS IN WHICH COMMERCIAL AGRICULTURE WAS FEASIBLE WITHOUT RAILROADS OR ADDITIONAL CANAL CONSTRUCTION

Fogel argues that water transportation, combined with short wagon hauls, could serve commercial agriculture adequately in the eastern half of the United States and swatches of the Great Plains and Pacific Coast.

Source: Robert Fogel, *Railroads and American Economic Growth* (Johns Hopkins, 1964), p. 81.

Fogel attacks the problem of measuring true social savings by applying the theory of rent. In the long run, the price of most resources—labor, capital—are determined by their value in other uses. But the return to land, a truly fixed factor, is in the nature of a residual: It is what is left over after the other, more mobile factors have been paid a competitive return. Land income thus captures the economic advantage of reduced transportation costs since, with or without good transport, the other factors command the same return. High-cost wagon and water transportation, Fogel computes, would have rendered uneconomical the use of the 24 percent of the country's farmland that was more than forty miles from existing waterway. This land was worth about $1.9 billion in 1890 and generated an annual income of about $153 million (see table 13.13). Fogel adds the $153 million to a more conventionally derived estimate of the increased cost of hauling goods to waterways for the 76 percent of farmland he figures would have remained in cultivation; his grand total is some $248 million annual social savings.

That figure, too, Fogel argues, is an overestimate of the social savings since more land could have been opened up by additional canal construction. Fogel actually proposes a system of 5,000 miles of canals that would have made cultivation profitable on 93 percent of 1890 farmland. Again combining an unconventional estimate of lost land rents (on the remaining 7 percent of land) with a conventional estimate of rail vs. water social savings, Fogel pares his social savings figure to just $175 million. Yet another pass at refining the counterfactual hypothesis—this time

TABLE 13.13

INCOME LOSSES DUE TO DECREASED LAND SUPPLY— FOGEL'S FIRST APPROXIMATION

Region	Land Value Lost (%)	Value of Lost Land (millions$)	Rental Income Lost (millions$)
North Atlantic	0.5	6	—
South Atlantic	21.1	118	8
North Central	29.2	1,442	110
South Central	21.5	159	14
Western	27.2	218	20
Total	23.9	1,943	154

Note: Column 3 is computed by multiplying the estimated mortgate interest rate prevalent in the state, times the reduced value of the land.

Source: Robert Fogel, *Railroads and American Economic Growth* (Johns Hopkins, 1964), pp. 82–83.

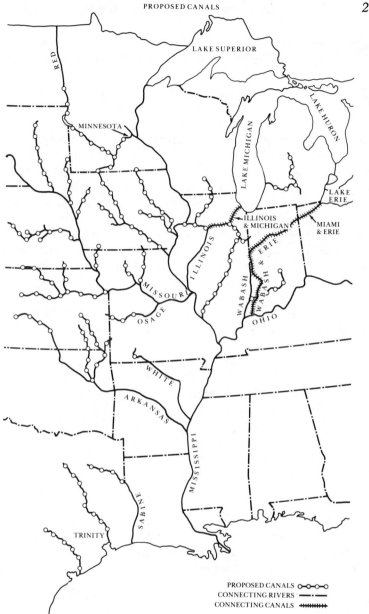

**A HYPOTHETICAL 5,000-MILE SUPPLEMENTARY CANAL SYSTEM
TO SERVE THE MIDWEST AND GREAT PLAINS**

Fogel's elaborate counterfactual hypothesis includes a set of supplementary canals to raise farmland value and open portions of the Great Plains otherwise inaccessible to commercial agriculture without railroads.

Source: Robert Fogel, *Railroads and American Economic Growth* (Johns Hopkins University, 1964), p. 93.

adding improved roads that would have allowed 96 percent of the land to be cultivated profitably—brings the social savings down to just $117 million.

Agricultural commodities represented only a modest fraction of total freight in 1890, only one-quarter of all ton-miles recorded. It is plausible, therefore, to simply multiply Fogel's agricultural estimates by a factor of four to get the total social savings for all freight. But this approximation, according to Fogel, is unnecessarily crude. Half of the nonagricultural freight by weight consisted of coal and iron ore—low-value bulk commodities where the social savings per ton could be expected to be far less than for grain or meat. The agricultural social savings, moreover, implicitly include a portion of the nonagricultural since all of the railroad overhead cost was attributed to agriculture. Yet shipment of the two kinds of commodities often complemented each other because they went opposite directions on the same routes. Fogel guesses that, overall, the social savings could have been no more than $560 million, or just 4.7 percent of 1890 GNP.

Why is Fogel's estimate so much smaller than Fishlow's? In part because Fogel does not include passenger savings. Hayden Boyd and Gary Walton estimate that, when the value of reduced travel time and improved comfort standards are included, passengers saved about $344 million in 1890. Combined with Fogel's own figure for freight traffic savings, the upper bound on total social savings reaches $904 million or 7.3 percent of GNP. Fogel argues that Fishlow overstates freight savings by being too generous in making assumptions. Fishlow, moreover, never considers the opportunities for nonrail adjustments—construction of new canals and roads—that would almost certainly have taken place if the railroad had not been around to help.

BACKWARD LINKAGES
Development economists call the demands that a growing industry makes on other industries "backward linkages." For Rostow and others, these linkages are a critical part of the case for railroads as the leading sector in the American growth process; the derived demand for coal, iron, and advanced engineering technology is thought to have given a push to the economy far beyond the direct benefits enumerated above. Does the case for backward linkages hold up under scrutiny?

Both Fishlow and Fogel are skeptical. Railroads did use large amounts of iron, but the impact on domestic iron demand was blunted by the use of imports and by the fact that scrap rails were a good substitute for virgin pig iron in the production of new rails. Fishlow calculates that from 1840 to 1850 *net* railroad iron consumption was just seven percent of the pig iron made in America. With the rail boom of the 1850's, though, that percentage was raised considerably, reaching twenty percent by the last half of the decade (see table 13.14).

TABLE 13.14

DERIVED RAILROAD DEMAND FOR PIG IRON

Demand Source	1840–45	1846–50	1851–55	1856–60
Net Demand for Rails (1,000 tons)	56	208	222	522
Demand for Locomotives (1,000 tons)	6	16	63	43
Other Railroad Demand (1,000 tons)	34	84	280	197
Total Railroad Demand (1,000 tons)	96	308	565	762
Rail Demand as % of Iron Consumed	4.5	7.9	15.8	18.9
Rail Demand as % of Domestic Production	4.7	8.6	18.6	20.6

Source: Albert Fishlow, *American Railroads and the Transformation of the Antebellum American Economy* (Harvard, 1965), p. 142.

After the Civil War, the industry's economic impact on ferrous iron-derived metals was even greater. It used roughly sixty percent of the Bessemer-process steel produced in the United States through 1880; and in 1889, twenty-nine percent of all the iron and steel production was devoted to the railroad. Note, however, that the post–Civil War linkage is irrelevant to the Rostovian thesis—it is the prewar experience that counts. By any reasonable interpretation of the statistics, economic growth was booming while the railroad was generating only a ripple in the iron industry's pond.

Rostow also tries to link the railroads to demand for coal, the great fuel of the industrial age. The figures, however, are hardly well suited for the part Rostow assigns to them. Before the Civil War, locomotives burned wood; only in the late 1850's did coal-powered trains enter service. Fogel points out that much of the iron consumed by the railroad sector was made with coal. But he estimates that only 12.6 million tons— just 6 percent of coal demand—could be attributed to the needs of railroads during the 1840–60 period.

Railroads absorbed large amounts of industrial machinery—locomotives, rolling stock, switching, signaling, and coupling equipment. Hence the temptation to infer a strong backward linkage to the machinery industry in general, and the steam engine industry in particular. Again, however, the numbers disappoint. The railroad's share of total machine production in 1859 was less than 10 percent. Locomotive production value in that year was slightly less than the value of machinery made for the textile industry. Locomotive producers were rarely brand-new firms coaxed into existence by specialized demand. Fishlow notes that most began as producers of marine engines, textile machinery, or as general machine shops. Indeed, Fishlow's estimates imply that steamboats, not railroads, were the largest purchasers of steam engines until at least the late 1850's.

FORWARD LINKAGES

Development economists are also interested in the "forward" railroad linkages, the impact of railroads on those who consumed rail services. There is a plausible list of many beneficiaries—farmers, miners, food processors, and manufacturers of equipment to serve all of them. It is important to be careful, however, in distinguishing the gross impact of railroads—the enormous movements in the location of economic activity—from the gain in real output. A new transport link that creates a meat-packing industry in Chicago or Kansas City is not a net gain to the economy unless the change also increases the productivity of the resources employed.

Fogel warns, moreover, that the forward linkage efficiency gains may be "double-counted." Railroads, for example, undoubtedly made it possible for some farmers in the Midwest and Plains to specialize in grain and wheat. Resources from inefficient eastern farms could thus be transferred, resulting in higher national income. But note that the value of efficiency gains, for a competitive economy, is precisely what Fogel is measuring in his land value calculation and in the direct calculation of social savings resulting from lowered shipping costs.

This does not mean that forward linkage gains can be dismissed entirely. At least some of the benefits may be captured as monopoly profits by the rail sector. And some could be diffused through the economy in the form of external benefits to the forward linkage industries—learning-by-doing,[3] training of skilled workers, technical research with applications outside the immediate purview of the researchers. But it should be remembered that the burden of proof rests with those who believe that rail forward linkages were important to pre–Civil War growth. Virtually any forward linkage case made for the railroads in the 1830's or 1840's can be made better by substituting canals or steamboats—or for that matter, cotton plantations.

Fogel, Fishlow, and the Critics

The attempts to measure railroad social savings and their significance to the economy has generated a flood of scholarly criticism. We certainly

[3]See chapter 5 for a discussion of this concept.

cannot do justice to the debate here; readers will have to settle for a synopsis of the highlights and a rather extensive bibliograhy.

TRANSPORT COSTS VS. FREIGHT RATES

Social savings consist of the reduction in real resources employed in providing a given amount of transport services. However the data Fogel and Fishlow were forced to use were not actually resource cost data at, all, but price data. Peter McClelland and Stanley Lebergott argue that the prices charged by railroads and canals are unlikely to be a good proxy for costs—in fact, McClelland notes, competition between the modes should guarantee identical fares on identical routes for equal service. In his view this explains why Fogel's first approximation of inter-regional rail savings was negative: Canals were forced to charge less because they provided inferior service.

Lebergott tries to avoid the cost/price problem by reconstructing cost per ton mile for typical rail and canal service. He estimates that in 1840 canal costs were already four times as high as railroad costs. This is roughly consistent with Fishlow's computation for 1859, confirming intrinsic resource savings roughly on the order of Fishlow's rather than Fogel's. Actually, Lebergott argues, this is probably an underestimate of the true social savings, since rail technology improved greatly after 1840 and railroads offered greater safety and speed.

UPWARD BOUNDS

Everyone agrees that social savings estimates are of necessity very crude. Thus, when in doubt, it is the obligation of the researcher either to provide some estimate of the margin of error around the estimate or to load the estimation procedure against the case he or she is trying to prove. Fogel believes that the significance of rail social savings has been overstated by others. He therefore accepts the obligation to find an "upper-bound" estimate of the range of plausible estimates of total social savings. That way, if the savings estimate turns out to be small, we will know *a fortiori* that he is right.

Unfortunately, the crudeness of the calculation makes it impossible for Fogel to really deliver on his obligation. As Fogel admits, however, his approach to measuring intraregional social savings embodies both upward and downward biases. And as Mark Nerlove and Paul David note, Fogel cannot legitimately assume that the two sorts of biases simply cancel out.

David claims that the waterways could not have handled the vastly increased quantities of freight at constant cost per unit, as Fogel assumes. It is at least possible that with crowding of facilities, secondary, less efficient water routes would have been needed to supplement the cheapest, most direct routes. He also argues that Fogel underestimates the cost of constructing loading facilities at points along rivers and lakes chosen solely to minimize wagon haulage. And he notes that Fogel probably underestimates the size of emergency storage facilities needed to handle inventories in transit during weather interruptions on water routes.

IDENTIFYING INDIRECT BENEFITS

To one degree or another, virtually everyone who writes about the rail social savings issue must wrestle with the way Fogel has constructed his counterfactual hypothesis. To measure social savings, it is necessary to construct a hypothetical world that never was and trust that it corresponds to the world that would otherwise have been. The bigger the counterfactual, the bigger the problem, and Fogel's is certainly very large.

This is really another way of saying that no one knows very much about the indirect savings attributable to railroads. It could be argued, as Paul David does, that forward linkages created substantial "learning-by-doing" among the railroads' customers. And unless a great deal is known about how an economy really works, it is hard to argue the point very forcefully one way or the other. Luckily for Fogel and Fishlow, Rostow probably offered the one counterfactual hypothesis that could be refuted—namely that railroads were important to growth before the 1850's. If Fogel and Fishlow have their troubles, Rostow is, by comparison, up to his ears in woe.

SOCIAL SAVINGS AND THE AXIOM
OF INDISPENSABILITY

Fogel's research on the railroads was motivated by an urge to debunk what he calls the "axiom of indispensability," the notion that the railroad was the critical institutional change upon which 19th-century economic growth depended. That turned out to be easy game. A mere glance at the timing of growth and the relatively late start of the railroads suggests that economic development and railroads were not inextricably linked. If railroads were indispensable to growth, so too surely were canals, steamboats, banks, power looms, and slavery. And Fogel's ambitious counterfactual construction of 5,000 miles of canals to open the Great Plains to commercial agriculture knocks the wind out of the psychological argument that railroads were literally critical to the physical expansion of the frontier.

But what is to be made of the axiom when it is rephrased in more cautious language—that is, that railroads were extremely important to economic growth? Fogel's calculation puts the direct social savings on freight haulage from railroads at 4.7 percent of GNP in 1890. Add the

Boyd-Walton estimated savings from passenger service, and the figure is up to 7.3 percent of GNP. That is perhaps less than might be guessed after a steady dose of cowboys and Indians and railroads movies. But can it really be said that 7.3 percent is not a lot of income?

The answer depends upon how you look at it. The figure 7.3 percent represents less than two years' growth in the late 19th century. On the other hand, it is nearly four years' growth in per capita terms—surely the more relevant benchmark if individual welfare is what economic systems are trying to maximize. Or consider the following test, suggested by Paul David. Technical innovations—among them, the railroad—raised incomes by about one percent per year between 1840 and 1890. Assuming that the railroad raised total income by 7.3 percent by the final year, it must have had an average annual impact on growth of about 0.14 percent—fully one-seventh of all progress attributable to technical change during the half century.

Another test would be to ask how much the railroad invention was worth in present dollars, how much contemporary investors would have paid for the right to a new product able to generate an annual income stream equal to the railroads' social savings in 1890 ($904 million). Discounted at 6 percent, that income stream has a present value of $15 billion, the total output of the 1890 American economy for about 14 months.

Then suppose the $15 billion worth of capital needed to generate $904 million each year had been set aside strictly for the benefit of future generations. If the $15 billion nest egg had earned just 3 percent interest a year in real terms, it would be worth $214 billion today in 1890 purchasing power, or about *$1.4 trillion* at today's prices. Thus, in a sense, for Americans alive in 1979, the opportunity cost of not building the railroads in the 19th century might be estimated at $1.4 trillion!

Such blue-sky calculations, however, can seem as relevant as Sonny & Cher. Many economists would just as soon back away from "indispensability"-style calculations and ask a more limited question: How did the average social rate of return on capital invested in the railroads compare with the return on other contemporary investments? Calculations for some individual railroads are quite impressive: Fogel's estimated average social rate of return for the Union Pacific (discussed earlier) was a whopping 30 percent, while Lloyd Mercer's estimated social return for the Central Pacific system is 24 percent. Fishlow calculates the average return for all railroads at 15 percent in 1859, at least twice the return to other secure assets. And David computes a comparable return of 12–16 percent for 1890.

Were the railroads important to economic growth? Yes.

Were they *very* important? It is all in the eye of the beholder.

The Puzzle of Farm Discontent

The years between the Civil War and World War I reveal a massive expansion of farm output as farming spread through the Midwest, the Plains States, and along the Pacific Coast. According to John Kendrick, gross farm output increased at an average annual rate of 2.5 percent between 1869 and 1909 (see table 13.15). That is much less than industrial growth but is still a remarkable achievement considering the immense changes in distribution and transportation required to link consumers in Boston or Pittsburgh with wheat farmers in North Dakota or cattle ranchers in central Texas.

In productivity terms, the record of the farm sector is less impressive. Grain yields per acre were virtually unchanged over the period; the opening of the West allowed crop expansion to take place without the

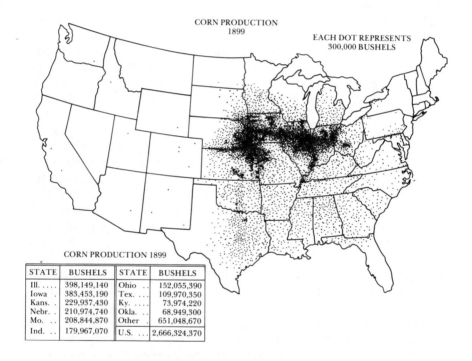

CORN PRODUCTION
1899

EACH DOT REPRESENTS
300,000 BUSHELS

CORN PRODUCTION 1899

STATE	BUSHELS	STATE	BUSHELS
Ill.	398,149,140	Ohio . .	152,055,390
Iowa .	383,453,190	Tex. . . .	109,970,350
Kans. .	229,937,430	Ky.	73,974,220
Nebr. .	210,974,740	Okla. . .	68,949,300
Mo. . .	208,844,870	Other .	651,048,670
Ind. . .	179,967,070	U.S. . . .	2,666,324,370

CORN PRODUCTION IN THE UNITED STATES, 1899

Although corn was grown almost everywhere there were farms, its commercial cultivation was centered in a broad belt of land from Ohio to Kansas and Nebrasks.

Source: Adapted by Robert Higgs, *The Transformation of the American Economy, 1865–1914* (Wiley, 1971), p. 84; from U.S. Department of Agriculture, *Yearbook, 1921* (Government Printing Office, 1922), p. 173.

TABLE 13.15

FARM SECTOR GROWTH 1869–1909
(average annual rate in percent)

	1869–79	1879–89	1889–99	1899–1909	1869–1909
Corn Production	8.7	1.9	2.3	−0.4	3.1
Wheat Production	4.8	0.2	3.5	0.3	2.2
Cotton Production	6.7	2.6	2.3	0.7	3.0
Cattle Stock*	3.3	3.6	3.6	0.8	1.8
Farm Output	4.9	1.5	2.7	0.8	2.5
Value of Farm Output (constant dollars)	4.4	1.9	2.5	—	—

*The rate of growth of number of cattle on farms is an underestimate of the growth in beef production because the amount of meat per steer grew over time.

Source: U.S. Bureau of the Census, *Historical Statistics of the United States*, Series K-240, K-414, K-503, K-507, K-554, K-564.

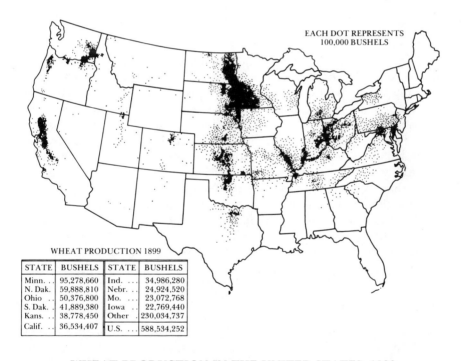

EACH DOT REPRESENTS 100,000 BUSHELS

WHEAT PRODUCTION 1899

STATE	BUSHELS	STATE	BUSHELS
Minn. . .	95,278,660	Ind. . . .	34,986,280
N. Dak.	59,888,810	Nebr. . .	24,924,520
Ohio . .	50,376,800	Mo. . . .	23,072,768
S. Dak. .	41,889,380	Iowa . .	22,769,440
Kans. . .	38,778,450	Other	230,034,737
Calif. . .	36,534,407	U.S. . . .	588,534,252

WHEAT PRODUCTION IN THE UNITED STATES, 1899

By the turn of the century, wheat production was heavily concentrated in the northern plains of the Dakotas and Minnesota.

Source: Adapted by Robert Higgs, *The Transformation of the American Economy, 1865–1914* (Wiley, 1971), p. 83; from U.S. Department of Agriculture, *Yearbook, 1921* (Government Printing Office, 1922), p. 332.

use of marginal croplands but did not actually raise average yields. Total factor productivity change lagged well behind the rest of the economy: Kendrick's estimate of the average annual improvement for the farm sector is only about 0.7, and just 0.6 for the Midwest grain belt. Nonetheless, massive doses of capital in the form of labor-saving machinery did allow substantial increases in labor productivity.

While these statistics may not quite paint a picture of a farm sector brimming with vitality, they hardly seem sufficient clues to the cause of the profound discontent expressed by farmers—particularly upper Midwest and Plains States' farmers—with their lot in life. That discontent spawned numerous organized protests, culminating in the populist campaigns of the 1890's. Until recently, historians were inclined to take the protestors' complaints at face value, accepting the notion that farmers were trapped by relatively sluggish growth in demand for their products and by the economic power of railroads, land speculators, and banks. These traditional arguments are, alas, only weakly buttressed by evidence.

LOW PRICES

Farm prices fell during most of the post–Civil War period. Corn that sold for about 70 cents a bushel in the early 1870's fetched only 30 to 40 cents in the late 1880's. Wheat prices slipped from about $1 to 70 cents during the same period, and cotton prices similarly declined by 20 to 30 percent. These figures are not very useful, even as a first approximation of the farmers' plight, however, for other prices fell as well. Conservative postwar monetary policies, interacting with enormous improvements in industrial productivity, led to a long decline in wholesale and consumer prices that ended only in the late 1890's. The important index, then, is what happened to the purchasing power of farm products, the terms at which farm output could be traded for other commodities.

The index shown in table 13.16 is far from perfect; prices were mainly sampled in New York, not in rural areas, and farm products cannot be separated from the all-commodity index to provide a price measure for the farm/nonfarm terms of trade. Nonetheless, it is hard to use this index as support for farmers' complaints.

Recent research by John Bowman and Richard Keehn is yet more damning. They computed terms of trade for four midwestern states in which farm complaints were loud and persistent. In table 13.17, farm commodity prices (columns 1 and 3) show trend change in favor of farmers, whether terms of trade are measured against national wholesale or retail prices. Farmers suffering from small harvests might, of course, be worse off, in spite of favorable price trends. So Bowman and Keehn calculate the trend in real income terms of trade—farm revenue divided by all commodity prices—for each state's farm crops (columns 2 and 4). Note the rapid growth in farm purchasing power for each state.

TABLE 13.16

FARMERS' TERMS OF TRADE 1870–1900

Year	All Commodities Price Index	Farm Products Price Index	Farmers' Terms of Trade (1870 = 100)[a]
1870	135	112	100
1872	136	108	96
1874	126	102	98
1876	110	89	98
1878	91	72	95
1880	100	80	96
1882	108	99	110
1884	93	82	106
1886	82	68	100
1888	86	75	105
1890	82	71	104
1890[b]	82	74	109
1892	76	73	116
1894	70	65	112
1896	68	58	103
1898	71	67	114
1900	82	74	109

[a]The price of goods farmers sold, divided by the price of goods they purchased.

[b]Two different wholesale price indices are spliced together in 1890; since they show different terms of trade, we include both for that year.

Sources: U.S. Bureau of the Census, *Historical Statistics of the United States*, Series E-40, E-42, E-52, E-53.

TABLE 13.17

FOUR STATE FARMERS' TERMS OF TRADE, 1870–1900
(average annual rate of change %)

State	Warren-Pearson Wholesale		Hoover Consumer	
	Commodity Terms	Income Terms	Commodity Terms	Income Terms
Illinois	0.83	2.70	0.50	2.36
Indiana	0.32	2.27	0	1.96
Iowa	0.52	4.30	0.19	3.98
Wisconsin	0.55	3.98	0.23	3.66

Interpretation: Each of the four columns shows a separate calculation of how, on average, farm purchasing power changed annually from 1870 to 1900. Note that in every state, and by virtually every measure, the trend was positive, favoring farmers over nonfarmers.

Source: John Bowman and Richard Keehn, "Agricultural Terms of Trade in Four Midwestern States 1870–1900," *Journal of Economic History* 34 (Sept., 1974), p. 602.

TABLE 13.18

PRODUCTIVITY-ADJUSTED TERMS OF TRADE, 1870–1900
(average annual rate of change)

	Warren-Pearson Wholesale		Hoover Consumer	
	Single Factoral	Double Factoral	Single Factoral	Double Factoral
Illinois	2.02	0.52	1.70	0.19
Indiana	1.60	0.07	1.25	−0.10
Iowa	2.52	1.01	2.20	0.69
Wisconsin	2.47	0.98	2.16	0.67

Interpretation: The columns follow the approach of table 13.17. But, here, a more refined measure of terms of trade is used, based on the purchasing power of the goods produced by a unit of labor rather than the purchasing power of the total crop produced. Again, the results suggest strongly favorable trends for farmers.

Source: John Bowman and Richard Keehn, "Agricultural Terms of Trade in Four Midwestern States 1870–1900," *Journal of Economic History* 34 (Sept., 1974), p. 602.

The income terms of trade do not tell much about the purchasing power of the average farmers' crop. Hence the virtue of the productivity-adjusted terms of trade shown in table 13.18. The "single factoral" indices (columns 1 and 3) offer the trends in the real purchasing power per unit of farm labor; the "double factoral" indices (columns 2 and 4) provide estimates of the trend in real purchasing power per unit of farm labor, relative to changes in output per worker for the manufacturing sector.

In each of the four states (and by either price index) the real income per farm worker rose at a trend rate between 1.25 and 2.5 percent per year. This does not mean that farm *wages* rose at this rate; some of the income gain must be imputed to farm capital and to land. But it does mean that the average farm worker saw his or her real gross income rise between 45 percent (Indiana-Hoover index) and 111 percent (Iowa-Warren Pearson index) over the 30-year period. And the positive trends in the double factoral indices shown for all states (save Indiana, gauged by the Hoover index) reveal that the real value of the product of a farm laborer's work rose relative to the real value of a manufacturing worker's daily output.

For those who have any remaining doubts, Robert Fogel and Jack Rutner's estimates of agricultural income and productivity should be decisive. Table 13.19 shows that real farm income per capita and per

TABLE 13.19

**TRENDS IN FARM INCOME AND
PRODUCTIVITY**
(average annual percentage change)

Years	Real Income per Capita	Real Income per Worker
1849–59	2.0	2.0
1859–69	0.8	0.9
1869–79	0.8	0.3
1879–89	0.7	0
1889–99	2.2	2.1
1849–99	1.3	1.0
1869–99	1.2	0.7

Source: Robert Fogel and Jack Rutner, "Efficiency Effects of Federal Land Policy, 1850–1900" in William Aydelotte et al., *Dimensions in Quantitative Research in Economic History* (Princeton, 1972), p. 396.

worker rose substantially in the postwar decades. The rates generally fell short of the 1.6 percent and 1.4 percent average annual gains for the economy as a whole (1849–99). But as table 13.20 reveals, the productivity gap disappears when the South is eliminated from the farm sector.

THE CAPITALIST SQUEEZE

The terms-of-trade evidence and the Fogel-Rutner income trend estimates cast doubt on the idea that farmers got the short end of the stick in the late 19th century. But there is no doubt that they perceived them-

TABLE 13.20

REAL AGRICULTURAL INCOME PER WORKER BY REGION
(average annual percentage change)

Years	North Atlantic	North Central	South	United States, Less South	United States, Less South and N. Atlantic
1839–79	1.3	1.9	0	1.4	1.8
1879–99	0.2	1.5	0.9	1.2	1.5
1839–99	1.0	1.8	0.3	1.3	1.7

Source: Robert Fogel and Jack Rutner, "Efficiency Effects of Federal Land Policy 1850–1900" in William Aydelotte et al., *Dimensions in Quantitative Research in Economic History* (Princeton, 1972), p. 397.

selves as victims and had no difficulty in identifying their oppressors. Enemy number one was the railroads, whom farmers were convinced stole the fruits of the land by charging monopoly freight rates.

The evidence on railroad rates is mixed. Where railroads were competitive with each other or with water routes—that is, east of Chicago—there seems little doubt that rates usually charged were no higher than the average cost of providing the service. And the special economics of the railroad industry—enormous initial investments, but low operating costs—often led to rate wars in which shipping prices fell below the levels needed to generate adequate rates of return on invested capital. Further west, however, there was less competition and, consequently, greater oportunity for profitable rate discrimination against local shippers. Undoubtedly there were times and routes where the railroads earned substantial monopoly profits at the expense of struggling farmers.

Overall, though it is difficult to translate the existence of some rate discrimination in to broad farmer victimization. According to Robert Higgs, the fall in average rates per ton-mile roughly paralleled the fall in farm prices through 1890, and thereafter fell much more rapidly. For the railroad industry as a whole, monopoly profits earned at the expense of some farmers were apparently frittered away in rate wars—Fishlow's estimates of the private rate of return on rail capital are no higher than might have been earned in other industries.

Douglass North argues, moreover, that when the railroads are seen as only one link in the distribution chain, the farmers' general case against the middleperson fades away entirely. A good portion of American wheat was exported, and over the 1870–1900 period, Atlantic freight rates fell by two-thirds. Increased competition and organizational efficiencies, note Morton Rothstein, guaranteed that reduced international distribution costs narrowed the gap between what consumers paid and what farmers got.

If the railroads were enemy number one, moneylenders and land speculators competed for the honor of runner-up. The populists believed that interest demanded on farm mortgages was a form of bloodsucking. Some of the agrarian writing of the 1800's is too confused to interpret. The core of the argument against financial intermediaries, though, seems to have been that monopoly power allowed the representatives of banks and insurance companies to charge interest above competitive rates. In fact, Allan Bogue's evidence suggests that the western mortgage industry was immensely competitive—thanks, ironically, to the entry of the hated eastern moneylenders into the western market. Interest rates reflected the risks of farming on the Great Plains in the 1880's and were thus higher than rates on gilt-edged securities. But they were far lower than interest rates had been in earlier years on the agricultural frontier.

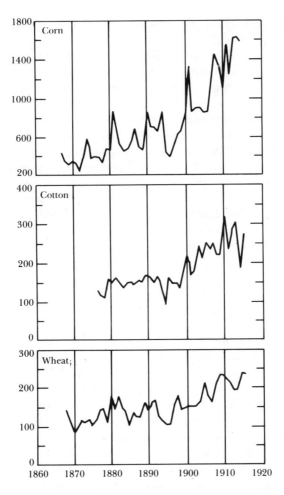

**INDICES OF FARM PRICES RELATIVE TO
RAILROAD RATES**

For corn, cotton, and wheat, railroad rates and market prices often moved in different directions. But Higgs's calculations show a mild treatment in favor of shippers over the 1870–1900 period.

Source: Robert Higgs, "Railroad Rates and the Populist Uprising," *Agricultural History* 44 (July, 1970), p. 295.

There is a subtler argument against agricultural creditors to be made here, one that, on initial hearing, appeals to economists. Mortgages are obligations fixed in money terms, not in real value terms. Hence in a period of declining prices, like the first three postwar decades, mortgage holders were paid back in increasingly valuable dollars by property owners whose incomes were not necessarily growing apace with the financial obligation.

The flaw here is that market interest rates adjust to anticipated price trends; only if debtors fail to anticipate declining prices do they truly lose out. And it is hard to believe that farmers' price expectations could have failed to adjust to a trend that lasted thirty years. Farmers were simply not likely to borrow at interest rates that they knew could not be supported by future crop revenues. There are other problems with this creditor-debtor redistribution argument, too. According to North, only 29 percent of farmers in 1890 were encumbered by mortgages, and among those that were, the debt averaged only 35 percent of their worth. Debt rates were higher in the troubled Plains States (60 percent in Kansas, 54 percent in Nebraska). But the average time to maturity for those mortgages was less than four years, suggesting that any losses due to unanticipated price changes were quickly worked through the system. Robert Fogel and Jack Rutner calculate that, since mortgages were short-lived and the ratio of debt to farm value was low, the overall wealth loss to farmers could not have been large.

TOWARDS A SOLUTION

If price trends generally favored farmers, and the intermediaries—banks, railroads—were generally unable to usurp their income, why did the farmers complain? One possibility is that generalities about price trends, railroad rates, and loan costs mask great variations in the experience of individual farmers. And it is surely plausible that the system produced large numbers of losers who had much to complain about. It would be little comfort to a North Dakota farmer that rates extorted by the local carrier would be returned to other farmers somewhere down the mainline in cut-throat competition. For farmers so foolish or unlucky as to become caught between expensive mortgages and declining grain prices, the general improvement of the agricultural capital market would be no comfort at all. Protest movements don't run on averages. The big losers can carry the majority, particularly when the majority consists of those near the bottom of the economic ladder.

Anne Mayhew extends this argument by taking special note of the institutional changes that exposed post–Civil War family farmers to greater risks. Prior to the war, most farmers tried—with varying success—to produce surpluses for market and were only somewhat at the mercy of market forces that determined crop prices, f.o.b. But postwar grain farmers—like postwar cotton farmers—were compelled by economic forces to sell a far greater proportion of their output in commercial markets. For example, machinery was needed to grow grain competitively, and with the machines came fixed debt obligations that required large cash crops to service. Furthermore, their incomes were subject to greater leverage by price changes in the distribution and financial system.

When wheat prices in the local market fell, say, by 10 percent in the 1850's, an Indiana farmer's total real income might fall by 3 or 4 percent; the blow is cushioned by the fact that the farmer consumes much of his or her own output as food, clothing, and shelter. Compare that to a western Kansas wheat farmer with a modest mortgage in the 1880's whose crop was marketed in Chicago. When the price of wheat in Chicago falls by 10 percent, the quarterly mortgage payment remains the same, and so does the railroad freight rate. Our Kansas farmers' net income after these unavoidable expenses might thus fall by 20 or 30 percent. The fact that both the interest rate and the freight rate the farmer pays might have been determined competitively does not change the reality of a sharp income decline. Nor does the fact that, in boom times, the leverage works in reverse, magnifying the impact of market grains.

North adds another ingredient to the protest brew. He observes that, in the decades following the Civil War, agricultural output growth was largely extensive. Some labor productivity gains were realized as grain farming mechanized, but nothing on the order of the productivity achievements of the industrial sector. Transport improvements opened vast new agricultural land areas that were capable of delivering grain to market at constant real resource cost. As a result, farm goods prices did not go up sharply with output expansion, denying established farmers the especially high profits they might otherwise have received by entering the business on the "ground floor". Agriculture expanded—and nobody got rich.

This line of reasoning, incidentally, can be generalized to help explain the thread of agrarian discontent that runs from the Whiskey Rebellion in 1794 to the American Agriculture Movement of 1979. In competitive labor markets, wages are determined by the minimum it takes to keep the marginal worker from moving to another industry or dropping out of the labor market altogether. Farmers are always unhappy with their wages, because other laborers are willing to work the land for very little return. When farm prices go up, raising the total return to farm enterprise, one of two things happens. Other workers move onto virgin land, driving down prices and farmers' incomes. Or, if more good land is unavailable (the current situation), the price of existing acreage is bid up to the point where the return to labor services is back to the competitive rate. Today's property-owning farmers, unlike 19th-century farmers, get the gravy in the form of capital gains on their land. But those agricultural workers who are not lucky enough to own land before the boom find their net incomes determined by their workaholic neighbors.

Appendix: Social Savings From Railroads

The measurement of the direct benefits from railroads appears to be simple enough in theory. In practice it has caused an immense amount of confusion among economic historians. We therefore offer a clarifying (we hope) graphical interpretation, courtesy of the highly organized mind of Albert Fishlow.

Before the railroads (say 1830), the marginal cost curve for transport services is MC_w, and the demand curve for transport services is D_0 (see figure 13.1). The quantity of services P_wF is therefore purchased at price P_w. With the coming of the railroad system (say 1890) the marginal cost curve shifts down to MC_r, while the demand curve has independently shifted out to D_1 due to increases in national income. Now P_RB services are purchased at price P_R. The social savings from the railroad consists of the extra rail services' value received by consumers, less the opportunity cost of the extra resources devoted to transportation. In graphic terms, this consists of the area carved out between the old and new cost curves and the new demand curve (P_wCBP_r).

This area is difficult to measure because all that is really known for certain is the new level of output. The observed market prices, before and after the introduction of the railroad, are only equal to the social cost if the transport industry is operating in competitive equilibrium. To find the point C, we would need to know what the old cost curve MC_w

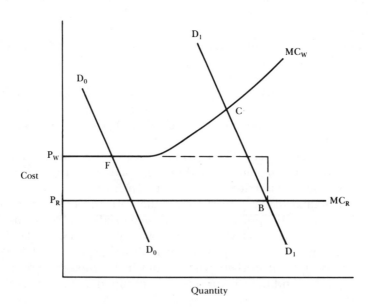

Quantity

FIGURE 13.1

and the new demand curve D_l looked like; or, failing that, at least some idea of the elasticities of MC_w and D_l.

Fogel and Fishlow measure the difference between unit costs for the two transport modes—that is, $(P_w - P_r)$, assuming prices equal marginal costs—and multiply this times B to approximate social savings. If P_w and P_r are indeed equal to marginal costs and the elasticity of transport supply under the old technology is high, the Fogel-Fishlow estimate will be a true upper bound on direct social savings.

That, unfortunately, is a lot of "ifs". As we note in the text, McClelland and Lebergott doubt that price is likely to be equal to marginal cost. Fishlow argues that they probably came close because neither the canal nor the railroad industry is thought to have earned monopoly profits for long. There is also the problem of the elasticity of MC_w. David argues that congestion would have caused the marginal cost curve for water-based transport to slope upward, as shown in the graph. Under this circumstance, it would be difficult to say whether the Fogel-Fishlow measure were larger or smaller than the true social savings.

Bibliography

**Derek Aldcroft, "Railroads and Economic Growth: A Review Article," *Journal of Transport History* 1 (Sept., 1972). Overview of rail social savings studies; useful here because of comparisons between American and British research.

**Fred Bateman, "Improvement in American Dairy Farming 1850–1910," *Journal of Economic History* 28 (June, 1968). Apportions the 50 percent increase in milk yield per cow among various factors.

**Fred Bateman, "Labor Inputs and Productivity in American Dairy Agriculture, 1850–1910," *Journal of Economic History* 29 (June, 1969). Estimates suggest that labor productivity actually fell in the dairy industry across the last half of the 19th century.

*Alan Bogue, *Money At Interest* (Cornell University, 1955). Evidence that the farm mortgage market was competitive in the midwest in the late 19th century.

**John Bowman, "An Economic Analysis of Midwestern Farm Values and Farm Land Income, 1860–1900," *Yale Economic Essays* 5 (Fall, 1965). Debunks the generalizations about farm distress, suggesting that it was crop and location specific.

**John Bowman and Richard Keehn, "Agricultural Terms of Trade in Four Midwestern States, 1870–1900," *Journal of Economic History* 34 (Sept., 1974). Careful statistical confirmation of the view that price trends generally favored midwestern farmers.

**Haydon Boyd and Gary Walton, "The Social Savings from 19th Century Rail Passenger Services," *Exploration in Economic History* 9 (Spring, 1972). Finds that passenger service social savings in 1890 were very large.

*Alfred Chandler, The Railroads: The Nation's First Big Business (Harcourt, Brace, 1965). Useful discussion of rail enterprise, as distinct from the railroads' contribution to improved transport.

**Phillip Coelho, "Railroad Social Savings in 19th Century American Economic Review 58 (March, 1968). Critique of (and exchange with) Hunt.

***Paul David, "Transport Innovation and Economic Growth: Professor Fogel on and Off the Rails," Economic History Review 32 (Dec., 1969). Critique of the method used by Fogel in estimating social savings.

**Richard Easterlin, "Regional Income Trends 1840–1950" in Robert Fogel and Stanley Engerman (eds.), The Reinterpretation of American Economic History (Harper and Row, 1971). Classic article examining regional economic growth and productivity.

**Albert Fishlow, American Railroads and the Transformation of the Ante-Bellum Economy (Harvard, 1965). Estimates pre–Civil War social savings for railroads and extrapolates to late 19th century; parallel to Fogel's work.

**Albert Fishlow, "International Transportation" in Lance Davis, et al., American Economic Growth (Harper and Row, 1971). Superb summary of the economies of 19th-century rail transport.

**Albert Fishlow, "Productivity Change and Technological Change in the Railroad Sector 1840–1910" in National Bureau for Economic Research, Output, Employment and Productivity in the United States after 1800, vol. 30, Studies in Income and Wealth (NBER, 1966). Basic rail data; measures total factor productivity trend.

**Robert Fogel, The Union Pacific Railroad: A Case in Premature Enterprise (Johns Hopkins, 1960). Social and private returns for one railroad computed here.

**Robert Fogel, "A Quantitative Approach to the Study of Railroads in American Economic Growth," Journal of Economic History 22 (June, 1962). Early, shorter version of the social savings estimate in Fogel's railways and growth book.

***Robert Fogel, "Notes on the Social Savings Controversy," Journal of Economic History 39 (March, 1979). Overview of the theoretical and practical debate over the measurement of social savings and the importance of railroads; hard reading, but ultimately provides a shortcut through the voluminous literature.

**Robert Fogel, Railroads and American Economic Growth: Essays in Econometric History (Johns Hopkins, 1964). Seminal research analyzing the impact of railroads on growth.

**Robert Gallman, "Gross National Product in the United States 1834–1909," in National Bureau of Economic Research, Output, Employment and Productivity in the United States After 1800, vol. 30, Studies in Income and Wealth (Columbia University, 1966). Basic resource on national income statistics.

**Robert Gallman and Edward Howle, "Trends on the Structure of the American Economy since 1840" in Robert Fogel and Stanley Engerman (eds.), The Reinterpretation of American Economic History (Harper and Row, 1971). Short, clear summary of trends in productivity, income, sectoral growth, and income distribution.

**Gerald Gunderson, "The Nature of Social Saving," *Economic History Review* 23, no. 2 (1970). Argues that social savings debate had missed the main issues.

*Robert Higgs, "Railroad Rates and the Populist Uprising," *Agricultural History* 44 (July, 1970). Analyzes the impact of railroad rates on changing farm income.

*Robert Higgs, *The Transformation of the American Economy 1865–1914* (Wiley, 1971). Overview of economic change.

**E. H. Hunt, "Railroad Social Savings in 19th Century America," *American Economic Review* 57 (Sept., 1967). Takes issue with the idea that Fogel's estimated social savings was "small".

*Leland Jenks, "Railroads as an Economic Force in American Development" in Thomas Cochran and Thomas Brewer (eds.), *Volume Two: Views of American Economic Growth: The Industrial Era* (McGraw-Hill, 1966). Classic statement of the indirect impact of railroads on economic development.

**Simon Kuznets, *Modern Economic Growth* (Yale, 1966). The growth process from a statistical perspective; particularly useful here for international comparisons.

**Stanley Lebergott, "Labor Force and Employment 1800–1960" in National Bureau of Economic Research, *Output, Employment and Productivity in the United States After 1800,* vol. 30, Studies in Income and Wealth (Columbia University, 1966). Standard reference on long term labor force trends.

**Stanley Lebergott, "United States Transport Advance and Externalities," *Journal of Economic History* 26 (Dec., 1966). Cost-benefit analysis of railroad innovation, casting doubt on general conclusions of Fogel.

*Anne Mayhew, "A Reappraisal of the Causes of Farm Protest in the United States, 1870–1900," *Journal of Economic History* 32 (June, 1972). Links farm discontent to increased commercialization of agriculture.

**Peter McClelland, "Railroads, American Growth and the New Economic History: A Critique," *Journal of Economic History* 28 (March, 1968). Challenge to Fogel's methodology and findings.

***Peter McClelland, "Social Rates of Return on American Railroads in the 19th Century," *Economic History Review* 25 (August, 1972). Perhaps the most rigorous statement of the methodological problems of measuring rail social savings.

**Lloyd Mercer, "Building Ahead of Demand: Some Evidence for the Land Grant Railroads," *Journal of Economic History* 34 (June, 1974). Test of building ahead of demand, with internal rates of return calculations.

**Lloyd Mercer, "Rates of Return for Land-Grant Railroads: The Central Pacific," *Journal of Economic History* 30 (Sept., 1970). Estimate of social rate of return for one major rail system.

**Mark Nerlove, "Railroads and American Economic Growth," *Journal of Economic History* 26 (March 1966). Review of Fogel's estimation procedure by a leading econometrician, with rough estimates of the marginal social return to railroads.

*Douglass North, *Growth and Welfare in the American Past,* ch. 11 (Prentice-Hall, 1974). Interesting summary of farm protest literature.

**William Parker, "Productivity Growth in American Grain Farming" in Robert Fogel and Stanley Engerman (eds.), *The Reinterpretation of American Economic History* (Harper and Row, 1971). Neat assessment of sources of change in farm productivity.

*Walter Rostow, *The Stages of Economic Growth* (Cambridge University, 1960). Rostow elevates the railroad to an exalted position in explaining American growth.

*Morton Rothstein, "America in the International Rivalry for the British Wheat Market 1860–1914," *Mississippi Valley Historical Review* 67 (Dec., 1960). Describes institutional changes that made international grain market more competitive.

‡**Donald Schaefer and Thomas Weiss, "The Use of Stimulation Techniques in Historical Analysis: Railroads vs. Canals," *Journal of Economic History* 31 (Dec., 1971). Applies statistical principles to uncertainty problem in estimating social savings.

*George Taylor, *The Transportation Revolution* (Holt, Rinehart, and Winston, 1951). Invaluable descriptive material on antebellum transportation.

**Thomas Weiss, "United States Transport Advance and Externalities: A Comment," *Journal of Economic History* 28 (Dec., 1968). Critique of Lebergott's findings.

***Jeffrey Williamson, "The Railroads and Midwestern Development 1870–1890: A General Equilibrium History," in David Klingaman and Richard Vedder (eds.), *Essays in 19th Century Economic History* (Ohio University, 1975). Ambitious model simulating the effects of railroads on growth and distribution.

Government
intervention

14

In searching for grand themes in American economic history—a dangerous mission—surely a prime candidate would be the Increasing Role of Government. For all the lip service paid to free enterprise, private markets today are typically partners, and often junior partners, of government. The price of beef, the sex of telephone operators, the crashworthiness of cars, the purity of streams, the wages of construction workers, the vocabulary of media entertainers, the design of ladders, the job prospects for teenagers—all of these are subject to government influence, if not total control.

That is well understood. What is less well understood is that government influence over the economy was not the invention of Franklin D. Roosevelt. Long, long, before New Dealers were closing banks and plowing under crops, government officials were making policy with substantial impact on the allocation of resources and the distribution of income. Economic historians, for the most part, have added to this misunderstanding by ignoring it. They have been reluctant to write about government and the economy because the issues involved are frustratingly complicated and the evidence is scarce. Thus, many of the relevant issues are considerably easier to identify thanks to research. To wit:

THE IMPACT OF SOCIAL INVESTMENT
Since colonial times, government has been investing public funds in social capital—roads, ports, prisons, military defenses, and so on. The rate of investment clearly accelerated with time. In fact, most of the canals constructed in the 1820's and 1830's were built with government resources; some of the research analyzing the impact of that investment was discussed in chapter 4.

After the Civil War, public school expenditures grew rapidly with the passage of compulsory schooling laws and the expansion of higher education. Albert Fishlow, Theodore Schultz, and Lewis Solmon have done some of the statistical spadework, measuring the size and timing of that investment. But we have only hazy notions about the social return of public education (see, for example, Engerman's work), or its impact on the distribution of income. In another important area of late 19th-century public investment—urban sewage and protected water systems—Edward Meeker offers estimates of the social return in the form of increased life expectancy and labor supply.

TARIFF PROTECTION

Tariffs were used as a revenue device in the first few decades after the Constitution, but there is little question that their intent became largely protective after 1815. Paul David's research touches on the efficiency effects of textile manufacturing protection. And research by Clayne Pope and others, reviewed in chapter 10, suggests that little can be intuited about their regional impact on income. For the post–Civil War era, even less is known. Long ago Frank Taussig catalogued the rise in nominal tariff rates during the war and the failure to reduce protection thereafter. Only recently, though, has the vacuum of analytic research on the allocative impact of postwar tariffs begun to be filled.

Jeffrey Williamson relates the relatively great protection afforded consumer goods to the rate of growth of 19th-century investment. V. Sundararajan, and Bennett Baack and Edward Ray have (independently) investigated the impact of tariffs on iron and steel protection. And Gary Hawke has taken the field a step forward by applying the theory of "effective protection" to assess the real impact of tariffs, industry by industry. But researchers are long way from firm conclusions about the role of tariffs on growth, efficiency, or regional and personal income distribution.

ANTITRUST POLICY

Industrial concentration, and more specifically, industrial monopoly, has been perceived by some as a national problem since the Civil War. Voluntary cartels—probably illegal under the common law—have been restricting output and setting up regional monopolies in manufacturing since the 1870's. In the 1880's, these informal, easy disrupted cartel arrangements were generally supplanted by formal trust arrangements in which corporate owners ceded control to trustees who ran the combined operations as a monopoly.

The trusts worked—that is, they eliminated competition and tended to increase profits by reducing output and raising prices. The congressional antidote was the Sherman Act of 1890, a spectacularly ambiguous piece of legislation that outlawed "conspiracy in the restraint of trade" and "attempts to monopolize trade." In 1914, Congress strengthened the government's potential antimonopoly power with the creation of the Federal Trade Commission and the passage of the Clayton Act, which more clearly specified what constituted anticompetitive behavior.

The Sherman Act was treated roughly by the courts, which at first refused to equate manufacturing with "commerce"—although it should be pointed out that twentieth-century decisions show just how difficult it is for courts to interpret anti-monopoly legislation. Indeed, a whole field of law has grown up around Supreme Court antitrust decisions, the body of which puzzles and exasperates economists. In recent years there have been signs that legal experts and economists are beginning to talk the same language when they define the goals of antitrust policy. But economic historians have yet to offer much in the way of analysis of evolving antitrust laws.

Ralph Nelson has documented the dimensions of merger activity since 1895; Carl Eis has looked closely at the merger wave of the 1920's. Eis and George Stigler have also independently tested the effect of the antitrust laws on merger activity; they find little impact in the 1920's, but Stigler does suggest that expanded enforcement since the 1950's has discouraged mergers. What is missing—and extremely difficult to find—is the effect of the antitrust laws and their enforcement on income distribution, economic efficiency or growth.

Post–Civil War Land Policy

As this chapter has suggested, most of the research on the government's role in economic history has yet to be done. There are, however, some questions to which we have tentative answers. One of the most interesting, and hotly debated, is how federal land policy affected growth, particularly during the second half of the 19th century. This section begins with a look at the land grants made to encourage railroad construction and then considers the more general efficiency issues related to land policy and agricultural expansion.

THE RAILROAD LAND GRANTS

Roughly three-fourths of the $190 million investment in canal construction before the Civil War was made with public funds—tax monies and revenues from bonds sold by state and local authorities. The most ambitious canal projects, however, were usually financial failures, and by the time it was the railroads' turn to look for government aid, few states were in a mood to cooperate. The void was in part filled after the Civil War by federal loan guarantees to the first transcontinental system; and more important, by a series of federal land grant subsidies that amounted to 131 million acres between 1850 and 1871. (Texas, which did not cede its public lands to the federal government when it joined the union, donated 27 million acres for a total of 158 million, or nearly a quarter million square miles.)These grants, with some very notable exceptions, were not a major source of capital for the railroads. Fishlow estimates that the gross investment in track and equipment between 1850 and 1880 was about a hefty $8 billion (in 1909 purchasing power). Land grants just don't stack up, although exactly how much the railroads' land grants were worth is debatable. Lloyd Mercer, following the convention set by a railroad apologist Colonel Robert Henry, argues that the true subsidy value is the market value of the land in the absence of railroads—perhaps just a dollar an acre. By this view, the fact that the land would be worth many times that after railroad construction is irrelevant, because the additional value should be properly called a capital gain to the railroad and thus would be considered part of the private return to rail construction.

This approach has a clever straightforwardness about it that masks underlying ambiguities. If the government had auctioned the land to a public savvy about a potential railroad, its value would have been determined in part by expectations of the success of the transport improvement. There was no auction, of course. But the entrepreneurs who accepted the land subsidies obviously did so in the belief that a railroad would be constructed. Hence the $1 per acre figure is, as a measure of value, quite conservative.

Railroad land, when actually sold, brought an average return of $3.38 per acre. This figure, however, surely *overstates* the subsidy for a number of reasons. First, the land was only sold after the completion of the railroads. Even the most optimistic rail entrepreneur must have had some doubt about the success of the project, and thus would not have been willing to pay full value in advance. Second, land sales occurred over many years—some of the land is still owned by the railroads today. Land that sold for $3.38 an acre in, say, 1880, was worth far less in 1869. Third, in return for the land, the federal government got the right to transport federal troops and property at less than market rates. The present value of this obligation at the time of rail construction is not known, but it certainly was significant.

For the want of a better number, Fishlow guesses the land subsidy was worth about $400 million. That is about 5 percent of the 1850–80 investment. Note, however, that these numbers are not really comparable because the periods of the subsidies and the investment are not identical: The land subsidies played a heavy role during the shorter period of 1865–70.

Why then did the land grants become a source of controversy in the

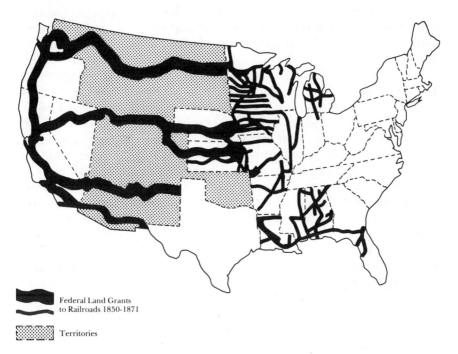

Federal Land Grants
to Railroads 1850-1871

Territories

FEDERAL LAND SET ASIDE FOR RAILROAD GRANT PROGRAMS, 1850–71

Federal lands set aside in conjunction with the railroad land grants comprised huge chunks of the public domain. Note, though, that the railroads received only a modest fraction of these lands. The rest was eventually auctioned or given away.

Source: Vernon Carstenson (ed.), *The Public Lands* (University of Wisconsin, 1962), p. 127.

1870's and continue as a hot debate a hundred years later? Many railroads, notably the Union Pacific, were shady financial enterprises from which a few intelligent, dishonest entrepreneurs made a great deal of money. To obtain the land grant legislation, votes were bought on a scale that was shocking even in that cynical age. Hence the public suspected that the land grants were giveaways, needless gifts of national treasure to begin or augment some of the great American fortunes.

Then, too, many people chaffed at the apparent effect of the land grant system on the availability of western land for settlement. The railroads received a narrow right-of-way through federal territory, plus the right to choose additional acreage from broad swatches of land along the right-of-way. Until the railroads were completed and their choices made, these federal lands—more than one-third of all land in the land grant states (see map) were held off the market. And when the transfers were completed, settlers found they still had to pay a special premium minimum price ($2.50 an acre) for the remaining public lands near the right-of-way.

Is the legend of the land grant giveaway justified? That is really not one question, but several. First it might be asked whether the railroads should have been built—that is, whether the social return (rail profits plus net gains to shippers and others) exceeded the opportunity cost of the invested resources. The evidence on this point, cited in chapter 13, is overwhelming. The social returns computed by Fogel, Mercer, and Fishlow are all well above the most reasonable measure of opportunity cost contemporary interest rates on equally risky investments. Thus there can be little debate over the fact that the nominal intent of the subsidies—to encourage construction of the western railroads—made economic sense.

This does not necessarily mean that every railroad, or every addition to the basic transportation network that received federal help, generated a superior social return. Nor does it necessarily mean that the land grants created incentives for the optimal time path of development: Perhaps, thanks to the subsidies, some of the railroads were built a few years early. With respect to this latter point, the evidence is ambiguous. By Fogel's estimates, the Union Pacific earned a social return on investment of 15.3 percent in its first year of operation, a rate that climbed steadily to 42.3 percent in 1879. Delaying the road would have retarded the flow of benefits, reducing their present value at the beginning of construction by more than the opportunity cost of the capital invested.

Mercer's computations of total annual costs and benefits from the Central Pacific reveal a similar pattern, and his survey of the *private* returns on six land grant railroads shows at least one other railroad, the Great Northern, generated immense social returns immediately. For three others, however, the private returns were initially very low, leaving open the possibility that the social returns for the early years were also below that of competing uses of capital.

Even conceding the premise that the railroads were worthy social investments, it does not follow that subsidies were needed to induce private parties to make the investment. The investments might have been made anyway—as the critics charged—meaning the subsidies program was just welfare for robber barons. The traditional test of this proposition is to estimate the private rate of return actually earned by the rail builders and compare that rate with returns earned on equivalently risky projects. If the rail return exceeds the private competitive return, the land grants are judged to have been unnecessary.

By this test, the public clearly was ripped off in some instances, and probably not ripped off in others. Mercer's estimates show the internal

TABLE 14.1

**PERCENTAGE RETURNS TO RAILROAD INVESTMENT AND
OPPORTUNITY COSTS**

System	Private Return (without aid)	Opportunity Cost of Capital
Central Pacific	10.6	9.0
Union Pacific	11.6	9.0
Texas and Pacific	2.2	7.7
Sante Fe	6.1	7.9
Northern Pacific	6.3	7.9
Great Northern	8.7	6.3

Note: The opportunity cost of capital is taken from the average earnings on all common stocks listed on the New York Stock Exchange, adjusted for inflation or deflation.

Source: Lloyd Mercer, "Building Ahead of Demand: Some Evidence for the Land Grant Railroads," *Journal of Economic History* 34 (June, 1974), p. 499.

rate of return on the Central Pacific, Northern Pacific, Union Pacific, and Great Northern should have been sufficient to attract investors without government aid, while the Texas Pacific, Sante Fe, and Northern Pacific needed help (see table 14.1).

For at least some railroads, the relatively modest private returns shown in table 14.1 are misleading in the sense that a few inside decision makers made far greater returns. Heywood Fleisig shows how the promoters of the Union Pacific were able to pyramid government loans and outside private capital into fortunes at minimal personal risk. They invested as little as $200,000 to $2 million of their own money—that estimated range is large because the promoters managed to pay an unspecified part of the original $2 million capital in potentially worthless paper obligations, rather than cash at risk. Yet within five years, they had received profits between $19 and $46 million—again the range is wide because no one knows for certain how much the railroad's financial holding company, Credit Mobilier, actually spent on construction. As table 14.2 shows, this works out to an annual rate of return between 65 and 1,207 percent—all before counting the value of the land grants!

There is a serious problem, however, in interpreting the meaning of these *ex post* (after-the-fact) returns to railroad construction. The observation that projects like the Union Pacific or Great Northern turned out to be immensely profitable without including the land subsidies value does not prove that these railroads would have been built without public aid. Nor, conversely, can it be said for certain that the low return to capital generated by the Sante Fe means that public funds were really

TABLE 14.2

PROMOTERS' ACTUAL RETURN ON THE UNION PACIFIC INVESTMENT, 1865–69

	Scenario 1		Scenario 2		Scenario 3	
Original Investment ($millions)	.211		1.6		2.0	
Total Profit ($millions)	19.1	46.1	19.1	46.1	19.1	46.1
Annual Rate of Return (%) Profit Flow Proportional to Construction Outlay	622	1207	148	277	125	237
Profit at End	172	231	74	111	65	101

Interpretation: If the railroad's promoters originally invested $1.6 million and earned a total profit of $19.1 million, every penny of which was received *after* the final rail was laid, the annual rate of return on the investment was 74 percent.

Source: Heywood Fleisig, "The Union Pacific Railroad and the Railroad Land Grant Controversy," *Explorations in Economic History* 11 (Winter 1973/74), p. 163.

needed to induce construction. What counts here is the *ex ante* (or expected) rate of return on the private investment before construction began. If promoters were pessimistic about the chances for profit in the Union Pacific they would not have gone ahead without help; if the Sante Fe's backers were overly optimistic, the subsidy was unnecessary.

Ex ante returns are thus really needed to decide whether the subsidies were required, and where they were required what amount was sufficient. Unfortunately *ex ante* returns are extremely difficult to estimate since we do not know what was going on in the minds of the promoters. Many observers simply fall back on the weak notion that *ex post* rates give a reasonable first approximation of what promoters expected. Robert Fogel, though, attempted a stronger test by observing the interest return demanded by purchasers of Union Pacific bonds before the railroad was completed. Fleisig notes, however, that this test is dependent on a number of essentially arbitrary assumptions. At least in the case of the Union and Central Pacific, it is fairly sure that the land grants were unnecessarily generous because the recipients spent a lot of money bribing Congress to pass the subsidy legislation. If the subsidy had been just the right amount—that is, just enough to raise the *ex ante* rate to the market return on alternative investments—the promoters would not have been willing to kick back a penny.

Enough is known, moreover, about the early financing and construction of the Union Pacific to allow Fleisig to make a highly plausible direct estimate of the minimum *ex ante* return. Under the terms of the government's loan guarantee (separate from the land grants), the promoters received a fixed amount of government bonds and were permitted to issue a like amount of their own bonds each time they completed twenty additional miles of track. They were also permitted to siphon off the top a profit equal to ten percent of construction costs as construction continued.

Hence, since the road was built on a pay-as-you-go basis, and the promoters were under no legal obligation to complete construction if they ever had difficulty covering ongoing costs out of borrowed money, the Union Pacific's managers risked very little to earn somewhere between $3.8 and $5.4 million in construction profits. Depending upon how much they actually did risk and how great construction profits might have been, the minimum *ex ante* rate was somewhere between 15 and 541 percent (see table 14.3).

TABLE 14.3

MINIMUM EX-ANTE RATE OF RETURN TO UNION PACIFIC'S PROMOTERS
(annual percentage rate)

	Scenario 1		Scenario 2		Scenario 3	
Original Investment ($ millions)	.211		1.6		2.0	
Total Profit ($ millions)	3.78	5.7	3.78	5.7	3.78	5.7
Annual Rate of Return (%) Profit Flow in Proportion to Construction	359	541	38	67	27	50
Profit at End	90	108	21	33	15	26

Interpretation: The columns show the return promoters could have expected under the most pessimistic plausible assumption—that the only profit would come from the government guaranteed return to the construction company. This minimum *ex ante* return varies from 15 percent, assuming a large initial capital investment and a small profit received at the end of construction in 1869, to 541 percent, assuming a tiny initial investment and a larger total construction profit received as work progressed.

Source: Heywood Fleisig, "The Union Pacific Railroad and the Railroad Land Grant Controversy," *Explorations in Economic History* 11 (Winter, 1973/74), p. 170.

It thus appears that further aid—the land grants—were unneeded to induce construction of the Union Pacific, and, as Fleisig has shown elsewhere, much the same can be said for the Central Pacific. Unfortunately, though, it is impossible to generalize from this evidence. Government loans were a critical part of the finance package for the first transcontinental railroad, but other builders lacked access to this form of federal largesse.

Assume for the moment that federal aid was needed to build some of the railroads whose *ex ante* social return was high, but whose *ex ante* private return was below market alternatives. Were land grants the best kind of subsidy, in the sense of providing the greatest social benefit for the smallest commitment of public resources? The answer is somewhat complicated.

The basic reasons for rail subsidy are (1) to raise the expected rate of return, and/or (2) to reduce the risk associated with the investment. The first pushes up the *ex ante* return to make it more attractive, while the second pushes down the market rate to which the investment return must be compared. A cash subsidy or government loans at low interest rates like those received by the Union Pacific do both, increasing expected profit and reducing the chance of losing money. But the railroad land grants mostly raised the expected return without affecting risk very much. If the railroads turned out to be unsuccessful in generating traffic, the land the government provided along the right-of-way would have minimal value. If, on the other hand, the railroad succeeded, the land would probably be worth a great deal, and the railroad's profits would be supplemented by large profits from the sale of the land.

Such a subsidy policy seems inappropriate, since the primary purpose of government aid was to shelter private enterprise from the financial risks of pathbreaking transportation improvements using state-of-the-art technology. This does not mean that subsidies raising the expected return alone, without significantly paring risk, would be ineffective. Give the promoters a high enough expected return, and they would presumably increase the amount of risk they would be willing to bear. But from the public's view, this sort of subsidy is unlikely to maximize the social bang for a buck. For society as a whole, investment risk is far easier to bear than it is for individuals. Hence subsidies that cushion private risk are cheap from the public's perspective compared to subsidies that simply induce individuals to bear greater risk.

The case against the land grant form of public subsidy is thus obvious—and it would be decisive, too, were it not for the peculiar economics of railroad operation. Railroads are (in the jargon of economics) "natural monopolies". That means most of the cost of operating railroads are overhead costs—the burden of the enormous investment in track, rolling stock and right-of-way needed before the first train can leave the station. To earn a profit, railroad rates must ordinarily include a large charge for this overhead, plus a small marginal charge for extra labor and use-related depreciation. Note, however, that the real cost of the marginal freight haul is the small cost of the variable factors (labor, wear-and-tear). Thus if the railroads (or any other natural monopoly) set prices equal to the average cost, they will effectively deny service to customers who would cost the railroads very little but are unwilling to pay the higher average cost for service.

This is a classic economic dilemma: To stay in business while charging everyone the same rate, natural monopolies keep prices above marginal cost; but, average cost prices (or more) reduce output below the efficient level. Economic theory offers a number of ways out of this bind. Public operating subsidies can be used to cover the fixed cost portion of total costs. "Two-part" pricing, requiring customers to pay a standby charge in advance to be eligible for service, and then setting the price of the service at marginal cost, effectively produces the same result. So, too, does price discrimination, in which the natural monopoly charges a lot to people who are willing to pay and a little to those who are not. None of these approaches was very practical, however, in the setting of the 19th century.

What was somewhat more practical—though not understood in these terms at the time—was giving railroads incentives to charge less than average cost in order to make the land they owned along the rail line more valuable. Agricultural land in the West, after all, was valuable only if shipping costs were low enough to allow farmers to get the crop to market and still make a profit. If the railroads had been given all the land within wagon-haul distance from the rail line, every dollar charged shippers above marginal costs would have been precisely offset by a dollar reduction in the competitive rental value of the land. Add $100 to profits by increasing a grain farmer's shipping bill by $100, and the return to the investment in land automatically falls by the same $100. Owning (and leasing out) the land would thus have been analytically equivalent to perfect price discrimination—that is, charging in rent the maximum all customers would be willing to pay for shipping. The discrimination would have been automatically built into the rental rate the land commanded in a competitive market.

Railroads, of course, did not get all the land whose value was affected by its presence; the government kept most of it for sale or for homesteading. Nor is it clear the railroads should on grounds of equity have gotten all that land: A large subsidy would have involved a huge wealth transfer to those who were already rich. Hence an extra dollar earned on freight rates meant far less than a dollar lost in land rents to the railroads. Only if the government had built and owned the railroads would the land efficiency mechanism have been reasonably equitable.

There is another problem in translating land ownership into efficiency-creating price discrimination. Railroads were mostly in the business of selling land, not renting it. Unless buyers received a guarantee that shipping rates would not be raised after the sale, the railroads would regain the incentive to act like old-fashioned profit-maximizing, output-restricting monopolists once sales were completed. Nonetheless, land subsidies may have worked to reduce the gap between the efficient price and the price railroads wanted to charge. The land grant railroads were in both the land business and the railroad business, and in a crude way, they may have practiced restraint in the latter to increase profits in the former.

Federal land grant subsidies, then, were a proposition of dubious value. They were an unnecessary incentive for some of the railroads and an unnecessarily expensive incentive for the others. Their only possible grace was their value as a deterrent to inefficient monopoly pricing by the carriers. And the practical impact of that deterrent has yet to be demonstrated empirically.

FEDERAL LAND POLICY:
THE GENERAL EFFICIENCY IMPACT

Land-hungry settlers complained about railroad land grants that slowed farm making in large chunks of the West. Economic historians, however, have generally held the opposite view. Federal policies which encouraged rapid agricultural expansion, argued Theodore Saloutos, directly led to overproduction and farm depression. And poor returns to farming created the agricultural distress from which the protest movements of the 1870's and 1880's were fueled.

The facts marshaled to support this case, however, are limited. High rates of farm failure in the West demonstrate that many farmers were unprepared for the risks of prairie farming. But personal bankruptcy, largely due to inability to outlast the vagaries of the weather, does not mean that resources were misallocated or that the government should have prevented individuals from voluntarily taking big risks. Farm prices did fall throughout the 1870's and 1880's, but Bowman, Fogel, and Rutner have demonstrated (see chapter 13) that the relative price of farm goods did not. Fogel and Rutner's estimates of healthy per capita growth outside the South are convincing, if indirect, evidence that overexpansion was not a problem.

Perhaps the most direct test of the proposition that agriculture expanded too rapidly is offered by Fogel and Rutner. The only rigorous definition of "overexpansion" is expansion at a rate that reduces the return on marginal invested resources below the return available in alternate uses. Estimates for the average return to agricultural capital are shown in table 14.4. In each decade the average return was substantial—

TABLE 14.4

THE REAL RETURN TO AGRICULTURAL CAPITAL
(average annual rate)

Source	1850–59	1860–69	1870–79	1880–89	1890–99
Current Production	5.8	11.8	10.6	7.2	8.1
Capital Gains on Land	2.9	− 2.0	3.1	3.0	− 1.3
Capital Gains on Livestock	6.0	2.5	5.4	5.8	2.9
Overall Return	8.5	10.1	13.4	10.0	7.7

Interpretation: In each decade, the average return to agricultural investment—land improvements, livestock, buildings, farm machinery—was equal to or above contemporary yields on other investments. Note that these yields did not depend on capital gains earned on land, which would partially reflect greater land rents associated with improved transportation.

Source: Robert Fogel and Jack Rutner, "The Efficiency Effects of Federal Land Policy 1850–1900," in William Aydelotte et al., *The Dimensions of Quantitative Research in History* (Princeton, 1972), p. 398.

equal to, if not above, the returns to alternative investment opportunities. Note, in particular, that the current return on farm output, as opposed to gains in farm value, dominates the return to capital; speculation was not the primary source of profit making on the farm. Remember that these figures are average returns, not marginal returns, which are more useful; even so, it is difficult to infer from the numbers any hint of overinvestment in agriculture.

Nor is it possible to argue that the aggregate return to American agricultural capital masked poor returns in the rapidly developing West. Table 14.5 breaks down the return by region for the last two decades of the 19th century. The return in the north central (midwestern) states is healthy, and the return in the West is downright startling. Again, profits are largely attributable to current production rather than to capital gains.

High returns on land, land improvements, agricultural machinery, and livestock might, of course, come at the expense of the return to labor—wages actually paid plus the implicit return to self-employed farmers. It might have, but it probably did not. As table 14.6 shows, the rate of growth of manufacturing wages did exceed the growth of farm wages during the 1859–89 decades. However, the aggregate statistics are

TABLE 14.5

REAL RETURN TO AGRICULTURAL CAPITAL BY REGION 1880–99
(average annual rate)

Source	U.S.	North Atlantic	North Central	South Atlantic	South Central	West
Current Production	8.1	6.4	5.8	10.9	10.4	20.3
Capital Gains on Land	0.9	−0.3	1.7	1.8	1.0	0.3
Capital Gains on Livestock	4.2	1.6	4.6	3.0	5.3	6.3
Overall Return	9.3	6.4	7.6	12.4	12.1	21.9

Interpretation: Breaking down returns by region does not suggest overinvestment in the West. The return to investment in the north central (midwest) states is relatively low, but higher than in the North Atlantic. Western and south central investment yields, moreover, are far above the national average.

Source: Robert Fogel and Jack Rutner, "The Efficiency Effects of Federal Land Policy 1850–1900," in William Aydelotte et al., *The Dimensions of Quantitative Research in History* (Princeton, 1972), p. 398.

heavily biased downward by inclusion of the South, where labor productivity was sharply reduced by changes in black work practices after Emancipation (see chapter 12). Fogel and Rutner recalculate real wage changes without the South in table 14.7—though unfortunately for time periods that make it difficult to draw exact comparisons with manufacturing wage growth. But it does seem fairly clear that non-southern wage increases equaled or topped manufacturing wage increases for the relevant periods. And if North Atlantic agriculture is also removed (leaving just the Midwest and Far West), the difference is yet more clearly delineated.

Midwestern and western agriculture, it appears, then, grew too slowly, not too rapidly. Greater investments in land improvements and other farm capital at the expense of the growth of inputs in other sectors might well have raised national income and the rate of national economic growth. It is difficult, thus, to condemn federal land policy for encouraging the development of western land after the Civil War. Some ambiguity remains regarding the impact of westward movement on the productivity of farm labor. The marginal product of labor (real wages) did grow faster on western farms than in eastern factories. But since manufacturing wages were much higher than agricultural wages at mid-century, the difference in growth rates only narrowed the gap. Hence

TABLE 14.6

AVERAGE ANNUAL REAL WAGE CHANGES BY SECTOR
(percent)

Decade	Manufacturing	Agriculture	Difference in Growth Rates
1849–59	0.5	1.2	− 0.7
1859–69	0.7	− 1.0	1.7
1869–79	0.5	0	0.4
1879–89	4.3	0.9	3.4
1889–99	− 0.2	1.2	− 1.4
1849–99	1.1	0.4	0.6

Interpretation: The rate of increase of wages in agriculture exceeded that of manufacturing in two of the five decades examined. Overall, though, manufacturing labor fared far better across the period.

Source: Robert Fogel and Jack Rutner, "The Efficiency Effects of Federal Land Policy 1850–1900," in William Aydelotte et al., *The Dimensions of Quantitative Research in Economic History* (Princeton, 1972), p. 403.

TABLE 14.7

AVERAGE ANNUAL REAL WAGE CHANGES IN AGRICULTURE, BY REGION
(percent)

Decade	South	U.S., Less South	U.S., Less South and N. Atlantic
1839–79	− 0.7	0.7	1.2
1879–99	0.9	1.2	1.5
1839–99	− 0.2	0.9	1.3

Interpretation: The relatively poor performance of farm wages suggested in table 14.6 is largely explained by the extremely poor performance of the South—most likely related to a reduction in the intensity of labor performed by emancipated slaves. Excluding the South, farm wages rose at about the same average rate as manufacturing wages.

Source: Robert Fogel and Jack Rutner, "The Efficiency Effects of Federal Land Policy 1850–1900," in William Aydelotte et al., *The Dimensions of Quantitative Research in History* (Princeton, 1972), p. 404.

every marginal worker engaged in agriculture, rather than manufacturing, reduced total measured output.

This, however, is different than arguing that every extra worker in agriculture reduced economic efficiency. Self-employed farm workers have been willing to labor for less than manufacturing workers for as long as wage data have been recorded. Some difference in wages between the two sectors reflects farm workers' nonpecuniary income—the pride of land ownership, insurance against unemployment, home-canned rutabagas. Fogel and Rutner argue that the wage differential in the 1850's reflects an efficient equilibrium: It was a prosperous era for farmers, and the agricultural labor force was still growing about as rapidly as the labor force as a whole. That is less than overwhelming evidence, of course—dozens of complex, unmeasured forces including immigration and technology were at work changing the farm/nonfarm wage ratio. But if one gives Fogel and Rutner the benefit of a doubt, the relative rate of growth of wages in the two sectors from 1850 onward is a reasonable index of the efficiency of labor force allocation.

Railroads and Government Regulation

Liberal opinion about the proper role of government regulation has changed enormously in recent years. Where it was once generally assumed that federal regulation defended the "public interest" against the antisocial tendencies of unleashed capitalists, there is increasing uncertainty about what that interest really is, and whether regulators are likely to serve it. The sheer cost and ineffectiveness of government control and oversight create obvious targets for the new critics of regulation. For example, OSHA, the federal Occupational Safety and Health Administration, has written thousands of rules about the proper distance between ladder rungs and the paint color on factory warning signs, neither of which have had a noticeable impact on industrial accident rates. Food and Drug Administration testing requirements are so onerous that life-saving medications take decades to be readied for distribution, and some never make it at all.

A less intuitively understood charge leveled against regulators is that they inevitably become the captives of the businesses they are empowered to regulate. The capture can be quite overt: An industry employee may simply switch to the public payroll without really changing bosses. Or it can be quite subtle: Dedicated, honest regulators may be overwhelmed by persuasive, well-paid lobbyists representing the regulated. Either way, the end result of regulation may be to shield business from the discipline of the marketplace or, ironically, from the discipline of more effective forms of legal regulation, like the antitrust laws.

The number one offending regulatory agency, in the view of many economists (liberal and conservative), is the Interstate Commerce Commission. Charged with the responsibility of ensuring safe, efficient, reasonably priced interstate transportation, the ICC has, in recent decades, watched helplessly as railroad freight service collapsed. Its major accomplishment, apparently, has been to guard the monopoly profits of licensed trucking firms at the expense of truckers without licenses, and of course, the public. One economist has estimated that ICC regulation costs the economy as much as $10 billion a year in wasted transportation services. No surprise, then, that economic historians have turned a jaundiced eye on the events leading to the establishment of this first and most important regulatory commission and doubt that the ICC has ever served the interest of the shipping public.

The conventional tale—a tale that hardly anyone still unqualifiedly accepts—goes as follows. By virtue of their monopoly position in the farmlands of the Midwest and the Great Plains, the railroads were able to exploit farmers, drawing off the profits of productive agriculture through high shipping rates. Where shippers were very large, they were able to fight back and even able to use rate discrimination to their own advantage. The Standard Oil Company played off the Erie, the New York Central, and the Pennsylvania railroads against each other, extracting secret rebates on published petroleum transport rates. But the only hope for farmers was to take collective political action to convince the government to intervene.

That political action was successful in the early 1870's; many states set up independent regulatory commissions with the mandate to bar unfair or discriminatory practices by railroads. Initially the Supreme Court accepted the constitutionality of state railroad regulation, relying on common law precedent for government intervention in private enterprises that greatly affected public welfare. But by 1886 the personnel (and with it, the opinion) of the Court had changed; the railroads were able to argue successfully that states could not interfere with interstate commerce, and thus could not regulate rates on interstate freight shipments. The only source of countervailing power against the railroads, it appeared, was the federal government.

In 1887, farmers acting in concert with other small shippers who found themselves at the mercy of the railroads, secured passage of the Interstate Commerce Act. The act prohibited rate discrimination among rail shippers buying the identical service—no longer could Standard Oil get cheaper rates shipping heating oil from Cleveland to Toledo, and so forth. It also forbade rate discrimination between long and short hauls unless a specific exemption were granted, and it established the Interstate Commerce Commission to ensure enforcement. The ICC was unable to exert much pressure on the railroads, however, because the courts remained obdurate. Judicial interpretations of the vague Commerce Act language all seemed to end up on the side of the carriers—so much so, that in 1897 the commissioners wrote that "the people should no longer look to this Commission for a protection it is powerless to extend."

Congress once more came to the aid of "the people" by passing a series of laws between 1903 and 1913 that considerably broadened the ICC's statutory authority. The Commission could now approve rates submitted jointly by several railroads, and prescribe rates themselves rather than bear the obligation to challenge railroad policies after the fact. The legislation did not end all abuses by the railroads. But in the words of historian Richard Hofstadter, regulation acted as a "counterpoise to the power of private business."

The biggest problem with this tale is that the facts do not quite fit. Organized farmers and shippers were surely instrumental in securing federal regulation over the railroads. But as Lee Benson pointed out, the railroads themselves were not always averse to federal intervention. The most eloquent general reinterpretation of the railroads and regulation is by Gabriel Kolko. For Kolko, federal regulation was initially viewed by the carriers as a means of outflanking more threatening state regulation. And eventually federal regulation evolved into a powerful protector of railroad privilege, enforcing anticompetitive collusion among the carriers where the railroads themselves had been unsuccessful.

Kolko is certainly correct in writing that railroads lent tactical support to federal railroad legislation efforts, and he is probably correct that the overall strategy of the railroads was to capture the ICC for their own use. This latter hypothesis should be qualified because the historical record is inconsistent; some railroads, some of the time, feared federal intervention. But there is little doubt that, at the very least, the industry landed on its feet, quickly adjusting to the concept of bargaining effectively with the government rather than with shippers in the marketplace.

Did, in fact, the railroads benefit from federal regulation before the First World War? Kolko argues that they did. Predatory price cutting on competitive, long-haul service was ended by ICC control. Rebates used by powerful shippers to best established rates were outlawed, and the law was enforced by the federal government. The establishment of formal federal authority, Kolko believes, also put the Congress and the president in the position of being responsible for the industry. Neither Teddy Roosevelt nor Woodrow Wilson ever "used regulation to attack the essential interests of the railroads . . ." This is not a consensus view, however; at least one prominent student of railroad history, Albro Martin, sees in early federal railroad policies the origins of the eclipse of railroads by other forms of long-distance transportation.

Paul MacAvoy has analyzed the role of regulation in enforcing group conformity to a cartel pricing scheme. MacAvoy looked closely at railroad price behavior on the potentially most competitive railroad routes where cartel pricing was attempted before regulation—eastbound transport from the Midwest's grain and hog belts to the East Coast. Using both statistical analysis and traditional historical record searches, he discovered that a voluntary cartel did operate successfully from 1871 to 1874. But with the entry of the Baltimore and Ohio into the Chicago market in 1875, agreements to keep prices high and limit capacity proved unworkable. Numerous agreements were formally made, but none lasted very long because of strong incentives for individual railroads to cheat.

By contrast, MacAvoy discovers that between the creation of the ICC in 1887 and the year 1893, the cartel seemed to work pretty well: Posted prices served as actual prices to shippers. Only in the 1890's when the Supreme Court denied the ICC the authority to enforce rebate prohibitions did the cartel again break down.

As Gavin Wright has demonstrated, MacAvoy's statistical analysis is not in itself compelling. MacAvoy tests (in a rough and ready fashion) the proposition that the *actual* price movements as reported by shippers' trade organizations (or inferred from the difference in the price of grain in New York and Chicago) reflected movements in the posted prices. That is not the same as testing the success of the cartel, however, where success is defined as keeping the actual prices near the profit-maximizing monopoly price. A very weak, unsuccessful cartel, after all, could "succeed" by posting very low prices, which provided no particular incentive for members to cheat.

Even without the benefit of special statistical insight, though, MacAvoy's study has much value. It shows that before the ICC, the actual prices were unstable and sometimes extremely low, while after the Commission was formed, overt signs of competition were successfully suppressed. This does not prove Kolko's point—proof would be too strong a word. Certainly, however, the burden of proof shifts to those who believe that the ICC was the natural enemy of the railroads.

There is one ironic footnote to the story of railroad capture of federal regulation. After World War I, the railroads lost much of their passenger traffic and most of the potential growth of their freight traffic to alternative transport modes. In part, this decline in rail use was inevitable—the railroad could not compete across-the-board for business with pipelines, cars, buses, trucks, and airplanes. But some economists believe that ICC regulation accelerated the decline by adopting price structures that made trucking far more attractive to shippers than railroads. The trucking companies, at least by this interpretation, played the railroads' game with federal regulation—only they played better.

Appendix A: The Simple Economics of Natural Monopolies

A natural monopoly is an enterprise whose marginal production costs remain below average costs at practical output levels. Public utilities—telephone companies, power distribution, railroads—often fit the description because they must have great amounts of capital invested to open shop, but can then accommodate users at relatively small cost.

From the viewpoint of efficiency we would like the natural monopoly to produce at output level A (see figure 14.1), where marginal cost just equals the value of the service to the marginal purchaser. If the enterprise produces less than A, some potential purchaser who values the service more than it cost to create will be shut out; if it produces more, the additional resources employed could have generated more value used in other ways. Unfortunately, this efficient output and price combination cannot be sustained without subsidy, since the utility will be unable to recover its costs in the long run; average cost exceeds price. The owner of the utility would most prefer to produce at output B, where marginal revenue equals marginal cost, and profits are maximized. Regulators often take a middle ground, requiring output C (Price = Average Cost), where prices are high enough to insure a fair return to the enterprise's investment, but lower than the profit-maximizing monopoly price.

Is there any way to reconcile the demand for efficiency with the need to pay a fair return on capital in order to keep the firm in business? Society as a whole (or the utility's customers, if they are a well-defined group) may underwrite the initial capital costs in return for a guarantee of a marginal cost pricing policy. This is effectively what happens when a town uses property taxes on residents to build roads and then opens the roads to general use at no extra charge. But it is rarely practical when the enterprise is privately owned.

The natural monopoly may be given the right to "price discriminate" on the condition that total revenues do not exceed total costs. This is often done in regulated transportation. Airlines, for example, charge business travelers more than average cost (because they will fly anyway) and charge vacationers less than average cost (because, otherwise, they will drive or stay home). Railroads charge shippers of valuable freight, like machinery, more per ton-mile than they charge coal or gravel shippers who have access to alternative barge transport. Price discrimination allows output levels closer to A without forcing profits below zero. But its use is often limited by popular opposition to market discrimination in any form.

Here is where the land grants fit in. Any agricultural shipper who would be able to pay a higher price than the railroad charges must be making a profit greater than the return needed to stay in business. And we can expect these profits to be capitalized in the value of the farmland.

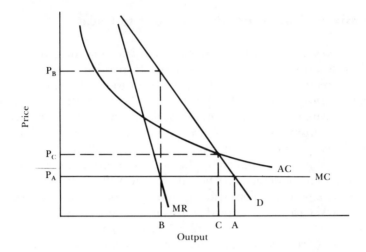

FIGURE 14.1

NATURAL MONOPOLY AND EFFICIENCY

Interpretation: At the efficient output A, where price equals marginal cost, the business will not break even. At output B, where marginal revenue equals marginal cost, the producer maximizes profit, but output is far below the optimal level. Regulators often compromise at output C, where the business makes an adequate profit (price = average cost). But note that output is still below the optimal level.

If the railroad owns the land, leasing it or selling it at a price contingent on guaranteed shipping fees, the profit-maximizing output of the railroad will change from the monopoly output (B) to the efficient output (A). Were the railroad to produce less than A, the competitively determined rent collected from the land would fall more than shipping costs would rise.

The obvious problem with this solution is that it is inequitable: Under all but the most unusual circumstances, the total profits earned by a perfectly price discriminating railroad will be excessive. We know that was the case for the western railroads as a group because Fogel's and Mercer's estimates of social rate of return are far above the opportunity cost of the capital invested. The social return from direct railroads benefits—the sum of railroad profits and net gains to shippers—really represents a lower bound on the potential return to a perfect price discriminator. Since railroads charged much more than marginal cost to their customers, output was surely below the efficient level. Hence the actual social returns measured by economic historians are below the private return that could, in theory, have been earned by a profit-maximizing rail-land conglomerate.

Appendix B: Cartels and the Incentive to Cheat

A cartel serves the interest of its members by allowing the group to maximize industry profits like a true monopoly. If members compete openly, the price would tend to fall to P_0 and output to be Q_0, where industry cost equals price (see figure 14.2). If the members collude to limit output to Q_m (where marginal cost equals marginal revenue), they can maximize profits by charging P_m; excess profits are earned equal to the cross-hatched portion under the demand curve. Naturally the cartel agreement must somehow apportion the limited output among member firms. This, in turn, determines how the profits will also be apportioned.

The more potential competitors there are, the greater the tendency for the market to move toward the competitive output level and the greater the collective interest in collusion. Unfortunately (for the firms anyway) the more members, the greater the incentive for any individual member to cheat. Figure 14.3 shows why. With many members, the car-

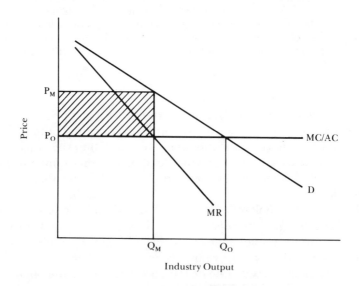

FIGURE 14.2

CARTEL PRICING

Interpretation: At output Q_0, the competitive market equilibrium, the efficient allocation of resources is achieved because price equals marginal cost. For the industry members, however, it is far better to produce at output Q_m (marginal revenue = marginal cost) where profits (shown in crosshatch) are maximized.

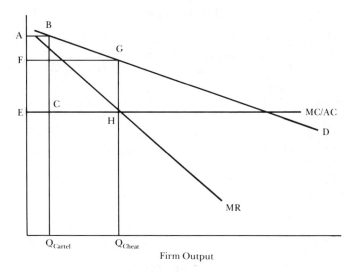

FIGURE 14.3

CARTEL CHEATING

Interpretation: It always pays for any individual member of a cartel to cheat by increasing output because the demand curve faced by the individual firm is very flat—and marginal revenue, therefore, far exceeds marginal cost.

tel output share is very small for any one member, yet the demand curve for that member considering lowering the price below P_m is very elastic (flat). That means a small cut in price will increase the cheater's sales (and therefore profits) enormously. Excess profits for the profit-maximizing cheater increase from area ABCE to area FGHE in figure 14.3. Note too, that in a very large cartel in which some members produce only a small fraction of total output, it may even be difficult for the honest cartel members to notice marginal cheaters. Today, in the case of the OPEC oil cartel, there is evidence that a few small hungry oil producers cheat regularly whenever their output falls below capacity.

In the case of railroads in the 19th century, the perceived need for a cartel (and the incentives to cheat) would be particularly great. These railroads were probably natural monopolies (see above). Thus without collusion, there would be a tendency for prices to fall toward marginal cost, well below even the long-run breakeven price. On the other hand, the alternatives to rail transport were limited on many routes, so the industry's demand curve is thought to have been inelastic and the possibilities for earning excess profits are thought to have been very large.

Bibliography

‡**Bennet Baack and Edward Ray, "Tariff Policy and Comparative Advantage in the Iron and Steel Industry 1870–1929," *Explorations in Economic History* 11 (Fall, 1973). Econometric estimates of tariff protection effect.

*Lee Benson, *Merchants, Farmers and Railroads: Railroad Regulation and New York Politics 1850–1887* (Harvard, 1955). Insightful analysis of who stood where on regulation, and why, by one of America's cleverest historians.

*Mary Jean Bowman, "The Land Grant Colleges and Universities in Human Resource Development," *Journal of Economic History* 22 (Dec., 1962). Impact of first federal aid to higher education.

*Vernon Carstensen (ed.), *The Public Lands* (University of Wisconsin, 1962). Essay by Colonel Henry and subsequent comments particularly interesting here.

‡*Lance Davis and John Legler, "The Government in the American Economy 1815–1902: A Quantitative Study," *Journal of Economic History* 26 (Dec., 1966). Attempt to measure the relationship between government involvement and regional economic growth.

*William Doezema, "Railroad Management and the Interplay of Federal and State Regulation 1885–1916," *Business History Review* 50 (Summer, 1976). Analyzes editorial content of railroad trade journals to see what railroads really thought of federal regulation.

‡*Carl Eis, "The 1919–1930 Merger Movement in American History," *Journal of Law and Economics* 12 (Oct., 1969). Develops statistical test of the effect of the antitrust laws on mergers during the 1920's.

**Stanley Engerman, "Human Capital, Education and Economic Growth" in Robert Fogel and Stanley Engerman (eds.), *The Reinterpretation of American Economic History* (Harper and Row, 1971). Estimates the social return and contribution of investment in education.

**Stanley Engerman, "Some Economic Issues Relating to Railroad Subsidies and the Evaluation of the Land Grants," *Journal of Economic History* 32 (June, 1972). Lucid theoretical analysis of the efficiency effects of various subsidy schemes.

**Albert Fishlow, "Levels of 19th Century American Investment in Education," *Journal of Economic History* 26 (Dec., 1966). Education expenditures, public and private, between 1840 and 1900.

**Heywood Fleisig, "The Union Pacific Railroad and the Railroad Land Grant Controversy," *Explorations in Economic History* 11 (Winter, 1973). Measures both the actual return and the railroad promoters' expected return on the Union Pacific.

**Robert Fogel and Jack Rutner, "The Efficiency Effects of Federal Land Policy 1850–1900" in William Aydelotte et al., *The Dimensions of Quantitative Research in History* (Princeton, 1972). Seminal analysis of the returns to factors in northern agriculture.

*Paul Gates, *History of Public Land Law Development* (Government Printing Office, 1968). Basic research reference, with enormous bibliography.

*Robert Harbeson, "Railroads and Regulation 1877–1916: Conspiracy or Public Interest?" *Journal of Economic History* 27 (June, 1967). Critique of Kolko from an economist's view.

**Gary Hawke, "The United States Tariff and Industrial Protection in the late 19th Century," *Economic History Review* 28 (Feb., 1975). Shows that effective rate of protection was far less than commonly thought.

**Anthony Herbst and Joseph Wu, "Some Evidence of Subsidization: The United States Trucking Industry 1900–1920," *Journal of Economic History* 33 (June, 1973). Assesses highway construction as an indirect subsidy.

**Reuben Kessel, "Economic Effects of Federal Regulation of Milk Products," *Journal of Law and Economics* 10 (Oct., 1967). Analyzes milk supply regulation designed to increase suppliers' monopoly power.

*Gabriel Kolko, *Railroads and Regulation 1877–1916* (Norton, 1970). The startling reinterpretation of business regulation; changed a whole field in American history.

**William Landes and Lewis Solmon, "Compulsory Schooling Legislation: An Economic Analysis of Law and Social Change in the 19th Century," *Journal of Economic History* 32 (March, 1972). Suggests compulsory education laws were the result of the demand for education, not the source of the demand.

*Lester Lindley, "Watered Stock and Control of Telegraph Rates: Early Proposals for Regulating a Public Utility," *Journal of Economic History* 32 (March, 1972). Early approach to regulating a natural monopoly.

‡* Paul MacAvoy, *The Economic Effects of Regulation* (MIT, 1965). Detailed quantitative history of late 19th-century railroad cartels and the impact of the ICC.

*Albro Martin, *Enterprise Denied: Origins of the Decline of American Railroads 1897–1917* (Columbia University, 1971). Concludes that ICC regulation damaged railroads by denying them the capacity to raise capital.

*Thomas McCraw, "Regulation in America: A Review Article," *Business History Review* 49 (Summer, 1975). Very interesting, broad review of interpretations of regulation.

**Edward Meeker, "The Social Rate of Return on Investment in Public Health," *Journal of Economic History* 34 (June, 1974). Measures social return to early public health investment.

**Lloyd Mercer, "Building Ahead of Demand: Some Evidence for the Land Grant Railroads," *Journal of Economic History* 34 (June, 1974). Estimates private return for each railroad.

*Lloyd Mercer, "Land Grants to American Railroads: Social Cost or Social Benefit?" *Business History Review* 44 (Summer, 1969). Shows that, while grants were needed to induce construction, the railroads generated very high yields.

**Lloyd Mercer, "Taxpayers or Investors: Who Paid for the Land Grant Railroads?" *Business History Review* 46 (Autumn, 1972). Sums up dollar impact of land grants on seven subsidized railroads.

**Jora Minasian, "The Political Economy of Broadcasting in the 1920's," *Journal of Law and Economics* 12 (Oct., 1969). Evolution of regulation of a new, poorly understood technology.

** Ralph Nelson, *Merger Movements in American Industry 1895–1956* (Princeton, 1959). Basic reference on mergers with some interpretation of their impact.

*Douglass North, "Government and the American Economy" in Lance Davis et al., *American Economic Growth* (Harper and Row, 1971). Nice summary of government role.

*Richard Posner, "A Statistical Study of Antitrust Enforcement," *Journal of Law and Economics* 13 (Oct., 1970). Analyzes trends in enforcement, remedies sought, justice department success rates, etc.

*Theodore Saloutos, "The Agricultural Problem and 19th Century Industrialization," in Joseph Lambie and Richard Clemence (eds.), *Economic Change in America* (Stackpole, 1954). Argues that rapid land distribution encouraged overproduction.

*Harry Scheiber, "Property Law, Expropriation and Resource Allocation by Government: The United States, 1789–1910," *Journal of Economic History* 33 (March, 1973). Sweeping survey of eminent domain law and its qualitative impact on efficiency and equity.

**Theodore Schultz, "Capital Formation by Education," *Journal of Political Economy* 68 (Dec., 1960). Estimate of the investment in education since 1900.

**Lewis Solmon, "Opportunity Costs and Models of Schooling in the 19th Century," *Southern Economic Journal* 37 (July, 1970). Model to explain state variation in education expenditures.

**George Stigler, "The Economic Effects of the Antitrust Laws," *Journal of Law and Economics* 9 (Oct., 1969). Shows that the Sherman Act had little impact on trend toward industrial concentration, but that Clayton Act amendments since 1950 have affected mergers.

‡**V. Sundararajan, "The Impact of the Tariff on Some Selected Products of the U.S. Iron and Steel Industry," *Quarterly Journal of Economics* 74 (Nov., 1970). The effect of late 19th-century tariffs.

*Frank Taussig, *Some Aspects of the Tariff Question* (Harvard, 1934). Classic treatise on the tariff; dated, but there are still no substitutes.

‡**Gavin Wright, "Econometric Studies of History" in Michael Intriligator (ed.), *Frontiers in Quantitative Economics* (London: North Holland, 1974). Valuable here for its analysis of MacAvoy's railroad research.

Economic distribution and equity

15

Economists, critics say with some justification, worry too much about efficiency and too little about equity. Radicals attribute this narrow concern to a profession dominated by apologists for the status quo: Free market economies, even those polluted by government interference, seem to do a better job pushing out goods than making sure that deserving folks end up with their fair share. And, according to the radical view, the "job" of economists is to help keep it that way.

Mainstream economists, many of whom are inclined to accept the validity of the general complaint, prefer a less conspiratorial explanation. The profession, at least the academic side, highly values the scientific method. Only by understanding the world can we hope to change it, and only by applying the scientific method can we hope to understand it. The job of economists, by this view, is to explain how things work and to provide society with the tools for reshaping it. Thus economists feel on safe ground in the essentially value-free territory of modern welfare economics,[1] where change is unambiguously good only in cases in which none suffer. By definition, that makes almost all practical "distributive" issues—who should have the right to what and at whose expense—off limits.

New Economic Historians are probably as guilty as any social scientist in giving short shrift to distribution. But today there is growing interest in distributional issues—not to fashion a morality play out of history,

---

[1] "Welfare economics" is the analysis of how economic activity affects people's happiness.

but to understand how economic forces of change have affected the lives of the majority. This chapter looks first at what is known about trends in the distribution of income and wealth, and then outlines research on socioeconomic mobility and approaches to poverty.

The Size Distribution of Wealth and Income

COLONIAL TIMES—1860

As indicated from earlier problems in pinning down trends in national income before 1840, the data on wealth and income distribution for early America are fragmentary. Thus generalizations about trends in income and wealth must be taken with skepticism. It is still possible to speculate, though, on the basis of a few specific studies.

From the early colonial years to the Revolution, the fraction of wealth concentrated among those at the top of the economic structure may well have increased substantially. James Henretta's research on Boston shows that 42 percent of taxable wealth—land, housing, business property—was in the hands of the top 10 percent of taxpayers in 1687, while about a hundred years later in 1771, that figure had increased to around 57 percent (see table 15.1).

Jackson Main's work suggests that the trend continued uninterrupted by the Revolution. He guesses that, for the country as a whole,

TABLE 15.1

DISTRIBUTION OF TAXABLE WEALTH 1687–1771

1687		1771	
Top __% of Taxpayers . . .	Held __% of Total Wealth	Top __% of Taxpayers . . .	Held __% of Total Wealth
0.5	15.1	1.4	10.7
2.9	33.6	3.0	19.3
4.6	44.1	4.9	26.8
9.6	55.4	9.8	41.9
19.6	70.6	19.3	61.0
52.9	89.9	51.5	88.7
77.4	96.5	80.5	97.3
89.4	99.1	85.4	98.2

Example: In 1687, the richest 52.9 percent of taxpayers owned 89.9 percent of the taxable wealth.

Source: James Henretta, "Economic Development and Social Structure in Colonial Boston" reprinted in Robert Fogel and Stanley Engerman (eds.), *The Reinterpretation of American Economic History* (Harper & Row, 1971), pp. 56, 59.

wealth ownership by the top decile was about 50 percent of total wealth in the 1770's. But Robert Gallman's systematic estimates for 1860 put the equivalent number for that year above 70 percent, a substantial trend toward concentration indeed. Unfortunately, not all of the evidence fits the case; Lee Soltow's investigation of the concentration of slave ownership, a key form of southern wealth that probably correlated highly with land wealth concentration, suggests that inequality was about as severe in 1790 as it was 70 years later.

Suppose, for the moment, that Henretta and Main are correct. Do we have any idea why the rich got richer so much faster than the poor? Main suggests that property concentration came with the increasing market orientation of the economy. In subsistence farming villages late in the 18th century, he found that the richest tenth owned only about 35 percent of total wealth. It is in the towns that property was most heavily concentrated, so the gradual transition of a nation of subsistence farming communities into one of medium-size distribution and manufacturing centers fed by commercial agriculture accounts for the change.

His hypothesis is consistent with Gallman's sampling of wealth distribution from different portions of the country in 1860 (shown in table 15.2). The most unequal sample is the one from the commercial sugar and cotton plantation region of rural Louisiana, where 10 percent of the families owned 96 percent of the wealth. (Actually, the concentration is even greater than the numbers show, since property in slaves is not counted as part of the wealth of slave owners.)

TABLE 15.2

SIZE DISTRIBUTION OF WEALTH IN THE UNITED STATES, 1860

Sample	Top 1% of Families	Top 5% of Families	Top 10% of Families
United States	24	53	72
Cotton South	30	58	79
Rural Louisiana	50	84	96
Rural Maryland	16	45	65
Three Large Cities (Baltimore, New Orleans, St. Louis)	45	73	85

Example: The richest 5 percent of families in rural Maryland owned 45 percent of the wealth.

Source: Robert Gallman, "Trends in the Size Distribution of Wealth in the 19th Century" in Lee Soltow (ed.), *Six Papers on the Size Distribution of Wealth and Income* (National Bureau of Economic Research, 1969), pp. 6, 7, 22, 23.

Enormous wealth inequality in that feudal setting fits almost everybody's expectations, but the contrast between the cotton-growing South and three large cities does not. In spite of the large numbers of propertyless slaves and the presence of some huge plantations, wealth was far less concentrated in the Cotton South than in Baltimore, St. Louis, and New Orleans. Just as striking is the (relative) egalitarianism of rural Maryland. Moreover, Gallman asserts that a sample from, say, the rural Midwest would show yet greater contrast with urban wealth concentration.

Note that this rural-urban wealth concentration disparity is consistent with the trend toward greater concentration, but it does not demonstrate cause and effect. Is greater concentration the result of urbanization, or is urbanization the result of the same forces causing greater concentration? In some measure great wealth created a demand for both the commercial services and the pleasures available in cities. It could be argued, however, that urban areas offered the opportunities for accumulation of great wealth that agriculture outside the Plantation South did not.

First, successful commercial or manufacturing firms rarely had to face diseconomies of scale[2]—they could expand, accumulating wealth as they went, as long as demand increased. Farmers, by contrast, faced a clear labor constraint: An expansion-minded farmer would be hard-pressed to find competent hired hands. Leasing land to tenants was a common means of escaping the constraint, but here the landlord was confronted with the same management efficiency problems discussed in chapter 12. Second, urban entrepreneurs had better access to capital markets and were thus able to lever their equity holdings. Leverage—stretching one's own investment with borrowed funds—increases business risk. But, in a rapidly growing economy, it is also a classic way of making a great deal of money very quickly. But the same token, risk factors also tended to reduce relative wealth inequality in rural areas. Farmers might be threatened by bad harvests or by crop price fluctuations, but the risk of losing everything was probably smaller than that faced by a skilled worker or a shopkeeper in a city during a severe business contraction.

Jeffrey Williamson's research on income distribution within cities complements findings based on rural-urban wealth differentials. He points out that the relative real wage paid to skilled and unskilled workers can fluctuate as a result of (1) changes in labor market conditions and (2) changes in the relative prices of goods consumed by high-income and low-income wage earners. In the 1818–60 period, Williamson calculates that average output per nonfarm worker rose by 2 percent a year, while the wages of the unskilled grew at only 1.2 percent. That implies a sharp

---

[2] Increasing unit production costs as the plant grows larger.

drop in unskilled workers' total income share: If that share was 50 percent in 1820 (a ballpark guess), it would have fallen to just 36 percent 40 years later.

CIVIL WAR—EARLY 20TH CENTURY

While the post–Civil War era was not exactly the triumph of industrial capitalism over some more primitive stage of economic development, vast new fortunes were, in fact, made from the transportation, banking, and manufacturing enterprises. And, never before or since have the contrasts in lifestyle between the rich and the poor been so visible in America. Can it thereby be inferred that wealth and income became more concentrated?

Not necessarily. Balanced against casual observations of conspicuous consumption by robber barons and the concentration of business enterprises, there are two factors to consider. One, slave wealth was redistributed from slave masters to the former slaves; and, two, the rapid growth of family farming on the western prairies where, it may be presumed, wealth ownership was reasonably egalitarian. Unfortunately, evidence presented by Soltow, Williamson, and Gallman does not offer any simple opinion on the net result.

Gallman does confirm one piece of conventional wisdom. Basing his findings on estimates of wealth held by the very, very rich in 1890, he argues that a reasonable reading of the data shows an enormous increase in concentration (see table 15.3). In fact, Gallman notes that his 1840–60 estimates are biased upward; more likely, the share going to the very rich increased even more during the post–Civil War era.

TABLE 15.3

**PORTION OF WEALTH HELD BY VERY
RICH AMERICAN FAMILIES**

Year	Richest 0.016 Percent	Richest 0.031 Percent
1840	5.2	6.9
1850	5.3–5.5	7.2–7.6
1860	3.6	NA
1890	9.6	14.3–19.1

Note: The richest 0.016 and 0.031 percent of families are the richest 2,000 and 4,000 families in 1890, respectively.

Source: Robert Gallman, "Trends in the Size Distribution of Wealth in the 19th Century," in Lee Soltow (ed.), *Six Papers on the Size Distribution of Income and Wealth* (National Bureau of Economic Research, 1969), p. 13.

Soltow, by contrast, uses fragments from income tax records to find that *income* distribution (within the relatively small group well enough heeled to be liable to income taxes) probably tended to become more equal from 1866–71 to 1894, and certainly became more equal between 1866–71 and the World War I decade. Williamson's estimate agrees with neither. Skilled and unskilled wages tended to drift together from the early 1870's to 1896. But 1896 to 1914 reveals "the last great surge in American inequality." Williamson notes that real wages for unskilled urban workers rose only 7.3 percent during a period in which real per capita income for the nation rose by 31.7 percent.

Is there a way to reconcile these stories? Remember that Gallman looked only at the remote summit of the wealth distribution, while Soltow's evidence come from a much larger portion (3 percent of the population) of the upper income tail. Soltow, moreover is looking only at distribution within the group; conceivably the distribution trend among the well-off was unrelated to the trend for society as a whole.

Williamson's concern is how middle and lower income groups shared the economic pie. Thus, the statistical impact of greater concentration of propertied millionaires, à la Gallman, might be washed out by the rise of a salaried and self-employed elite, à la Soltow—managers, lawyers, doctors, engineers—just below the top. And trends in the real income of unskilled workers need not be closely related to the fortunes of either group.

1914—WORLD WAR II

The data are much better for this period, but the story is more complicated. During World War I, there was a sharp movement toward equality in income distribution, probably as a consequence of the differential demands the war placed on skilled and unskilled labor. Williamson points out that war demand was for commodities, rather than for professional services or for capital goods requiring large doses of skilled inputs. Hence unskilled manufacturing labor was in relatively short supply, and the gap between skilled and unskilled wages narrowed. Williamson calculates that the real wages of the urban unskilled jumped 19 percent between 1917 and 1920, and 14 percent in 1917–18 alone. From 1914 to 1919, the real wages of skilled workers actually fell by 11 percent.

In the 1920's, however, the rich bounced back. Real wages of unskilled workers dipped to 1915 levels before recovering their 1920 peak in 1927. The contrast with the luckier classes is particularly vivid because total personal income grew substantially; real wages for the urban skilled rose by 11 percent between 1920 and 1927. Trends in the share of income going to the upper economic classes are shown in table 15.4, while the uneven impact of prosperity is more sharply illustrated in table 15.5.

TABLE 15.4

PERCENT OF INCOME RECEIVED BY ECONOMIC ELITE

	Variant 1*		Variant 2*	
Year	top 1%	top 5%	top 1%	top 5%
1919	14.04	26.10	12.21	24.27
1920	13.64	25.76	11.80	23.96
1921	16.15	31.70	14.20	29.32
1922	15.58	30.39	14.39	29.04
1923	14.02	28.08	13.08	27.05
1924	14.69	29.06	14.28	28.73
1925	15.74	30.24	16.54	31.09
1926	15.77	30.21	16.26	30.78
1927	16.46	31.19	17.22	31.92
1928	17.18	32.06	19.12	34.06
1929	17.15	31.88	18.92	33.49

*Variant 1 includes wages, salaries, self-employment profits, rents, dividends, and imputed rent on owner-occupied houses. Variant 2 deducts federal taxes and adds capital gains from property sales to Variant 1.

Source: U.S. Bureau of the Census, *Historical Statistics of the United States* (Government Printing Office, 1975) Series G339–342.

TABLE 15.5

REAL DISPOSABLE INCOME PER CAPITA 1920–29
(1929 dollars)

Year	U.S. Average	Non-Farm Average	Top 1% Non-Farm Average	Lower 93% Non-Farm Average	All Farm Average
1920	543	659	7,962	513	269
1921	477	599	8,397	435	183
1922	548	683	9,817	497	213
1923	613	754	9,641	566	244
1924	613	745	10,512	542	256
1925	633	761	12,719	521	280
1926	640	769	12,606	531	270
1927	649	775	13,563	525	278
1928	675	807	15,666	527	280
1929	693	825	15,721	544	295
% Change 1920–29	28%	25%	97%	6%	10%
% Change 1923–29	13%	9%	63%	−4%	21%

Source: Charles Holt, "Who Benefited from the Prosperity of the Twenties?" *Explorations in Economic History* 14 (July, 1977), p. 283.

The real income of the top one percent left after income taxes nearly doubled in the 1920's, while that of the lower 93 percent of the nonfarm population crept up by only 6 percent. Farmers, interestingly, did better than might have been expected from the tales of the 1920's agricultural depression. The most reasonable explanation here is that farmers, though doing relatively well, were unhappy—and vocally so—about returning to relative humdrum prewar incomes after their extraordinary success during the war.

The trend during the next two decades has been labeled the "distribution revolution." From 1929 to 1946, the share of disposable income going to the top one percent fell from 18.9 percent to 7.7 percent; the share going to the top five percent slipped from 33.8 percent to 17.7 percent. According to Williamson's figures, while real family incomes for the upper fifth were rising 26 percent during the period, real wages for the urban unskilled were going up by a whopping 53 percent. The inequality of urban wealth, moreover, declined dramatically. By Robert Lampman's calculations, one percent of adults owned 36 percent of private wealth in 1929, and only 21 percent in 1949. The top 0.5 percent saw their fortunes decline from 32 percent of total private wealth to just 19 percent.

What accounts for the movement toward equality dating from the end of the 1920's? There is no easy answer. Progressive taxation of income and wealth has probably had some impact. So too has the steady decline in the percentage of the population—most people in the South and the Border States—marginally existing in subsistence agriculture. But economists generally believe that the key is the large, seemingly permanent, shift in the fraction of national income going to labor.

Employee compensation as a percentage of national income crept up from about 59 percent in 1929 to about 64 percent in the years after World War II. This accounts for a good portion of the shift in the size distribution of income because labor's income is so much more evenly distributed than is the return to capital or land. In 1948 the top 5 percent of wage earners took home 10.9 percent of total wages and benefits. In the same year, the top 5 percent among those receiving dividends collected 69.8 percent of all dividends paid out; the top 1 percent of dividend recipients collected 53.6 percent of total dividend income.

This still amounts to a description, not an explanation. Unfortunately, the forces that have redistributed income toward labor are difficult to isolate. One obvious candidate is the trade union movement— more on that in a following section. Two other possibilities come to mind. First, it is quite possible that the underlying technical relationships between capital and labor have changed as both technology and the amount of capital per worker increased. This could result in making labor relatively more valuable than capital goods, thereby raising the income share of the labor force. Such a result might not seem obvious to the non-economist, but it is by no means difficult to construct models of production relationships that generate this conclusion.

The second possibility relies on the notion of "human capital." Labor, as it is generally pictured, is not "raw" in the sense that individuals are selling brute force without any skill attached. It is more useful to think of "labor" as a surrogate for many different kinds of inputs connected to specific skills—plumbers, dentists, quarterbacks, and so forth. Or, labor may be thought of as an amalgam of two factors: raw labor and "human capital."

The advantage of the human capital approach is that it makes quantitative research more practical. Rather than worrying about thousands of separate factors, only two are needed: labor, as measured by work-hours, and human capital, as measured by the flow of productive services from an investment in formal education or training. Seen in this way, the distribution revolution can be at least partially explained by returns to a large investment in human capital, whose ownership is fairly evenly distributed through the population. The distributional share of raw labor might, therefore, be stable, but the average skill level (and thus the total return to human capital) may have increased considerably.

The Impact of Unions

Until recently, ideology made it difficult for practically anyone—economists and historians included—to assess the role of unions objectively. Either one approved of unions because they spearheaded the struggle for justice in the workplace, or one disapproved because they led the nation down the road to collectivist ruin. The only belief held in common was that unions were very important. Ironically, that consensus view is probably not correct. The labor movement has probably done less good (or harm) than either its defenders or detractors imagine.

It is possible to pick out instances of collective labor activity in American before the Civil War, but they were few and far between. According to Stanley Lebergott, there were only 26,000 union members in 1834—about 0.5 percent of the labor force (see table 15.6). Lebergott argues that these early unions are best thought of as local trade associations of small business owners. They had little success in fixing prices (read wages); when they did succeed, it was due to the extremely narrow geographic range of markets for skilled crafts. The plumbers in Philadelphia might raise their wages by 10 percent because no Philadelphian would bother to hire a plumber from Trenton.

After the Civil War, unions went national along with the rise of national product markets. In the 1860's some 300,000 members were en-

TABLE 15.6

UNION MEMBERSHIP, 1830–1960

Year	Union Members (thousands)	Total Labor Force (thousands)	Percent Organized
1830	26	4,200	0.6
1860	5	11,110	0.1
1870	300	12,930	2.3
1880	50	17,390	0.3
1883	210	NA	NA
1886	1,010	NA	NA
1890	325	23,320	1.4
1900	791	29,070	2.7
1910	2,116	37,480	5.6
1920	5,034	41,610	12.1
1930	3,632	48,830	7.4
1935	8,728	52,600	16.6
1940	8,944	56,290	15.9
1945	14,796	65,600	22.6
1950	15,000	65,470	22.9
1960	18,117	74,060	24.5

Source: Stanley Lebergott, "The American Labor Force" in Lance Davis et al., *American Economic Growth* (Harper & Row, 1971), p. 220.

listed, virtually all of them skilled crafts workers, in what is generally viewed as a defensive move against the relatively new phenomenon of national competition for jobs. If labor was still relatively immobile, goods were not. And the movement of goods to regions other than their place of manufacture meant that crafts workers everywhere could not exact compensation that was out of line with pay in other regions without the risk of losing sales. Labor first exerted force as a single movement in their collective condemnation in 1859 of the use of Chinese immigrant labor to keep down wage rates.

The first genuine attempts to exercise national monopoly power on behalf of members failed miserably, however, and led to a temporary drop in union membership. The deep economic recession of the 1870's created a substantial amount of unemployment and saw wage rates decline by about one-fourth. Prices were falling roughly as fast, so real wages (for those who kept their jobs) probably did not decline with the union movement. Strikes, including a bloody railroad strike in 1877, were virtually always unsuccessful however; management had the law, and more important a large, hungry workforce—what Marx called the reserve army of the unemployed—on their side.

Organized labor made a big comeback in the 1880's, principally in the meteoric rise of the Knights of Labor. The Knights looked more like European socialist unions than most American labor efforts. They claimed broad political goals—progressive taxation, child labor restrictions—and recruited unskilled as well as skilled workers. Their big break came when a railroad union associated with the Knights won a modest victory against the infamous robber baron Jay Gould's Wabash Line. That led to a sevenfold increase in national membership; in 1886, seventy percent of the nation's million union members were affiliated with the Knights of Labor.

Again, though, when the chips were down, unions failed because they did not have the monopoly power to deliver. The national leadership of the Knights was unable to constrain locals from striking and unable to support them politically or financially when they did strike. Recruitment of unskilled workers swelled their ranks. But these numbers ultimately proved a liability, since the unskilled had minimal power to stop production and minimal personal resources to outlast management in strikes of attrition. The Knights faded in the 1890's almost as rapidly as they had come to prominence. Some would blame the leadership for tactical errors; from the perspective of nearly a century, though, it simply appears that they were outgunned.

The one enduring 19th-century labor organization of significance was the American Federation of Labor, and the reasons for its endurance say much about the history of the labor movement. Founded in 1881 as a loose federation of stable crafts unions, the AF of L never set for itself ambitious goals that would eventually have to be lived down. The only issue that counted was bread and butter for the members; the AF of L eschewed radical causes. Growth for the sake of growth was resisted, and affiliation was generally limited to skilled crafts. The big exception was the United Mine Workers, many of whose members could not be called skilled. But even here the pragmatism of the decision to welcome an enormously successful industrial union, regardless of the precedent, is what shines through.

Under Samuel Gompers, the AF of L became steadily more important. From a total membership of 100,000 in 1890, it reached a half million by the turn of the century, two million by 1914, and four million by 1918. Probably its most important achievement was to reduce competition among individual crafts unions, reorganizing craft job definitions along artificial lines when crafts overlapped. The AF of L put its real muscle behind conservative, easily understood issues like the eight-hour day, which it managed to win for several stronger affiliate unions before World War I.

Contrast the AF of L with the prototype ideologically minded industrial union, the International Workers of the World. The Wobblies, as they were known, believed that the general strike was labor's best weapon, and saw their goal as the betterment of all who worked for a living. Organized in 1905, they welcomed any willing worker to the ranks and specifically called for labor ownership of the means of production. However, for all the class antagonism they triggered in the American middle-class soul, their numbers never amounted to much. The Wobblies' membership peaked at about 100,000 and the organization floundered on its exceedingly unpopular dissent against fighting the "international capitalists' war" (World War I). Probably the Wobblies only lasting contributions were (1) to scare conservative politicians enough to wrest occasional concessions on social legislation and (2) to provide a touch of romance to a decidedly unromantic movement, and thereby attract allies for labor among intellectuals and minorities.

If there is a watershed in American labor history, it came with the Depression and the administration of Franklin Roosevelt. Until the New Deal, government had been hostile to labor, or, at best, neutral. The power of the state was enlisted to preserve employers' ability to use substitutes for strikers; court injunctions against labor coercion effectively made specific questionable labor practices a matter of criminal contempt rather than the grist for civil damage actions. A long series of Supreme Court decisions threatened the legal right of unions to organize. And, at the local level, police were rarely to be found when labor meetings were broken up or pickets assaulted by company goons. With New Deal legislation, however, unions gained a formidable ally in the federal government. The National Labor Relations Act of 1935 (the Wagner Act) formally established the rights of workers to bargain collectively. As important, the New Dealers set up the National Labor Relations Board with broad powers to enforce the letter and spirit of the law.

The Wagner Act gave unions the right to organize; the Depression provided the incentive. The conservative leadership of the AF of L was reluctant, however, to organize aggressively outside traditional craft areas. And more militant affiliates, led by the United Mine Workers' John L. Lewis, broke away to form the Committee for Industrial Organization (CIO) in 1935. The CIO won titanic battles to organize the auto workers of General Motors and Chrysler in 1937; Ford fell in 1941. Its other big target, the steel industry, collapsed with hardly a fight.

Unions became socially and politically acceptable. Their membership grew from 9 million at the start of World War II to over 18 million in the early 1960's. They were counted equally as allies in the fight for social justice and in the holy war against communism. They were damned as monopolies and as refuges for gangsters. But all the propaganda, pro and con, aside, how did unions affect the American economy?

The first effect that can be identified with some confidence is their impact as market makers. The terms of employment usually are quite complex. Compensation includes wages, of course, but also paid holidays, sick pay, medical benefits, life insurance, and retirement. Individuals could negotiate an optimal compensation package on their own, and in a competitive labor market would be at no bargaining disadvantage in the negotiation, but the process would be expensive and time consuming.

Much the same thing can be said about working conditions and grievance procedures. In big companies with enormous managerial hierarchies, it becomes difficult to define worker-manager responsibilities and to enforce contractual agreements with minimal friction and misunderstanding. Through collective bargaining and formal grievance mechanisms, unions reduce the cost and uncertainty of contract enforcement. Workers can be protected from capricious supervision and punishment; working conditions can be negotiated by specialists. Collective actions may give workers little or no monopoly power over management in deciding money issues—the price of a longer lunch hour or a new gymnasium or a slower pace on the assembly line may well be a smaller paycheck. But unions are probably a reasonably efficient means of communicating worker preferences to employers.

The bigger, more controversial question, of course, is whether unions have also increased wages. Probably the classic study on this subject is by H. G. Lewis, who argues that the impact of unionization has varied greatly by industry, and by historical period. The well-organized, well-led mine workers in the bituminous coal fields have always done much better than the competitive market wage. Lewis believes that the coal worker's wage advantage may have been as high as 40 percent at the turn of the century. In general, Lewis suggests that union wages may have exceeded nonunion by over 25 percent during the early years of the Depression, but not at all in the late 1940's. A 10–15 percent advantage is probably as good as guess as any for most of the post–World War II decades.

Industrial unions, and the hybrid amalgamated craft unions that represent a range of skill groups, may have had a very substantial impact on the relative wages of skilled and nonskilled workers. The standard view is that democratic pressures within unions tend to narrow the acceptable range between skilled and unskilled compensation; this pressure is, of course, self-limiting since the unity of the union is endangered by attempts to redistribute income within the group. Historical evidence is slim here, but Sherwin Rosen's recent estimates for the late 1950's suggest a somewhat different picture. He argues that unions have, on balance, raised the wages of the very highly skilled and very unskilled workers much more than the wages of the unionized semiskilled workers in between.

It is important to remember that, so far, we have limited consideration to *relative* wages. Evidence of the effect of unions on the average wage of the labor force—union and non-union combined—is harder to come by. Even harder is evidence of the effect of unions on labor's fractional share of national income—that is, the product of wages and employment. It is a matter of faith among union supporters that unions have worked to the benefit of all working people, rather than skimming the cream from others. And, as noted earlier, there is clear evidence that, since 1929, labor's share has grown substantially.

Economists, also as a matter of faith (somewhat leavened with indirect evidence), prefer alternative explanations basing the shift in labor's favor on structural changes in the economy or investments in human capital. The debate can degenerate to a kind of religious warfare when organized labor's supporters argue that, without strong unions, corporations would have been able to grab all the gains as profit.

When one sorts through the claims and counterclaims with a skeptical eye, there is a short list of changes brought about by unions which clearly stand up. Unions have done best where (1) they have been able to exert monopoly power through disciplined organization of the workforce and (2) they have been willing to accept reduced employment opportunities as the price of high wages. These areas include construction crafts, printing trades, mining, and railroads. Unions have done worst where their monopoly power is inherently limited by foreign competition or interregional competition from nonorganized firms. Textiles, clothing, and shoes all fit this description well.

On the issue of the effect of the general condition of labor, unions have probably had their greatest impact in improving the efficiency of the local bargaining process. These gains have probably been as great for management as they have for labor—if the United Auto Workers disappeared, General Motors would invent another union so they would have someone to bargain with over which Monday to take off for Easter. It is not certain that unions have been ineffective in raising the return to labor, but both theory and a smattering of evidence points that way. At the very least, the burden of proof is on those who believe they have raised total labor compensation.

Social and Economic Mobility

If a goal of American society is economic equality, it is a long way off. Americans tolerate, even apparently approve, the existence of enormous disparities in income, and still greater inequality in the distribution of wealth. Casual observation suggests that "leveling" has never had much of a constituency in America; even the poorest Americans seem to define a major distributive goal as equality of *opportunity.* We approve of sending the smart, well-motivated children of the poor to college so they may grow up to be rich. We do not approve of giving scholarships to the dumb or ill-motivated children of the poor, who, of course, must therefore go through life with financial as well as genetic and environmental handicaps. Seen from this perspective, "equality of opportunity" comes close to arbitrarily turning an efficiency standard—getting the most value from productive resources by not blocking individual advancement—into an equity standard.

Arbitrary or not, equality of opportunity is the basic equity standard to which American society aspires. Does the historical record permit any generalizations about success? It is not possible to know what percentage of talented hard-working Americans have been able to advance to their potential, since it is impossible to know how hard they worked or what their potential was. But it is possible to measure the next best thing: the rate at which Americans have succeeded in overcoming the accident of birth by advancing in social and economic position. Recent research suggests that Americans have not been as mobile as peddlers of the American Dream suggest. But, for most, there has been some real opportunity to change relative economic position.

INTRAGENERATIONAL MOBILITY

Stephen Thernstrom, a pioneer in social and economic mobility research, neatly summarizes the results of a dozen historical mobility studies. The earliest economic mobility data come from Boston in the 1830's and 1840's. They paint a rather depressing picture of the likelihood of changing status across a decade: Less than one blue-collar Bostonian in ten had managed to advance to a white-collar job, and virtually no white-collar workers lost their status. From 1850 onward, however, there are distinct signs of increasing mobility. The percentage of Bostonians moving up was nearly double the pre-1850's rate, while the percentage moving down became statistically significant.

This pattern seems to hold in a rough way for both big cities and small, and across the entire 1850–1920 period (see table 15.7). There are a few exceptions among the studies—Boston in the 1880's, Poughkeepsie in the 1870's, Norristown after 1910. Thernstrom has no real explanation for these anomalies. The sense of the research, though, is that for most urban Americans, at most times, there have been opportunities to change social and economic status.

This sense is reinforced by more ambitious research showing mobility over a lifetime career, rather than within a single decade. In 19th-century Boston and Poughkeepsie, the job status one began with was the status one was most likely to end with (see table 15.8). Those who began at the top were almost certain to remain there. Notice, however, that an

TABLE 15.7

CAREER MOBILITY IN URBAN AMERICA

City	Years	Blue-Collar Climbers (%)	White-Collar Skidders (%)
Boston	1830–40	9	3
	1840–50	10	0
	1850–60	18	7
Poughkeepsie	1850–60	17	7
	1860–70	18	8
	1870–80	13	9
Atlanta	1870–80	19	12
	1880–90	22	7
Omaha	1880–90	21	2
	1900–10	23	6
Norristown	1910–20	8	4
	1920–30	9	8
	1930–40	10	19
	1940–50	10	15
Boston	1910–20	22	10
	1930–40	11	16
Los Angeles	1910–20	16	13

Source: Stephen Thernstrom, *The Other Bostonians* (Harvard, 1973), p. 234.

TABLE 15.8

CAREER MOBILITY—FIRST TO LAST OCCUPATION
(percent)

	Last Occupation			
City/First Occupation	High White Collar	Low White Collar	Skilled Blue	Low Manual
Boston Men (born 1850–59)				
High White Collar	92	8	0	0
Low White Collar	25	61	9	6
Skilled Blue Collar	4	22	60	15
Low Manual	4	23	13	59
Poughkeepsie Men (born 1820–50)				
High White Collar	93	5	1	1
Low White Collar	25	61	6	8
Skilled Blue Collar	8	23	60	10
Low Manual	2	13	17	68

Source: Stephen Thernstrom, *The Other Bostonians* (Harvard, 1973), p. 237.

TABLE 15.9

CAREER MOBILITY OVER ONE DECADE
(percent)

City/Occupation 1910	Occupation 1920			
	High White Collar	Low White Collar	Skilled Blue Collar	Low Manual
Boston Men				
High White Collar	90	7	0	3
Low White Collar	10	79	2	10
Skilled Blue Collar	2	21	66	11
Low Manual	2	19	6	73
Los Angeles Men				
High White Collar	88	8	4	0
Low White Collar	7	78	11	4
Skilled Blue Collar	0	13	79	9
Low Manual	0	21	12	67

Source: Stephen Thernstrom, *The Other Bostonians* (Harvard, 1973), p. 238.

unskilled manual laborer in Boston had a 40 percent chance of moving up, and a skilled blue-collar laborer in either city had at least a 25 percent chance of graduating to a white-collar job. Poor people did not grow up to manage railroads or to become college professors very often. But they did frequently become clerks and shopkeepers.

One striking conclusion from Thernstrom's survey is how little difference there was between mobility in mature eastern cities and the boomtown west. Table 15.9 compares what happened to the careers of a sample of Boston and Los Angeles workers between 1910 and 1920. In neither city, naturally, did many people lose status. The surprise comes in the fact that 21 percent of Boston's skilled manual laborers changed collar color, while only 13 percent of their counterparts in Los Angeles managed the trick. Perhaps this only reflects the fact that the blue/white collar social distinctions meant less to Los Angeles residents. Perhaps it reflects, as Thernstrom suggests, different age distribution patterns for the two cities. But surely it puts in doubt any 20th-century version of the frontier thesis, in which the urban West represents the land of opportunity.

INTERGENERATIONAL MOBILITY

In the more conservative variation on the American Dream, the father toils not for his own advancement, but for that of his son. And here, too, the numbers show that he did not always toil in vain (see table

TABLE 15.10

INTERGENERATIONAL OCCUPATIONAL MOBILITY
(percent)

Study	White-Collar Sons of Blue-Collar Fathers	Blue-Collar Sons of White-Collar Fathers
Poughkeepsie 1880	22	30
Boston 1890	43	20
Boston 1910	39	17
Indianapolis 1910	22	35
Boston 1920	46	24
San Jose 1933	29	39
U.S. Non-Farm 1946	24	19
U.S. Non-Farm 1962	29	28

Source: Stephen Thernstrom, *The Other Bostonians* (Harvard, 1973), pp. 246, 249.

15.10). The percentages moving up vary greatly, suggesting differences in social structure among American cities. Thernstrom is persuaded that the variations mostly reflect age differences among the samples. Twenty-year-olds just entering the labor force were, of course, less likely to hold better jobs than their fathers than were fifty-year-old sons at their peak of seniority.

The real surprise is the high percentage of white-collar fathers who saw their sons in blue-collar jobs. ("Skidding" was not a typical experience in American families; but for middle-class Americans today whose children have regressed to driving vans, making cabinets, and drinking apple wine, there may be some comfort in the continuity of historical experience.)

QUALIFICATIONS
Three sorts of qualifications are in order. First, the intragenerational studies show less than a complete picture because they only follow individuals and families who remained in a single city. Unfortunately, that eliminates a high percentage of Americans from the samples: During the 19th and 20th centuries, only one-half to two-thirds of those living in one place (large city, small city, rural village) were there to be inspected ten years later. On the farm frontier of the 19th century, fully two-thirds of adult Americans failed to stay put for a decade.

This would not matter much, if the groups that stayed and groups that moved had similar chances for success. We don't really know, though, whether people moved because they were likely to get a better job elsewhere, or whether they moved because they were trapped in low-grade, insecure work like today's farm migrants, or whether success stories among movers canceled out failure stories.

Second, the relatively bright prospects for advancement found in these statistics mask enormous variations in mobility among ethnic groups, and don't touch at all on the occupational mobility of women. Thernstrom's estimates show far less mobility among Irish and Italians in Boston, and qualitatively different circumstances for blacks. Blacks were not simply the last of a series of poor ethnic groups to begin the climb up the ladder; they had a different ladder to climb—one with the top rungs missing. Until World War II, blacks had virtually no chance of entering the white-collar class.

Women are rarely even mentioned in occupational mobility studies. A charitable view is that their absence from the middle-class labor force is not important since they shared the social and economic gains of successful husbands and fathers. An uncharitable view is that, in contrast to their view of the experience of ethnic minorities, social historians are not yet prepared to acknowledge the importance of discrimination against women as an historical issue.

Third, there is only a loose standard by which to judge the American mobility record a success. There is some very modest evidence that there was greater mobility in the United States than in Europe. But even if the evidence was overwhelming, it would not prove much about relative equality of opportunity. It is possible, even probable, that Europeans had less economic incentive to change class because of substantial social security programs, and were thus less likely to test barriers to mobility. It might also be argued that a different standard should apply in the United States, anyway. During the 19th century, extensive economic growth meant there was always plenty of room, in absolute terms, at the top. Mobility was possible even in a very rigid social setting because the rich could not reproduce fast enough to keep their class full. Europe, by contrast, had no equivalent room for additions to the elite, and no equivalent of Kansas City or Los Angeles in which to house them.

Poverty in America

Even the most dedicated enemies of egalitarianism, those who see a mildly redistributive tax system as a deadly threat to productivity incentives, accept some social responsibility for people who end up at the bottom of the economic heap. Almost all would agree that serious deprivation—inadequate access to basic amenities—should not be anyone's lot in life. This view has prevailed through much of American history—the real differences over time have been in what constituted the minimum acceptable income level.

Stanley Lebergott's comparisons between the consumption standard of very poor families in 1970—those earning under $4,000 a year—and the standard of the *average* American family in 1900 illustrate this point (see table 15.11). By the table it appears that today's poor have a higher material standard than all but the elite 80 years ago. Skeptics might argue, of course, that the items left off the list would change its appearance greatly—food, for example. But there are additional methodological and philosophical problems in comparing living standards. According to Lebergott, a 1965 Agriculture Department survey showed that 14 percent of families with incomes below $3,200 failed to eat enough calories to be healthy. Trouble is, 10 percent of those with incomes above $10,000 also failed to eat enough.

Americans generally reject a subsistence definition of poverty in favor of a relative definition. This is really the basis for minimum-decency standards, or poverty standards, that have been around in one form or another since the early 19th century. Once biological objectivity is abandoned, of course, there is no telling what follows. Senator John Dreyden, writing in 1907, decided that "a minimum of subsistence in conformity to the American standard of life requires at least an annual income of $360" (about 70 percent of the average contemporary wage), while economist Robert Chapin found that families living on twice that much were frequently "underfed, overcrowded, and underclad."

In the 1920's the U.S. Bureau of Labor Statistics formally defined the cost of "decency" in terms of an exhaustive consumption list, which,

TABLE 15.11

LIVING STANDARDS 1900–1970

Percentage with . . .	Among All Families in 1900	Among Poor Families in 1970
Flush Toilets	15	99
Running Water	24	92
Central Heating	1	58
One (or fewer) Occupants per Room	48	96
Electricity	3	99
Refrigeration	18	99
Automobiles	1	41

Source: Stanley Lebergott, *The American Economy* (Princeton, 1976), p. 8.

Lebergott notes, included 23 pounds of canned peaches, 2 pounds of canned pineapple, and a butter knife. BLS "decency" has since evolved (1947) into the "prevailing standard of what is needed for health, efficiency, nurture of children, social participation, and the maintenance of self-respect and the respect of others."

That comes close to giving up and declaring the bottom X percent of the income distribution as poor—after all, can people get the respect of others if they are in the bottom five percent of the income distribution? In fact, in spite of regular updates of the official standard, there has been headway made against Labor Department-defined poverty. Note, from table 15.12 that the minimum standard has not grown as rapidly as per capita GNP. Unfortunately, what is really necessary to know here— the percentage of the population living below the poverty line—is not available for the early years. It is fairly certain, though, that the size distribution of income has become more equal since 1929, so the percentage of families earning less than the poverty minimum has probably dropped too.

Interestingly, society's perceived obligation to help the poor has more faithfully mirrored economic changes over the long pull than has the bureaucratic definition of poverty. Stanley Lebergott has amassed data on poor relief since 1850 (table 15.13). Note that, insofar as price level comparisons over 120 years make any sense, the real value of poor relief has gone up five-fold. Lebergott speculates that legislators have balanced many political forces to arrive at poor relief figures that reflect a slowly increasing fraction of the earnings of the working poor. These

TABLE 15.12

NEW YORK CITY INCOME DECENCY STANDARDS
(1959 dollars)

Year	Minimum Comfort Cost per Capita	Real GNP per Capita	Minimum Comfort as Percent of Average
1903–5	555	1,096	.51
1914	740	1,217	.61
1918	618	1,315	.47
1935	705	1,383	.51
1947	984	2,213	.44
1951	1,021	2,493	.40
1954	1,011	2,520	.40
1959	1,082	2,721	.40

Source: Eugene Smolensky, "The Past and Present Poor" in Robert Fogel and Stanley Engerman (eds.), *The Reinterpretation of American Economic History* (Harper & Row, 1971), p. 87.

TABLE 15.13

GOVERNMENT POVERTY AID AND UNSKILLED WAGES

Year	Annual Poor Relief per Person (current dollars)	Real Value of Poor Relief (1970 = 100)	Poor Relief as Percentage of Common Labor Earnings
1850	59	20	22
1860	87	28	26
1870	119	27	24
1903	125	40	23
1929	269	45	31
1940	287	59	28
1950	568	68	29
1960	826	81	28
1970	1,344	100	29

Source: Stanley Lebergott, *The American Economy* (Princeton, 1976), pp. 55, 57.

figures are considerably more than is necessary to keep poor people alive and healthy, but sufficiently small so that they would be unlikely to have significant efficiency effects. Hence, welfare payments have not discouraged those on relief from looking for jobs or—until recently—threatened to demoralize those just over the self-sufficiency line.

Appendix: The Theory of Marginal Productivity Distribution

Behind much of the analyses of income distribution changes is a single theory about the way free markets divide up income. Marginal productivity theory associates the return to a factor of production to the extra output that the marginal (last) unit of the factor adds to total output.

Consider the example of a company that uses machines and labor to produce beach balls. The company's demand for labor will be determined by the amount of labor which will allow it to maximize profits. The company will hire an additional worker if the extra beach ball sales that the worker's output generates (the worker's marginal revenue product) exceeds the wage the worker will need to be paid. Conversely, if the cost of paying an additional worker is greater than the revenue thereby gained in the product market, the company won't bother.

Hence it appears that the company's demand schedule for labor— the amount of labor the firm will hire at any given wage—is the company's marginal revenue product (MRP) for labor (see figure 15.1). Note

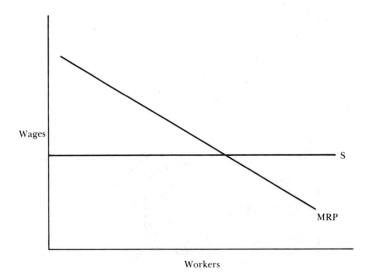

FIGURE 15.1

that the MRP is sloped downward; this follows from the fact that the number of beach balls each additional worker can add to the factory's output falls as the total number of workers in the plant goes up. The equilibrium wage and quantity of labor hired is determined by the intersection of the MRP and the supply curve of labor faced by the firm.

If we know the equilibrium wage and the number of workers hired, we can show the distribution of income from beach ball sales on the same graph. The entire area under the MRP curve is the company's total revenue; this follows deductively from the definition of the MRP. Total wages paid consist of the wage rate, times the number of units of labor the firm buys—that is, the area in the cross-hatched rectangle (see figure 15.2). The total income for the other factors of production—in this case just capital—is the remaining area under the MRP.

Figure 15.2 shows us the share distribution for one company. To determine the distribution of income among factors for the economy as a whole we generalize from the profit-maximizing behavior of one company to all employers. In Figure 15.3, the demand curve for labor represents the amount each marginal worker can add to national income. Again, the demand curve slopes downward because the number of beach balls (or corn or steel) produced by each extra worker declines as the same quantity of complementary factors—land, machines, raw materials—is spread thinner. An individual employer faces a labor supply curve that is nearly flat—any reasonable amount of labor is available at the going wage. For the whole economy, however, the labor supply

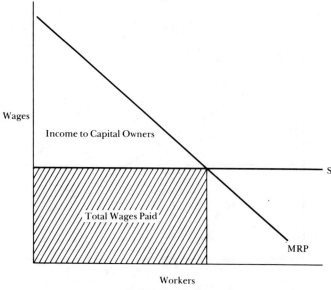

Wages

Income to Capital Owners

S

Total Wages Paid

MRP

Workers

FIGURE 15.2

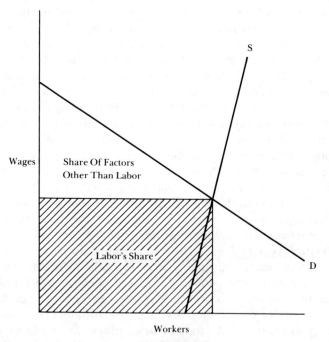

S

Wages

Share Of Factors
Other Than Labor

Labor's Share

D

Workers

FIGURE 15.3

curve slopes upward, reflecting the limited dimensions of the total work force. Labor's share of national income is the analogous cross-hatched area, while other factors divide up the remaining revenue under the demand curve according to their marginal products.

Income distribution for the society as a whole is thus determined by a two-step process. Step 1: Technological relationships about the way factors can be combined to make products, plus demand conditions for the various products, generate factor demand functions. The stock of factors available for productive use—plus in the case of labor, personal attitudes toward work vs. leisure—generates factor supply functions. Markets then allocate factors to their highest value use, and in the process, set wages and other factor prices according to marginal productivity. Step 2: Individuals collect income according to their factor ownership rights. Since the ownership of land and that of capital are, as a matter of historical fact, concentrated, a shift in distribution away from land and capital toward labor tends to reduce income inequality. This need not be true at all times and all places. In the antebellum South, for example, we expect that higher slave labor income ended up in the hands of the rich.

Note especially two unintuitive properties of marginal productivity distribution:

• Pay is determined by the productivity of the last worker employed, not by the productivity of the typical or average worker.
• Marginal productivity—and thus wage rates—has as much to do with technological relationships among factors as it has to do with how diligently labor works. That is fine for General Motors workers, who get more each year at least in part because GM continues to install more productive machinery. It was not so fine for the skilled hand loom operators during the early 19th century whose marginal product fell with the introduction of water-powered textile looms.

In a marginal productivity distribution world, can unions change the distribution of income? The answer is yes—but the "yes" is qualified:

• They can raise wages in a unionized firm or industry by restricting the supply of labor, as in figure 15.4. However, higher wages come at the cost of fewer jobs.
• They can change the difference between wages paid to different skill levels within an industry by bargaining on the collective behalf of all workers. Employers may thus be forced to buy a mix of skills as a package and then let the union informally determine who gets the money. This won't work very well, though, unless the union can restrict the movement of workers. Otherwise skilled workers who are paid less than

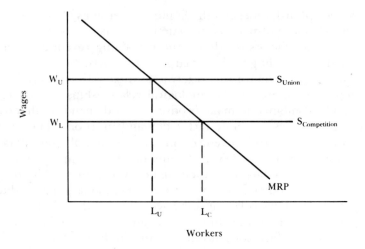

FIGURE 15.4

Explanation: A firm buying labor in a competitive market hires L_c units of labor at wage W_L. A union may impose a higher wage (W_u) on the firm, but as a result, the firm reduces its workforce to L_u.

their marginal products will move to employment where they can collect the full competitive wage.

 • They can raise wages by raising the demand for the product they make through collective action. Garment workers urge other union members to buy only union-made clothes; steel workers pressure the government to restrict steel supplies from foreign competitors. One must carefully distinguish here between members of individual unions and labor as a group. Tariffs on auto imports, for example, may raise American auto workers' incomes, but the resulting higher prices for cars may reduce the total purchasing power of labor in general, and actually shift the distribution of income toward capital.

 • They can raise wages—at no cost in jobs—in industries where the competition for labor is very limited. If the labor market has failed to equate wages with the marginal product of labor, a union can sometimes effectively enforce competitive wages through collective bargaining.

Not everyone believes that income is, in fact, distributed via the marginal productivity market mechanism:

THE MARXIST CRITIQUE
Marx predicted that wages would tend to fall to the subsistence level; labor's equilibrium share of national income would thus be whatever amount was needed to keep the working class in potatoes. This is a

prediction, however, not a theory; Marx's alternative to classical marginal productivity distribution theory is, lamentably, presented in only very ambiguous terms in *Capital*.

With or without a theory to back it up, the prediction hasn't come true in the industrialized world. Real wages have risen in Europe and America with increases in the quantity of complementary factors per worker and with technical improvements in production processes. Unfortunately, the Marxist prediction is all too accurate for the really depressed portion of the less developed world, countries like India, Haiti, and the Central African states. Note, though, that marginal productivity distribution theory makes the same prediction for those desolate lands.

Some people confuse the "iron law of wages" with Marx's ethical theory of what distribution *ought* to be. Labor deserves the entire pie, not just a slice, according to some Marxists, since ultimately all value is created by the sweat of the brow. The problem here is that labor may deserve more, but the free markets won't give them more. The conflict between Marxist and neoclassical economists only begins when the former argue that market power should be used to get for labor what it ethically deserves.

TECHNICAL CRITIQUES

Quite separate from the Marxist attack on neoclassical marginal productivity distribution is the challenge from within mainstream economics. Joan Robinson, Nicholas Kaldor, and others question the applicability of the theory, particularly the relevance to distribution for an economy as a whole. One big problem, it is argued, is generalizing from the standard textbook marginal product function for a firm to the real world. If, for example, it can be shown that lower wages sometimes lead to less labor-intensive production, the relevance of the whole mechanism is in doubt.

These critics have scored a lot of academic points against traditionalists. It is hard now to find a sophisticated economic theorist who will buy marginal productivity theory exactly as it was laid out early in the 20th century. On the other hand, the great majority still believe that the practical reality of income distribution is remains consistent with the theory as sketched above.

Bibliography

‡***Orley Ashenfelter and John Pencavel, "American Trade Union Growth: 1900–1960" *Quarterly Journal of Economics* 83 (Aug., 1969). Statistical model of the determinants of union membership change.

‡***Barry Chiswick and Jacob Mincer, "Time Series Changes in Personal Income Inequality in the United States from 1939," *Journal of Political*

Economy 80 (May/June, 1972). Relates changing distribution to investments in human capital.

*Howard Chudacoff, *Mobile Americans: Residential and Social Mobility in Omaha, 1880–1920* (New York: Oxford, 1972).

**Martin Estey, "Trends in the Concentration of Union Membership 1897–1962," *Quarterly Journal of Economics* 80 (Aug., 1966). Explains reduced union membership concentration in America, with comparison to Britain.

**Robert Gallman, "The Pace and Pattern of American Economic Growth," in Lance Davis, Richard Easterlin, William Parker (eds.), *American Economic Growth* (Harper and Row, 1972). Valuable here for its summary of income and distribution trends.

*Robert Gallman, "Trends in the Size Distribution of Wealth in the 19th Century," in Lee Soltow (ed.), *Six Papers on the Size Distribution of Income and Wealth* (National Bureau of Economic Research, 1969). Basic reference material showing distributions for mid-century.

*Selma Goldsmith, "Changes in the Size Distribution of Income in Edward Budd (ed.), *Inequality and Poverty* (Norton, 1967). Summary on distribution changes from 1929 until early postwar years.

*Sidney Goldstein, *Patterns of Mobility 1910–1950: The Norristown Study* (University of Pennsylvania, 1958). Social history of mobility in one sample city.

*James Henretta, "Economic Development and Social Structure in Colonial Boston," *William and Mary Quarterly* 22 (Jan., 1965). Documents trend toward increasing inequality from 1687 to 1771.

*Charles Holt, "Who Benefited from the Prosperity of the 1920's?" *Explorations in Economic History* 14 (July, 1977). Careful new look at the annual data on income distribution.

*Richard Hopkins, "Occupational and Geographic Mobility in Atlanta 1879–1890" *Journal of Southern History* 34 (March, 1968). Social mobility calculations for a southern city.

**Robert Keller, "Factor Income Distribution in the United States During the 1920's," *Journal of Economic History* 33 (March, 1973). Evidence of the distribution away from labor during the 1920's; fits underconsumption theories of the Depression.

*Peter Knights, "Population Turnover, Persistance, and Residential Mobility in Boston 1830–1860," in Stephen Thernstrom and Richard Sennett (eds.), *19th Century Cities: Essays in New Urban History* (Yale, 1969). Essay on mobility before the Civil War.

*Robert Lampman, *The Share of Top Wealth-Holders in National Wealth* (Princeton, 1962). Good summary data and interpretation since the 1920's.

*Stanley Lebergott, "Are the Rich Getting Richer? Trends in U.S. Wealth Concentration," 36 *Journal of Economic History* (March, 1976). Witty essay explaining why extreme concentrations of wealth tend to dissipate over time.

*Stanley Lebergott, "Changes in Unemployment 1800–1960" in Robert Fogel and Stanley Engerman (eds.), *Reinterpretation of American Economic His-*

tory (Harper and Row, 1971). Pieces together evidence on unemployment trends over the business cycles.

*Stanley Lebergott, *The American Economy* (Princeton, 1976). Essays on income distribution, including a highly provocative one on poverty.

‡**H. Gregg Lewis, *Unionism and Relative Wages in the United States* (University of Chicago, 1963). Classic estimates of the effects of unions on wages.

**Peter Lindert and Jeffrey Williamson, "Three Centuries of Inequality" in Paul Uselding (ed.), *Research in Economic History: An Annual Compilation of Research, Volume I* (Greenwich, Conn.: JAI, 1976). Superb overview of the basic equity issues.

*Jackson Main, "Trends in Wealth Concentration Before 1860," *Journal of Economic History* 31 (June, 1971). Controlled speculation on the trend toward greater concentration to mid-century.

‡***Sherwin Rosen, "Unions and the Occupational Wage Structure in the United States," *International Economic Review* 11 (June, 1970). Estimates suggest that very highly skilled and unskilled benefit at the cost of the semi-skilled.

*Bernard Sarachek, "American Entrepreneurs and the Horatio Alger Myth," *Journal of Economic History* 38 (June, 1978). Study of the social and economic origins of 187 American entrepreneurs.

*James Smith and Stephen Franklin, "The Concentration of Personal Wealth 1922–1969," *American Economic Review* 64 (May, 1974). Straightforward wealth estimates show strong trend toward equality and reduction of extreme wealth concentration.

*Eugene Smolensky, "The Past and Present Poor," in Robert Fogel and Stanley Engerman (eds.), *The Reinterpretation of American Economic History* (Harper and Row, 1971). Discusses problems in defining poverty and surveys changes in the perceived poverty problem.

**Lee Soltow, "Economic Inequality in the United States from 1790 to 1860," *Journal of Economic History* 31 (Dec., 1971). Weight of the evidence here suggests little change in distribution pattern between Constitution and Civil War.

‡**Lee Soltow, "Evidence on Income Inequality in the United States 1866–1965," *Journal of Economic History* 29 (June, 1969). Uses tax data to infer that distribution became more equal between the Civil War and World War I.

*Stephen Thernstrom, *Poverty and Progress* (Atheneum, 1969). Pioneering measure of social and economic mobility in 19th-century Newburyport, Mass.

*Stephen Thernstrom, *The Other Bostonians* (Harvard, 1973). Mobility study for 1880–1970; especially valuable for its survey of the whole field of mobility studies.

**Jeffrey Williamson, "American Prices and Urban Inequality Since 1820," *Journal of Economic History* 36 (June, 1976). Measures trends in real income for the urban poor.

The great depression

16

Apart from the two great armed conflicts, the Civil War and World War II, it is hard to find a disaster in American history equal to the Depression of the 1930's. Between 1929 and 1933 real output fell by 29 percent and then took five years to inch back to pre-Depression output rates. Gross investment fell from an historical average of about one-sixth of GNP to less than one percent in 1932 and 1933 and remained far below the long-term trend rate until World War II rearmament. Net investment—gross investment, less depreciation—probably was negative from 1932 through 1934.

If the economy had continued in the 1930's along the moderate growth path of the 1919–29 decade, GNP would have been $147 billion (1929 dollars) in 1939. Instead, it was only $111 billion. To put it another way, if the American economy had grown at an average annual rate of three percent from 1930 to 1939—an historically conservative rate—total GNP for the decade would have been $1.232 trillion (in 1929 prices). In fact, the decade GNP amounted to just $932 billion, a shortfall of almost one-quarter.

Actually these aggregates hide the appalling impact the Depression had on the lives of many Americans. The Standard and Poor's composite index of common stock prices collapsed from an average of 26.02 in 1929 to just 6.93 in 1932, a loss of nearly three-quarters. Tens of thousands of investors lost *all* their assets because they had borrowed heavily to increase their stock purchasing power in the booming twenties. Even harder hit by the Depression were the millions who lost their livelihoods as well as their assets. In 1929, 3.2 percent of the labor force—1.5 million workers—were unemployed, mostly between jobs. By 1933, 10.6 million Americans were pounding the pavement looking for work, and another 2.2 million had make-work emergency jobs (at low pay) from state, local, and federal governments. That adds up to 21 or 25 percent of the labor force unemployed, depending on whether those in government make-work programs are counted.

Even these figures partially mask the trauma by their failure to measure the inequitable burden of the economic collapse. Although hard numbers are difficult to come by, there is little question that urban blacks and other racial minorities living in cities were more severely affected than the population as a whole. They were fired first both because of discrimination and because a disproportionate number worked in the particularly hard-hit service sectors—household domestics, restaurant and hotel workers, and so on.

Then, too, the overall unemployment rate does not distinguish between the unpleasantness of a month or two out of work and the catastrophe of a year or two without work. In good times, most unemployment is transient in nature—people are between jobs. During the Depression, when unemployment remained at least double the 1929 rate for ten straight years, a large fraction of the unemployed had no reasonable prospect of ever again making a living without government aid. In retrospect, then, it is no wonder that the Depression brought the most serious challenges to the established political and social order in America since the Civil War.

For all the significance of the Depression and the long recovery, the subject has escaped rigorous analysis by economic historians until recently. Happily, the vacuum is now being filled rapidly. This chapter looks first at the lively debate over the cause of the contraction, and then surveys the recovery process—more explicitly, the government's part in the recovery. A final section examines the political economy of New Deal spending policies, and research which provides clues on how Roosevelt managed to weather the social and economic storm.

Economic Collapse

Before we take the plunge into interpretation, it makes sense to provide a chronology of what happened.

THE 1920'S AND STRUCTURAL WEAKNESS

The decade of the 1920's began with a brief recession that sharply cut industrial production and investment, but had little effect on consumption or on GNP (see table 16.1). Prices fell remarkably rapidly, but thereafter followed a nine year period in which they were nearly perfectly stable. From the recovery of 1922 to the last good year (1929), GNP grew at an average pace of 4.7 percent a year.

There were several changes in the economy in the 1920's that might have indicated some structural vulnerability. The distribution of wealth

TABLE 16.1

AN ECONOMIC PROFILE OF THE 1920'S
(Indexes, with 1929 = 100)

Year	Real Consumption	Real GNP	Real Gross Investment	Real Industrial Production	GNP Price* Deflator
1920	66.7	70.2	79.0	65.9	121
1921	71.0	68.6	54.7	53.2	103
1922	73.5	72.6	65.4	66.9	98
1923	80.3	82.2	96.3	76.7	100
1924	86.2	84.7	77.8	73.1	99
1925	83.7	86.7	101.2	81.3	101
1926	90.5	92.3	105.6	86.6	101
1927	92.7	93.2	96.3	87.4	99
1928	94.7	94.3	89.5	91.2	100
1929	100	100	100	100	100

*The GNP Price Deflator is a price index that covers all goods and services in the economy, rather than just wholesale goods or consumer goods. It is the measure most appropriately used in adjusting the effects of price change on national income.

Source: Peter Temin, *Did Monetary Forces Cause the Great Depression?* (Norton, 1976), p. 4. U.S. Department of Commerce, *Long Term Economic Growth* (Government Printing Office, 1966), p. 169.

and income which had taken a hard left toward equality during the war years, turned around completely (see chapter 15). Charles Holt shows that the great majority of Americans—those whose income was dependent on earnings from blue-collar, non-farm labor—did not get any piece of the twenties action. More remarked upon at the time, farm income growth lagged far behind that of the non-farm sector. It fell more sharply in the postwar recession and recovered more slowly. From 1920 to 1929, real per capita income for the economy as a whole grew by 28 percent, while per capita farm income rose only 10 percent.

It does not seem likely, though, that such modest absolute gains would have been sufficient to cause so much perceived distress among farmers. The real key to the farm sector's malaise probably lay in its financial structure. Thomas Johnson notes that farm real estate values were bid up enormously (along with farm prices) during World War I and the years immediately following (see table 16.2). The real estate was heavily mortgaged, so farmers and the banks that lent them money suffered from the relatively poor performance of the sector after 1920. Farm bankruptcies led to growth in the rate of farm tenancy at the expense of family ownership and an extraordinary rise in small bank fail-

TABLE 16.2

FARM FINANCE DURING THE 1920'S

Year	Value of Farm Real Estate (index 1912–14 = 100)	Farm Mortgage Debt (index 1910 = 100)	Farm Mortgage Foreclosures (per 1,000 farms)
1914	103	119	3.1
1916	110	133	3.5
1918	130	166	2.8
1920	173	214	3.8
1921	160	259	6.4
1922	140	271	11.2
1923	136	274	13.6
1924	131	271	15.6
1925	128	251	16.2
1926	125	246	17.0
1927	120	245	16.6
1928	117	248	13.9
1929	116	248	14.9
1930	114	244	18.0
1932	103	238	27.8

Interpretation: Mortgage debt increased enormously while the value of farm real estate actually fell during the twenties. Note, too, the spectacular increase in mortgage foreclosures beginning in the early twenties.

Source: Thomas Johnson, "Postwar Optimism and the Rural Financial Crisis of the 1920's," *Explorations in Economic History* 11 (Winter, 1973/74), p. 176.

ures in the 1920's—hardly a sign of financial health for the economy as a whole.

Another oft-cited sign of structural weakness was increased speculative activity, particularly on the part of the middle-class savers, in the stock market. A broad index of stock prices rose 67 percent from May 1926 to May 1928, dipped slightly in the early summer, and began another spectacular 14-month climb that put average stock prices 40 percent higher in September, 1929 than they had been in May of the previous year (see figure 16.1). A few dozen favorite industrial stocks did even better—the Dow-Jones industrial average doubled between early 1928 and the fateful autumn of 1929.

A long, almost uninterrupted stock price climb proved—as it has since—to be an enormous temptation to small savers who might otherwise have invested their money very conservatively. And there is little

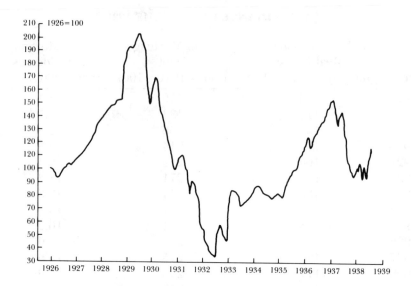

FIGURE 16.1

NEW YORK STOCK PRICES, 1926–1938

The Standard Statistics Index of New York stock prices shows the magnitude of the market crash. From an index level of 100 in 1926, the market soared to a high of 216 in September, 1929 before collapsing to 34 in June, 1932.

Source: Charles Kindleberger, *The World in Depression, 1929–39* (University of California, 1973), pp. 110–11. Bottom graph adapted from League of Nations, *Statistical Yearbook*, to 1934, 1935–38, Standard Statistics (1934–36 index converted to 1926 base).

	1926	1927	1928	1929	1930	1931	1932	1933	1934	1935	1936	1937	1938
Jan.	102	106	137	193	149	103	54	46	84	81	114	148	100
Feb.	102	108	135	192	156	110	53	43	88	80	120	154	99
Mar.	96	109	141	196	167	112	54	42	85	75	124	154	96
Apr.	93	110	150	193	171	100	42	49	88	79	124	144	86
May	93	113	155	193	160	81	38	65	80	86	118	138	86
Jun.	97	114	148	191	143	87	34	77	81	88	119	134	92
Jul.	100	117	148	203	140	90	36	84	80	92	128	142	106
Aug.	103	112	153	210	139	89	52	79	77	95	131	144	103
Sep.	104	129	162	216	139	76	56	81	76	98	133	124	104
Oct.	102	128	166	194	118	65	48	76	76	100	141	105	114
Nov.	103	131	179	145	109	68	45	77	80	110	146	96	114
Dec.	105	136	178	147	102	54	45	79	80	110	144	95	112

doubt that the great majority of those who took a fling at the market in those heady days were "speculating" in the sense that they paid little attention to the earning power that lay behind their equity.

As both Charles Kindleberger and Peter Temin point out, however, the get-rich-quick feel to the era does not necessarily mean that great market forces determining stock prices were ever overwhelmed by speculative frenzy. The average ratio of stock prices to earnings—the rate at which current earnings are capitalized in stock prices—rose only modestly through the late 1920's and never exceeded the optimistic levels achieved in the less ominous bull markets of the 1960's. Happy days on Wall Street only reflected confidence that corporate earnings gains in the 1920's could be sustained in the 1930's.

More disturbing—though really only with hindsight—was the extensive use of credit to finance stock purchases. Confident that three years of rising stock prices meant ever more of the same, many stock buyers levered their holdings by borrowing money from brokers to finance stock purchases. The brokers, in turn, financed these loans by borrowing from banks, which were, of course, lending on behalf of depositors. Brokers' loans increased from $4.4 billion at the end of 1927 to $8.5 billion at the beginning of October, 1929.

There was nothing immoral or truly irresponsible about buying stocks "on margin." But heavy borrowing made the financial system as a whole less liquid and more vulnerable to shocks. Individuals who borrowed 80 to 90 percent of the money to buy stock could rarely afford to watch prices fall very far before being forced to sell the stock to cover the loans. If purchased with 90 percent margin credit, a fall in value of Consolidated Transnational Widget from 19 to 17 would wipe out every penny of the investor's equity. Hence, in a falling market, the rate of descent can be accelerated by panic selling on behalf of illiquid margin investors.

Two other structural weaknesses in the 1920's deserve mention. The American economy was relatively self-sufficient during this period, but the emphasis should be on "relative" not "self-sufficient." Both real demand and domestic finance were tied to the rest of the world through export and capital markets. Europeans, in particular, could cut U.S. output—and employment and corporate earnings—by buying less in America. This is, in fact, precisely what happened to agriculture in the 1920's, as world supply and demand shifts reduced the foreign demand for grain. And net movements of foreign funds into American stocks, bonds, and bank deposits could greatly influence securities prices and the quantity of money.

International links between markets generally increase economic efficiency by allowing resources and goods to flow to where they generate the most value. Why, then, could these links be considered a structural weakness in the 1920's? Because the big European economies were extraordinarily unstable, and because a tangled web of debt arrangements arising from the World War I peace treaty had become extraordinarily dependent on flows of financial capital from America to allow war recovery. Hence any shock to the financial ties binding New York to London, Berlin, and Paris could be magnified by reactions on both sides of the Atlantic.

A final weakness concerns one particularly unstable component of investment outlays—construction. Real expenditures on construction rose from $5 billion to 1920 (39 percent of gross investment) to a peak of $10.7 billion in 1926 (63 percent of gross investment), and then eased back to just $8.7 billion in 1929. This has prompted many economists to cite "overbuilding" or market saturation in housing as a foreboding economic phenomenon of the late 1920's. We leave the issue of whether the construction cycle was a precipitating factor for the Depression until later. But there seems little dispute that the factors leading to very large swings in construction investment were inherently destabilizing to the economy.

THE ECONOMIC CONTRACTION

Things went remarkably sour for the economy during the second half of 1929. The stock market peaked in mid-September and started slipping in earnest on October 3. Decline turned to rout in the last week of October, with the market finally bottoming out in mid-November, down about one-third from the September highs. A modest market recovery during the winter brought the stock average about half-way back, before the beginning of the long, long slide to oblivion. From an index high of 216 in September, 1929 (1926 = 100), the market fell to 102 in December, 1930, to 54 in December, 1931, and finally bottomed out at 34 in June, 1932.

Actually, the market decline was preceded by a decline in business activity. Auto sales fell from 600,000 in March, 1929 to 400,000 in September; industrial production, overall, peaked in June. Real output dipped by 9 percent from 1929 to 1930, another 6 percent between '30 and '31, a sickening 15 percent for 1931–32, and a final 3 percent in 1933 before starting back up. GNP fell by 29 percent from 1929 peak to 1933 trough. As in every business cycle, investment changed more than consumption, but here the relative decline was remarkable: Subsistence demand held the consumption drop to 18 percent, while gross investment fell by 98 percent! (See table 16.3.)

Financial institutions were strained, and finally broken, by the economic catastrophe. A wave of bank failures hit the midwest and border states in October, 1930, and one big private New York bank, the Bank of

TABLE 16.3

ECONOMIC COLLAPSE, 1929–34

Year	Real GNP (billion '29 $)	Real Consump-tion (billion '29 $)	Real Gross Investment (billion '29 $)	Unemploy-ment (percent)	Unemployment* Including Relief Employees as Part of Workforce (%)
1929	104.4	79.0	16.2	3.2	3.2
1930	95.1	74.7	10.5	8.7	8.9
1931	89.5	72.2	6.8	15.9	15.7
1932	76.4	66.0	0.8	23.6	22.9
1933	74.2	64.6	0.3	24.9	20.9
1934	80.8	68.0	1.8	21.7	16.2

*After 1930, government work-relief programs reduced the number of people literally without jobs. Thus Michael Darby's calculation of the labor force, including those in temporary make-work, may provide a useful measure of personal hardship—and in Darby's view also yields insights into why competitive market forces failed to reduce private unemployment more quickly.

Source: Peter Temin, *Did Monetary Forces Cause the Great Depression?* (Norton, 1976), p. 4. Michael Darby, "Three and a Half Million U.S. Employees Have Been Mislaid . . . ," *Journal of Political Economy* 84 (Feb., 1976), p. 8.

the United States, collapsed in December, 1930. Then, in the spring of 1931, a second wave of failures swept the banking community, And a final, more drastic run on banks began in January, 1933, terminated only by President Roosevelt's "bank holiday"—the moral equivalent of 19th-century specie suspensions—in March, 1933. All told, Friedman and Schwartz report that 9,000 banks suspended operations from 1930 to the bank holiday, ultimately resulting in losses for depositors and stockholders of about $2.5 billion.

In itself, the $2.5 billion was trivial—over the same period total stock market losses amounted to $85 billion, and New York Stock Exchange stocks lost $15 billion in value in October, 1929 alone. But accompanying this failure of financial intermediaries was an enormous fall in the money supply, M_1—currency and checking deposits—and the price level (see table 16.4). Note that M_2, defined as outstanding currency, checking and bank savings deposits, fell by one-third between 1929 and 1933, while prices fell by one-fourth. By contrast, high-powered money—currency plus commercial bank deposits with the Federal Reserve—actually grew across the period. Clearly, people were leery of using banks as financial intermediaries (just why they became suspicious is part of the debate over the cause of the Great Depression).

TABLE 16.4

MONEY AND PRICES 1925-34

Year	M_1 (billion $)	M_2 (billion $)	High-Powered Money (billion $)	Consumer Prices (1929 = 100)	GNP Price Deflator (1929 = 100)
1925	25.5	41.8	7.0	102.3	101
1926	25.9	43.3	7.1	103.1	101
1927	25.9	44.5	7.2	101.2	99
1928	26.2	46.1	7.1	100.0	100
1929	26.4	46.2	7.1	100	100
1930	25.4	45.2	6.9	97.4	96
1931	23.6	41.7	7.3	88.7	85
1932	20.6	34.8	7.8	79.7	77
1933	19.4	30.8	8.2	75.4	75
1934	21.5	33.3	9.1	78.0	80

High-powered money is bank reserves on deposit at the Federal Reserve plus outstanding currency. M_1 is the traditionally defined money supply—currency plus checking deposits. M_2 is M_1 plus savings deposits.

Source: Peter Temin, *Did Monetary Forces Cause the Great Depression?* (Norton, 1976), pp. 5–6.

RECOVERY

Once bottom was touched in 1933, the pace of recovery was, by historical standards, reasonable. Between 1933 and 1937, the American economy grew at an average annual rate of 10 percent, and real consumption recorded a 6 percent average annual gain (see table 16.5). The recovery of the banking sector was equally brisk, as the nominal money supply M_2 nearly regained its 1929 level by 1937. And since prices were much lower, the purchasing power of money balances was actually substantially greater than in 1929 (see table 16.6).

Unfortunately, though, even 10 percent growth wasn't adequate in an economy that had fallen so far below operating capacity and in which capacity continued to expand. Private net investment may have become negative for a few years—that is, the private stock of machines and structures and improvements to land may have begun to shrink. But the labor force grew about 12 percent from 1929 to 1937, and continuing investment in human capital, plus improvements in technology, helped to raise productivity. Hence the 47 percent increase in output between 1933 and 1937 still left 9 percent of the labor force unemployed—14

TABLE 16.5

UNCERTAIN PATH TO RECOVERY, 1933–39

Year	Real GNP (billion '29 $)	Real Consump-tion (billion '29 $)	Real Gross Investment (billion '29 $)	Unemploy-ment (%)	Unemployment Including Relief Employees as Part of Workforce (%)
1933	74.2	64.6	0.3	25.2	20.9
1934	80.8	68.0	1.8	22.0	16.2
1935	91.4	72.3	8.8	20.3	14.4
1936	100.9	79.7	9.3	17.0	10.0
1937	109.1	82.6	14.6	14.3	9.2
1938	103.2	81.3	6.8	19.1	12.5
1939	111.0	85.9	9.9	17.2	11.3

Source: Peter Temin, *Did Monetary Forces Cause the Great Depression?* (Norton, 1976), p. 4. Michael Darby, "Three and a Half Million U.S. Employees Have Been Mislaid . . . ," *Journal of Political Economy* 84 (Feb., 1976), p. 8.

TABLE 16.6

MONEY AND PRICES 1933–39

Year	M_1 (billion $)	M_2 (billion $)	High-Powered Money (billion $)	Consumer Prices (1929 = 100)	GNP Price Deflator (1929 = 100)
1933	19.4	30.8	8.2	75.4	75
1934	21.5	33.3	9.1	78.0	80
1935	25.5	38.4	10.7	80.1	79
1936	29.2	42.9	12.2	80.9	82
1937	30.3	45.0	13.4	83.8	83
1938	30.0	44.9	14.6	82.3	83
1939	33.6	48.7	17.6	81.0	82

Source: Peter Temin, *Did Monetary Forces Cause the Great Depression?* (Norton, 1976), pp. 5–6.

percent including underemployed workers on temporary governmental payrolls.

As if things were not bad enough, the economy took another nasty plunge in the autumn of 1937. Industrial production fell from an index level of 116 for the first eight months of the year (1923–25 = 100) to 83 in December. Kindleberger reports that steel producers who had been operating at 85 percent of capacity in August were down to 26 percent by December. And the stock market average, which had crawled back up to 1928 levels, took a 30 percent dive. Overall, output dipped 5.4 percent, and the unemployment rate rose from 14 percent to 19 percent.

Mercifully, however, the 1937 recession was just that—a recession. Output surpassed the 1937 level in 1939, regaining, if making no particular advance over, the 1933–37 recovery path. Unemployment (including temporary public service employees) stayed above 10 percent until well into 1941. Only by late 1942 was the American economy fully employed. And not an inconsiderable number of the newly employed were either making ordnance in defense plants or chucking it at the Japanese and Germans.

Why Did It Happen?

Dozens of theories have been offered. Marxists have argued that the Depression was caused by internal contradictions in capitalism that lead to increasingly unstable cycles in business activity. Another school of thought ties the Depression to long swings in investment opportunities. The depression of the 1870's came at the end of an investment cycle in railroads, while the 1920's marked the end of the initial growth of the electric power and auto industries. By this reckoning, the special severity of the 1929–33 contraction is explained by the coincidence of the "long-wave" downturn in investment with an independent, shorter-wave downturn—the latter perhaps the product of the natural cycle in business inventory accumulation.

Still another approach, presented by George Soule, connects the very substantial redistribution of income and wealth in the 1920's with the economic system's failure in the 1930's. This, by the way, fits into a Marxist view of the inherently self-destructive nature of mature capitalism. But it is also consistent with Keynesian "underconsumption" theories tying maldistribution of income with the saturation of the market for consumer durables such as autos, appliances and housing.

Peter Temin offers a simple taxonomy of Depression theories. It cannot account for fringe explanations—God's Wrath, or 11 anonymous billionaires in the boardroom of a bank in Basel—but it sorts out the evidence in a methodical way. Temin classifies two types of explanations: those that see the prime cause of the economic collapse in the reduction of the money supply, and those that tie the collapse to a fall in autonomous spending—capital goods, consumer goods, exports.

This division is particularly apt, for the two camps are generally also split on how the Depression might have been sooner ended, as well as by how it began. Monetarists, inspired by Milton Friedman and Anna Schwartz's seminal *Monetary History*, pin the blame on the Federal Reserve's failure to save the banks, and argue that a sound monetary policy would have speeded recovery. Keynesians and assorted post-Keynesian allies fault the government's failure to fill the shortfall in private spending with government outlays or tax-cut-induced private purchasing power.

Cause and cure, however, need not be seen as inextricably linked. Aggressive fiscal policy—government spending and/or tax cuts—might have saved an economy battered by the Federal Reserve's monetary errors; expansionary monetary policy—increasing the money supply—might have saved an economy slowed by shifts in spending. The emphasis following will be on outlining competing theories of causation, not on competing approaches to recovery.

THE MONETARY HYPOTHESES

By the monetary view, large, government-induced changes in the money supply turned an ordinary, short-lived recession into a decade of deep depression. In the first phase of the downturn, dating from the second half of 1929 to the fall of 1930, the Federal Reserve pursued a policy of vaguely malevolent neutrality. External factors tended to expand the money supply, as an inflow of gold from abroad and a slight shift by the public in favor of checking deposits over currency swelled the loanable funds base of the banks. The Fed, however, chose to more-than-offset these outside factors by allowing borrowing by banks from the Federal Reserve system to decline.

So far, it is hard to give the Fed much credit or blame—nothing special had happened, and the Fed had a long record of bumbling its way through recessions. But the game changed radically in the last quarter of 1930. The wave of bank failures in rural areas (now thought to have been related to bad crops, on top of an overextended credit structure) and the failure of the Bank of the United States changed both public and internal bank perceptions of the stability of the banking system. The Fed allowed the failures to trigger a search for liquidity by depositors, who converted demand deposits into currency, and by banks as well, which tried to prune risky and illiquid loans from their assets.

The banking system was stable enough to survive the first liquidity crisis without Fed help, but a second wave of failures, starting in March 1931, made both depositors and bank managers dangerously sensitive to the risks of bank illiquidity. The psychological impact of the second crisis was heightened by the failure in May of Austria's largest private bank, the Kreditanstalt, and the subsequent suspension of all deposit withdrawals from German banks. In spite of public alarm, the Federal Reserve took no decisive action to prevent specific bank failures, or to improve the overall liquidity of the system. And once again, the crisis was weathered without a wholesale run on private banks. But this time the liquidity squeeze did reduce the national money supply sharply; public preference for currency over deposits—for shoeboxes and safe deposit boxes over checking accounts—cut the money supply by 5.5 percent. Fears of illiquidity and business risk, moreover, drove up the interest rates charged on business loans and corporate bonds.

Until this point, those who wish to give the Federal Reserve the benefit of a doubt would label its sins as those of omission. But in September, 1931, as the result of Britain's decision to abandon the Gold Standard, Federal Reserve policy became an unmistakable burden on the domestic banking system. Britain had effectively floated the pound sterling, refusing to convert its currency into gold at a fixed rate and letting supply and demand determine the Pound's exchange rate with gold and other currencies. To allay fears that the United States would follow suit, the Federal Reserve tried to attract investments in dollar-denominated currencies by forcing up interest rates.

It "worked"—interest rates shot up; but the action helped set into motion another drive for individual liquidity. Depositors scrambled to convert unsafe checking account money into safe paper; banks pared their loans and holdings of corporate bond obligations. The money supply fell at a faster rate between August, 1931 and January, 1932 (31 percent annual rate) than it had for any previous five months on record.

By early 1932, everyone with an I.Q. above 80—and most members of the Federal Reserve Board of Governors—knew something was dreadfully wrong with the economy. Prodded by an election-year Congress, the Fed used its most potent medicine for increasing liquidity, open market operations. The Fed purchased $1 billion worth of government bonds from the marketplace, thereby injecting cash into private bank deposits and into currency. But it is difficult to know whether any conceivable effort at this late stage of the banking system's illness would have saved the patient, or whether the decline was irreversible.

In any event, after a few months the Fed stopped trying. From July, 1932 until the final panic in early 1933, the Federal Reserve pursued a neutral monetary policy, buying about as many bonds as it sold. A separate government agency set up by the Hoover Administration, the Reconstruction Finance Corporation, made $900 million in loans to distressed banks, but sporadic bank failures during the last half of 1932 pushed the system ever closer to total collapse. When the Roosevelt Administration finally closed all the banks in March, 1933, half the states had already independently suspended bank activity.

By the monetary hypothesis, first the Fed's inaction while confidence in fractional reserve banking slowly ebbed and then its perverse action (in defense of the gold standard) in 1931 destroyed the system and, along the way, cut the money supply by one-third. That turned a nasty recession into an economic calamity. In fact, the monetarists argue that bad government regulation turned out to be much worse than no regulation at all. Though the point cannot be proved, the existence of a federal agency with the muscle to maintain bank liquidity through any conceivable panic led banks to drop their own defenses. Thus we got the worst of both worlds: a banking system dependent on government for its stability, and a government with little sense of its powers or responsibilities.

THE SPENDING HYPOTHESIS AND TEMIN'S TEST

The spending hypothesis—that the Great Depression was initiated by changes in aggregate demand—is older than the monetary hypothesis. And its association with the prestigious Keynesian economists of the 1940's and 1950's has almost automatically prejudiced generations of economic historians in its favor. The most systematic statements of the spending hypothesis, those by Robert A. Gordon, emphasized the inherent instability of investment demand—the fact that there are natural cycles in investment that cause cycles in business activity. The Depression is thus laid at the feet of the investment decline in housing, autos, tires, and textiles. Formal statistical models of the structure of the economy in the interwar years, most notably those by Lawrence Klein, showed that the evidence was consistent with the spending hypothesis. The contraction could be explained through simple Keynesian relationships, with hardly any references at all to the bank failures or to changes in the money supply.

How does this square with the Friedman-Schwartz blow-by-blow account of the road to hell in the Federal Reserve's handbasket? The key, Keynesians reply, is the direction of causality. By the monetarist interpretation, the Federal Reserve's failure to protect the banks led to a reduction in the money supply, which in turn reduced aggregate demand. Falling prices and wages might eventually make the new reduced stock of money adequate to support full employment output again—but in the interim employment and output suffer.

By the Keynesian view, it is demand factors that cause the fall in the stock of money, not independent shifts in the money supply function. Companies doing less business tend to borrow less money from banks. The impact on outstanding loans may be offset by competition among banks: They lower interest charges in order to compete for whatever loan business is left, and the lower interest charges encourage investment. But the offset will not be complete if banks choose to keep a higher proportion of their assets as reserves as the low returns make the loan business less lucrative.

That scenario seems a little lame, however. There is no empirical evidence that banks actually do react to lower interest rates by raising their reserves. But Keynesians have something more to back up the direct effect of demand on the money supply. A fall in income, caused by shifts in spending, reduces business profits and increases defaults on bank loans. Friedman-Schwartz may be right that bank failures caused the money supply to fall, the Keynesians argue, but the initial cause of the bank failures may be business bankruptcies caused by reductions in the demand for goods. This is not a pure spending hypothesis, in the sense that the financial system's structural weakness magnifies the impact of the initial spending reduction. It does qualify, though, as a spending hypothesis "hybrid" because the initial source of the crisis comes on the spending side.

What disturbed Temin about the monetary-spending controversy and led to his own research was the symmetric weakness to be found on both sides. Friedman and Schwartz's detailed narrative convinces because it is consistent with the facts so relentlessly thrown at the reader. So, too, the spending hypothesis is attractive because it is plausible and because it is not apparently contradicted by evidence. The opposing camps do not debate; they talk to themselves and past each other. Is it possible, Temin wonders, to devise empirical tests that will allow rational choice between the alternatives?

For the monetarist position to hold—that is, for monetary events to be the cause of changes in output—the reduction in the supply of money should be seen as higher interest rates on loans. Scarce money would raise its "price," reducing investment, and, in turn, reducing production and employment. But, Temin notes, interest rates fell amost without interruption from the stock market crash to the Federal Reserve's move to shore up the international standing of the dollar in the fall of 1931. Thereafter, tight money may have exacerbated the contraction; but the Depression was already two years in the making before the interest rate pinch was felt.

Monetarists don't like the money supply-to-interest rates-to-spending line of reasoning. Although there is no real contradiction in the alternative approaches, they prefer to think of the deflationary impact of a reduction in the supply of money as working through movements along a stable demand for money function. When the money supply function shifts backward, supply and demand for money should equilibrate only at a lower level of national income.

But here too, Temin finds the monetarist case lacking. The "money" the monetarists are talking about is "real money" or purchasing power. Even if the nominal stock of money declines, the equilibrium level of income, where the demand for money equals the supply of money, won't decline unless the nominal money stock actually buys less. It turns out, however, that prices—both wholesale and retail—fell roughly as fast as

TABLE 16.7

THE REAL MONEY SUPPLY
(index, 1929 = 100)

Year	M_1	M_1/WPI	M_1/CPI	M_2	M_2/WPI	M_2/CPI
1925	96.6	88.8	94.3	90.5	83.3	88.5
1926	98.1	93.4	95.1	93.7	89.3	90.9
1927	98.1	97.8	96.7	96.3	96.0	95.0
1928	99.2	97.5	99.1	99.8	98.2	99.8
1929	100	100	100	100	100	100
1930	96.2	106.2	98.8	97.8	107.9	100.4
1931	89.4	116.8	100.9	90.3	117.8	101.8
1932	78.0	114.8	98.0	75.3	110.8	94.6
1933	73.5	106.5	97.3	66.7	96.2	88.2
1934	81.4	103.3	104.2	72.1	91.7	92.5

The nominal money supply (by either the M_1 or M_2 definition) did indeed fall rapidly after 1929. But in purchasing power terms, the changes are less visible. M_1 adjusted to account for falling wholesale or consumer prices (columns 2 and 3) reveals no clear movement. M_2 after similar adjustments (columns 5 and 6) only really falls after 1931—and even then the magnitude of the fall is relatively small.

Note: Columns (1) and (4) show a nominal money supply index (unadjusted for price changes) for purposes of comparison with the purchasing power indexes; WPI = wholesale price index; CPI = consumer price index.

Source: Peter Temin, *Did Monetary Forces Cause the Great Depression?* (Norton, 1976), pp. 5, 141.

the quantity of money, at least through the initial agony of the collapse (see table 16.7). The real money stock changed between −1.2 percent and 7.9 percent in the first year of the contraction, depending on which definition of money is used. And it grew sharply in 1930–31, thanks to the unprecedented decline in prices. Only after 1931 does the real money supply fall, but even then only M_2 clearly sinks below the real level of 1929.

Can similar tests be applied to the spending hypothesis? In a sense, the logic of the debate does not require positive proof if the monetary alternative is counted out. The hypotheses are drawn so broadly and inclusively, that once the monetary approach is shown to fail, all that is left is a spending explanation. Still it would be nice to be more specific, and Temin's research aims at differentiating explanations based on independent shifts in investment—the traditional Keynesian view—from explanations based on shifts in consumption.

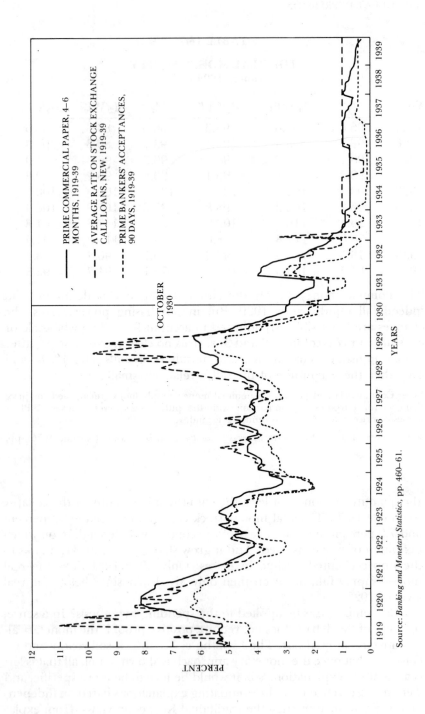

PRIME COMMERCIAL PAPER, 4–6
MONTHS, 1919-39

AVERAGE RATE ON STOCK EXCHANGE
CALL LOANS, NEW. 1919-39

PRIME BANKERS' ACCEPTANCES,
90 DAYS, 1919-39

OCTOBER
1930

PERCENT

YEARS

Source: *Banking and Monetary Statistics*, pp. 460–61.

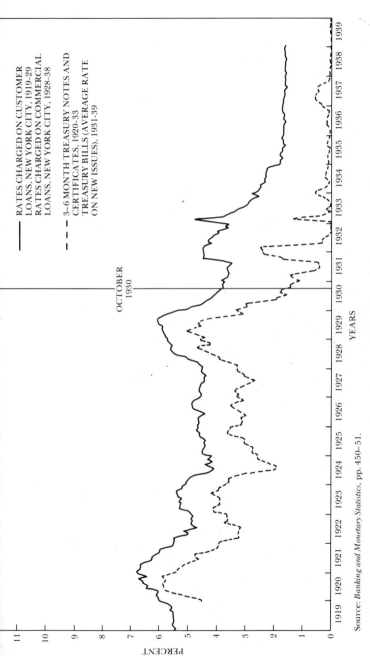

Source: *Banking and Monetary Statistics*, pp. 450–51.

Five Interest Rate Series, Monthly 1919–39

No single interest rate tracks like any other. But, within reason, all five examined by Temin tell the same story. Interest rates fell from mid-1929 to mid-1931, then rose briefly in 1931 as the Fed moved to protect the dollar's exchange value abroad.

Source: Peter Temin, *Did Monetary Forces Cause the Great Depression?* (Norton, 1976), pp. 124–25.

TABLE 16.8

CHANGES IN COMPONENTS OF REAL INCOME
(percent)

Years	GNP	Consumption	Investment	Exports
1920–21	−2.4	+6.4	−41.7	−14.2
1919–21	−3.5	+11.6	−30.7	−19.7
1929–30	−8.9	−5.4	−35.6	−19.1
1928–30	−3.4	−0.2	−27.8	−15.7
1937–38	−5.4	−1.6	−53.1	+1.7
1936–38	+2.3	+2.1	−26.4	+29.8

Source: Peter Temin, *Did Monetary Forces Cause the Great Depression?* (Norton, 1976), p. 64.

As table 16.8 reveals, investment did fall in the first year of the contraction, but not in a way that makes the beginning of the Great Depression look different from the short-lived recessions of 1920–21 or 1937–38. In fact, the investment component of the initial contraction was relatively small. The *composition* of the investment fall was unusual though; construction accounted for a much larger portion of the reduction, and inventories far less (see table 16.9). With hindsight, this could be taken as an ominous sign. Cycles in construction take a long time to work through, while inventory cycles are typically quite brief. If a construction depression were the source of the severe contraction of 1929–30, it might explain why the recovery was unusually long in coming.

That story has a nice ring to it, but Temin forcefully argues that it does not bear up well under examination. The construction cycle peaked in 1926, three years before the Depression began, and no slowdown in the economy is evident between 1926 and 1929. No doubt construction fell further during the 1929–33 contraction than it would have under more normal circumstances, but the direction of causality seems to be from income fall to construction decline, not the reverse. The inherent complexity of the economy, particularly the lags of unknown length between changes in independent factors and income declines, makes it necessary to qualify practically every conclusion about the cause of the business downturn in 1929. Thus it is hard to pin the Great Depression on the construction cycle.

What, then, caused the Great Depression? Temin is fairly confident that the culprit lies in independent changes in *consumption* demand. His best version goes something like this. In 1929 the economy was heading for a recession. Two phenomena made this recession special: the agricultural decline and the stock market crash. The fall in agricultural income,

TABLE 16.9

**SOURCES OF DECLINE IN GROSS INVESTMENT
DURING ECONOMIC CONTRACTION**
(percent)

Years	Total	Construction	Equipment	Inventories
1920–21	100	6	19	75
1919–21	100	−9	20	89
1929–30	100	12	22	36
1928–30	100	82	18	0
1937–38	100	10	28	62
1936–38	100	−33	28	106

Interpretation: One special feature of the fall in investment at the beginning of the Depression was the enormous decline in construction relative to inventories. From 1928 to 1930, 82 percent of the investment fall was in construction; during the 1920–21 recession construction investment hardly changed.

Source: Joseph Swanson and Samuel Williamson, "Estimates of National Product and Income for the United States 1919–41," *Explorations in Economic History* 10 (Fall, 1972), p. 70.

related to a nasty combination of small harvests and low prices (due to good harvests abroad), reduced consumption demand. And so, too, did the change in wealth associated with the bust in stock prices.

But taken together, these factors could not account for a very large fraction of the total independent change in spending observed by Temin. Based on econometric estimates of the consumption function—the mathematical relationship between consumer spending and variables such as income and wealth—only about one-third of the total consumption decline can be linked to predictable reactions to the crash or to the crunch in agriculture. Most of the rest has to come from still unidentified forces that made Americans less willing to spend their incomes than they had been in the 1920's.

TEMIN AND HIS CRITICS

The most telling criticism of Temin is by Temin. He offers an explanation of what did not cause the Depression—monetary forces, investment changes, consumption changes related to the stock crash and rural distress—but he remains agnostic about what autonomous spending changes did cause the contraction. We are left—literally—with a statistical residual from an estimated consumption function as the prime cause. Temin does not apologize for serving these scraps—he claims that the meat so confidently proffered by both monetarists and Keynesians should never have been on the menu.

Yet, it should not be thought that Temin has totally demolished his opposition. Thomas Mayer presents a skillful rebuttal, largely on behalf of the monetarist camp. His points are worth summarizing:

• Temin argues that a reduction in the supply of money should raise interest rates. Rates did not go up, so Temin claims that the observed drop in the stock of money must have been initiated on the demand side. Mayer acknowledges the power of the argument, but provides monetarists with possible routes of escape. First, the *real* interest rate—the difference between nominal rates and the expected rate of overall price change—is not observable. It is possible, if not proven, that a part of the drop in prices was anticipated by potential borrowers, who thereby became reluctant to accept loans that would have to be repaid in much more valuable dollars later on. In effect, this means real interest rates might have soared in 1930, even as observed rates fell.

Second, the rush to make assets more liquid after the stock market crash and the rural bank failures may, perversely, have lowered the interest rates depositors and other lenders demanded on short-term securities. Normally, strong preferences for cash over illiquid assets raise interest rates. But Mayer points out that it is at least theoretically possible for the drive for liquidity to favor short-term securities; savers may prefer to go halfway, from stocks and bonds into more liquid interest-bearing liquid assets like treasury bills, rather than all the way into non-interest-bearing paper currency or gold.

• "Real" money gives the monetarists as many headaches as "real" interest rates. If money had been tight in 1930, asks Temin, how could it be that the purchasing power of the money supply remained the same, or even increased a bit? More fancy footwork by Mayer provides at least a theoretical escape. Suppose short-term interest rates really fell, as a monetarist might argue, because at the beginning of the crunch the search for liquidity led savers from the stock market into savings accounts and other short-term securities. Low interest rates would encourage business to borrow money and thereby keep the total real money supply large. The argument can be expressed more formally: The monetarist reduction in the supply of money might *temporarily* have been offset by an increase in the demand for money associated with lower (rather than the expected higher) interest rates. None of this could last very long—but long enough to rescue the monetarists from an empirical mess.

• Temin's own search for an explanation for the Depression finally lands on unexplained shifts in the demand for consumption goods. Mayer argues, however, that the statistical case for an unpredicted shortfall in consumption is questionable. This is not the place to air a debate over econometrics. Suffice it to say that Mayer is probably right, in the sense that Temin's case is not overwhelming. A neutral observer would probably accept Temin's findings. But for an observer already predisposed to accept other explanations for the contraction, there is room left for skepticism over the consumption shift.

• For Friedman and Schwartz, many blundered in 1929–33, but there is only one true villain: the Federal Reserve. Not so, implies Temin. The Depression was caused by an independent fall in demand; the Fed was an ignorant, but innocent, bystander. Mayer believes he scents a whiff of sophistry here, for just how the blame is allocated in the Depression depends upon how responsibility is defined. Suppose Temin is correct about the facts: The fall in income, the bank failures, the contraction of the nominal money supply were all the result of an autonomous shift in consumption. Should the Federal Reserve still not be blamed for standing on the sidelines watching the show, rather than aggressively opposing the downturn?

Mayer is not sure. The answer turns on what the Fed could have done to make things better in 1930. Extensive open market purchases of government bonds by the Fed might have slowed the fall in the money supply, blunted the fall in income, and speeded the upturn. Or it might have done nothing but drag out the fall in the real money supply a while longer. Still, assertions that expansionary monetary policy would have done no good should be treated skeptically. There is no evidence that it would not—surely it was never seriously tried in the 1929–33 contraction. And only the most rigid, pre-1950 Keynesian models of the economy (and the most avant-garde "rational expectations" models) deny monetary policy some role in changing aggregate demand.

Regrettably, no clean and quick explanation for the Depression survives close examination. Temin's attack badly damages the monetarist defenses. His own case lays a fragile foundation for an explanation based on shifts in consumption demand. But as Temin is first to argue, honest results come very hard in macroeconomics. A lot of economists have been embarrassed into this view in recent years, as they have watched Keynesian and monetarist models fail to predict economic behavior. So too, must economic historians adjust to the inherent complexity of macroeconomic events in the past.

Depression, Fiscal Policy, and the New Deal

Conventional histories provide no answer to the question of why recovery took so long, other than a sense that the immense structural damage done to the economy was exceedingly difficult to repair.

The anecdotal nature of the structural damage case does not, however, reduce its force. The Depression, it could be argued, destroyed institutions as well as income. Capital markets were unraveled by disintermediation—people, with good reason, distrusted banks after 1931 and were thus reluctant to use them again. Bankrupt corporations, including many banks, were immersed in legal proceedings which made it difficult to use their underlying assets productively. And the stock market crash brought home the inherent risks in equity investments, as well as exposing the degree to which the market was vulnerable to stock price manipulation and securities fraud. All this increased the cost of raising capital for businesses that wanted to increase production.

Note, moreover, the damage done to the economy by rapidly falling prices. Deflation—like inflation—is an uneven process; some prices go down faster than others. The uncertainty created by unpredictable changes in relative prices made investment and production decisions extremely difficult. If changing prices were poorly anticipated, businesses exposed themselves to great risks—costs could exceed revenues by the time a contract was completed. The only predictable result of deflation is inefficiency: a tendency for business to pass by investment opportunities with high expected returns, allowing some firms that produce poorly but guess right to survive, and bankrupting other firms that produce efficiently but guess wrong.

In retrospect, though, it is interesting how little standard historical accounts blame government for the long agony of recovery. In part this may follow from the fact that the Depression's cast changed after the first act. The Roosevelt Administration, bulging with activist plans and slogans, replaced the discredited Hoover Administration. Roosevelt promised a major role for the government in ending the Depression and generated a flood of legislation that made the first hundred days. . . . the First Hundred Days.

Appearances betray reality. The federal government certainly had the basic weapons with which to fight the Depression—fiscal and monetary policy. But, monetary policy was in the hands of the same folks—the Board of Governors of the Federal Reserve—who had never smelled the smoke in 1930, and then refused to help put out the fire in 1932. They did little from 1933 to 1937 that could be construed as policy of any sort. This left fiscal policy for the president to exercise, and it is still popularly accepted that Roosevelt played his part aggressively, adopting the new interventionist approach called for by Keynes and his crowd.

Now, John Maynard Keynes, Cambridge University's premier economic theorist and controversial adviser to several British governments, did once meet Franklin Roosevelt. But that meeting came off badly— neither found his audience sufficiently respectful—and there is not a hint that Roosevelt was influenced by Keynes. However, it took the analysis of E. Cary Brown, writing in 1956, to bury the myth that Roosevelt was the first American Keynesian.

If fiscal policy in the 1930's is to be judged, there must be a standard by which to judge it. This is not quite as simple as it sounds. Politicians are fond of using the size of the budget deficit as a gauge of fiscal impact: If federal expenditures exceed tax revenues, the government must be stimulating the economy. But note the problem here. The same set of tax rates and government spending programs may generate either a budget surplus or a budget deficit, depending on the vigor of the private sector. If businesses and individuals spend aggressively on their own, tax collections go up and government spending tends to fall as welfare, unemployment, and jobs programs are automatically phased down; the federal budget will be in surplus. If, on the other hand, private spending is slack, tax revenues fall and government social spending accelerates; the federal budget slips in the red. This explains why an economically conservative government, like the Eisenhower Administration, could run up big deficits without half trying. During the 1958–59 recession, Ike's advisers were horrified to find that federal expenditures exceeded federal revenues by 16 percent, the largest deficit since the crisis years of World War II.

Brown avoids this problem by judging fiscal policy by its relative impact on aggregate demand at full employment income.[1] It might be intuitively argued that a tax and expenditure policy that generated a balanced budget at full employment is a neutral fiscal policy. Intuition is a little misleading here too, but not as misleading as measuring fiscal impact by the size of the actual deficit. And the size of the full employment budget surplus (or deficit) relative to total economic capacity is surely a useful measure for comparing fiscal policy changes over time.

Brown, of course, did not know exactly how large the government deficit or surplus would have been at full employment. However, by assuming that (1) government expenditures were virtually unaffected by income levels, (2) tax collections were roughly proportional to increases in income above actual income levels, and (3) full employment income was growing at 3 percent a year, he was able to construct counterfactual full employment budgets (see table 16.10).

Federal fiscal policy was, on balance, expansionary during six or the seven Roosevelt Administration years shown (1933 on). But that should be cold comfort, indeed, for Roosevelt partisans. For on close inspection, it becomes clear that expansionary fiscal policy was hardly used in any year. At the trough of the Depression, when Brown calculates that actual output was 39 percent below full employment capacity, the full employment deficit would have been only 0.3 percent of GNP. In 1936 the Roosevelt budget reaches its expansionary peak (2.1 percent)—but only because Congress, over White House objections, sweetened the veterans'

---

[1] Actually Brown used a somewhat different measure; for purposes of clarity and consistency with other research we translate his calculations into full employment terms.

TABLE 16.10

IMPACT OF FISCAL POLICY ON AGGREGATE DEMAND 1929-39

Year	Actual GNP (1947 prices, billions $)	Full Employment GNP (1947 prices, billions $)	Federal Deficit(+) as % of F.E.GNP	All Government Deficit(+) as % of F.E.GNP
1929	149.3	149.3	−0.6	+0.8
1930	135.2	154.0	−0.1	+1.4
1931	126.6	159.0	+2.0	+3.1
1932	107.6	163.9	+1.0	+0.9
1933	103.7	169.1	−0.3	−1.0
1934	113.4	174.4	+1.6	−0.2
1935	¹27.8	179.9	+1.6	+0.1
1936	142.5	185.6	+2.1	+1.1
1937	153.5	191.5	−0.7	−1.8
1938	145.9	197.5	+0.6	−0.6
1939	157.5	203.7	+0.8	+0.1

Note: The signs are reversed from the common sense notion of a deficit to illustrate more clearly whether the budget was expansionary (+) or contractionary (−).

Source: E. Cary Brown, "Fiscal Policy in the Thirties: A Reappraisal" in Robert Fogel and Stanley Engerman (eds.), *The Reinterpretation of American Economic History* (Harper & Row, 1971), pp. 484-85.

compensation program. And the following year, political pressures to balance the budget pushed fiscal policy into its most conservative stance since the late 1920's.

Note, too, that the extremely moderate stimulus of the Roosevelt budgets was offset by increasingly conservative financial policies of state and local governments who were up to their capitol domes in debt. During the last three disastrous years of the Hoover Administration (1930–32), state and local governments maintained a slightly positive fiscal stance, raising the net stimulative impact of all government activity. But after 1932, efforts to stem growing deficits made non-federal government budgets a net deflationary force, fully offsetting Roosevelt's cautious expansion. As a result, the net impact of all government on aggregate demand was negative in four out of seven Roosevelt years and was surely less expansionary overall from 1933 to 1939 than it had been from 1930 to 1932 (see table 16.10)! By Brown's standard, Herbert Hoover was a better Keynesian than FDR.

Larry Pepper's recent reworking of Brown's computations puts Depression fiscal policy in even worse light. Pepper adjusted Brown's estimates of full-employment income and made more sophisticated projections of tax revenues and expenditures at the full employment level. He discovered that the federal budget would have been in full employment *surplus* in every Depression year, with the exception of 1931 and 1936 (see table 16.11).

Why was fiscal policy so perversely practiced during the Depression? The simple—and nearly complete—answer is that policy makers did not know any better. To be fair, ignorance was a reasonable excuse in the early 1930's. Monetary policy makers at least had intuition working in their favor: By doing the obvious thing (saving the banks by pumping liquidity into the system), the Federal Reserve would have been doing the right thing. Fiscal planners, by contrast, had only classical macroeconomic theory, which prescribed nothing but increased labor market competition as the answer to unemployment, and the false analogies of private business to guide fiscal planning. Government budget deficits were seen as a threat to stability in the same way operating deficits were seen as a threat to the stability of the corporation. The only proper course, it appeared, was to batten the hatches and head into the wind.

It could be said, too, that government was hostage to these homilies even if policy makers were not fully taken in by them. Radical departures from accepted policies could have further weakened confidence in the economy, and thereby defeated their own purpose. All in all, Her-

TABLE 16.11

PEPPERS' FULL EMPLOYMENT BUDGET CALCULATIONS, 1929–39

Year	Potential Budget Surplus (+) in billion $	Potential Taxes (% GNP)	Potential Expenditures (% GNP)	Full Employment Surplus (% GNP)
1929	1.3	3.75	2.55	1.20
1930	0.9	3.57	2.67	0.90
1931	−0.5	3.78	4.32	−0.54
1932	0.8	4.43	3.56	0.87
1933	1.7	6.34	4.44	1.90
1934	0.1	6.59	6.45	0.14
1935	0.8	7.10	6.34	0.76
1936	−0.7	7.57	8.14	0.57
1937	3.2	9.31	6.50	2.82
1938	3.4	10.09	7.17	2.92
1939	2.6	9.53	7.32	2.21

Source: Larry Peppers, "Full Employment Surplus Analysis and Structural Change: The 1930's," *Explorations in Economic History* 10 (Winter, 1973), p. 203.

bert Hoover comes out looking a tad better than Franklin Roosevelt as an economic leader. As historian (and fiscal planner under the Nixon Administration) Herbert Stein argues, Hoover had no hope of breaking with conventional policies that had yet to be demonstrated ineffective to the business and financial communities.

Roosevelt, on the other hand, inherited policies that had obviously not worked at all. But he resisted an expansionary approach out of the conviction that the economy's problems were structural, rather than fiscal. In the short run, budget deficits might be tolerated in order to provide emergency relief for the unemployed. But Roosevelt believed—or at least acted as though he believed—that the country could not spend its way out of the Depression. Salvation could only be had through structural reform.

This goes a long way toward explaining the passions of Roosevelt's economic advisers in defending the New Deal's emphasis on structural change—and the painful surprise liberal economists get today when they look back and see what the first modern liberal attempted. For, while New Dealers of the 1930's and mainstream liberal economists of the 1970's share a common commitment toward income redistribution, contemporary liberal economists have far greater respect for the value of competitive market mechanisms in making sure there is something to redistribute.

We won't take the space here to run through the chronology of New Deal programs; the point can be better made by examining one major New Deal reform, the National Recovery Act (1933). The NRA mandated the formation of planning boards for critical sectors of the economy, staffed by representatives from business and labor. The boards were supposed to set output goals as well as prices and wages for the industry. That way, the uncertainty associated with private planning in those dark days could be overcome. With the approval of the government, the boards restricted production and raised prices and wages— what better way, the New Dealers asserted, to fight the spiral of deflation that had lowered prices and wages?

Many of the contemporary complaints about the NRA were about its impact on income distribution. It was suspected (perhaps correctly) that business could dominate the boards and increase capital's share of the pie. But for those who respect the allocative advantages of competitive markets, there were other, and perhaps deeper, problems. The NRA was a license—no, an order—to cartelize. The planning boards were supposed to raise wages and profits by raising prices and reducing output. Now that just isn't likely to end up producing a higher national income. If only some of the sectors of the economy are allowed to construct cartels, their members will be better off, but at the expense of the rest of the economy and possibly of their own unemployed workers.

On the other hand, if everybody joins a cartel, two results are possible. Suppose everyone's prices go up by the same percentage; this leaves relative prices the same and has no effect on resource allocation or the real income of those working. Much more likely, some cartels will be more successful than others, and relative prices will change. That leaves some firms (and perhaps workers) better off but distorts resource allocation. The successful cartels will produce too little, and real national income will surely fall.

The NRA was thus a short-lived (it was declared unconstitutional in 1935) attempt to gain the freedom from uncertainty offered by state socialism without public ownership or direct government control of business. At best it should be viewed as the product of misguided economic theory. At worst it can be seen as part of America's flirtation with the rigid anti-libertarian mercantilism sweeping Germany, Italy, and Spain in the thirties.

It is fashionable to argue that FDR saved the United States from right or left wing totalitarianism, that his radical actions were profoundly conservative in the sense that they held a disintegrating political-economic system together. There may be some truth to the argument. But it is well to remember that his fiscal policy was not in the slightest helpful in saving anything. And that the residue of misguided New Deal structural reforms—minimum wages that eliminate jobs for unskilled workers, farm price supports that discourage production, pork barrel public works, expensive and inefficient regulation of private business—still plagues efforts to keep the American growth economy on track.

The Objectives of New Deal Spending

By the standard of the times, enormous resources were invested in New Deal programs. This investment seems reasonable as part of the Roosevelt Administration's attempt to cope with the impact of the Depression on real incomes. But what seems less reasonable is the great variations in per capita allotments of funds among the states (see table 16.12); Nevada residents averaged $1,499 per person, while North Carolinians managed only $228.

Don Reading argues that the New Deal's goals were more specifically defined by the president as, first, relief and recovery, and then, reform. For Reading, relief and recovery mean repairing the immediate economic damage done by business failure and unemployment. Reform means attacking the structural causes of poverty—low productivity, racial discrimination, unequal wealth distribution. To measure the New Deal's goals in practice, Reading chooses variables that show the states' relative relief needs (percent decline in income, unemployment) and the state's relative reform needs (per capita income, percentage of tenant farmers, percentage of blacks). He then statistically regresses these variables (plus others to allow for the practical problems of setting up aid programs) against per capita New Deal aid to see if they explain state-by-state variations in spending.

TABLE 16.12

NEW DEAL OUTLAYS PER CAPITA, BY STATE 1933–39

Region/State	Rank	Allocation (dollars)	Region/State	Rank	Allocation (dollars)
Northeast	6	301	Indiana	34	333
Connecticut	47	237	Iowa	15	467
Delaware	36	310	Michigan	21	389
Maine	32	336	Michigan	21	389
Massachusetts	39	286	Minnesota	17	426
New Hampshire	45	248	Missouri	31	340
New Jersey	35	330	Ohio	22	383
New York	33	335	Wisconsin	20	390
Pennsylvania	42	261			
Rhode Island	46	247	*Great Plains*	3	424
Vermont	19	390	Kansas	16	434
			North Dakota	6	708
Southeast	5	306	Oklahoma	30	343
Alabama	37	31	South Dakota	7	702
Arkansas	18	396	Texas	26	362
Florida	23	377			
Georgia	40	273	*Pacific*	2	536
Kentucky	44	251	California	10	538
Louisiana	23	370	Oregon	12	536
Maryland	28	345	Washington	13	528
Mississippi	27	358			
North Carolina	48	228	*Mountain*	1	716
South Carolina	38	306	Arizona	4	791
Tennessee	29	344	Colorado	14	506
Virginia	43	255	Idaho	5	744
West Virginia	41	265	Montana	2	986
			Nevada	1	1499
Midwest	4	380	New Mexico	8	690
Illinois	25	365	Utah	9	569
			Wyoming	3	897

Source: Don Reading, "New Deal Activity and the States 1933–39," *Journal of Economic History* 33 (Dec., 1973), pp. 794–95.

His results show a much deeper dollar commitment to relief than to reform. Expenditures were greatest where, other factors equal, unemployment and the rate of decline of income were greatest. Loan dollars appear to be related to income declines, but not unemployment. This follows, Reading argues, from the fact that the programs specifically targeted against unemployment—welfare, public works, were all grant programs.

Surely the most striking result from the study is the apparent failure of New Deal administrators to pass out funds according to the single clearest measure of need—per capita income. The poorest region of the country, the South, got relatively little, while the richest, the Pacific states, averaged 75 percent more per capita. In a sense, this fits the recovery vs. reform dichotomy; the New Deal simply never got as far as reform. But it also adds weight to the argument that Roosevelt was most concerned with defusing political and social unrest. Within bounds, it is logical that people would react more strongly to changes in income than to their absolute level of purchasing power. Thus an Oregon orchard owner, who lost half of his or her substantial income, would be a better candidate for aid than a dirt-poor North Carolina sharecropper, whose income fell only marginally during the contraction.

Leonard Arrington suggests that Roosevelt may have had something more prosaic in mind, too: getting himself and other Democrats reelected. This idea is elegantly developed by Gavin Wright, who econometrically tests several alternative models of spending for votes. A smart politician with limited resources to offer does not simply reward loyalty—a dollar spent on a sure vote is a dollar wasted. Rather, the politician tries to maximize the clout of expenditures, spending where the money is most likely to change the course of an election. This implies that more should be spent in states where, other factors equal, (1) the voting is expected to be close and (2) there have been substantial swings in voter sentiment, suggesting that voters can be persuaded to switch party allegiance in return for favors.

Even without formal statistical testing, the predictive power of this approach is clear. The South, ever loyal to the Democratic Party, got little, while the western states that switched allegiance frequently were heavily courted with dollars. Wright's regression analysis bears out the intuitive: adjusting for the "ruralness" of states, the combination of electoral votes per capita, variability in previous elections, and the closeness of the 1932 election vote, explains 80 percent of state-to-state variations in New Deal spending.

These three variables dominate the statistical analysis so completely that plausible alternatives—like Reading's relief hypothesis—wash out. When the percentage decline in per capita income, the percentage of families on government relief, and the unemployment rate are added to the basic "political" model, they have no statistical impact on the spending equation. Wright's political explanation works differently, however, in accounting for one important component of New Deal spending, public jobs. Here, the political variables all make some difference in 1936, but even in that year collectively explain just 37 percent of state-to-state variations in how the administration apportioned some 2.5 million Works Progress Administration jobs.

Did Roosevelt's political spending strategy work? It is not enough to show that he was reelected three times. It is necessary to demonstrate that New Deal funds changed the share of Democratic votes in the states. Here Wright's statistical analysis produced more ambiguous results. Improvements in income raise the percentage of Democratic votes, all right, but the effect of government spending *per se* is barely visible in the 1936 election and disappears entirely in the 1938 and 1940 elections. It can be argued that government spending raised incomes, so that the indirect effect of spending was still there to be seen. But that isn't very persuasive, because the link between government spending and per capita income is not tight. Clearly a more complex model of voting behavior is needed—or, as likely, a different model for each election. Wright notes that the European war probably dominated other issues in the 1940 election: Indeed the single variable with the most power to explain votes is the percentage of German Americans in the state population.

Roosevelt, then, probably tried, and less probably succeeded, in using New Deal spending to keep Democrats in office. Economic goals were either secondary or did not figure in decisions on how to allocate funds. Roosevelt need not be judged harshly for this preoccupation with politics, though. It would take an unreconstructed cynic to claim that FDR did not believe that his reelection and the election of New Deal Democrats to Congress would help the economy. However the New Deal is judged, there was certainly more to it than the maximization of Franklin Roosevelt's political power.

Appendix: The Hicks-Hansen Synthesis of Income Equilibrium Models

Much of this chapter concentrates on alternative explanations of why the economy contracted so sharply in 1929–33. The two classes of hypotheses suggested by Peter Temin—spending and monetary—can best be understood with the help of the graphical synthesis first offered by John Hicks and Alvin Hansen. The Hicks-Hansen, or "IS-LM," synthesis applies equally well to Keynesian and monetarist views of macroeconomic relationships and events. We develop the bare bones of the Hicks-Hansen model and then show how spending and monetary explanations of the Depression fit.

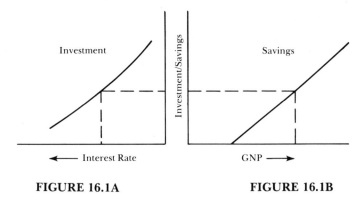

FIGURE 16.1A   **FIGURE 16.1B**

Interpretation: On the left, investment demand is shown as a function of interest rates—the higher the interest rate, the less companies will find it profitable to invest.

On the right, savings is shown as a function of GNP—the higher national output, the more people are willing to set aside before consuming the rest.

Thus, for a given level of GNP, intended savings will equal intended investment only at a specific rate of interest.

Hicks-Hansen focuses in turn on the conditions for income equilibrium requiring (1) that intended investment equal intended savings and (2) that the desired quantity of money assets held by the private sector equal the amount of money actually available. First, consider the Investment-Savings (IS) equilibrium condition. As figure 16.1a suggests, the amount of investment spending is related to interest rates on loans. The lower the interest rate, the higher the rate of investment.

Figure 16.1b shows the familiar relationship between savings and income: The more income people have, the more they wish to save. Now, in order for national income to be in equilibrium, it is necessary that the amount investors wish to invest to equal the amount of income left over after income recipients decide how much they wish to consume. Hence figures 1a and 1b indirectly reveal what interest rate (and therefore investment rate) is consistent with what level of national income (and therefore savings rate). The so-called IS relationship is shown in figure 16.2. It slopes downward because high interest rates mean little investment, and thus a low equilibrium level of income.

Now consider the other condition that must be met if national income is to be in equilibrium. The demand for money is determined both by the level of business activity and interest rates. The more business, the more money individuals and firms feel they must hold to meet day-to-day expenses. By the same token, the higher the interest rate on securities, the more income they give up by holding their assets as non-interest-bearing money. The higher interest rates are, the greater the motive to pare down non-interest-bearing cash balances.

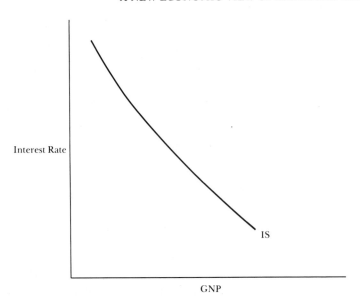

FIGURE 16.2

Interpretation: The IS relationship is derived from underlying savings and investment functions shown in figure 16.1. The curve slopes downward because, other things equal, the higher GNP is, the more people will wish to save. This higher savings will equal higher investment only if interest rates are low enough to accommodate the higher investment.

Suppose the supply of money is fixed independently—it is usually a convenient simplification to think of the Federal Reserve as controlling the money supply completely. Suppose, too, that at current income and interest rates, there is just enough money to go around to satisfy cash holders. The only way this fixed quantity of money will be able to accommodate a higher income (and higher rate of business transactions) is for interest rates to go up. This will give cash holders an incentive to economize by switching into interest-bearing securities and freeing the cash for use by others. Hence, for a fixed money supply, higher interest rates will be consistent with a higher level of national income. The so-called LM relationship is shown in figure 16.3.

Only one point, the intersection of the IS and LM curves, satisfies both equilibrium conditions, and thus the intersection represents the equilibrium interest rate and income for the economy. Note that expansionary fiscal policy works to increase equilibrium income by lowering the amount of private investment needed to support a given level of income. Increased government expenditures or reduced taxes tend to shift the IS curve to the right. Equilibrium income goes up, and interest rates rise to accommodate the LM side of the system (see figure 16.4).

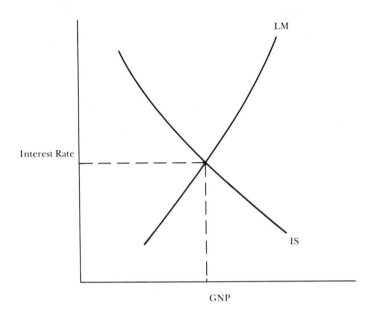

FIGURE 16.3

Interpretation: The IS curve comes from figure 16.2. The LM curve shows the possible combinations of GNP and interest rate in which the quantity of money available equals the quantity of money people wish to hold. The IS slopes upward because, as interest rates are higher, businesses and individuals keep smaller cash balances to maintain a given level of business activity.

Both the IS and LM equilibrium conditions are met where the two functions cross. At that point, intended savings equals intended investment and desired money balances equal the quantity of money supplied.

Expansionary monetary policy works by increasing the quantity of money available for cash users, thereby raising the level of national income supportable at any given interest rate. All other factors equal, an increase in the supply of money raises equilibrium income. But it also *lowers* equilibrium interest rates, as investors must be given an incentive to invest more (see figure 16.4).

Now we are ready to see how the Depression theories may be classified. Spending theories, in one form or another, translate into backward shifts of the IS curve:

• Reduced investment opportunities, due to the saturation of the housing or auto markets, mean that investors will invest less at any given interest rate; thus a lower rate of interest will be needed to equilibrate the same level of investment and savings.

• A stock market crash reduces the wealth of individuals and makes them more conservative consumers. This means that savings will be

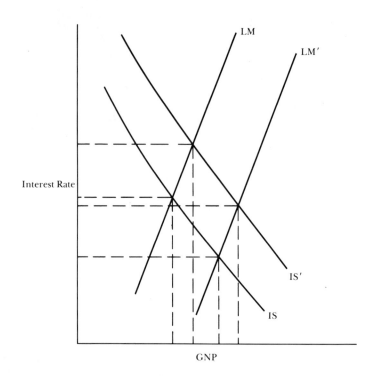

FIGURE 16.4

Interpretation: Expansionary fiscal policy works by shifting the IS curve to the right (IS'); at the new equilibrium, both GNP and the interest rate will be higher.

Expansionary monetary policy works by shifting the LM curve to the right (LM'); at the new equilibrium, GNP will be higher but interest rates will be *lower*.

Private, as well as government-induced, changes in the IS an LM curves will change equilibrium income. Temin uses the fact that a reduction in private spending and a reduction in the money supply should have opposite effects on interest rates to test monetary vs. spending hypotheses.

higher at any given level of income, and investment will have to be higher also to use up the economic resources left over after desired consumption rates. The higher investment level will be attainable only at lower interest rates; thus the backward shift in the IS curve. The stock market crash could also reflect changing expectations about the profitability of corporate investment. Analytically, this would have the same effect on the IS curve as housing market saturation, or any other perceived reduction in investment opportunity.

Monetary theories work by shifting the LM curve to the left. Bank failures reduce confidence in the banking system, leading depositors to turn their funds into currency, and leading banks to call in loans. Both actions reduce the money supply, and thus make it necessary to have a higher level of interest rates to keep money holders satisfied with their balances at a given level of income—that is, the LM curve shifts backward.

If one wishes to emphasize the role of the Federal Reserve, the same basic analysis applies. The Fed can prevent the money supply from shrinking by compensatory open market operations, trading Fed cash for publicly held government securities. Or it can lend reserves to the banks directly, encouraging them to borrow from the Fed by charging a low "rediscount" rate on Fed-to-bank loans, and then putting the borrowed reserves to work in business loans. The Fed's failure to do either may have allowed destabilizing forces to contract the money supply, shifting back the LM curve and lowering equilibrium income.

Does the Hicks-Hansen synthesis provide a means of choosing between spending and monetary hypotheses? Yes and no. Yes, because of the difference in the predicted effect of each on interest rates. A reduction in aggregate demand shifting the IS curve to the left should lower interest rates, while an autonomous contraction in the money supply should raise interest rates. Temin's research supports the spending side since he finds that interest rates fell sharply in 1930.

No, because the test is not definitive. The Hicks-Hansen structure is too simple to accommodate the complexities of the real world. As noted in the text, real interest rates are not observable because they depend upon private expectations of future price changes. There is not a single interest rate to measure, moreover, but a whole series of interest rates that may not move together. Hence the somewhat contorted monetarist explanation that falling interest rates on some securities may not reflect the scarcity of loanable funds. In short, the Hicks-Hansen synthesis can only be used on the first step in analyzing the macroeconomics of the Depression. And as Peter Temin explains in great detail, the subsequent steps are exceedingly difficult to make.

Bibliography

*Leonard Arrington "Western Agriculture and the New Deal" *Agricultural History* (Oct., 1970). Examines alternative explanations for wide variations, state-by-state, in New Deal spending.

**E. Cary Brown, "Fiscal Policy in The Thirties: A Reappraisal," *American Economic Review* 46 (Dec., 1956). Classic refutation of the legend that FDR's fiscal policy helped end the Depression.

‡**Michael Darby, "Three and a Half Million U.S. Employees Have Been Mislaid: Or, an Explanation of Unemployment, 1934–41," *Journal of Political Economy* 84 (Feb., 1976). Explains persistence of high unemploy-

ment after 1934 partially by measurement errors in the unemployment rate.

**Milton Friedman and Anna Schwartz, *The Great Contraction 1929–33* (Princeton, 1965). The portion of the famous *Monetary History* which gives a monetarist interpretation of the causes of the contraction.

*John Galbraith, *The Great Crash* (Houghton Mifflin, 1972). Witty anecdotal history of the stock market collapse.

‡**Arthur Gandolfi, "Stability of the Demand for Money during the Great Contraction, 1929–33," *Journal of Political Economy* 82 (Sept./Oct., 1974). Econometric evidence showing stable money demand function for money; evidence in he monetarists' favor.

‡**Arthur Gandolfi and James Lothian, "Review of 'Did Monetary Forces Cause the Great Depression'," *Journal of Money, Credit and Banking* 9 (Dec., 1977). Critique includes reestimate of Temin's consumption function, using a permanent income model.

*Robert Gordon, *Economic Instability and Growth: The American Record* (Harper and Row, 1974). Sober, reasoned Keynesian statement of the causes of the Depression.

‡***William Gramm, "The Real Balance Effect in the Great Depression," *Journal of Economic History* 22 (June 1972). Argues that falling prices led to a *reduction* in the real value of monetary assets, deepening the impact of the Depression.

*Alvin Hansen, *Fiscal Policy and Business Cycles* (Norton, 1941). Early Keynesian view of the Depression.

*H. Thomas Johnson, "Postwar Optimism and the Rural Financial Crisis of the 1920's," *Explorations in Economic History* 11 (Winter, 1973/74). Attempts to explain the wave of rural bank failures in the 1920's that were a prelude to the national downturn.

**Charles Kindleberger, *The World in Depression 1929–39* (University of California, 1973). Masterful, nontechnical survey emphasizing the international aspects of the collapse.

‡**John Kirkwood, "The Great Depression: A Structural Analysis," *Journal of Money Credit and Banking* 4 (Nov., 1972). Econometric model of the Depression in the Keynesian spirit.

‡**Lawrence Klein, *Economic Fluctuations in the United States 1921–1941* (Wiley, 1950). Classic Keynesian econometric model of the Depression.

‡**Thomas Mayer, "Consumption in the Great Depression," *Journal of Political Economy* 86 (Dec., 1978). Estimates consumption function for the Depression period to see if autonomous shifts explain the 1930 downturn.

‡**Thomas Mayer, "Money and the Great Depression: A Critique of Professor Temin's Thesis," *Explorations in Economic History* 15 (April, 1978). A careful assessment of the damage done to Friedman-Schwartz by Temin.

**Allen Meltzer, "Money and Other Explanations of the Start of the Great Depression," *Journal of Monetary Economics* 2 (Oct., 1976). Defense of the monetarist view by a leading monetarist.

‡**Lloyd Mercer and Douglas Morgan, "Alternative Interpretations of Market Saturation: Evaluation for the Automobile Market in the late 1920's," *Explorations in Economic History* 9 (Spring, 1972). Defines and measures saturation to see how it connects with the economic contraction.

‡**Lloyd Mercer and Douglas Morgan, "The American Automobile Industry: Investment Demand, Capacity, and Capacity Utilization 1921–40," *Journal of Political Economy* 80 (Nov./Dec., 1972). Econometric measure of the industry, suggesting that overcapacity was not as serious a problem in the late 20's as previously thought.

‡**Lloyd Mercer and Douglas Morgan, "Housing Surplus in the 1920's: Another Evaluation," *Explorations in Economic History* (Spring, 1973). Focuses on the overbuilding hypothesis and its effect on the downturn.

**Lynn Muchmore, "The Banking Crisis of 1933: Some Iowa Evidence,"*Journal of Economic History* 30 (Sept., 1970). Research is unable to connect failures with structural instability.

**Larry Peppers, "Full Employment Surplus Analysis and Structural Change: The 1930's," *Explorations in Economic History* 10 (Winter, 1973). Sophisticated reworking of E. Cary Brown's article on depression fiscal policy.

‡*Don Reading, "New Deal Activity and the States 1933 to 1939," *Journal of Economic History* 33 (Dec., 1973). Tries to explain state variations in New Deal expenditures by Roosevelt's economic goals.

*Arthur Smithies, "The American Economy in the Thirties," *American Economic Review* 36 (May, 1946). Standard source for the view that fiscal expansion proved effective in the thirties.

*George Soule,*Propserity Decade* (Holt, Rinehart, 1947). History of the 1920's, with emphasis on structural weaknesses preceding the Depression.

*Herbert Stein, *The Fiscal Revolution in America* (University of Chicago, 1969). Nontechnical history of fiscal policy since the 1920's.

*Joseph Swanson and Samuel Williamson, "Estimates of National Product and Income for the United States Economy 1919–1941," *Explorations in Economic History* 10 (Fall, 1972). Up-to-date estimates of interwar trends.

‡**Peter Temin, *Did Monetary Forces Cause the Great Depression?* (Norton, 1976). Seminal effort to reassess the alternative explanations of the contraction.

**James Tobin, "The Monetary Interpretation of History," *American Economic Review* 55 (June, 1965). Review of Friedman-Schwartz by one of the eminent post-Keynesians.

‡**Gavin Wright, "The Political Economy of New Deal Spending: An Econometric Analysis," *Review of Economics and Statistics* 56 (Feb., 1974). Econometric explanation of New Deal spending in terms of Roosevelt's attempts to win votes.

Epilogue

Economic history, of course, does not end with the Great Depression—though in the darkest hours of the 1930's not a few pessimists thought it might. It seems a suitable place to stop, however, for a number of reasons. The first is purely pragmatic. This is a book based on the work of the New Economic Historians, and they have had relatively little to say about events since the Depression. For scholars with an otherwise refreshing disregard for the boundaries between social sciences, economists show an excessive respect for each other's turf. What has happened post 1939 is generally marked "current events," to be left as raw material for applied macro and micro-economists rather than economic historians.

We could still follow textbook conventions here, ending with our own interpretation of what Modern Life Is All About. There is no shortage of tempting tunes to whistle: Is the American economy, like Britain's, fated to go to hell in a handbasket? Have two centuries of growth fueled by limitless natural resources left us ripe for a fall? What good is growth anyway, if all it means are more Pringle's New Fashioned Potato Chips and more time to watch The Gong Show? But we think it would be truer to the spirit of the book to reserve these waning moments of your attention for a few paragraphs about the discipline of economic history, rather than the content.

Even the most loyal readers of the last sixteen chapters must have been taken aback by the number of questions posed and left unanswered. We make no apologies, for we believe that this only reflects the state of the art/science. Today's economic historians are better at raising issues than resolving them. When firm historical interpretation is offered, it is usually taken as a provocative act begging for a counter-interpretation. No doubt, the next decade will be filled by pitched battles over the causes of the Great Depression, the sources of Populist discontent, the economic impact of Emancipation, the relationship between industrialization and changes in income distribution. Just how these controversies will end is anybody's guess.

Some take this confusion and restless movement within economic history as a sign of failure. A little perspective, however, suggests the opposite. Consensus within an intellectual discipline should be taken as a warning that practitioners have stopped exercising their curiosity and independence. The unwillingness of German physicists to listen to new ideas early in the twentieth century cost that country its preeminence in physics—and, some argue, even cost Hitler the ability to develop an atomic bomb. The complacent acceptance of Keynesian fiscal fine-tuning as the means to achieve stable economic growth has left contemporary economists unprepared to deal with inflation and anemic growth in the 1970's. Even within the history profession, the pitfalls of a strict party line are clear. The "Whig" interpreters of English history chronicled the rise of liberal constitutional government with no sense of the explosive forces brewing in Victorian England. Nationalist celebrations of the American past have probably helped to shield Americans from knowledge of social injustices perpetrated in their name.

It would be pretentious to argue that ferment among economic historians will render the world safer for democracy, or help Sara Lee to perfect a noncaloric cheese cake. We have little doubt, though, that dissension in the ranks makes for better history in the long run . . . and no doubt whatever that it makes history more fun.

Index